Water Conservation Techniques in Traditional Human Settlements

Water Conservation Techniques in Traditional Human Settlements

Pietro Laureano

COPAL PUBLISHING GROUP
New Delhi

Published by Copal Publishing Group
E-143, Lajpat Nagar, Sahibabad,
Distt. Ghaziabad, UP – 201005, India

www.copalpublishing.com

First published in 2001 by Bollati Boringhieri editore s.r.l. Corso Vittorio Emanuele II, 86 – Turin

New Edition 2013 published by Copal Publishing Group
© Copal Publishing Group, 2013

This book contains information obtained from authentic and highly regarded sources. Reprinted material is quoted with permission. Reasonable efforts have been made to publish reliable data and information, but the authors and the publishers cannot assume responsibility for the validity of all materials. Neither the authors nor the publishers, nor anyone else associated with this publication, shall be liable for any loss, damage or liability directly or indirectly caused or alleged to be caused by this book.

Neither this book nor any part may be reproduced or transmitted in any form or by any means, electronic or mechanical, including photocopying, microfilming and recording, or by any information storage or retrieval system, without permission in writing from Copal Publishing Group. The consent of Copal Publishing Group does not extend to copying for general distribution, for promotion, for creating new works, or for resale. Specific permission must be obtained in writing from Copal Publishing Group for such copying.

Trademark notice: Product or corporate names may be trademarks or registered trademarks, and are used only for identification and explanation, without intent to infringe.

ISBN: 978-81-924733-7-6 (hard back)
ISBN: 978-81-924733-3-8 (e-book)

Typeset by Bhumi Graphics, New Delhi
Printed and bound by Replika Press, New Delhi

CONTENTS

1. **The Cycle of Life** — 1
   1.1 The Mystery of Water — 2
   1.2 Traditional Techniques: A System of Local Sciences — 7
   1.3 Socio-Cultural Formations and Intensification of the Use of Resources — 11

2. **Hunter-Gatherers** — 17
   2.1 Migratory Nomadism — 18
   2.2 Weapons, Tools and Traps (Mobility – Multipurpose function) — 20
   2.3 Surfaces and Heaps of Stone, Caves, Fire, and Water — 20
   2.4 Drainage Systems and Labyrinths — 22
   2.5 Women, Their Knowledge of Plants and First Forms of Cultivation — 28

3. **Farmer-Breeders** — 30
   3.1 The Great Neolithic Transformation — 31
   3.2 Settlements Without Agriculture — 33
   3.3 Land and Water: The Origins of Urban Civilisation — 34
   3.4 From Huts to Stone: The Water Systems of Beida — 37
   3.5 Drainage, Condensation, Harvesting, and Fertilisation: A Multipurpose System — 40

4. **Metal-Using Agro-Astoralists** — 59
   4.1 Transhumant and Warring Nomadism — 60
   4.2 The Gates of the Waters of Heaven — 63
   4.3 The Civilization of Hidden Waters — 76
   4.4 Condensers, Atmospheric Wells, and Water Extraction Walls — 81

5. **Oases** — 93
   5.1 The Cycle of Autopoiesis — 94
   5.2 The Water Mines — 98
   5.3 The Structure of the Oasis — 110
   5.4 Water Genealogy — 112
   5.5 The Great Caravan Nomadism — 115

6. Urban Ecosystems — 120
  6.1 Complexity and Stratification — 121
  6.2 The Society of Waters — 121
  6.3 Flood Management Communities — 134
  6.4 The Mother of the Cisterns — 140
  6.5 Water and Urban Shape — 154

7. Water Techniques and Landscape Building — 166
  7.1 Permanency of Traditional Techniques in the Mediterranean Area — 167
  7.2 Hydraulic Structures of the Indian Subcontinent — 174
  7.3 Water Pyramids of the Ancient Mayas — 181
  7.4 Local Knowledge in the Hydraulic Societies: China — 184

8. The Water Crisis and the Decline of the Civilisations — 192
  8.1 Water Distribution and Climate Changes — 193
  8.2 The Desert and Desertification — 194
  8.3 Calamities, Cultural Shock, and Urban Exoduses — 200

9. Traditional Knowledge for A New Technological Paradigm — 204
  9.1 Interest and Studies on Traditional Knowledge — 205
  9.2 Critiques and Biases Against Traditional Knowledge — 206
  9.3 Tradition as a Dynamic System Able to Incorporate Innovation — 212
  9.4 The Future of Tradition — 218

Appendices — 223
Appendix 1: Hunter-Gatherers — 223
Appendix 2: Farmer-Breeders — 224
Appendix 3: Agro-Pastoralists — 232
Appendix 4: Oases — 249
Appendix 5: Urban Ecosystems — 257
Appendix 6: Local Knowledge in Hydraulic Societies — 274
Appendix 7: The New Paradigm — 282
Appendix 8: Technologies and Projects for Their Application — 290

Bibliography — 305

Index — 319

FOREWORD

In this beautifully illustrated work, Pietro Laureano shares with us the fruits of more than a quarter of a century of careful observation of traditional knowledge and techniques applied to urban settlements and landscape resources management in all regions of the world. The book introduces us to very sophisticated, thousand-year-old, capacities developed by local communities and civilizations around the world, amongst which water harvesting techniques, recycling of organic wastes and used waters for soil fertility conservation or, in more general terms, the ecosystemic approach to town planning, are anything but new! The volume is also the most convincing illustration of the fact that, whereas modern technological solutions rely on separation and specialization and for most of the time imply the mobilization of external resources, traditional knowledge, which by its very nature applies the principle of integration and uses internal renewable inputs, has proved over time to be effective in the daily struggle of civilizations against adverse environments and, more recently, against desertification.

Pietro Laureano's work is not exclusively oriented towards the past, describing solutions on the margins of our "progressive world". It is also suggesting that the looming water crisis which threatens our societies at the beginning of this new millennium is first of all a cultural one, in the widest sense of the word, and that to face it adequately, traditional local knowledge and techniques inherited from the past have to be brought together with our present technological capacities in order to assure the diffusion of more sustainable ways of dealing with territories in general, and water scarcity in particular.

We are honoured to have been invited to contribute to the diffusion of the present work. It is, in our view, destined to become a reference for all those – experts, stakeholders, decision makers – who have committed themselves to the fight against desertification and the promotion of more sustainable development solutions for our societies. We hope that it might be transformed very soon into a web-based tool for the sharing of this knowledge worldwide.

Howard Moore
Former Director
UNESCO Regional Bureau for
Science in Europe (ROSTE)

In the memory of Mariena Mondelli Montandon

The Cycle of Life

1

FIGURE 1.1 Stonehenge (England) is one of the most well-known and investigated megalithic monuments which date back to prehistory. The several interpretations of its mysterious meaning hardly ever give special importance to the evident water use of the ditch surrounding the complex structure, which was dug out before creating the big stone masses. The stone circles, which were progressively built throughout different ages, did not look as they do today. They were probably structures which supported a wooden circular roofing with an impluvium in the middle. The atmospheric condensation and the conservation of humidity in the soil were probably favoured by the big stone masses. As shown in the suggestive picture, the meaning of the monument was connected to the cycle of water and the latter functioning as a catalyst of its ethereal shape in the sky and its liquid state in the soil.

1.1 The Mystery of Water

According to the legend, after his conquest of the Egypt, Alexander the Great went into the vaults under the pyramid of Gizeh where the tomb of Hermes Trismegistus, the mythical founder of the ancient science, was discovered. There, he brought to light an emerald tablet with the most important secret of the universe impressed on it. The enigmatic inscription starts by stating that "what is above corresponds with what is below" and then mysterious words reveal the essence that is the origin of everything:

"Its father is the Sun, its mother is the Moon, the Wind carries it in its lap, and the Earth nourishes it. It generates all wonders of the universe. Its power is perfect. It gently separates land from fire and what is thin from what is dense. It slowly ascends from the earth to the skies and comes down to earth again by collecting in itself the strength of superior and inferior things".

Medieval alchemists considered that document to be the most important in the Hellenistic tradition and the foundation of their doctrine; its meaning was kept secret for generations. Indeed, it is one of the many enchanting but nonsensical lucubrations, which drove the vain search for the philosophers' stone.

Nevertheless, the alchemists' doctrine is wrongly considered as a mere esoteric abstraction: it was based on intense experimental work and, above all, it involved a load of learning that was a part of the knowledge gathered through tradition and throughout human history. Likewise, this provided the basis for modern science that, in spite of its undeniable success, is still a recent thin layer of the long and deep human cultural evolution. The traditional heritage is an inexhaustible source of techniques, discoveries, and solutions; it indicates research pathways and unconventional ways of operating and conceals fascinating possibilities of overturning models of existence previously thought to be sound and self-evident.

The present study is an immersion into the abysses of the remote past by the exploration of habits and customs as well as faraway places. It has been conceived to contrast environmental catastrophes and emergencies, the negative effects of which branch out from a local to a worldwide level. Climatic change, desertification, glaciers melting, the disappearance of biological and cultural diversity, the exodus of entire populations, the shortage of food, and the loss of role and identity of continuously increasing sections of the population are calamities which cannot find an answer in modern technology which very often is, paradoxically, the main cause of these situations. So that, international organizations such as the United Nations Convention to Combat Desertification (UNCCD), the FAO and UNESCO question traditional knowledge by calling back the deep streams of history and by comparing the most different and remote situations (UNCCD, 1998ab, 1999b–d; FAO, 1997; UNESCO, 1994ab). The discovery of appropriate knowledge and techniques in the societies and the environment previously considered as living in primitive and ignorant conditions overturn commonly shared convictions.

Distances become shorter: in time, because the discovery of plenty of notions and practices making it possible to live in and admire the environment and the landscape dates back to prehistoric ages; it brings us closer to our ancestors and more critical towards modernity in space, because the awareness of the existence in remote societies of knowledge to which we can refer demonstrates the importance of diversity. And, above all, a new way to consider culture and its values is conceived: technology linked to common welfare, art, and symbols.

Modern science classifies and separates, while traditional knowledge joins together and flows. The foundation of a dynamic knowledge embracing each single science in a continuous flow and gathering them into a unity is a possibility pursued by the most advanced contemporary reflection and it was a part of our ancestors' thought pattern.

The 6th century BC Ionian philosopher Thales of Miletus, whom Aristotle pointed out as the first to develop physical science, propounded the materiality of knowledge and the necessity to found it on the unity of nature. Thales, who had travelled and questioned Egyptian and Babylonian wise men, pointed out water as the principle behind everything. Nowadays, the Greek philosopher is commonly considered as the initiator of scientific reflection: before him the creation of universe was explained by mythology. He explained the origin of the cosmos as a concrete substance and attributed its essence to a material basis and to unitary laws from the physical world. Nevertheless, Thales' thought has a wider meaning and range.

Water is undoubtedly the most widespread and strangest element on the planet. Its multiform nature, liquid, solid, and gaseous, allows it to convert from one condition into another, and with a sudden change of state it can even be sublimated. It is the substance which forms oceans, permeates the atmosphere, and even determines the formation of certain types of

FIGURE 1.2 Eritrea, the steep slopes going down to the coast from the high altitudes of the African highland. Water is a constant element of the landscape in the shape of vapours and clouds. The condensation from the high evaporation of the Red Sea due to the thermal currents in the atmosphere creates moisture used for the cultivations.

rocks: indeed, perennial glaciers should be considered as authentic rock formations. Its volume increases when it solidifies and this property, enabling ice to float, allows the present climatic balance and the spread of dry land. The physical characteristics of water are exploited to calibrate instruments that measure temperature, volume, and mass. From the remotest times water has been at work moving water mills, in recent times with steam power, in the future supplying clean energy through fuel cells. All living beings are composed of and fed with water. Most of the species of our planet live in the sea whereas all the others colonized the land by absorbing the primordial ocean. By taking the liquid component away from all animal or vegetable organisms, the dry residue is negligible in comparison with the original weight of the organism. It was through the decomposition of the water molecules in the primordial seas by cyanobacteria that oxygen was released and our atmosphere was created. We are born in water but we can drown in water as well.

Water is always mixed with other substances because of its diluting property, yet it is a symbol of purity. It is a universal solvent that can melt and coagulate. Thin and malleable, it carves out stone and destroys metals. By its strongly destructive power and weak building strength, it, constantly, shapes the earth eroding mountains, making grooves and digging caves. In damp areas, it falls as rain, condenses into frost and dew, falls as hailstones, and assumes the impalpable and crystalline form of snow. In desert areas, minuscule water particles penetrate even the hardest stone that disintegrates

FIGURE 1.3 The collapse of the rocks in the Algerian Sahara. In spite of the great aridity of the soil, water is the main landscape-shaping agent. The haloclasty and cryoclasty are important phenomena of demolition of the mountains. In the first case, the salts contained in the rocks absorb the atmospheric moisture and swell. In the second case, moisture absorbed by the rocks in the cold night temperature freezes. In both circumstances the volume increases and causes even the hardest stone formations to disintegrate.

in the cold night temperature when water freezes. Otherwise, in the heat of the day water surges to the rocky and sandy surface, transports and deposits salts or creates oxide layers creating the beautiful painted deserts, canyons and multicoloured dunes. Water energy shapes coasts, demolishes embankments, and destroys forests and towns. Its weak and insinuating tenacity allows it to build geological formations, fill up valleys, and enable plants to stand. It chisels and forms the landscape: in stone, by accumulating rocky layers on the earth's surface; subterranean, infiltrating the deep tunnels and shaping an architecture of stalactites and stalagmites; ethereal in the skies by the continuous movement of the clouds. The weather would not exist without water. Indeed, it operates as a general thermal regulator with the masses and the streams of the oceans on a worldwide level and by the perspiration and evaporation on the skin of the human body. Water's perpetual flow and change engage the world in a vital cycle, involving the seas, the atmosphere, and underground by filtering through everywhere and vitalizing everything.

FIGURE 1.4 Erosion of the Jordan desert in the Wadi Rum. Moisture condensed on the rocks owing to the differences in temperature has a slow but constant action of dissolution. Water penetrates the rocks in the night and is drawn to the surface in the heat of the day. During this process water dissolves the salts deep in the rocks, transports and coagulates them on the outside walls. Faults form inside the rocks and ochre-coloured layers are created on the surface due to oxidation.

Although the contrary is believed, water is widely spread over the universe. In the galaxy of Andromeda great vaporous water masses have been observed. Comets are 70% water, and it is possibly because of the comets that water is present on earth. Although it is so widespread, water is enormously precious. In proportion, if we were to pour the total water of the globe into a 5-litre tank, the quantity of non-salty drinking water would be no more than a spoonful. If we ignored the water in the glaciers, the proportion of drinking water would be reduced to just a drop. The geographic distribution of this quantity is so unequal that the largest areas are in conditions of complete aridity.

These features perfectly suit the enigmatic descriptions of the essence pursued by the alchemists. In the 6th century AD, the Greek Zosimus questioned "that precious thing without any value, that polymorphous thing without any form, that unknown thing everyone knows". The Emerald Tablet in the legend of Alexander refers to the same mysterious force permeating nature. It is enough to take the indications literally, ignoring their esoteric meaning, to understand the practical sense of the formula. Raised up by the sun's heat, condensed by the cold moonlight, and brought by the wind, water falls into the ground and then resumes its ascending cycle. It nourishes the living beings and allows them to generate: it corrupts the seed and converts rottenness into plant energy making the plants blossom under the sun.

This is the perspective from which Zeno, the main character in Marguerite Yourcenar's novel *The abyss*, contemplated the world, and observing the forest "Found in each of the vegetal pyramids the hermetic hieroglyph of the ascending forces, the sign of the water wetting and nourishing the beautiful wild living beings and of the fire whose virtuality they bear and that may destroy them one day. But those ascents were balanced by descents: under its feet, people, blind and sensitive to its roots, imitated in the darkness the endless division of the twigs in the sky and cautiously took the direction towards who knows which nadir. Here and there, a prematurely yellowed leaf revealed from beneath the green, the presence of the metals with which it had formed its own substance and of which it was operating the conversion".

His way of thinking according to which inert and organic elements, energy and life, are considered as a part of a process of continuous transformation where earth and sky, microcosm and macrocosm, the individual and the universe are not separate, is typical of traditional knowledge. From the early prehistoric paintings in the caves to the Neolithic demographic increase, due to the development of the skills of tilling, harmony with the lively power of nature is more a vital necessity than a speculative conception. The conviction of an indivisible relationship between humanity, nature

FIGURE 1.5 The effects of desertification in the Sahel. The lack of water inhibits vegetation and cohesion of the soils. The dry soil, no longer protected, disintegrates and feeds the sandstorms.

and the universe is the basis of all traditional technical solutions. The most widespread knowledge is that relating to water supply and likewise knowledge relating to the cultivation and the structure of the land are closely linked to water. In history, the success of both powerful hydraulic civilisations and smaller communities of local and family nature was based on the activities of water harvesting, conservation and diffusion. Therefore, water could be the key element to the secret quintessence sought by the ancients, but not as a substance. In fact, water is already one of the four main traditional elements: air, water, earth and fire. The essence sought after does not have a material nature but is a process and an extraordinary lesson: the cycle of water.

In the 1st century BC, the Roman essay writer Vitruvius narrated that in the most hidden and deepest place of the pyramid the pharaohs prostrated themselves before an urn full of water, the origin of everything (Vitruvius, De Architectura, VIII, 4). The Egyptian priests used to knead a statue of "humus" and incense embellished with all the regal attributes in the Nile – explained the Greek writer Plutarch in the 1st century AD. The statue was the demonstration that the neter, the primordial spring of energy, the only principle of nature is nothing else than an earthy and water essence. Now that modern science can make the most incredible dreams of the shamans and the alchemists come true by charging human deeds with a never fulfilled constructive or destructive potential, the ancient wisdom needs to be recovered. The water cycle is responsible for the earth's physical and morphological transformation process, for the development of its forms of life and the harmonious self-regulation system maintaining the conditions for the preservation of the human presence. It is also the metaphor of a way of thinking of nature according to which all elements and beings are linked to each other in an endless mesh of symbioses and dependences, the physical example of a process involving a continuous use of resources without garbage or waste, a model of productive dynamics and environmental management based on sustainability. It is a cycle of life that modern technology is able to imitate in order to found a new paradigm of coexistence.

1.2 Traditional Techniques: A System of Local Sciences

In 1992, the United Nations organized the World Conference on the Environment and Development in Rio de Janeiro with the participation of 178 governments and 120 heads of state. The importance of that meeting was such that it is described as "The Earth Summit". The Conference, which aimed to reconcile the dramatic world environmental conditions with the development and the welfare of people, issued three world conventions on the climate, on biodiversity and on desertification. Each of these conventions experimented an innovative approach to the question of development and technology and considered the necessity of taking into account and re-enhancing traditional knowledge and practices. More specifically, the United Nations Convention to Combat Desertification and the Degradation of Soils (UNCCD) founded a Science and Technology Committee composed of the most outstanding experts from all countries to argue the issue of an inventory and classification of such knowledge. Thus, the Convention Secretariat began a huge research activity in all of the approximately 200 member countries.

The work of synthesis (UNCCD, 1998a) based on the reports on traditional knowledge sent in by the different countries and by the experts specifically sent on missions, proposes an inventory of traditional knowledge in a 78-item list of techniques or practices classified into seven different topics:

- water management for conservation
- improvement of soil fertility
- protection of vegetation
- fight against wind or water erosion
- silviculture
- social organisation
- architecture and energy

However, an inventory with this structure and classification, based on a separation of functions due to the need to present such a vast subject, risks weakening the theme and not catching the meaning and the way of operating of the traditional techniques. Thus, the Science and Technology Committee decided to continue to extend the research by setting up a special team of experts on the topic, which has drawn up the following definition:

Traditional knowledge consists of practical (instrumental) and normative knowledge concerning the ecological, socio-economic and cultural environment. Traditional knowledge originates from people and is transmitted to people by recognizable and experienced actors. It is systemic (inter-sectorial and holistic), experimental (empirical and practical), handed down from generation to generation, and culturally enhanced. Such a kind of knowledge supports diversity and enhances and reproduces local resources.

Based on this definition, the Italian Ministry for the Environment, within the framework of the Action Plan to combat desertification, has promoted the work on an inventory of the traditional knowledge and techniques on which the present survey is based. Traditional and local knowledge are part of a complex system; therefore, they cannot be reduced to a mere list of technical solutions and restricted to a series of different applications according to the results to be attained. Their efficacy depends on the interaction between several factors. These should be carefully considered in order to understand the historical successes achieved by the use of traditional knowledge and to use its internal logic to find modern solutions.

FIGURE 1.6 Sand dunes in the Great Western Erg in Algeria. The lack of water courses flowing down to the sea prevents the disposal of sands which as a consequence accumulate. The sands, in their turn, by absorbing water further prevent it from flowing along the surface.

FIGURE 1.7 Sebkha of Timimoun (Algerian Sahara). The sebkha are deep depressions where the underground microflows converge. Due to the high evaporation on the surfacen, the salts rise and form completely barren crusts.

Each traditional practice is not an expedient to solve a specific problem, but always a complex and often a multifunctional method involved in an integrated approach (society, culture, and economy) closely linked to a concept of the world based on the careful management of local resources. Terracing, for instance, is a method used to protect slopes, replenish soils, and harvest water. But it is also something else. It takes on an aesthetic value and works within a social organization and a shared system of values supporting it and based on it as well.

Modern technology aims at an immediate efficiency through a high specialization of knowledge supported by dominant structures able to mobilise resources external to the environment. Traditional knowledge proficiency is appreciable over long and very long periods by resorting to shared knowledge, created and handed down from one generation to another, and also to social practices; and it exploits renewable internal inputs. Thanks to modern technology; for instance, very deep wells have been dug out to pump water up to the surface. The results have immediately been visible, but have dried up bordering resources and sometimes by drawing water from fossil pockets, with the passing of time they completely exhaust them. On the contrary, traditional knowledge uses systems for harvesting meteoric water or exploits run-off areas by using the force of gravity or water catchment methods allowing the replenishment and increasing the durability of the resource.

FIGURE 1.8 Sebkha of Timimoun (Algerian Sahara). The natural dynamics of the sebkha are used by the desert people who by intercepting the smallest quantities of water create the oases and the soil, reverse the process of aridity and transform the desert into a palm tree forest.

Modern technological methods operate by separating and specializing, whereas traditional knowledge operates by connecting and integrating. According to the usual meaning of words such as forest, agriculture, and town, they are completely distinct from each other and meet similarly different needs: wood, food, and housing. They correspond to specialized scientific systems: silviculture, agriculture, and town planning. Local knowledge does not make an artificial distinction within the world of plants between the forest supplying commercial wood and tilled land supplying food (Shiva, 1993). Forests, fields, and dwellings are unitary ecological systems. Forests and other marginal apparently nonproductive areas, such as steppes and marshes, provide large quantities of food and water resources, and fodder and fertilizers for agriculture. They are also convenient to live in. The traditional town, in its turn, integrates with agriculture by replacing the forest in desert areas, by collecting fertilizers produced by the inhabitants' organic waste and through its production of water collected on the roofs. The humus thus produced in the fields provides the colloidal material indispensable to build adobe towns. The cavity resulting from the excavation is used as an impluvium for water, a ditch for the transformation of excrement into humus, a productive garden protected by the outside excavated walls. This is a continuous cycle of activities in which the result of one forms the basis for the next. The buildings, right down to the smallest detail, conform to this necessity.

This principle, so close to the way in which nature works, where everything that remains of a system is reused by other systems and the concept of waste and the possibility of resorting to external resources do not exist, has allowed human beings to survive throughout history. Multipurpose and multiuse techniques have guaranteed successful results even in harsh conditions. Collaboration and symbiosis resulting from the reuse of everything produced within a system have allowed autopoiesis (self-reproduction) and a self-propulsive development independent of exogenous or occasional factors.

By this logic, when a strong cohesion between society, culture, and the economy is created, this leads to positive development leaps in history. The synthesis of traditional knowledge and social systems strengthens the proper use of all resources and, consequently, determines positive changes of status and builds rural or urban ecosystems. This is the process that generated the success of the great civilizations, built on the traditional techniques that led to their economic, social, and monumental results. The prosperity of the magnificent Angkor civilisation is due to the digging of colossal canals and ditches surrounding human settlements with several concentric rings in north-eastern Cambodia, a traditional practice in use since prehistoric times. These landscape-shaping techniques are usually explained as drainage or irrigation systems, but this is too narrow an interpretation. Their use as a means of defence, owing to the ease with which the ditches could be crossed, is not a convincing reason. Only an understanding of their multipurpose use (van Liere, 1980) as water reservoirs in the cold season and as a protection against floods in the humid season, and of their value as a symbol and as a form of identification of the community can explain the success of this practice.

Aesthetic and ethic values complete the interaction between environmental, productive, technological, and social aspects. Traditional procedures operate a harmonious fusion between the landscape and the traditional aesthetic canons. A device for collecting or conveying water is never a merely technical structure but it also has its own beauty. Fields in the oases are systems of production and relaxing places for contemplation as well. Little agricultural fields in desert areas are called gardens, just as in Southern Italy, eliminating the separation between the vegetable garden and the pleasure garden. Often, the works and procedures have a deep symbolic meaning and are a continuous game of suggestions and analogies between techniques, art, and nature. Systems of water distribution in the Sahara are reproduced in carpet drawings and in women's hairstyles. They are part of a complex symbolism linked to life, fertility, and the generations. Spiritual principles make rules sacred and guarantee their perpetuation as in the case of the African sacred woods with their restricted access and of the whole set of taboo-objects, practices which guarantee the regeneration of forests, the saving of environmental resources and the land as reserves for nature and human communities.

Therefore, traditional technique is an integral part of a strongly consolidated network of links and relations, supported by a global framework of signs and meanings. It works within a socially shared cultural structure: the historical system of science and local knowledge. It is therefore wrong to isolate each single technology, which is always highly contextualised, linked not only to an environmental situation, but to a precise historical moment and a complex social construction. These are decisive reflections in the perspective of the dissemination, the reproducibility, and a modern re-proposal of these traditional practices. Really, the use of traditional technique is not always and everywhere successful. The practices known as slash and burn or as itinerant agriculture allowed the survival of human communities in perfect harmony with resources over a very long time. But, it can be disastrous if applied in a completely different environmental and demographic context.

Therefore, traditional knowledge should not to be understood as a series of devices replacing the usual knowledge background, since it can generate a new paradigm. Traditional and local knowledge do not suggest miraculous solutions, which would mean to follow the modernity logic, but put forward a method to be also re-proposed through modern technologies.

1.3 Socio-Cultural Formations and Intensification of the Use of Resources

The fact of not reducing traditional knowledge to a mere series of techniques means considering it as part of the overall environmental, productive, and cultural conditions of the societies. The inventory of the technologies, knowledge, and the traditional and local practices, therefore, becomes an investigation of the social groupings. The technological dimension of these formations is based on a series of resource usage practices that are an integral part of the cultural system and

FIGURE 1.9 In the Tassili n'Ajjer, in the Algerian Sahara, the natural cavities such as this one, called guelta, have been used since the prehistoric ages as precious water reservoirs.

FIGURE 1.10–1.11 Water is the most precious resource of nomadic people who constantly move from one place to another. They must know, therefore, the places where water can be found in nature or drawn by means of the devices built by the nomads themselves. Above, a Saharan Tuareg near a guelta. Below, a young nomad from the Dahalac isles in the Red Sea who is drinking the fresh water produced by catching the sea evaporation in the artificial basins.

TABLE 1.1 **Characteristics of modern and traditional knowledge**

Modern knowledge	Traditional knowledge
Specific solution	Multifunctional
Immediate efficacy	Functional over long period
Specialisation	Holism
Dominant powers	Autonomy
Separation	Integration
External resources	Internal inputs
Confliction	Symbiosis
Monoculture	Connection and complexity
Uniformity	Diversity
Inflexibility	Flexibility
Costly maintenance	Self-regulation and labour intensity
Internationalisation	Consideration of the context
Costliness	Saving
Attention to mere technical details and rationalism	Symbolism and full of significance
Dependence	Autopoiesis

guarantee the maintenance of a relationship between the social groupings and nature. Such knowledge, technologies, and environmental transformation devices supply people with a larger quantity of resources than the naturally available ones. Centres aimed at the amplification of the benefits to guarantee optimal life conditions and open to further positive changes are set up. Those communities that are in harmony with the resources remain stable for a very long time. Deep transformations spreading over long periods or condensed into sudden status revolutions may also occur, thus determining the passage from one social formation to another.

Therefore, the object of the present study involves both human history and knowledge, without any limitation in space and time. Consequently, the classification is not supposed to be an exhaustive inventory but an open scheme of reference to be filled in gradually with new contributions. Like the ancient portolanos, this book contains pictures exemplifying places and situations, whereas still unknown large areas are left for future exploration.

The traditional knowledge system has been drawn up on the usual classification of the social groupings adopted in the fields of archaeology and anthropology: hunter-gatherers, farmer-breeders, and metal-using agropastoralists. These three categories are completed by two superior syntheses composed of complex traditional social systems intensifying and integrating knowledge: oases and urban ecosystems. In them the previous social groupings technologies are stratified and variously combined, according to the different social and environmental conditions.

The first synthesis of complexity is the oasis intended as an artificial accomplishment deriving from a perfect knowledge of the environment. In the desert, dryness is interrupted by singular situations that give rise to niches and microenvironments contrasting with the overall cycle. A slight depression collects humidity, a stone provides shade, and a seed flourishes. Thus, favourable dynamics develop: the plant generates its protection from the sun's rays, concentrates water vapour, attracts insects, produces biological material and the soil from which it subsequently draws its nourishment.

A biological system used by other organisms bringing their contributions is created, and a microcosm is generated as the result of their co-existence. By using these processes people from the Sahara create the oases. They often originate from a single palm tree, planted in a hollow in the ground and surrounded by dry branches, which protect it from the sand. As the time goes by, large tilled fields develop along terraced canyons or on green archipelagos among the dunes, thanks to complex and diversified techniques of water production, land organization, and microclimate formation. On a different scale, the oasis effect works following the same principle: the installation of a self-propulsory and self-generating virtuous cycle. This process can be held as a model and the term oasis can be generalised to any situation

FIGURE 1.12 Oasis of Tozeur (Tunisia). The courtyard dwelling synthesises the traditional knowledge spread all over the Mediterranean and ensures better conditions for living in arid areas by building a protected space in the middle and arranging an impluvium for harvesting the water collected on the terrace roofs.

where a life-sustaining island is created, even in non-desert areas, according to the following definition: "An oasis is a human settlement in harsh geographic conditions which exploits scarce local resources, to trigger a growing amplification of positive interactions and to create a fertile and self-sustaining environmental niche, in contrast with its hostile surroundings" (Laureano, 1988). There are, therefore, adobe oases in the Sahara, and also stone oases in rocky uplands and sea oases in the islands as well. Even the Maya settlements in the rain forests of Yucatan can be considered as an oasis system since, due to the karstic conditions of the area, they had no surface water courses.

Niches of intensification on the oasis model can be found in all climatic conditions and historical ages. These habitat systems are located along the Southern Mediterranean coast and in the Southern part of the EuroMediterranean area in particular, on islands and peninsulas and in all environmental circumstances where alternate and catastrophic climatic conditions, rainfall concentrated in a few months of the year and followed by dry seasons, make it necessary to manage the water resource with great care, due to its unavailability in a free state, in lakes or rivers, using technological devices to monitor its variability in time (Laureano, 1995).

The urban ecosystem is the next level of complexity. It is the model of the oasis that has grown into a city. They are great caravan cities in the desert or urban agglomerations that have grown larger than the first oasis model. Favourable geomorphologic circumstances are exploited to create irrigated areas in specific geographic systems. An important capital dominates each landscape unit: isolated basins in the middle of the desert; large plains among the mountain peaks; strips of oases along hydrographic networks, international and intercontinental crossroads. Making the most of the available resources, even traditional habitat systems develop into historical centres of regional importance and with urban features.

The classification chronologically outlines the continuous process of knowledge accumulation and stratification, since the first three social groupings correspond to the passage from the Palaeolithic and Neolithic Ages to the Iron Age and to the upper levels of complexity of oases and urban ecosystems. But even if this is useful for classification purposes it would be misleading as a theoretical definition. The social groupings of our model are not conceived as phases in the evolution of human history but rather as typical conditions of specific ages. They can, however, co-exist within the same historical background and indeed they guarantee continuity, stratification and interpenetration.

Socio-cultural formations that prevailed in early human history still largely exist within human groupings, where the practice of knowledge is similar to that derived from palaeontological and archaeological surveys. Obviously there are differences, but these are largely already present within those communities belonging to the same social grouping and living in the same historical period. The types of social-cultural formation should not be intended as universally shared models: they develop depending on the geographical background and the dominant conceptions. Classification is a scientific principle, but it conceals the succession and stratification, in time, of levels of technology and culture, the different climatic and environmental conditions simultaneously occurring and the synchronic existence in history of human experiences and different social models. Both the environment and a community's conception of the world contribute to the creation and maintenance of specific characteristics. Both these factors continuously vary in time and from one place to another, thus creating and preserving cultural diversity.

Hunter-Gatherers

2

FIGURE 2.1 Cueva Pintada (Baja California in Mexico). The cave, included in the UNESCO World Heritage List, is the figurative synthesis of the hunter-gatherers' knowledge and rituals in the Palaeolithic age. The enhancement of the artistic skills was an astonishing element of affirmation, creating places of social cohesion and identity, and leading to the elaboration of symbols and rituals essential to the memorisation and transmission of knowledge.

2.1 Migratory Nomadism

The hunter-gatherers were the first colonisers of the whole planet [216, 217]. This social formation allowed the human species to spread all over the continents, from Africa to America, and Australia which the first hominids never reached and to which man was to return only in recent times. Low coastal lands and ridges arising from the watershed of river basins were the privileged itineraries. The paths along mountain ridges and uplands are not interrupted by long watercourses, which, instead, originate in the lower valleys, and the environment is generally more salubrious and free from pests. The Rift Valley is a great historical ridge considered as the crossroads for the spread of the human race all over the world, due to its geographical conformation stretching across Eastern Africa for over 4,830 km, from the south to the north, from Mozambique to the Mediterranean Sea. The slope caused two systems of symmetrical rises and uplands on both sides of the tectonic depression. These systems are a natural passageway vertically running up through various climatic and ecological barriers, such as the desert, forests, and the savannah, which horizontally cross the continent.

The Rift Valley has been a vehicle for the spreading of humankind through its ramifications, both eastern, formed by the Gulf of Aden, the Red Sea, the Gulf of Aqaba, the Dead Sea, and the valley of the River Jordan up to Lake Tiberias, and western, from the Nile, across the Libyan desert, to the Saharan Atlas and the Tell Mountains, the Atlantic coast and the Straits of Gibraltar. The first great world communication network was created by the hunter-gatherers who hunted game, followed migrating animals' tracks across the seas, through natural pathways formed after the glaciations as a result of lowered water levels, or on the ice formations themselves, or by means of rudimentary rafts. For ages, important knowledge was developed and passed on from generation to generation, crossing through this great world communication network.

FIGURE 2.2 Janet (Algeria). The Tuareg, the great Saharan nomads, perform a propitiatory ritual dance in which they look like vultures.

Human communities experienced a constant accumulation of knowledge and their ability to observe nature. In fact, they collected a lot of information through contact with plants and animals, and their harmonious integration into the environment enhanced an astonishing cultural heritage. This was gradually lost when advances in agriculture and industrialisation inevitably influenced people who were dependent on specialisation and on a decreasing variety of means of support. We can have an idea of those ancient skills by making an anthropological observation of surviving cultures and by looking at Palaeolithic pictures. Still now, in the Amazon and in Guinea, what the hunter-gatherers left behind acts as "a botanical library" through a recording process of the characteristics, the properties, and the habitat of hundreds of plants, whose classification and use remain still unknown to modern science. The recurring subject in American prehistoric art is the flight of the condor with spread wings that you find painted, for example, on the walls of the "Cueva Pintada", a cave in the Baja California in Mexico. These paintings have been associated with symbolic pictures of shamanistic flights. The hunter-gatherers obtained vital information from the birds. The flight of the birds was, for example, an important signal of pools of water and edible vegetation and, in particular, the wheeling of the vultures signalled dead animals and or appetising carcasses. Still now, the Tuareg, the great Saharan nomads, perform a ritual dance in which they look like vultures. The drawings of these dances can be seen in Saharan rock paintings.

FIGURE 2.3 Cueva Pintada (Baja California), pictures of condors. These paintings recur in Meso-American wall art and result from shamanistic experiences and concrete benefits. The flight of the birds is an important signal indicating prey and pools of water during migrations.

As a matter of fact, the hunter-gatherers were more often gatherers of plants and carrion rather than hunters. Improved skills in carving tools out of stone, the development of language, religion, as well as art were all due to the hunter-gatherers. The early practices of taming and tillage, which were successfully applied throughout the following ages, had already been introduced in the Late Palaeolithic Age. Owing to prejudice and common places, the hunter-gatherers' living standards and knowledge have usually been underestimated, but scientific research has recently reappraised them.

The hunter-gatherers are commonly thought to have led a miserable and poor life. However, the long lasting presence of this social grouping throughout time and the observation of people living at present in this way prove that belief wrong. Starting from its study in the 60s and 70s, science has accepted the idea that the hunter-gatherers enjoyed flourishing conditions of plentiful food and leisure (Lee and De Vore, 1968; Sahlins, 1968 and 1972). Evidence of this emerges from the study of the Native American groups living along the northwest coast of North America. They were hunter-fishers who had enjoyed time and resources enough to develop their culture both artistically and socially (Orme, 1981). Salmon fishing, in fact, provided them with an amount of food that was greater than any farmer's contribution. Likewise, in the Palaeolithic age, hunters had developed such an astonishing ability in hunting, fishing, and cropping as to assure them a high living standard and plenty of time, as is shown by the quality of the art in the caves and the time that was dedicated to it.

Confirmation of this comes from studies on the way of life of modern Australian Aborigines and Bushmen from the Kalahari. As to the former, they do not spend more than 3 or 5 hours a day on finding food; in spite of their living in desert areas, the latter maintain wealthy conditions, without much striving, and spending 4–5 days a week on activities other than looking for food (Lee, 1969). During the cropping, they can also allow themselves to leave out many edible plants, for cultural and symbolic reasons. The Mbuti Pygmies from Ituri, in the Democratic Republic of Congo (former Zaire), as well, live comfortably and lazily using the forest as a reserve they can get food from.

These results only depend on the occurrence of particular conditions of prosperity, which, therefore, do not require knowledge and skills. In fact, it is generally believed that the periods preceding the Neolithic age enjoyed prosperity and demographic development, proportional to the available resources rather than to skills and technology. By analysing traditional knowledge and, particularly, the practices of water harvesting, distribution, and use, early examples of the intensification of resources, thanks to their proper use through specific knowledge and appropriate applications of technologies can be found dating back to the hunter-gatherers' time.

2.2 Weapons, Tools and Traps (Mobility – Multipurpose function)

In these forms of societies, high productivity of hunting and fishing depended on the application of sophisticated techniques in manufacturing weapons, tools, and traps. Most of these tools have not lasted in time up to the present day, since they were made of perishable materials. In fact, though the Palaeolithic Age is commonly understood as "The Ancient Stone Age", the most widely used material at that time was wood. Many of the several Palaeolithic stone tools discovered were used for cutting and carving trees or branches in order to make objects or buildings, no trace of which exists at present. The wide variety of these tools and their refinement are meaningful. They were of high quality and were so elaborate as to seem works of art. Besides, they are multipurpose tools. An Australian throwing tool could serve, for example, both as a table to eat on, and as a tool to light a fire or dig and hoe the soil. Multipurpose tools favoured hunter-gatherers' mobility. In fact, heavy tools were not carried away during migration but left behind and were found in the same place by other migrating groups. Only multipurpose tools were worth carrying. The hunter-gatherers' mobility was such that right up to the modern era, only in that period was humanity able to reach the farthest corners of the earth. This tendency to move, together with a good knowledge of the environment, allowed a diversified use of the space according to the season. Rules forbidding certain sorts of food and taboos in some areas guaranteed the saving of nature's resources and the regeneration of the ecosystem, at the same time providing useful supplies in case of need.

2.3 Surfaces and Heaps of Stone, Caves, Fire, and Water

The oldest example of land organisation is the Palaeolithic site in Isernia dating back to between 700,000 and 500,000 years ago and ascribed to hunter-gatherer hominids, not yet belonging to the Homo Sapiens species. A Palaeolithic area with thousands of bone splinters, stone tools, limestone, flint and travertine cobbles (Peretto, 1991) was discovered. Over an area of approximately 2 m in diameter, the limestone cobbles have been intentionally arranged next to each other, like primordial paving. The fragments gradually become fewer, up to an area where it is supposed they were laid under the water. Although at present, this Palaeolithic site has not been actually proved to be the oldest water harvesting area, a clear relationship between land and water underlies the site of El-Guettar 15 km from the oasis of Gafsa, in Tunisia. An artificial heap of hewn spherical limestones along with cut flintstones and bone splinters has been found in a layer dating back to 150,000 years ago (Camps, 1974). The spherical stones form a conical structure, which is 0.75 m high and 1.30 m wide, with long stone splinters, intentionally stuck into its top. A mass of manufactured flint consisting of more than 4,000 tools, stone weapons, and fragments of bones and teeth have been found within the structure. In the middle, a little triangular plate had been placed on another lozenge-shaped one. Research has demonstrated that the heap of stones was piled in a pool from which the tip emerged. A direct connection of this structure with water management cannot be proved but it was certainly dedicated to water. Like the cairn, heaps of stones that nomads still build in the desert, and the hermaion, typical of the ancient pastoral world, the site of El-Guettar is, at present, the oldest non-funeral monument in the world, a boundary line, water architecture, and a Palaeolithic nymphaeum.

The space organisation underling religious or economic needs can be ascribed to the hunters-gatherers who used caves, fire, and water for these purposes. Animals had been the first to exploit natural underground environment and used them as shelters from inclement weather and temperate dwellings in all seasons, as well as places for rest, because of the comfortable guano to lie on and puddles to drink they were provided with. Owing to the presence of water, the cave

FIGURE 2.4 Algerian Sahara. The barrows and the stone arrangements disseminated all over the Sahara refer to a prehistoric civilisation based on the capability of catching the quantity of water contained in the atmosphere, which in the presence of colder stone masses condenses and is retained in the soil.

FIGURE 2.5 The cave of Pertosa (Cilento), used for its pools of water and as a holy place since Palaeolithic times.

dwellings were used not only by fierce beasts known as cave dwellers, together with bears and sabre-like teeth tigers, but also by any kind of herbivores. Still now, in Kenya, large herds of elephants go into deep caves to drink and bathe in the puddles.

Lightening and heating those natural places up with jealously and protected fires were the first way to occupy and artificially manage them. The next action was the harvesting of seeping water, as well as of water dripping from stalactites into specially made cavities. Management of water, light, and heat energy in the caves played a key role in the process through which man started to shape the landscape. As first form of shelter and threshold from the unfriendly outside world into a protected, intimate, and cosy dimension, the cave was the favourite place for artistic representations and rites and the archetype of temples.

2.4 Drainage Systems and Labyrinths

Hunter-gatherers used to dig pools under the stalactites in the caves to harvest and store drinking water exuding or dripping from the rocks. In the proximity of the areas where useful wild herbs grew, they dug out pits and little streams, on slopes or before caves, in order to replenish spontaneous vegetation and improve its yield by creating the first artificial irrigation system (Drower, 1954). The hunter-gatherers' ability to manage environmental mechanisms regulating water resources on a large scale has been proved, as demonstrated by archaeological research on Palaeolithic sites and studies

FIGURE 2.6 The cave of Loltun (Yucatan), where in prehistory pools of water were carved out under the stalactites to collect the dripping water. Paintings referring to fertility rites and graffiti depicting concentric circles bear witness to the ritual power of the place.

FIGURE 2.7 The cave of Nakuto Laab (Ethiopia). The cave equipped in prehistory for the catchment of the dripping water is still now a holy place of the Coptic religion because of its healthy and salvific water.

made on Australian drainage systems introduced by the Aborigines. The hunter-gatherers reached both New Guinea and Australia 40,000 years ago when these lands were still joined, but were separated from the Asian continent by at least 80 km of sea. The distance was overcome with bamboo rafts, requiring considerable knowledge and navigational skills that were not equalled by later groups in any other part of the world for tens of thousands of years until the Neolithic migrations. New Guinea and Australia thus developed a society cut off from the continent, with a high level, independent culture, almost a Palaeolithic Mediterranean civilisation in the South Seas. Archaeological excavations in New Guinea have brought to light a complex system of drainage channels, built 9,000 years ago, that reached their fullest development around 6,000 years ago (Diamond, 1997).

The Australian district of Southwestern Victoria is a mild area with humid winters and hot seasons. People's survival was greatly affected by the highly variable climate, so that the lands where they lived were flooded during humid seasons and became arid in the dry seasons. Generally, human groupings faced up to this situation by seasonal mobility and by practising fishing, hunting, or harvesting, according to the circumstances. The Aborigines from Victoria introduced a water regulation system on a territorial scale, like the systems used by the sedentary Neolithic groupings (Lourandos, 1980).

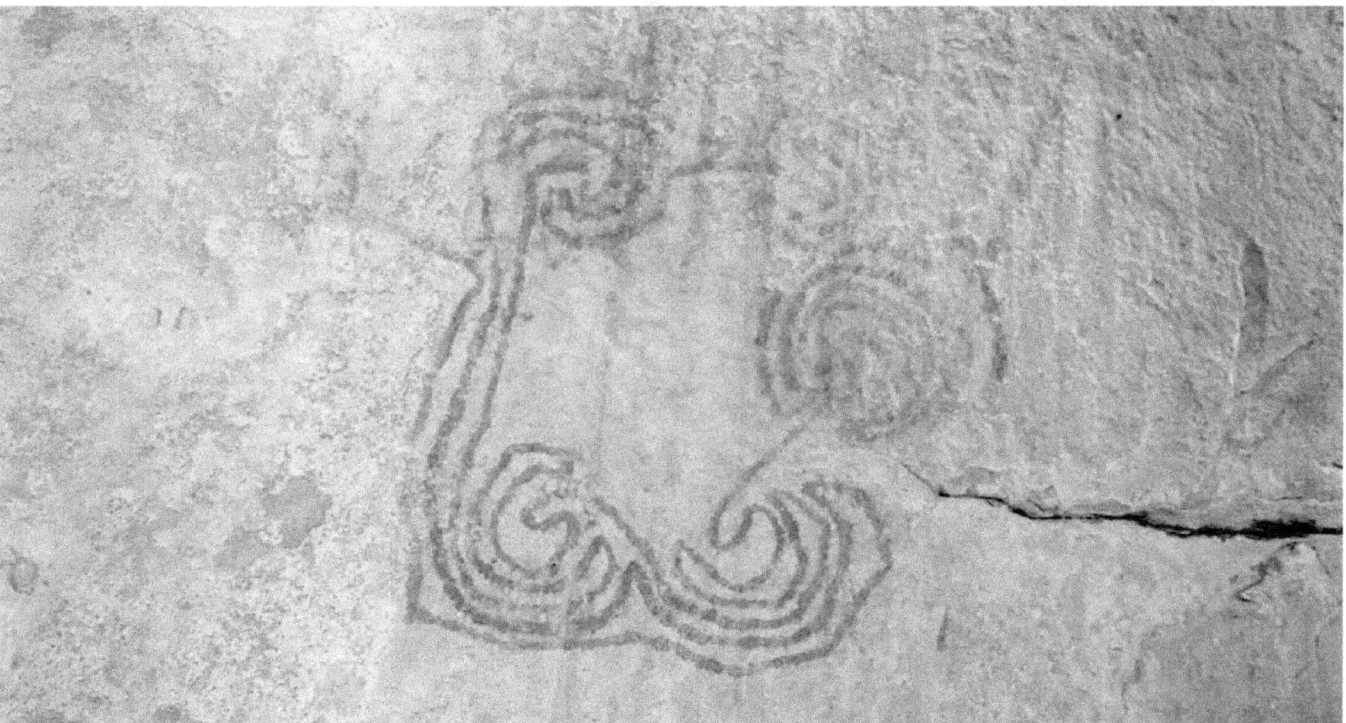

FIGURES 2.8–2.9 Tassili n'Ajjer (Algeria). Paintings of concentric circles, meanders, and labyrinths recur in Saharan prehistoric art: above (the site of Tin Tegherghent) a graffito of an ox decorated on the inside and all around with concentric circles and meanders; below (the site of Sefar) painting of a labyrinth.

A complex network of ditches and embankments crosses a 6-hectare area bordering on the mountain slopes on one side and the lands subject to flooding on the other side. The hunter-gatherers carried out this massive work only by means of the digging-sticks used for fishing eels, which were an important source of nourishment. It consists of a network of channels conveying water from the mountains, drainage systems, regulating moisture levels in humid areas, and a huge maze-like network of ditches, understood to have been a trap for eels. This series of massive works was completed probably because of a gradually worsening of environmental conditions. About 3,000 years ago the store of water was exhausted, forcing large social groupings to manage and preserve marshlands by a system of embankments, diversions, and the water labyrinth.

In Australia, this kind of work on the landscape dates back to about 10,000 years ago, though similar constructions made by hunter-gatherers since the Palaeolithic Age have been found. On the highlands of Tassili N'Ajjer, in the Algerian Sahara desert, many enigmatic graffiti and paintings of labyrinths similar to the Australian water systems network appeared among the prehistoric cave paintings. In the Palaeolithic Age, the management of a gradually collapsing humid environment and the capability to exploit fishing resources provided Saharan people with the surplus to develop their cultural knowledge, as wall art is witness of. Drawings representing fishes prove the concrete relationship between

FIGURE 2.10 Tassili n'Ajjer (Algeria), the site of Tin Tazarift. Figures of the Saharan wall art, dating back to the archaic period called "the age of the Round Heads", appear to be hovering in the air. They are probably swimming in water coursers and are recurrent in the humid period of the Sahara.

FIGURE 2.11 Tassili n'Ajjer (Algeria), the site of Sefar, the so-called painting of "the Sowers". Female figures with short skirts and ornaments made of vegetable fibres appear to be busy harvesting, sowing, and arranging dams and channels.

Saharan people and water. Two graffiti along Wadi Jerat on Tassili N'Ajjer represent a man and a woman, with a reticulate tool in one hand stretching downwards, while the other hand is ready to catch something. This is a fishing scene using a wicker tool to catch the prey, probably performed in a channel of the water labyrinths.

2.5 Women, Their Knowledge of Plants and First Forms of Cultivation

Pictures of labyrinths are frequent in Aboriginal cave painting and are to be found in all prehistoric wall art. Maze-like water systems favoured the hunter-gatherers' demographic growth and prosperity, irrespective of climatic and environmental conditions. They included a series of works aiming to take benefit from environment: the creation of sites for food storage (plants, meat, and dried fish); the use of fire to regulate the spread of plants and generate new ones; attempts to increase the edible insect and larva species; the transport and cultivation of tubers. Wooden dikes or stones were put across streams to decrease their strength; animal remains were used as fertilisers.

In this framework, women played a significant role as bearers and conveyers of knowledge. Berries, roots, seeds, and edible larvae were first recognised by women and children, owing to their natural bent for taking and tasting whatever they

FIGURE 2.12 The cave of Loltun (Yucatan). The name of the cave which means "stone flowers" still today recalls the practice of using these cavities in the first attempts to cultivate the plants gathered during the migrations.

found, out of curiosity or simply for fun. As a matter of fact, the most widespread plants had bright colours and forms, such as leguminous plants, datura and belladonna, or an intense smell, such as aromatic herbs. In the modern age as well, such plants as tomatoes, potatoes, and tobacco were introduced to Europe for merely ornamental use at first. Women learnt about the plants' powers: their vegetative energy, the power of life in a seed and its disposition to reproduce and be cultivated; and they learnt to store and carry plants as well.

Likewise, animal breeding probably started in the Palaeolithic age with the same non-utilitarian origins; insects, rogs, and birds were collected and kept for fun and curiosity or to absorb their qualities through imitation or sympathetic magic. Domestication of animals originated from such practices as keeping mammals' young in captivity aiming at no practical purposes but out of a maternal instinct to help the weakest ones, which would certainly not overcome the struggle for life. This explains the graffiti that have been found, dating back 14,000 years, which represent domesticated horses and dogs.

The caves, as Palaeolithic temples of memory and central elements of stability in the network of mobility, were the places where the vestal virgins kept their transportable gardens containing aromatic, medical, or hallucinogenic plants; guarded the fire, harvested the water, decorated the walls, and looked after the first animal-marvels that were the result of domestication. These caves were the centres of subsequent productive changes in the environment.

Farmer-Breeders

3

FIGURE 3.1 Tassili n'Ajjer (Algeria), emblematic Neolithic Saharan drawing. The circle, surrounded by oxen and probably made from the hide of the same animal, recalls the building of a circular hut of animal skins and the organisation of a settlement around a common centre which is the symbol of sedentary life.

3.1 The Great Neolithic Transformation

The main accomplishment of the farmer-breeders was their passage from a nomadic to a sedentary way of life, settling on cultivated plains, and their demographic growth which underlay the large-scale process of transformation and productive exploitation of space. In the relatively short time of 10,000 years since they appeared, the way of life of most human beings changed. People spread all over the planet, colonizing and shaping lands. As a result, the hunter-gatherers progressively disappeared and, currently, they are reduced to a few endangered groups. Urban society, which has been the heart of a productive, technological, and demographic dynamism in modern age, originated from the Neolithic process of adopting a more sedentary life. As a matter of fact, on a worldwide scale farm workers are still 50% of the work force, although in western countries they are less than 7%.

The practices of plant cultivation and animal husbandry were first introduced in the Neolithic age in those areas, which are now undergoing processes of degradation and desertification. The start of agriculture in tropical and subtropical environments and in arid and semi-arid climates, which were apparently the least suitable to develop it (Childe, 1954),

FIGURE 3.2 Tassili n'Ajjer (Algeria), scenes of Saharan Neolithic breeding. The attitude, the coat and the swollen udders of the animal suggest domestication.

was due to the fact that high temperature and the long sunny days are the best conditions to allow even a small strip of land to feed a significant human community. Without these convenient conditions, the first agricultural activities carried out on small areas would have been abandoned before demonstrating their potential applications on a larger scale. Thus, the social revolution in the Neolithic period occurred in the arid areas with a catastrophic water regimen, alternating floods with drought. These particular environmental conditions require social cooperation and working commitment to dig out embankments and canals, harvest water, shape and protect fruitful soils, in order to gain the most benefit from any favourable conditions (Drower, 1954).

However, most of these areas had a much larger tree stock in the past than today. Immediately after the ice age, a greater water supply, coming from the melting of perpetual snow, started a humid phase in desert areas. Later, the climate became warmer but this alone cannot explain the disappearance of forests and plant cover from the once-fertile and populated areas. The Palaeolithic economy, based on a limited exploitation of natural resources, developed, in the Neolithic age, into an economy founded on the productive exploitation of the land. This triggered a deterioration of the environment, which in borderline geographical circumstances had an amplified effect. It follows that the phenomenon of desertification was not due to natural climatic changes but to man's destructive interaction with nature.

In the Neolithic age, man developed certain practices because of three essential conditions: (a) the availability of fruitful seeds and domestic animals; (b) fertile soils; (c) water. The organisation of productive and sedentary life depended on the existence of these conditions. Indeed, the efforts to maintain them in periods of shortage of water and in harsh environmental circumstances explain the development of technology, the creation of habitat systems, and the introduction of complex forms of social organisation. The selection and classification for use of crop seeds and domestic animals required the building of grain storage spaces and shelters for animals and human beings: this laid the bases for architecture. The need for fertile soils fostered the acquisition of practical know-how for applying manure, humus formation and soil structure, soil protection and maintenance: on these principles depended the organisation of space. Water harvesting and management demanded knowledge of the laws of liquid physics and environmental dynamics, the elaboration of methods of numbering, calculation, transcription, and memorisation, and this led to the formation of legal and social systems. Successful solutions to all these issues and, in particular, to the harvesting and distribution of water led to the birth and development of the first societies.

The development of agriculture and its direct connection with water management can be summarized in the following phases:

- small plots in alluvial semi-arid regions, naturally inundated with water (nomadic cultivation);
- development in Iraq and on the Anatolian plains of ditches and floodwater diversion dams (use of floods for irrigation), since the 6th millennium;
- locations on higher slopes to exploit the force of gravity for irrigation (garden horticulture);
- excavation of cisterns and water intakes for the irrigation of fields located on arid hills, since the 4th millennium (villages with ditches);
- creation of wells from the middle of the 3rd millennium (urban extension);
- water catchment in the desert through drainage tunnels (qanat, foggara, falaj) and distribution on a large-scale of irrigation systems in the inter-fluvial basins, in the 1st millennium (oases and towns on caravan routes).

In dry areas, early methods of cultivation were subject to the availability of water resources in nature: moisture in the atmosphere and in the sediments in the soil. Moisture, seeping into the soil, played a significant role in the cultivation of small vegetable gardens, in the areas next to basins and watercourses or geological situations and heaps of stones that helped the collection of moisture and the condensation of dew. A nomadic type of farming is still practised today in the Sahara, simply scattering seeds in suitable areas and returning to these places in the harvest season. By observing the best growth cycle of spontaneous plants, it was possible to find the most suitable zones. It was also possible to discover the areas where the second water resource was available, the water in the sediments in the soil. Alluvial soils, loess and dry wadi beds make the most suitable places for water to be stored in the upper layers. Because of the aridity of the soils, the rain runs off the barren slopes, so that large quantities of water collect in natural depressions and in the wadi beds, and are preserved in the sediments. Under these conditions a rainfall of 50–150 mm a year, an insignificant amount for non-irrigated farming that relied just on rain, provide a 125 million cubic metre groundwater reserve. Thus, plants directly soak up water from the soil or from hollows and puddles that are small enough not to need stone reinforcements.

These conditions explain the distance of the early Neolithic settlements from a water spring, which was very often completely absent or could be from 1 to 5 km away. Drinking water, which was needed in smaller quantities than for agriculture, could be carried in skins or wicker jars, waterproofed with clay, and poured into the pools near the huts. Plant cultivation on the other hand needed hydromorphic soils and this condition determined their choice of location.

Many African villages are settled near cropping areas, even though this implies long hikes up to the well or the drinking water spring, still now.

In the Middle East, in Anatolia, Africa, and Europe, the early forms of agriculture were practised on soils which where naturally water-logged, thanks to humid or marshy lands, and with other resources such as fishing, snails, and shellfish, in order to make small, highly productive areas without too much effort. Meaningfully, already in the Mesolithic Age, the first forms of sedentary life developed under the same conditions.

3.2 Settlements Without Agriculture

The first forms of cultivation and domestication are usually thought to have been introduced in the Near East, more precisely in the Fertile Crescent, stretching over a semicircular area from the Dead Sea up to the Iranian highlands. The archaeological site of Jericho in Palestine, in the depression of the Dead Sea, is commonly known as the first stable human settlement in the world. The Natufian civilisation was the most archaic example of settlement, which developed from 10,000 to 8,000 BC and was characterized by a process towards a sedentary existence, before the Neolithic age. The next settlement, dating back to 8,350–7,370 BC, consisted of many round-shaped raw earth-brick constructions, surrounded by a ditch and a 3 m thick, 5.75 m high wall, with a stone tower about 9 m high. At the time of these constructions, belonging to the pre-ceramic Neolithic age, wild barley and probably wheat were cultivated, while game largely consisted of gazelles and frogs. Starting from 7200 BC, dwellings developed into rectangular shapes, with plastered walls and floors (Çauvin, 1994). The finding of human skulls covered with plaster and, sometimes, with shells in the place of the eyes, suggests the practice of a religious cult of the dead. Goats, rams and, probably pigs were bred, while oxen had already been domesticated. Peas and lentils were grown, besides barley and wheat.

Water channels and irrigation systems already existed in this phase, when ceramics had not yet been introduced, but the structures of Jericho were probably used as water systems in far more ancient times. Actually, it is not yet clear what purpose the ditch, the wall, and the stone tower served. Recent research tends to discount the initial theories about their defensive function. They are more likely to have been used for water harvesting. In fact, being located on low hills that were subject to landslides along the slopes that lead down to the depression, the site must have needed continuous works of soil reinstatement and collection of rainwater before they mixed with the salty and useless waters of the Dead Sea. Previously, the most ancient construction of Jericho, a high platform in natural clay supported by walls, dating back to the pre-Neolithic age, had been likewise conceived. Though not yet breeders and farmers, the Natufians were already a sedentary people, able to make tools for the organisation of space. Similar works of soil embankment have been found in the Negev desert, where the Hedomites introduced the first agricultural techniques later used by the Nabateans.

Thus, the current belief that sedentariness was the outcome of farming is overturned. Human groupings, holding knowledge that was not applied to productive farming purposes, led a sedentary life. They used their knowledge to carry out works for supporting the habitat, or to arrange symbolic places for their cults and gatherings. The birth of agriculture is conventionally considered as a revolution. However, both sedentariness and knowledge necessary for farming and breeding preceded agricultural practices.

Furthermore, it is important to understand that people began farming lands not to improve their living standards, but rather due to environmental changes. In fact, hunting, fishing, and gathering were much comfortable and effortless means of subsistence, compared to the hard work of farming. Agriculture, therefore, was a necessity. At the end of the Ice Age, global warming and a greater amount of moisture, due to the melting of perpetual snow, created mild and irrigated areas. The hunter-gatherers took advantage of these favourable conditions, which allowed them to settle and exploit local natural resources. As a consequence of this the birth rate increased. The nomadic tribes, subject to continuous migrations, had been limited to one or at most two children. Later, the demographic growth led to a gradual decrease in natural resources by hunting and gathering wild fruits, snails, shellfish, and frogs, that along with natural catastrophes and the unfavourable climate, eventually forced these sedentary groupings, who were not yet farmers, to undertake actions to organise space and start farming.

3.3 Land and Water: The Origins of Urban Civilisation

The process leading to sedentary life took place simultaneously in different areas. Like the Natufians of the Middle East, at the end of the Palaeolithic Age the Capsians of North Africa lived in large sedentary communities based not only on hunting and eating plants, but also on snail gathering and consumption. It was the abundance of this local resource, resulting from the environmental changes that occurred in those areas at that time that turned the Palaeolithic Capsians into a sedentary people. Huge heaps of ashes can still be seen where incredible quantities of snails were roasted for more than 2,000 years. Studies carried out on hundreds of Capsian villages have put forward the hypothesis of north-African "neolithisation'" as a whole process involving people from the Mediterranean to Senegal and from the Atlantic to Libya (Vaufrey, 1939). Therefore the Capsians and the Natufians are thought to have been the common ancestors of all the Mediterranean people.

The first productively used areas are likely to have been more numerous than commonly believed. Recent genetic surveys have shown that domestication of cattle probably took place in two different regions of south-western Turkey,

FIGURE 3.3 Oasis of Taghit (Algerian Sahara). The compact and clustered urban agglomeration made up of adobe houses recalls the first forms of proto-urban settlement found in Anatolia.

east of the Iranian desert, and in a third African area (Cavalli Sforza et al., 1994). A further independent area of cattle breeding was located in India. Even if cattle taxonomy is more recent than goats' and rams', it confirms the hypotheses put forward by archaeological research: the first process of neolithisation took place not only in the Middle East, but also in Africa, Anatolia, and the Pakistan–India area. In Africa, the existence of pre-historical societies characterised by developed forms of culture has been proved by rupestral evidence found in Tanzania, Namibia, all long the Rift Valley, and up to the Sahara, where it is most concentrated. It is highly unlikely that the world of farmers and breeders beautifully represented in these works with the same artistic skill as in the Palaeolithic ones did not have local centres of dissemination. In the Sahara, species of cultivated millet dating as far back as the 7th millennium have been found during the limited research carried out there (Camps, 1974); despite the high level of the artistic representations, few traces of constructions dating back to that period have been found up to now. The question can be resolved by studying evidence found in the other sites that underwent the neolithisation process. The sites of Çatal Hüyük in Anatolia near Konya and of Jarmo at the foot of the Zagros mountains in Iraq are all Neolithic settlements, made of adobe bricks only, just like the first constructions in Jericho. Perhaps the very perishability of the materials used has made the Saharan sites difficult to find during archaeological excavations.

In particular, due to its size and the complexity of its structures as well as to the quality and quantity of findings, the site of Çatal Hüyük is so important that it is thought to have been the first town ever built, the cradle of civilisation. Buried in a tell of about 7 hectares, only a very small part of which has been excavated and with huge difficulties, the large built-up area consists of a series of closely clustered habitats made of adobe bricks only. This kind of close-built structure has made archaeologists think that doors and entrances did not exist at all, and that the ways in were made through stairs from the terraces (Mellaart, 1967). In fact, excavations are not of much aid in understanding how this village was built, since adobe constructions are not easily identified. The site plan and the materials used in Çatal Hüyük are very similar to those of the thousands of adobe-construction settlements in the Saharan oases, which are still inhabited. Adobe constructions and clustered habitats are used here because they suit the local environment and climate conditions and the need for a careful use of natural resources.

Adobe constructions allow fuel saving which would otherwise be necessary to fire bricks, and also provide better thermal insulation of the buildings. The material used is easily found and treated. In the Sahara, the red soil of the desert is still ground and mixed with water and with straw that increases its binding capacity. By means of wooden moulds it is shaped into rectangular bricks, the so-called Arabian tub. Through Andalusian Spain the term adobe (al-toub) derives from tub, which is generally used to indicate raw earth-brick structures. Dried in the sun, the bricks become resistant, thus no trees need to be cut down for firing them. The thick walls of the dwellings are made of these bricks, which create a perfectly insulated inner environment, suitable for both torrid summer days and cold winter nights. The rooms inside the dwellings do not have an exact function, but their use depends on the seasons and climate changes, according to a sort of nomadism inside the houses. The terraces too, surrounded by high adobe walls, turn into ventilated bedrooms with the starry sky as a ceiling on hot summer nights.

In the Sahara, the most archaic building system of adobe walls uses semi-spherical raw earth-bricks. This technique is still used for the perimeter walls of the cropping areas. Both their shape and the method of laying them make these walls very similar to the "herringbone" masonry work, made of plano-convex bricks and produced in Mesopotamia in the 3rd millennium. A wicker basket is used as a mould, and the bricks, after having been dried in the sun, are arranged in alternate oblique strips, thus shaping a herringbone design. The interstices in the wall form a sort of decorative "open-work", which is above all the most suitable protection against sandstorms. A completely closed barrier, in fact, would cause heaps of materials carried by the wind and the plots would be progressively buried in sand. This building technique is supposed to provide gardens with a greater water supply. At night, the wind blows against the convex sides of the bricks and releases humidity into the earth the walls are composed of. During the day, the hot wind penetrates the interstices in the wall and reaches the garden, where heat is absorbed and the temperature decreases.

Other types of bricks still in use in sub-Saharan Africa are mere hand moulded spheres. In southern Arabia, instead, by directly pressing wooden moulds on the rolled-out mud mixture, wide and flat bricks are made. Long muddy "sausages" are also made, hand shaped and arranged in consecutive spirals to form a wall. However, a technique that does not use bricks is the so-called pisé: the raw earth mixture is poured into wooden moulds and pressed. Once the mixture has dried up, the wooden planks are taken off and used again to make another form. This practice is shown in the ancient Egyptian drawings.

Entrance to dwellings is a series of roofed tunnel-like paths running across the built-up area, which is thus given the appearance of an inaccessible maze, typical of underground cave-dwellings. Meaningful defensive and climatic functions underlie this technique. The use of such a system could explain the apparent lack of entrances in Çatal Hüyük. Here, the practice of irrigated cultivations shows the careful use of natural resources, as in the Saharan oases. Apart from the building materials, the methods used in the organisation of space for climatic purposes could be similar as well. In fact, excavations at Çatal Hüyük have not reached the barren layer of the ground; therefore, the maze of paths may not have been found yet.

In Çatal Hüyük the vast decorated rooms are significant. Their importance and quantity make them the social places of the whole village. There, big cattle horns reliefs and the first wall paintings stand out. These spaces were probably devoted to rites where oxen or bulls and female statuettes representing "the lady of animals" had an important function. Similar sculptures have been found in the Neolithic hypogea of Malta, devoted to the cult of the great mother goddess, and in some tombs in Sardinia. The paintings represent bulls, scenes of hunting and landscapes. In one of these, the outline of the impressive and threatening volcano of that region dominates the scene. That is the first known drawing of a landscape which is painted on built walls. The volcano is probably portrayed for ritual purposes deriving from man's fear of the force of nature. Perhaps it was the pressure on the environment and the threat of cataclysms relating to the

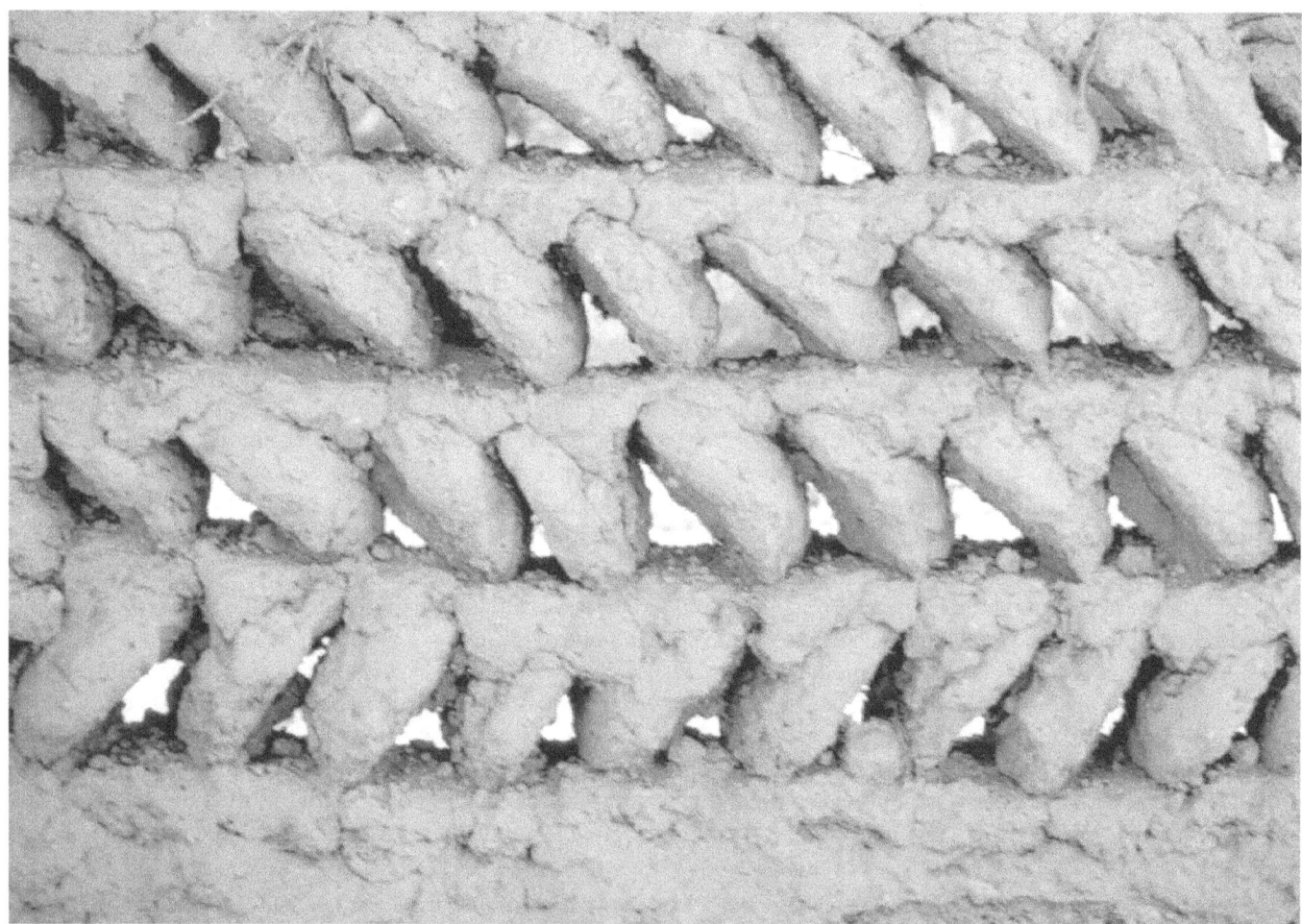

FIGURE 3.4 The adobe walls surround the small tilled parcels and contribute to the water balance. When the wind penetrates the narrow interstices in the plano-convex bricks, it accelerates and expands making the temperature decrease. The raw earth mixture absorbs and releases humidity into the soil.

volcano that fostered social grouping and cult practices, leading to the building of such a striking site as Çatal Hüyük. It is proved that the favourable conditions of Çatal Hüyük were created precisely by the volcanic eruptions. As a matter of fact, the fertility of the soils is due to the volcanic ash layers deposited over time. Due to their flexibility, adobe buildings and clustered habitats reproducing underground structures are, absolutely, the most resistant to earthquakes and volcanic activity and the best protected against volcanic ashes and lapilli. Otherwise they easily deteriorate under ordinary atmospheric conditions: torrential rains or floods can wholly destroy them, without leaving any trace. Therefore they need constant maintenance. Every season, fresh mud is added to mould the structures and the surfaces. Maintenance of dwellings is such a rite, and the town turns into an anthropomorphic and living thing. "Building a house means giving life to something dead" say the inhabitants of Saharan villages, showing how close their relationship with their dwellings has been since ancient time. This explains why the Egyptians would bow down with religious respect before a mixture of water and mud. They built up their civilisation by using that material. The first Pyramids were made of adobe bricks, using the material that remained from the digging of irrigation canals. It was probably the experience previously gained by the Saharan people in the building similar constructions that allowed the Egyptians, in the Neolithic age, to show to the world such astonishing achievements as the Pyramids.

3.4 From Huts to Stone: The Water Systems of Beida

A widespread use of stone has been observed in the partially excavated pre-ceramic Neolithic village of Beida, as well as in a number of still untouched sites, such as Shakaret Musei'ed located like Beida near Petra in Jordan. People were established in Beida for 500 years, as is clear from the six levels of stable settlement, dating back to between 7,000 and 6,500 BC. Throughout that period, the village developed and new kinds of building structures were added about every 70 years. Now it is possible to study how all these structures evolved throughout the ages. Level VI, the most archaic, had been preceded by some forms of semi-permanent settlement around fires in certain periods of the year. It consists of circular stone constructions with floors half dug into the subsoil. The outside bearing walls stand closely together in order to support each other, while the interstices between constructions are filled with rubble. On level V, the dwellings are still in the form of circular stone huts, but they also appear standing alone. Level IV shows the passage from circular to square shapes, with slightly rounded-off corners. This innovative structure led to the development of new and greater skills to build rectilinear walls, which were much more difficult to support. The interiors show carefully plastered ceilings and walls, and are provided with fireplaces. Levels III and II show an extraordinary innovation that has made archaeologists believe that foreign groups had come and introduced different building techniques, as proved by the fact that the types of construction on the following level, which is the last settlement level, are similar to those of level IV. The innovation consists in the so-called corridor-dwellings, because of their rectangular plan, with six small rooms laid out three on each side of a central corridor. Perhaps these buildings were only used as craftsmen's workshops, while people lived on the upper floors, which were made of lighter structures and supported by the massive walls of the workshops. In corridordwellings, elbow-shaped courtyards were built along both sides of very large rooms, where a fire was placed and common meals were eaten. The structure resembling a "b" recalls the structure of the dwellings of Jarmo. It is the original pattern of the Phoenician dwellings called beit, whose form originated the letter "b" of the alphabet.

The Neolithic period of Beida also preceded the introduction of fired clay. However, besides the many stones found, which were used for the hand grinding of grains, raw earth-objects were also made in that period, such as a cup or a statuette representing a ram. Near a large complex that is known as "the sanctuary", with finely plastered floors, there is a wide flat stone for draining water, which might be evidence of rites connected to water and pastoral life. Recent excavations in the larger area of Beida have unearthed a long stone wall surrounding the whole of level VI. It is only 1 m high, so that excludes any military function. It is more likely to be a structure built for soil consolidation and land arrangement, which raises a series of significant questions.

During the 500-year period when Beida existed, most of the Neolithic changes occurred, from animal breeding to food production and the land organisation for dwellings and farming. Anthropologists have always wondered how prehistoric farmers maintained soil fertility, lacking any knowledge of crop-rotation techniques. The answer to the issue lies in the great mobility of the villages, which were abandoned once the surrounding fertile soils were exhausted. This also explains the many traces of Neolithic villages found in Africa or southern Italy. Assuming that the same human

FIGURE 3.5 Oasis of Taghit (Algerian Sahara), the narrow streets are built like tunnels through the built-up area. This practice has an important climatic function, providing protection from the strong sun's heat and dissuading strangers who are not able to find their way across this maze of streets only lit up by rare light wells, mostly built in recent times.

FIGURE 3.6 The site of Beida (Jordan desert). Construction of a semi-hypogeal circular house from the more archaic level and dating back to the 7th millennium.

FIGURE 3.7 The impressive archaeological vestiges of Beida and the structures of the so-called corridor-dwellings, the embankments, and the water protection systems.

FIGURE 3.8 The site of Beida. Above on the left a large semi-elliptic stone may be distinguished. Now, it is broken into two parts and a bush has partially grown over it but in the past it clearly had a water function.

grouping frequently moved and settled in different sites, it is easy to understand why so many of these sites have been found, without drawing the necessary conclusions about their demographic and cultural importance. Migration was actually practised only by people using moveable wooden shelters or quickly reassembling ones on the new site, without any waste of time or work. It is probable that human groupings using adobe buildings also migrated. The stone structures of Beida on the contrary required too much work for groups to rapidly abandon them. The duration of this site proves that it had been inhabited for ages. Therefore the problem of maintaining soil fertility had probably been overcome by the building of structures such as fences and ditches, or the famous tower of Jericho. They had always been understood as serving war purposes, but recent studies have recognised their important use as systems for water and environmental protection.

3.5 Drainage, Condensation, Harvesting, and Fertilisation: A Multipurpose System

The so-called entrenched villages in the Apulia district of Daunia and on the plateau of the Murgia, in Basilicata, settled from the 7th to the 4th millennium, are the first Neolithic sites in Europe, where human communities achieved massive constructions, thanks to a large production surplus. Simple stone tools were used to dig deep ditches in the rocky ground to make enclosures comprising several concentric circles, meanders, and crescents.

In the Neolithic settlement of Murgia Timone, near the town of Matera, an area of about 2 hectares is enclosed by a large elliptic excavation having in one of its two focuses a smaller inner circle. Its longer diameter stretches from east to west and the two entrances to the village are perfectly oriented at these two extremities. As in Jericho and Beida, these ditches were not used for defensive purposes, as had been supposed at the time of their discovery (Ridola, 1926). As a matter of fact, no remains of arrowheads or other prehistoric weapons have ever been found. Furthermore, groups of humans or wolves could very easily cross them during their attacks. In the Neolithic Age their function was more likely to have been connected with breeding and farming practices.

Surveys made of some villages of Daunia, which are characterised by a number of semi-circular trenches, have proved that they were used as drainage systems (Tiné, 1983; Leuci, 1991) to reclaim the land for use. This region, at the bottom of the Gargano promontory, in Apulia, because of its hydromorphic soils, was suited to Neolithic agricultural practices that needed soft and fertile soils. The large quantity of moisture made it necessary to dig out ditches regulating the surplus water. Later on, when the resources of Daunia were exhausted, and perhaps under the pressure of micro-environmental pollution due to the demographic growth, the process of neolithisation moved to the healthier areas on the Murgia plateau. Here the ditches were dug in the limestone using tools made of stone extracted from the Gargano flint mines. Aerial photographs of the village of Murgia Timone show its perimeter, now covered with vegetation that grows more thickly thanks to the moisture in the ditch, showing that on these limestone plateaux one of the purposes of the trenches was to collect water (Laureano, 1993).

FIGURE 3.9 The Neolithic ditch of Murgia Timone (Matera). The thicker vegetation makes the ditch visible. On the right the double ring mausoleum of the Bronze Age is evident.

An evocative case is the ditch of Toppo Daguzzo, in Basilicata, where massive works were destroyed between the end of the Aeneolithic Age and the beginning of the Bronze Age (Cipolloni Sampò, 1999). Especially, remains of a fence and a wall standing up on mounds of heavy stone blocks and river cobbles have been found. This proves that the setting up of an outside wall surrounding the ditch was probably intended for the preservation of water collected in the ditch.

The digging of ditches developed around cave-dwellers' habits that were widespread and continued in these areas until the modern era. In the south of Italy, the climate ranged from freezing winters to scorching summers. Water shortage fostered practices for meteoric water collection and underground storage. Caves keep a constant temperature throughout the year and are the ideal shelters for human beings and animals, for the storage of grain and mainly of water. The latter is the most precious underground resource: water dripping from walls, seeping out from the rocks, forming puddles, and, though always drawn, "miraculously" keeping at a steady level, just as in the cave of Manduria described by Pliny (Natural History, II, 226). Each underground cavity can be related to water-harvesting techniques or to water-related rites. Evidence of such practices, dating back to the 4th millennium (Tiné and Isetti, 1980), were found in the Grotta Scaloria, along the Gargano slopes, in Apulia, in the form of ceramic pots, which were placed under stalactites to harvest dripping water.

FIGURE 3.10 Murgia Timone. Two ellipses mark the partially visible perimeter of the large Neolithic settlement. Only hard work and collective cooperation, using only stone tools, can have made the excavation possible.

In some caves, vapour-laden air caused by the heat coming up from the magma under the earth's crust is condensed along the walls to produce water. This method that was described by the Latin writer Vitruvius (De Architettura, VIII, 4) can be seen among the ruins of the Roman town of Tiddis, in North Africa. In Eritrea, on the highlands and in the region of Afar, the fumaroles, which are called boina (Dainelli and Marinelli, 1912) by the Danakils and originate from the faults of the Rift Valley, produce moisture that is harvested in the open air by means of a device made of tree branches. This technique involves building hut-like structures with conical roofs made from plants right over the volcanic fumaroles. Vapour rises up to the branches where it condenses into water and drops down. Then it is collected in basins. A similar method is used to collect dew from the straw and leaves covering deep trenches dug into the ground. This technique was applied by the Nabateans in the Negev Desert and in the underground Roman town of Bulla Regia in Tunisia (Pignauvin, 1932).

In the south of Italy the places which were first settled by human communities, are the dolines that consist of the circular depressions locally called puli, and the canyon cracks called gravine. Dwellings of this basic type have then been modified in different ways in other areas. A pulo, which is similar to a big funnel, harvests water and keeps the soil fertile, preserving vegetation. In south-eastern Murgia, in Conversano, a small town in the province of Bari, the so-called laghi (lakes) are still used; these are shallow depressions and dolines provided with pit-like cisterns at their bottom to catch seasonal rain (Palmisano and Fanizzi, 1992). The natural caves are the dwellings, set out in circles all around the walls and open towards the inside, thus resulting in a system of tunnels radiating out from a central courtyard. A similar but artificial structure can be found in the Neolithic flint mines, of which the largest examples in Europe are on the Gargano promontory (Di Lernia et al., 1990). On this model, a new type of dwelling was made consisting of an open-air semicircular

FIGURE 3.11 Natural dolinas and sinkholes are the environment favoured by the prehistoric habitat of the Apulian and Lucanian highlands of the Murge. Altamura, the aerial photograph of a massive karstic formation locally called pulo. Nearby is a sheepfold: its two rings evoke the structures of the Neolithic settlements. Drystone walls, embankments, and pathways are proof of the organisation of space.

FIGURE 3.12 A dolina used as garden-threshing floor, impluvium and pastoral shelter in the area of Matera. The dolina is the basic natural matrix of the agro-pastoral structures of the enclosures and the pit-courtyards.

common courtyard dug vertically downwards on a flat surface; this is a communal pit-courtyard, the vicinato a pozzo, and from its walls a system of underground rooms are tunnelled through, parallel to the ground. In the Mediterranean area it can be found on the highlands near Matera, in the Turkish region of Cappadocia, along the limestone banks of the River Loire in France, on the clayey shelves of Matmata in Tunisia, in the Libyan desert and in the south of Spain. In Lybia in the gebel Nefusa and Garian, the dwelling of the patriarchal family, of pre-Islamic origin, comprising a pit-courtyard with radially excavated rooms, is called damùs, a term that can be connected with dammusi, which is the name used in Pantelleria for the traditional passive architecture dwellings. In the most complex systems of this type, the tunnels are connected underground with other tunnels that radiate from other pit-courtyards, resulting in the landscape showing a number of large holes connected by a starry network of underground passageways. In China, on the loess plains along the Yellow River, even more complex systems can be found. There, the vertical hollow is not semicircular, but it is dug in precise rectangular shapes. These dwellings are still inhabited by millions of Chinese people. Similar structures can also be found in North America, all along the Chaco Canyon, in the Anasazi Indian villages called pueblo, which existed from the prehistoric age up to the 12th century AD. However similar structures are much more technologically advanced, consisting of pit-courtyards called kiva and made of massive dry stonewalls.

A pit-courtyard acts as an impluvium and provides an open-air sunny space, surrounded by walls, which can be used for agricultural work and preparation of food. Some of these courtyards are used for collecting waste and produce humus, and form gardens carved out of the rock. This technique solves the problem of in fertile soil and the need to protect plants. Very similar cultivation methods have been found in Petra, in the Jordanian desert. A space hewn in the rock,

FIGURE 3.13 Matmata (Tunisia). Dwelling consisting of a pit courtyard dug out of clayey soil. The rooms overlooking the courtyard have underground connections with others of the same kind.

closed towards the outside and open towards the sky, was the origin of courtyard dwellings used by the Sumerians, the Egyptians, in the Etruscan and classical world, and in the Islamic world too. A courtyard dwelling arrangement is actually the equivalent in buildings of what can be observed from cave dwelling architecture.

In Ethiopia, underground dwellings and churches are used by the Agau people at Ucrò, whose name derives from the root waqara, standing for "to dig", as well as at Dongollo, which means "stone". These are very characteristic structures since they were built by digging wide-open pits with a big block of stone left in the middle. This was then hollowed out and worked on the outside to build a church, which is therefore a monolith, having the roof at the level of the plain, from which the deep ditch separates it. The most massive structures of this type are in the site of Lalibela. They were made by using both the techniques of open-air excavation of pit-courtyards, peculiar to North Africa and southern Italy, and of hollowing underground rooms out, as in Egypt, in Petra, in the Sassi of Matera and in Cappadocia. Churches are provided with impluviums and systems supplying water to baptismal fonts. A network of open-air ditches, tunnels, and channels surrounds these monumental structures. The town derives its name from King Lalibela, who is traditionally believed to have built it during the Middle Ages. The Chebra Neghest, meaning "Glory of Kings", which is the holy book of the Ethiopian kings, has it that Lalibela performed fabulous feats such as for example, diverting the Blue Nile to deprive Egypt of water, thus endangering the life of the whole country. Even if this action seems exaggerated, the king was a great expert on water systems; his expertise was based on ancient knowledge and practices, still in use in that region.

FIGURE 3.14 Petra (Jordan). The carved sandstone rock contains hypogeal rooms arranged throughout the whole height of the rock. The different levels are connected with each other by means of external stairs carved out of the wall.

FIGURE 3.15 Cappadocia (Turkey). The troglodyte settlement is dug out of the rock. Water harvesting and the collection of guano produced by the pigeons enable productive gardens to be arranged at the foot of the built-up area on the protected valley floor that is free of buildings.

Farmer-Breeders 47

FIGURE 3.16 Lalibela (Ethiopia), monolithic hypogeal church of Biet Ghiorghis (12th century AD). The roof of the church is level with the surrounding plain. The building technique of the monolithic hypogeal structures consists of a courtyard dug in the plain and a block of rock left in the middle which is worked into architectural forms. The windows are hollowed out and through them internal storeys with colonnades, capitals, and architectural orders are excavated. The result has the appearance of built architecture which is actually dug out of a monolith.

FIGURE 3.17 Deep ditches surround the underground monumental complexes of Lalibela. Their water drainage and harvesting function is proved by the reservoirs for conserving the precious liquid in the dry seasons.

On the Ethiopian highlands, on the slopes of the Rift Valleys ridges, in the sunny lowland valleys, there are thousands of villages, where unchanging practices and knowledge are handed down. It is like seeing the original landscape of entrenched villages on the Murgia highlands in the south of Italy, reproduced on a very large scale. Each cluster of huts, located on a land rise higher than the surrounding fields or on a slight incline, is surrounded by elliptic ditches, sometimes consisting of concentric circles, one inside the other. These structures are still used. However, their utility will be appreciated only after several seasons or, maybe, years of constant observation aimed at understanding how they are used in different circumstances, either recurring or extraordinary. During the rainy season, the ditches serve as drainage systems that keep the soil dry, thus protecting huts and orchards. Once harvested, water is stored in the lower part of the ditches to be used during drought periods. In this way, they turn into linear-shaped cisterns for water harvesting that can also be very easily used as drinking troughs for cattle in emergency situations.

All along the walls of the ditches there are chambers and other rooms where food can be stored and kept fresh and safe from pests. Being free from water, the upstream sections of the ditches can be used to count cattle and sheep, to milk or shear them, sometimes to shelter and hide them. Waste from the village, animal carcasses and manure end up in these trenches as well. In this way, when irrigated, the fields are also fertilized. It is the same process as the Nile leaving fertile silt on lands while flooding them. Another method, adopted on a smaller scale, is the so-called flood recession technique, still used all along the river Niger, which was developed in ancient Egypt in the huge water system that created this country.

FIGURE 3.18 Lalibela (Ethiopia). A complex network of underground tunnels, most of them yet unknown, connect the different ditches and contribute to the preservation of the hypogeal monuments during the rainy season and to the conservation of the water resources during the dry seasons.

FIGURE 3.19 Village on the Ethiopian highland. The general view shows the elliptic ditch like that of the Neolithic villages.

FIGURE 3.20 Detail of the ditch whose multipurpose function still now enables the built-up area to be kept dry and drained, creating a water reservoir and a sewage collection system for soil fertilisation.

In some cases, the ditches branch off or are doubled by further semicircles. These can be used to intercept greater flows or to channel water into particular areas. They serve as outlets for the overflow in the case of particularly violent floods, or are used to clean an area by making water flow into it while channelling manure into other areas in particular seasons. The many Neolithic ditches and their branches found in Matera were probably dug out for these purposes. They were also provided with sluice gates or walls, placed not across the channel, so as to block it, but following its direction, thus functioning as flow shearing devices. Similar structures were unearthed during the excavation of a Neolithic site in the Apulian town of Gravina, near Matera, and of the Neolithic village of Casaldolce, near Rome, where the use of ditches for water purposes has been confirmed by recent archaeological research (Zarattini and Petrassi, 1997). In northern Italy the excavation of the Neolithic village of Piancada di Palazzolo dello Stella in the province of Udine enabled a large drainage channel to be identified. Used between the first half of the 5th and the beginning of the 6th millennium, it had an average width of 1.5 m and a depth of 50 cm. Confirming the many uses they had in Ethiopian village life, it was found to contain animal skeletons and carcasses.

Ditches probably originated from smaller pits that were used for storing water and dumping rubbish, of the type seen in the Neolithic and farming communities of Matera. These practices may have helped select cultivated domestic species and understand when the sowing season of each plant was. In fact, the seeds ingested ended up with the excrement in the pits, where they spontaneously germinated in the appropriate season. Wetting fields with water from the pits also helped to understand that manure could be used as a fertiliser.

FIGURE 3.21 Eritrea, oxen drinking from a ditch. The linear water structures are the most useful to the pastoral practices of watering and washing the herds of cattle.

FIGURE 3.22 Saharan Neolithic paintings seem to come to life in usual scenes of Eritrean pastoral life.

FIGURES 3.23–3.25 The Neolithic village of Murgia Timone, cavities carved out of the limestone for water harvesting and other agropastoral activities. The cavities in Fig. 3.23 are connected with each other forming a water decantation and filtration device. The micro-cistern on the right (see Fig. 3.24) fills up with rain water and acts as a drinking trough for the animals; the graffito of lyre-shaped horns and a cross mark the place and make it sacred. The device in Fig. 3.25 is a further example of a cavity for water collection and decantation.

FIGURE 3.26 These cavities in the Murgia that are both agricultural works and burial places in the rock, fill up with soil, humus, and water, allowing plants to grow.

This theory is underpinned by a particular technique that is still used in Burkina Faso. It is called zai and is able to regenerate highly degraded soils by means of water pits and waste, as well as through combined action of other living organisms. The soil is dug with holes that fill up with water in the humid season and are used as dump-sites for rubbish and manure in the dry season. This practice attracts termites that digest rubbish, thus its absorption by the plants' roots. Furthermore, the tunnels dug by the termites increase the soil's porosity. Seeds are then sown in the holes, giving very high crop yields. On the Murgia uplands in Italy, the practice of digging ditches so that soil collects in them has continued from the Neolithic era up to recent times.

Multipurpose functions are therefore the major characteristics of Neolithic structures, thus making the development of the first communities successful. Sedentary life forced them to devise and build the structures necessary to maintain favourable conditions in the face of environmental, seasonal, or catastrophic changes. Towers were raised, embankments dug out, walls built to condense and channel water, to make the soil fertile and preserve it. The tendency towards a sedentary life was then strengthened by the fact that these works, continually improved through the generations, offered too many advantages and too much hard work had been put into their construction for them to be abandoned. They represented important devices for adapting to and controlling the changing environmental conditions, thus reducing the uncertainty of human life. Successful models were handed down and reproduced in different times and places. Techniques were improved and practices took on a symbolic meaning and sacredness.

FIGURE 3.27 Tassili n'Ajjer (Algerian Sahara). The Neolithic painting represents a scene of the ancient technique of sowing by means of a perforated stick, which has remained unchanged until the present day (see Fig. 3.28–3.29).

FIGURES 3.28–3.29 In the Hadramaut valley and the isle of Ibiza women follow the plough and sow seeds straight into the drills by means of a perforated stick.

Since every kind of activity was considered as sacred, from sowing, fertilisation, and irrigation of lands, to digging procedures, the techniques used were perpetuated and spread unchanged to very distant places.

Women of very distant cultures use the method of sowing seeds straight into the ground by means of a perforated stick. It is of Neolithic origin, with the seed being dropped carefully into a hole in the ground made with a stick. It is represented on a Babylonian seal of the 2nd millennium in the scene of two oxen ploughing the soil. This technique is still adopted in the Hadramaut valley in Yemen, where a hollow stick identical to the one in Babylon is used, and on the Spanish isle of Ibiza, where men prepare the drills while women follow them and sow.

Spirituality and ritual fulfilled an important function in making people accept the hard work needed to preserve the balance of things. Besides, they permeated the techniques that, being considered as sacred, have been handed down through the ages. The great Neolithic circles, the ditches, and the activities connected to them were the reasons for the success of human communities and were also their identity marks. The use of these structures changed in each different season, thus emphasizing the seasonal climatic changes. For this reason, the village perimeters were traced according to specific astronomic orientations, while time elapsing was believed to depend on the organisation of space as codified in traditional knowledge that was itself an image of the harmony of the universe.

Metal-Using Agro-Astoralists

4

FIGURE 4.1 The Jordan desert the graffito of a hunting scene dating back to the Metal Age. A character of high rank with an impressive hairstyle and armed with a long javelin is hunting on horseback a gazelle. Stylised characters and an enigmatic symbolic representation is visible at the below portion.

4.1 Transhumant and Warring Nomadism

At the end of the Neolithic Age, great innovations in the way of life and in agriculture had already been introduced. In the following period, metal-working techniques were disseminated as well as mobility and the ability to organise the environment increased. Neolithic societies were replaced by new cultures adopting carts pulled by horses, boats able to sail long distances, new weapons, and stouter tools. Their spread over Europe and the Mediterranean depended first on the search for copper and tin used to make bronze at the end of the 3rd millennium, and, later, on the search for iron. Bellows, pipes, wrenches, and hammers were the new technological tools needed to reach melting point in the furnaces and to beat and forge weapons. The ease with which they could be carried enabled human groups to move from one place to another, thus gaining advantages over other societies. Today, in Africa metal objects are still worked by itinerant smiths carrying their goatskin bellows. They are welcomed with reverential awe in the villages. This triggered such processes as class stratification and privatisation of the means of production, which are the basis of the division of labour, trade, and competition to gain control over nature's resources, over other groups and individuals.

The term "metal" derives from the Greek metallao meaning "to search", while metallon means "the place where metals are extracted, a mine or a quarry". Greed for this precious mineral caused feverish prospecting and mining. The introduction of new weapons ensured military supremacy for people who had gained better means of moving thanks to the use of wheels, carts, and horses. These people, organised in family clans, had a pastoral, transhumant, and semi-nomadic type of economy. Everybody was the owner of his own mount, turning those people into extremely mobile and powerful war organisations. A new idea of the world spread from central Asia to Europe and the Mediterranean. It was based on a greater confidence in man's ability to explore, find, and profitably use natural resources. The female principles of fertility and fertilisation typical of the Neolithic economy were replaced by the power of metal, vigorously dug out and forged by fire. On that aggressive and penetrating power, a male aristocracy of warriors and conquerors was founded, proud of gaining control over the forces of nature. A typical example of a master of metals is the Homeric king-shepherd, a hero, and a conqueror attacking Troy, the Bronze Age town par excellence.

The passage from the animism of traditional societies to the modern age was actually performed by the birth of monotheism in that period. In the Book of Job in the Bible, this passage is impressively and poetically described: the feelings and fears of this farmer, whose communion with nature is bound to be broken by a greedy and violent civilisation, are openly expressed:

"Iron is drawn out of the earth and copper is smelted from ore. [...]

As for the earth, out of it comes bread, but underneath it is turned up as by fire. [...]

They put their hand to the flintstone rock and overturn mountains by the roots and their eyes see every precious thing. The sources of the rivers they probe, hidden things they bring to light. But where shall wisdom be found? And where is the place of understanding?" (Book of Job, 28, 2–12)

A result of the oral tradition that was only later recorded, that poem proves a concrete knowledge of the precious-stone deposits of Sinai exploited by ancient Egyptians, as well as of copper mines of the Arabah Valley between the Dead Sea and the Gulf of Aqaba.

The Fertile Crescent was the meeting and trading area of the great fluvial empires of that period, which were also the originators of the first monumental architecture: the Egyptian Pyramids in the Nile valley and the ziggurats in Sumeria, between the Rivers Tigris and Euphrates. In the Metal Age, thanks to the agricultural surplus, those powerful hydraulic organisations engaged a number of highly productive craftsmen and tradesmen. Egypt periodically sent expeditions of people on foot and donkeys across the desert up to Sinai to mine turquoise and to the Negev desert to mine copper. Firstly, they were organised as military groups accompanying miners and their supplies and food but soon, they evolved into caravans of merchants using local people. The Sumerians arranged caravans of carts pulled by oxen and onagers loaded with goods to be traded in the villages along their routes. The presence of mineral resources that seismic quakes had unearthed made the region of the Rift Valley a very interesting area. The bitumen of the Dead Sea had been used and traded since the Neolithic period, though copper mining was the greatest resource.

The copper mines in the Arabah Valley, located one day's walk from Petra, are among the first ones ever dug out. First the Hedomites and then the Nabateans exploited them in the early and middle Bronze Age and from the 18th to the 13th centuries BC. Later, they increased the economic power of Solomon's kingdom and were used up to the Islamic age. Mining methods and the availability of finer tools supported the development of excavation techniques. Open-air pits evolved into square- or round- section tunnels, provided with shoring pillars, ventilation systems, and drainage of groundwater tables. Expertise in mining is the technological basis for digging quarries and cave dwellings out of sandstone walls and tunnels intended for massive water works. Ventilation tunnels were built together with drainage systems and hydraulic devices to dam groundwater tables, "the most secret parts of nature and its hidden treasures were avidly sought and brought to light". Brave conquerors driven by their greed for precious minerals moved by land and sea and followed ancient routes, all over the Planet. Fast two-wheeled carts pulled by horses replaced the slow pace of oxen. Representations of these fast-running chariots driven by warriors, leaning out in the so-called flying gallop, have been found in the farthest regions of the Sahara. All over the Mediterranean, drawings of armed men, called bi-triangular because of their schematic forms, stylised images of horses, swords, and spoked wheels throughout the Mediterranean overlapped the representations of nature of the previous period. Stone barrows, kurgan, and tholos, developed and spread. These are mausoleums devoted to the leaders of the clan leaders, warriors with virile and solar symbols decorations that are also painted on pots, hewn out of monolithic phallic steles or on the entrance to the tombs that were decorated with ornaments dedicated to male burials.

The cult of the Great Mother Goddess, however, did not completely disappear. Throughout the early Bronze Age, she reigned supreme in Crete and other civilisations.

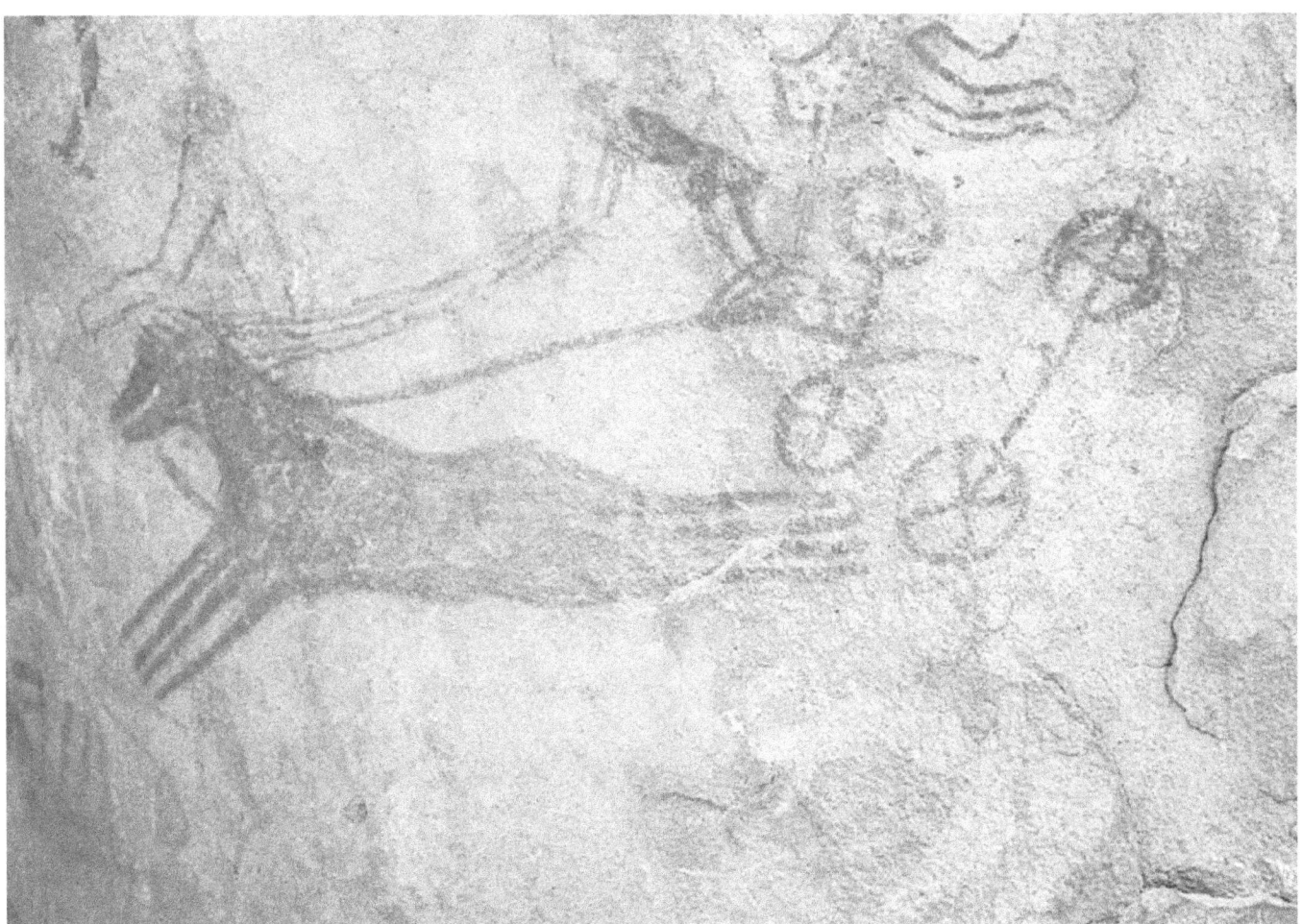

FIGURE 4.2 Saharan painting of a cart pulled by a pair of horses. These representations of light chariots driven by audacious warriors have been found in the most inland areas of the Sahara.

Afterwards, dethroned from the main seats and deprived of her dominion over society, she remained as the wife of the male divinity, the female antithesis to the dominant power. She took shelter in ravines and caves, where mysterious rituals devoted to underground waters perpetuated her cult. Underground waters dripped down the walls of cavities until they eroded the hardest rock, emerged in springs and pools and even dissolved the best-forged iron. They represented the gloomy side of the human condition, its weak and most elusive dimension that is incessantly at work and re-emerges. In the hidden recesses, the religions of Mother Earth were perpetuated. At present, in many traditional societies, male predominance is just like a gloss on a layer still operating in the depths.

The pride of the kings had the technical structures of local cultures and built as monuments and took control of them. In this context, in the middle of the 2nd millennium Pharaoh Thutmosis I fulfilled a highly symbolic work. On the left bank of Thebes, he dug out the "underground chambers in the wadi", the first monuments in the area which is now the world-famous Valley of the Kings. The setting of the underground structures just along the branches of the dried-up river of the desert proves that excavations had previously been accomplished in those areas, in order to locate the hydrographical network or at least to build monuments by using the expertise reached in the course of these activities. Thus, understanding which further functions such structures took on with the passage of time is going to be harder and harder, though they continued to be used for their original purpose. Warrior-shepherds, masters of metals, used their new and more powerful tools and improved excavation techniques to cut the stone. They penetrated the rocks, raised

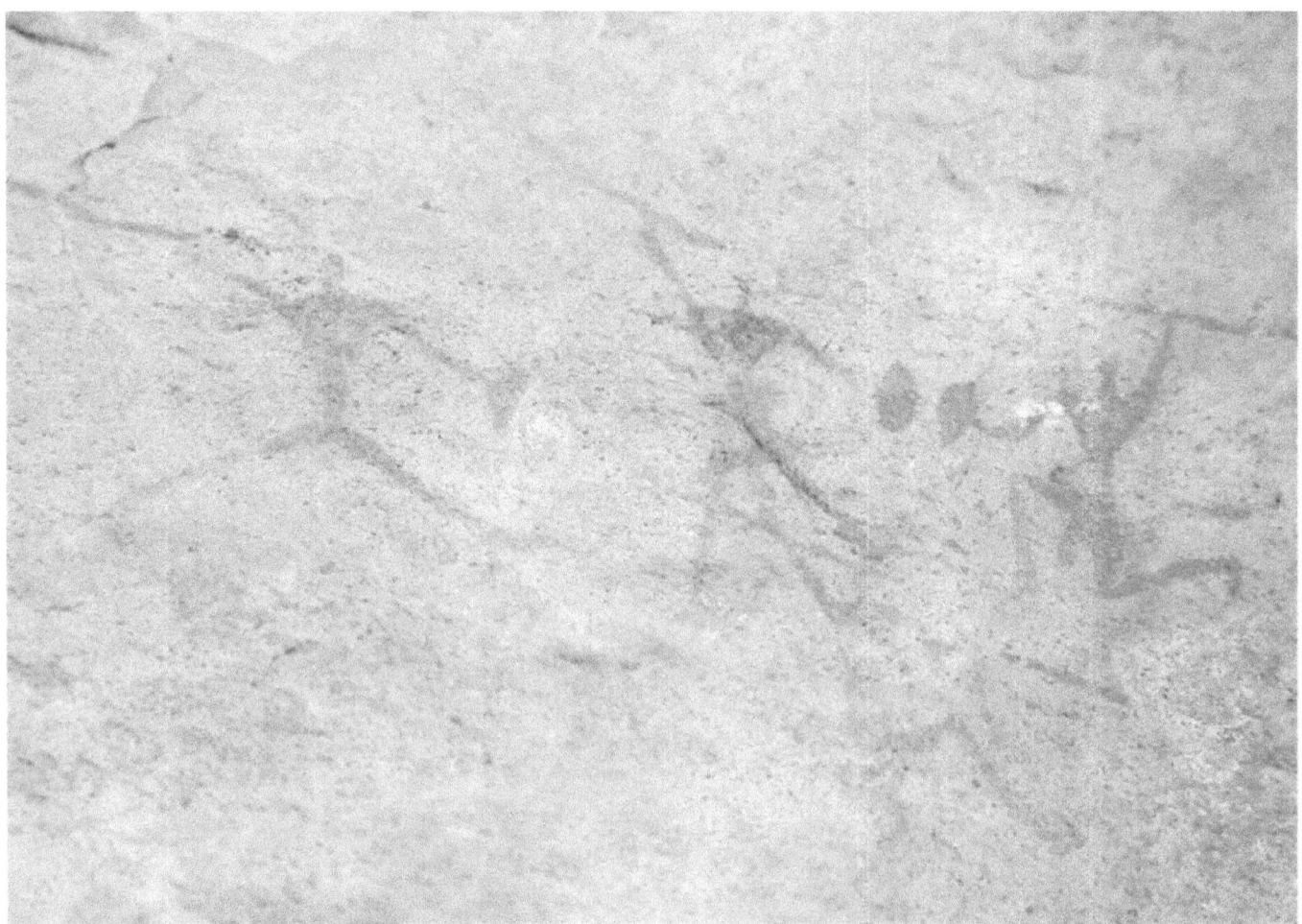

FIGURE 4.3 Saharan painting of fighters dating back to the Metal Age. The bi-triangular stylised forms replace the representations of nature of the previous period.

mausoleums, and built up fortresses and walls. By organising slopes and draining coastal plains, they colonised all those regions that had not been included in previous expansions. A wise use of natural resources and the application of the principles of catchment, harvesting, condensation, and distribution of water made all these works possible.

At that time, the concept was developed of territory built on a network of centres which enable different environments to be exploited by operating in an integrated way. Based on bioarchaeological data, Graeme Barker (1981, 1988–89) demonstrated that in central Italy the practice of seasonal transhumance was already used from the 2nd millennium BC, and that it was connected to a complex system of mountain villages, paths, stopping places, and pastures. Therefore, even monumental constructions take on a different meaning. The leaders in the Metal Age used to consecrate their weapons by dipping them in water pools. Then, they kept them in underground votive hiding-places dripping with humidity. In that way, they paid homage to water, which held the secret to both tempering and corrupting strong iron.

4.2 The Gates of the Waters of Heaven

Fortifications and the buildings for the consolidation of the soils were the models for the organisation of space in the Metal Age. Urban centres were functional to a trade network, which used metal bars smelted in the shape of oxen's skin for money. In the 7th century BC, the prophet Ezekiel listed the far-off markets that traded "the most exquisite spices, valuable stones and gold" (Ezekiel, 27, 21–24) with Palestine and among them he mentioned the markets of Cannae,

FIGURE 4.4 Beyt Bows (Yemen). Stone settlement on the upland with an open-air cistern for harvesting water.

Eden, and Sheba. The massive architectures of these centres were not only intended for war purposes. All over the Arabian Peninsula, from the Mediterranean to the Indian Ocean, the arid climate forced urban settlements to deal with the problem of water above all. In the Negev desert, on a hill overlooking the eastern side of the Beersheba valley, the excavation of the site of Arad has provided the most accomplished example of a settlement dating back to the early Bronze Age (Amiran, 1962). The topography of the hill outlines a large semicircle draining the whole runoff area that is closed in by a wall, and the water is conveyed into a reservoir in the middle to be harvested. Still now, in the Saudi Arabian villages, the houses gather around a cistern, bir or birkeh and the fortification, that was raised up to protect the impluvium, surrounds an area much larger than the built-up area. Similar systems can be found in the site of Teleilat Ghassul in the Jordan valley and in the town of Jawa, in the eastern desert. There, since the Early Bronze Age in 3,000 BC, a system of embankments conveyed water from mountains into the basins that supplied a population of about 2,000 inhabitants. The Nabateans in the town of Umm al-Jamal bordering on the Syrian Desert used the same technique.

Cannae is another name for Qana, the ancient outlet situated on the Indian Ocean on the incense route, where a steep volcanic promontory overlooks the warehouses and the ports. This outlet can be reached by crossing a rough passage turning into a large and comfortable ramp, after some meanders. At its entrance there is a cave inscription, in the ancient Sabean language, which records the works of maintenance ordered by the sovereign in the town of Qana, which is situated on the rock called Ma-hayat. According to current translations the town was fortified for defensive purposes. On the top of the hill there are ancient buildings, but none of them seems to have been erected for military purposes. The peak is levelled in a circular depression sloping towards the ramp that goes down to the port. The higher southern edge is occupied by a larger building which overlooks the central area that, in its lower part, is surrounded by a series of basins dug in the ground and having different shapes and sizes. The largest one is square and is more than 3 m deep. Another one has a rectangular shape and is 15 m long and 4 m wide. Both of them have round edges and before the entrance there are smaller basins. A third reservoir has a crescent shape whereas the fourth is divided into two compartments. It is clearly a hydraulic system used to keep water after it has undergone a process of decantation into the other basins. The area of water harvesting spread over the whole central area, dominated by the most important building probably dedicated to propitiatory offerings and religious activity. The water harvested does not come from periodic rainfalls, but rather from the condensation of sea vapours carrying a large quantity of humidity, which is collected in a large hollow that is used as an air source. Architects from Qana had thus solved a much trickier problem than the military one, because it enabled the town to survive ensuring supplies to ships, thanks to the production of water. It is likely that the name mentioned in the Sabean inscription indicates this function: *Ma* = water and *hayat* = life, that is, the rock of the water of life.

This explanation of the use of the Qana rock helps to understand the water supply system in the town of Aden. Located on an isle, which is now linked to the mainland, the town is made up of the cone of a huge extinct volcano. Aden is built on the breaking point of the edge of the big crater that opens with a depression towards the sea. The volcanic cone was used as a huge basin to harvest the rainfall and humidity particles that were conveyed to the depression from the lower slopes that had skilfully be made impermeable. Harvesting reservoirs had been built against the sides of the sloping walls in order to catch the smallest runoff. Tunnels and channels fed a series of 50 big open-air cisterns having a capacity of 1,400,000 hl of water and connected with each other, along the slope towards the sea.

Today, the archaeological site of Qana is a neglected place and the ancient cisterns of Aden are empty, thus the town is supplied with water by long aqueducts and expensive desalination plants. Maintenance of those cisterns is no longer carried out since their ancient working has been forgotten and water is not conveyed through them any more. Therefore, the previous abundance is now ascribed to the magic power of the mythical Queen of Sheba to whom those systems were dedicated.

The Queen of Sheba's Arabian capital is Marib, a town situated in the North of Yemen, now completely deserted. There, among the pillars of the temple of the moon, the beautiful Bilkis, which is the Yemenite name of the Queen beloved by Solomon, celebrated all the propitiatory rites for the fertility of the fields and the prosperity of trade. The remembrance of that propitious time lives on in the epic poetry of the Arabian civilisations and in the literary transcriptions. The Koran dedicates to Sheba sura XXXIV where "the delightful country" is mentioned as being composed of two gardens, one in the north and the other in the south. Tradition says that when Abraham was shown the Kingdom of Heaven he asked to preserve just two earthly things: the farming area of the Ghuta of Damascus and the two gardens of Sheba in Marib. The mediaeval historian al-Masudi wrote that the oasis of Marib was so large that a traveller took one month to cross it

FIGURES 4.5–4.6 Archaeological site of Qana (Yemen). The Qana promontory on the Indian Ocean is equipped with various types of water-harvesting devices. The cisterns are provided with filtration and decantation systems (see Fig. 4.5) and have particular shapes like the crescent shape in Fig. 4.6. The water comes from sporadic rainfalls and from the condensation of sea humidity.

Metal-Using Agro-astoralists   **65**

FIGURE 4.7 Aden (Yemen), the so-called cisterns of the Queen of Sheba. An impressive system of reservoirs is placed at the outlet of the crater of Aden, which in the past was made watertight and acted as a huge moisture catchment device to fill the pools.

FIGURE 4.8 Detail of the cisterns of Aden made watertight by means of the traditional plaster that is particularly water resistant.

riding a horse in the shadow of the palm trees (Gold Grasslands, III, 367). Other authors said that if women crossed the two gardens bearing baskets on their heads they would find them full of fruit, which ripened so plentifully that they did not need to gather them from trees or pick them up. The historian al-Hamdani said that the tilled land stretched over the desert up to Shabwa and the Hadramaut valley (Iklil, VIII, 98).

The titanic ruins of the irrigation and cultivation systems that made this miracle possible can be still admired. Cyclopean masonry positioned on the right and left shores of wadi Dhana, upstream of the archaeological site of Marib has been established as the starting point of the powerful dam. Considered as one of the wonders of the ancient world, it harnessed the floods, enabling them to be wisely used for agriculture. The several Sabean inscriptions carved out of stone blocks clearly refer to the massive structure called aram, meaning fortification. However, the definition of the hydraulic installations of Marib as a dam is misleading. In fact, it stopped the flow of wadi Dhana running east-west by means of an embankment 620 m long, 16 m high, and 60 m thick at the base. It had not been built to create a water basin upstream of the wall, but rather to lift water and spread the floods on both the shores of the wadi. Huge sluices and channels conveying water to the north and the south of the town were built, in fact, at the two extremities of the wadi. Thus, it is easy to understand the meaning of the two gardens mentioned by all the authors: the flow sharing system created two tilled areas and fanned out the deposit of fertile land beyond both the shores. Taking into account the accumulation of mud that can reach even 30 m in height and its sedimentation rate equivalent to 1.1 cm per annum, the period of activity of the water system can be calculated at 2,700 years, at least. As the water control practice has not been adopted since the end of the 6th century AD, the gardens are estimated to have existed since the 3rd millennium. The recent excavation of similar

FIGURES 4.9–4.10 The southern and northern sluice-gates of the Marib dam (Yemen). It was a complex sharing system of the water intercepted by a dam which spread out perpendicular to wadi Dhana between the two sluices.

shearing systems that had been covered with sediments and abandoned in archaic time shows that the Sabean civilisation dates back to even more ancient times.

The Marib dam is a flow sharing system that allows gardens to be created, producing tilled lands, supplying humus, and watering soils. It is part of a complex water system developing in several distribution systems, measuring devices, embankments, and canals, which attest to an advanced hydraulic technology applied in more ancient times. The sharing systems of Marib worked at full capacity during floods, otherwise other water production systems assured drinking water. In fact, ancient inscriptions celebrate mysterious canals, areas built on the top of the dam, massive fortifications and towers that have actually been found all over the desert. Those works always bear a dedicatory inscription where kings and dignitaries called Mukkarib boasted of the construction of the mahfid, valuable works to be worshipped. The archaeologist Jacqueline Pirenne, whose research has focused on the best interpretation of the Sabean language and civilisation, put forward the hypothesis that the term mahfid, usually translated with the word "towers", had a very different meaning. Jacqueline Pirenne noted that "the epigraphists and the archaeologists themselves do not pay very close attention to the techniques, since art, architecture and the cult are much more important to them" (Pirenne, 1977). Furthermore, researchers who were mostly European completely ignored the ecological system of arid countries. They knew about the systems for water use made up of dams, canals, and wells. As a result, all the constructions were interpreted as mausoleums and temples, or as towers and structures built for military purposes.

A famous dedicatory inscription where God is asked to "bring rain in autumn and in winter" did not have any meaning in Sabean time because of the dry climate. While, if the term "rain" is translated as "dew" the concerns of those populations become clear and the mahfids are understood as water harvesting systems using masonry and its double wall circle as a condensation chamber. A mahfid was built by raising up a second wall in front of the original masonry in order to produce shade and humidity. In ancient times, the same technique was used for the construction of the Nuraghi, in Sardinia, and more recently for Islamic architecture. It can still be admired in the Arabian mediaeval palaces and castles as well as in the Arabian-Norman buildings such as the Zisa of Palermo, in Italy.

Thus, structures such as stonewalls, channels, and smooth surfaces intended for water harvesting and the relative terminology can be better understood. Marbid is a low dry stone wall producing moisture which is harvested on the flat surface it surrounds. Tu'rat is a mound of stones in the shape of a crescent that catches winds full of fog and conveys them condensed to the neqaba, cisterns carved out of the limestone rock. Man-hal is the arrangement of flat stones along the edges of a relief. Resaf is a series of basins arranged along the slopes to harvest the rainfall that is usually destined for the temple. In fact, the resaf often mixes up with the surface of the courtyard or with the terrace where the rite takes place. Several inscriptions mention resaf sanctuaries, whose Hebrew equivalent term risefa is also used in the Biblical descriptions of Solomon's temple.

The Queen of Sheba's capital city lies under the sands, as do her innumerable other towns. Since there was no maintenance of the water systems, the desert spread over the whole area. But some communities living at the top of the highlands of the Yemen still use those amazing hydraulic practices. In the current Arabic language ancient Sabean terms describing hydraulic works, cultivations, and constructions are still alive. Harrah is a word commonly used to indicate the low walls or the stone embankments in the fields; masraf is the dam built across the river to lift the water level; iglamah is a device which conveys water to the fields through a hole; zabur stands for an adobe construction; and ma'had is the ablutions room in the mosque. Other words accurately describe the huge variety of geographical shapes (Rossi, 1940); the depressions on the slopes, the watersheds, the range of drainage surfaces and the areas subject to flooding. Even the single parts of a valley are differently named according to their degree of usefulness for water harvesting. In fact, the most useful part is called "core".

Along each mountain range, peak, and valley, the complex system composed of citadels, look-out towers, and Samsara, the buildings for caravan stops, is organised to control and protect the trade routes, but it is above all a system for meteorological observations. On the highlands rainfall is irregular but violent, inundating one valley and leaving the nearby one completely arid. "Matar! Matar! Rain, rain" the guards on the towers shout and hurry to move the stones and close the embankments, irrigate the fields and fill up the cisterns. In Zafar, the ancient capital, there are 365 cisterns, one for each day of the year, and only when they are wholly filled up with water can people peacefully live until the next season. In Hababa the surfaces of the terraces harvest the rainfall, which is conveyed to the large cistern-square that is surrounded by the whole town looking like a water amphitheatre.

FIGURE 4.11 Nuraghi of Palmavera (Sassari). The massive double wall circle has the practical purpose of condensing humidity and preserving water in the underground hydraulic devices, like the principle on which the southern Arabian mahfid are based.

FIGURES 4.12–4.13 Yemen. Ploughing the soil enables the field to absorb the humidity from the atmosphere. In Fig. 4.13, the water distribution to the fields by means of a device which conveys water through a hole, the iglamah.

FIGURES 4.14–4.15 Yemen. In Fig. 4.14, at the bottom of the marbid the stone walls which organize the terraced slope and collect humidity. In Fig. 4.15, the stone walls and dams called harrah which share out the water quotas.

FIGURE 4.16 Yemen. A large system of organization of valleys by means of water devices. Along the natural water course the dams called masraf intercept the flows running down the steepest slope and deviate them towards the cultivated terraces on both sides.

FIGURE 4.17 Yemen. As rain approaches, stones are arranged to block and channel the flows. The flows are conveyed to small cisterns placed along the edge of the slope and at the top of the terracing systems.

FIGURE 4.18 Hababa (Yemen). Even the smallest mosque has its resaf, terrace, or courtyard for collecting the water that is stored in the open-air cistern and the underground rooms for ablutions.

At an average altitude of 3,000 m the rocky surfaces of the highland are the watershed conveying water or the night dew to the edges where the slope starts. There, the fortifications store and distribute water into the valley where the most important urban settlement is located. The acropolises of Thula and Kawkabam have open-air cisterns and large underground cavities. The peak of the rock towering above Thula is equipped with still used water harvesting systems, which are very similar to those found in Qana. Underground cavities used as chambers, barns, cisterns, and passageways have been entirely carved out of the rocky buttress. A tunnel carries water to the urban settlement at the foot of the slope at an altitude of 2,700 m. It ends in the subsoil of the mosque which has large chambers with pools for ablutions, thus representing an authentic monument dedicated to water. The shapes of the places of the Islamic cult still seem to show the ancient Sabean temples with the resaf, the courtyard for water harvesting and the holy altar. Water used for holy rites is soon after distributed for the irrigation of gardens by gravity, thanks to an accurate land organisation that follows the orographic lines for harvesting on the highland, the channelling along the slopes, and the distribution in the fields. When the enemy threatened to attack the outlying buildings, people abandoned them and sheltered in the high citadels where they managed the complex systems of water condensation and harvesting. Furthermore, they did not defend their town by means of military fortifications, but rather by controlling the water supply and closing the gates of the waters of heaven.

FIGURE 4.19 Hababa (Yemen). The town surrounds the large cistern-basin where the water coming from the terraces of the buildings is collected. The little building at the water's edge is a mosque with pools inside supplied with water by the big arches.

4.3 The Civilization of Hidden Waters

In his last song Moses starts by asking the rain and the dew for inspiration and consecrates to Israel the following mysterious words "a high land where honey is sucked from the rock and oil from the cobbles of the rock" (Deuteronomy 32, 13). A correct interpretation of these words depends on their reference to the desert practices of producing water by condensation systems based on mounds of stones. According to modern Israeli research, in the Negev desert very ancient remnants of olive trees and vineyards were irrigated by means of dry stonewalls harvesting dew. In Arabic those devices are called teleylat al-anab, which stands for hillocks for vineyards. Plants grew within small enclosures whose stones were purposely arranged with large interstices to catch the wind full of moisture. Thus, the vineyard and the olive tree did not need springs or groundwater tables in order to grow and the sweet raisin juice, which in ancient times was often referred to as honey, could be tasted as well as oil; thanks to the activity of solid rocks (Keller 1955).

The Nabateans founded a commercial empire that started from their safe seat of Petra and passed through Hegra, which is called today Medain Saleh, in the south of the deep Arabian desert up to Damascus and the well-known fertile depression of Ghuta. They settled their trading posts in Alexandria and on the isles of Kos and Delos. Nabatean temples were raised up in Sinai and in Egypt, but also in Rome and in Pozzuoli. The dynamics of soil erosion was kept under control over the whole landscape to build areas suitable for tilling deep in the Negev desert (Dentzer et al, 1989). Each riverbed of the fossil water system was equipped with little embankments, the khaur, arranged perpendicularly to the runoff area so that when water sporadically flows, it is conveyed to the two shores to deposit the mud and create arable areas supported by dry stonewalls, the sleisel (Evenari 1971). The application technique that those populations adopted was defined as that of the "Nabatean farms" (Evenari et al, 1971) and is still in use in Tunisia where the embankments are called jerud.

Pliny the Elder referred in amazement to the Essenes, another community living in the same area who were able to make the desert fertile. They dwelt in the caves along the slope of the Dead Sea, and turned their shelters into green vegetable gardens smelling of balsamic plants (Pliny, Natural History, V, 17, 4). The excavations at Qumran, where the famous manuscripts were found, have confirmed the existence of ascetical communities building underground dwellings and hydraulic systems, to supply the bathrooms used for the ablutions, and large tilled lands. Their experience, that was handed down to monastic orders which built similar stone towns all over the Mediterranean area, originated from a life spent in the desert, the ancient wisdom of breeder patriarchs and farmer prophets. They were devoted to the production and harvesting of water.

At the opposite side of the incense route, Pliny (XII, 63) talked about Shabwa, a mysterious town that was reported as Sabota in the Ptolemy's planisphere. This caravan city situated deep within the Ramlat as Sabataynm desert is linked to the South through the port of Qana on the Indian Ocean, and to the North with Gaza on the Mediterranean Sea after a 2,000 km journey that was made up of 65 stops, as Pliny said. Nowadays, that region is completely deserted. The archaeological research and excavations carried out by Jacqueline Pirenne all over the region in 1975 and in 1977 unveiled an endless evidence of water harvesting and condensation devices on the jol, the stony highland at the foot of which the region is situated. According to Pirenne, these structures made up of stones arranged along the edges and of mounds of stones with cavities inside, were used to catch moisture coming from the ancient palm tree cultivations and orchards surrounding the town of Shabwa. Those methods were passed on by nomadic and transhumant pastoral civilizations that watered the herds and ensured the survival of merchant caravans that used them. Those practices played a key role in history. Herodotus reported that the Persian Emperor Cambise invaded Egypt in 525 BC crossing the desert, thanks to an agreement with the Arabs who revealed to him where the cistern-jars were situated. However, the agreement was never finalised because Cambise failed in his attempt to conquer the oasis of Siwah in Libya, because his caravan never reached it and still lies buried in the sands of the Sahara.

Some mysterious cistern-jars are still used in the more than 300 Dahalac isles in the Red Sea where sea nomadism is practiced. Young shepherds and their herds are transported on rafts to the deserted isles where they stay for all the period needing for grazing. At the end of their stay, they call the rafts by sending light signals in order to be picked up and transferred to another desert isle. The way they get water on these coral soils, completely lacking in fresh water tables, where rains are very irregular, is a sample of condensation and survival techniques used in dry environments. Open-air cisterns are built on the sandy surfaces by means of large jars, which are wholly sunken into the sand. Heaps of stones catch the atmospheric moisture that drops into the surrounding reservoir. In the porous madrepore soils, large

FIGURE 4.20 The large reservoirs for water conservation on the acropolis of Thula (Yemen) had sufficient dimensions to supply water to the fields and the surrounding houses and to withstand sieges.

FIGURES 4.21–4.22 Cisterns and rain-water harvesting and decantation systems on the rock of Thula.

FIGURE 4.23 In Petra (Jordan) the stone-terracing systems called khaur, typical of the Nabatean agriculture used in the Negev desert, are still visible. In rural environments, they are mere semi-circular terracing systems which retain the soil, whereas in urban areas they are more complex building systems. Some examples of these systems made with carbon layers to filter water and make it fit for drinking have been discovered.

FIGURES 4.24–4.25 Water-harvesting systems in the Dahlac isles (Red Sea). Figure 4.24 shows cistern-well in the Great Dahlac. Figure 4.25 shows desert isle of Schuma: the shepherd, a sea nomad, shows how the rows of stones are able to produce water as proved by the flourishing vegetation.

craters carved out of the rock in a circular way have mounds of stones in the middle. Underneath, there is a watertight cistern that is always full of clear water taken from the sea breeze through the pores in the walls of the artificial craters and miraculously appears in the pond seeping out of the rocks. On flat surfaces any small depression is used to store the moisture needed for grazing and the leaves of the trees also collect the dew, which is conveyed to ditches protected from the heat by their own shade. Furthermore, tiered stone masses drive the runoff along the slopes towards the openings of the cisterns or tiers of stones catch the winds full of humidity and transmit it to the soil to irrigate the grass for grazing. This is how the populations of the villages of the Great Dahalac still find sustenance today. It is the only inhabited island, though it is now a mere shadow of the enchanted garden that it once was.

4.4 Condensers, Atmospheric Wells, and Water Extraction Walls

Monuments commonly ascribed to funeral use were used to manage water resources both for practical and ritual purposes. During the Bronze Age, in the site of Murgia Timone near Matera, some double stone ring constructions, crossed by a corridor leading to a central underground chamber, were arranged along the ditch around the archaic Neolithic enclosures. These constructions are very similar to the Saharan prehistoric barrows and concentric rings and to the rows or mounds of stones in the Negev desert and in the Yemen, where they were used both for moisture condensation and for dew storage. Likewise, the structures at Murgia Timone are supposed to have been used for water harvesting or for the worship of water, as their association with the ditches of the archaic Neolithic villages proves. The latter had been definitively abandoned in the Bronze Age although the ditch carried on to convey moisture used by the underground chamber. If the concentric rings were surmounted by mounds of stones, the remains of the tholos and the passageway would be found. In this case, the barrow could have both a real function as a further moisture collector and an evocative purpose in the mausoleum of the dead, symbolically recalling the shape of water devices, sources of water and life. The absence of stone coverings over the double ring mausoleums is justified by the fact that at Murgia Timone water is provided by the ditch, and water is directly harvested in the underground chamber.

In the Bronze Age, the use of metal tools made excavation work easier. They followed the edges of the canyon, the gravina, whose vertical wall could be smoothly dug horizontally. The Neolithic farmers had neglected these impenetrable areas. Thanks to the technique of the supporting dry stone walls, even the steepest slopes could be tilled. The walls prevent the erosion caused by the torrential rainfalls and afford the creation of embankments where humus is collected. In summer, the walls trap atmospheric moisture, which is conveyed to the soil they shade, and they protect against the wind and the heat. The material for the building of the wall is provided by the digging of caves on the terraces. Inside the caves, large bell-shaped cisterns are dug to harvest water dropping from the slope, which is conveyed by a network of little channels. In some circumstances, a cistern built at the bottom of the cave fills up with water even though it is not connected to channels. In that case the cave soaks up the exterior moisture which condenses on the colder bottom wall and drops down into the cisterns.

Therefore, excavation is multipurpose: it drains the rock by soaking up micro-infiltrations and capillary moisture making it salubrious for living or for grain storage; it provides material for the building of external terracing walls; it condenses atmospheric moisture and produces water. Each terrace has many caves that open up in a horseshoe shape onto a courtyard supported by dry stone walls. They can reach more than 10 storeys of caves and cisterns overlapping and connected with each other by means of channels and narrow streets, in a network shaping the whole canyon slope. The cavities carved with a slanting inclination often have side-benches and a niche at their ends, with various engravings, hewn out in the bottom wall. Sunbeams strike the niche differently according to the time of year. These cavities were probably used by the family clans as places of worship: they celebrated the principle according to which the Sun joining the Mother Earth in the core of the rock generates the miracle of life: water which condenses within the cistern.

The architecture of the caves with an underground passageway leading to a vaulted chamber is the prototype of the conic or semiconic vaulted circular construction, which is the most archaic example of a monument. This shape is the stone version of the wooden huts that are still in use in Africa and can be found in the religious and sepulchral architecture, typical of the ancient Mediterranean populations. The early shapes consist on hypogeal constructions with a rectangular entry, called dromos, and leading to a pseudo circular dome that is called tholos in Greek. They spread all over the Aegean area and attained the height of architectural accomplishment in the so-called Treasure of Atreus in Mycenae in the 15th century

FIGURE 4.26 A Bronze-Age monument on the limestone highland of Murgia Timone which stands in front of Matera. Two concentric rings are crossed by a linear corridor which leads to the central underground cavity. Inside there are separate rooms divided by a pillar carved out of the limestone and deposition beds.

FIGURE 4.27 Massive dry stone walls protect from the effects of the rainfalls and create the space for cultivations organised on artificial terraces along the slopes of the Palomba of Matera.

FIGURE 4.28 Bell-shaped cistern in the Sasso Barisano of Matera subsequently reused as an underground room. Note the orifice at the top for the water, and the watertight plaster of a reddish colour due to the pottery shards used in its making.

BC. The dome, made out of megalithic stone blocks, was 13.2 m high and 14.2 m wide. It represents the passage from the passive Neolithic building technique, which was inspired by the natural Palaeolithic cavities, to built architecture.

The barrow, which is a structure with pseudo domes having a circular base and an outside mound-shaped profile, is used in the typical constructions of the Apulian Murgia landscape, known as trulli. The well-known little town of Alberobello (Allen, 1969) is an example of an urban conglomeration of trulli. However, they are common in various types of rural shelters throughout the low and coastal Murgia (Ambrosi et al, 1990). The shapes of these pagghiari, casali, chippuri, and casedde are so far from the rural architecture that in the 18th century travellers who crossed through Apulia described a landscape scattered with monumental and funerary constructions full of important archaeological reminiscences (Saint-Non, 1781–1786). The name trullo derives from the Greek term *tholos*, i.e. dome. Similar structures found in the Balearic Islands, the talayotes, have the same etymological origin. The term recalls the name of the Nabatean stone mounds that allowed the humidification of the vineyards and the olive groves, the teleylat (Arabic plural of tell which stands for heap of stones, hillock) al-anab (vineyard). The elevations are reminiscent of ancient Mesopotamian and African monuments such as the earthen and straw cones that can still be admired in the regions of Aleppo and Harran as well as the stone barrows, the medracen, in Northern Africa. The plan is very similar to the lobes of the nuraghi or the meanders of the Cretan labyrinth.

However, the analogies are not fortuitous. In fact, many megalithic monuments such as the dolmen, the menhir, and the specchie, terraced heaps of stones like the ziggurat and the early pyramids, cover the Apulian countryside. The presence of Cretan and Mycenaean tradesmen in the Late Bronze Age, all over the area which later became the Greek civilization, is a real fact. Between the 14th and the 13th century BC, Mediterranean international trade developed along with large movements of people who the Egyptians called "People of the Sea". The places where Aegean manufactured products were found correspond to the settlements of these human groupings that were established in the new lands, such as the Philistines in Palestine and the Tyrsenois in Etruria. The Egyptians mentioned the Lycians, the Sicilians, and the Sardinians as tradesmen of the islands of the sea. Also the inhabitants of Daunia, the Peucetians, and the Messapians who are the populations who occupied Iapigia, the ancient name of Apulia, were probably involved in that important trade movement.

However, the horizon of reference may extend even further. The tholos is a typical African shape and starting from a linguistic, mythographical, and historiographical survey; Martin Bernal asserts a direct influence by the Egyptians and Phoenicians on the origins of the Cretan and Mycenaean civilizations (Bernal, 1991). This hypothesis is supported by the archaeologist Theodore Spyropoulos' discovery in Thebes, in Greece, of a monument dating back to the Early Helladic period around 2800 BC. The structure consisted of a terraced adobe barrow and was identified as the tomb of Amphion and Zetes, the mythical builders of the town walls. Because of his study on the architecture of this structure, so similar to the terraced pyramids, Theodore Spyropoulos, who worked as the superintendent of Boetia in the 1970s, was persuaded that Greece underwent a former colonization by the Egyptians (Spyropoulos, 1972). The Greek tragicians associated Thebes to the Sphinx and Cadmus, the mythical founder of Thebes who was of Phoenician origin. Sophisticated hydraulic works, which enabled the nearby Lake Kopias to be drained during the winter and water for irrigation to be stored during the dry summers, date back to the same age as the barrow. According to classical studies, the elaborate hydraulic engineering consisting of ditches, embankments, and canals, and which was unknown to the natives was introduced by the Egyptian King Danaus, the mythical founder of Argus or by the Minoans, a group that settled in the city of Orcomeno, at the north of Lake Kopias. Bernal asserts that both terms have an Egyptian etymology. The name Danaus probably derives from the Egyptian word dni that means "to irrigate" and Minoans from mniw that means "shepherds". The relationship existing between the pastoral groups who were familiar with the irrigation technologies and the migratory people coming from Africa and the East is meaningful.

It is also possible to establish an analogy with Minos and the mythical pharaoh Menes or Mendes who, according to Diodorus, built the first Egyptian labyrinth, a place for the worship of the holy bull (Historical Library, I, 66). The construction of the catavotre, semi-natural underground tunnels of the Orcomeno Lake in the Peloponnese, which turned Arcadia into an irrigated and fertile region, is ascribed to Heracles whose mythical tradition is found in the epic poems of different countries. The hero, who was educated by the cowherd Teutaro, revealed his pastoral origins by cleaning the stables of King Augeas with a device that is still used in the sheepfolds of southern Italy: to arrange a water canal on the manure and then to convey the canal into a system of ditches. The toponym Orcomeno occurs both in Boetia and in Arcadia, since these are two regions characterized by the use of water systems. The term appears on the Cretan tablets in Linear B and is composed of orch that means closed place, cultivated enclosure; and menos that is the Greek participle of

FIGURE 4.29 Gravina in Puglia. The channel carved out of the slope provides water for the cistern dug out in the hypogeal room of the troglodyte settlement.

FIGURE 4.30 African hut in Ethiopia, an archetype of the false-vaulted circular constructions. It is the first form of built dwelling. It may have a semi-hypogeal base or be built with a wall structure and may evolve into a complex variety of types (see fig. 254-59).

Metal-Using Agro-astoralists **85**

FIGURE 4.31 The trulli spread in the region of Apulia draw their origins from the Mycenaean tholos of which some archaeological traces were actually found in the area.

FIGURE 4.32 The interior of a trullo. Like the tholos, the covering of the trullo is a false dome which does not need a keystone on the top to support itself.

Metal-Using Agro-astoralists

FIGURES 4.33–4.34 Above, Cleopatra Selene's mausoleum (Algeria). The construction derives from the megalithic barrows of the Numidian tradition called medracen. Of the same typology are the Apulian barrows and specchie (see Fig. 4.34), whose masonry enables the moisture absorbed by the tree roots to be conserved in the soil.

FIGURE 4.35 A "jazzo", an enclosure for the herds, on the Murge. The vertical excavation into the plain creates a large artificial pit; cavities and horizontal tunnels can be cut into its walls.

FIGURE 4.36 Olive tree moistened by a dry stone wall similar to the Nabatean teleylat in the quarry of Fantiano in Grottaglie (Apulia).

FIGURE 4.37 The dry stone walls and the specchie of the Apulian countryside are a titanic work organizing the landscape and useful for catching moisture and maintaining the hydromorphic capacity of the soil.

the Aramaic mayn stands for "water". Therefore the word means "enclosure to control the water" and recalls the Neolithic water systems found in Apulia and in Lucania. Also the most well-known megalithic construction with concentric circles, Stonehenge, is correlated to water. In fact, a great ditch surrounds the famous upright stones whose building mass could have been useful to trigger the phenomena both of condensation and precipitation.

Most of the dry stone constructions spread throughout the Apulian barren lands, where mounds of porous stones absorbs the night frost and replenish the soil with moisture, can be considered as water producers (Cantelli, 1994). As a matter of fact, the roots of the ancient olive trees all stretch towards the dry stone walls which are typical of the agricultural landscape. Still now olive trees wholly bounded by dry stone walls exist. It is meaningful that in the most imposing structures, the parieti, the rows of stones that close the upper part of the two faces of the walls are arranged with slabs leaning towards the inner part in order to allow the frost to drop down the mound of stones filling the interior.

The walls, the mounds of stones, the barrows, the trulli, and the heaps of limestone rock called specchie like the talayotes, the nuraghi, and the teleylat al-anab act as constructions for the condensation and storage of the water. The mounds of stones work both during the night and during the day. Under the broiling sun, the wind carries traces of moisture and seeps into the interstices of the mounds of stones where the internal temperature is lower than the outside temperature because it is not exposed to the sun or because it has an underground room. The fall in temperature causes the condensation of the drops, which are either soaked up by the soil in the case of the walls or fall down into the cavity. The water accumulated finds further moisture and coolness, thus improving the efficiency of the condensation construction.

FIGURE 4.38 Roofed cistern, a water-production device on the Murge. The slope of the roof emerging from the ground catches water which pours into drinking troughs for the animals. Micro-flows of water from the subsoil collect in the hypogeal chamber.

FIGURE 4.39 Archaeological vestiges of Paestum. The heroon, the mausoleum of the holy ancestor has the same shape as that of the roofed cisterns still in use in Apulia and Lucania.

During the night the process is reversed and condensation occurs outside, even though the results are the same. The external surface of the rocks is cooler and condenses moisture so that dew settles on the surface; the dew slides into the interstices and is collected in the underground room. It is remarkable that the construction of each trullo starts with an underground cistern excavated right under the trullo itself and tiered stones convey water into the cistern. In a prehistoric graffito found in Valcamonica a large, geometrically perfect hut is depicted. The structure of the roof with its symbolic motifs and the storey used as the living area are clearly represented. Beneath the latter is an element to which some signs starting from the slope of the roof convey. It seems to be the representation of the cistern set under the house as for the trulli.

All over the Murgia area, underground cisterns shaped as monuments plunged into the ground with just the slopes of their roofs emerging above the surface are still in use. They were built at the bottom of a little impluvium to catch and harvest water mi-croflows and the moisture of the soil. Thanks to their pitched roof and the frontons almost shaping a tympanum, these constructions gain architectural dignity and the form of temples or mausoleums. On the Tyrrhenian coast, the mythical founder's sacellum of Paestum, a city dating back to the Greek civilization, has a structure very similar to the underground cisterns, which comes out of the ground with a sloping roof covered with limestone slabs. No archaeological survey has been carried out to prove the hydraulic function of this construction. However, the thickest vegetation marks the route of moisture towards the underground room. This structure supports the thesis of the direct relationship between the funeral forms and the water devices, which has been proposed for the double ring mausoleums of the Metal Age. It also confirms the process of appropriation that the monuments of celebration and commemoration perpetuate on the water works.

Oases

5

FIGURE 5.1 The birth of an oasis. A slight depression collects humidity; the palm tree flourishes and provides shade and biological material which attract the other organisms; the humus produced gives rise to further cultivations.

5.1 The Cycle of Autopoiesis

Modern biological science has demonstrated that organisms survive, thanks to the processes of symbiosis and alliance. Complex species have evolved by combining their respective characters and not by destroying each other. This principle also underlies the process of evolution of the social formations. Those communities which have learned to gather their resources and exploit them usefully have had more long-term chances of success. In particular, these situations of a careful relationship with nature tend to occur in the most impenetrable areas, where the effort required to create the conditions for living generates and passes on from generation to generation the rules of humility and of respect for the environment. Oases are typical of the desert, but can also be assumed as a wider model, and a theory of the oasis can be drawn up: the study of closely linked processes between man and nature that, under the hardest living conditions, can create vital cycles and autopoietic ecosystems, which are able to continuously regenerate and perpetuate themselves.

The environmental features of the desert can be ascribed to the conditions of high aridity of the soil and to the sparse vegetation. It is the soil, which is the surface layer produced by the continuous action of chemical, physical, and above all biological factors that makes plant life possible, and this in its turn, protects the soil and ensures its constant regeneration. Due to the absence of vegetation, the desert surface undergoes the violent process of atmospheric agents that crush the rocks and produce sand along with erosion and poor drainage. Sand, in its turn, worsens drought and causes the disappearance of run-off water. As a consequence of this, sterile saline outcrops accumulate on the soil. Therefore, land degradation and biological impoverishment intensify within an ever increasing aridity cycle.

However, the general picture is studded with specific environmental situations that are in contradiction with the overall framework. They break the negative cycle of aridity and trigger phenomena that augment humidity and fertility. The oases, as vital niches, are not the natural upshot of spontaneous occurrences but rather the result of mankind's work: they are the practical application of techniques suited to the environment and passed on from generation to generation the product of skilfulness and knowledge. It is enough to consider that the date palm, which is a typical oasis plant, is not a spontaneous tree but the result of domestication and cultivation. In the desert each palm-grove has been planted and lovingly tended and watered. In the oases, water resources too depend on special techniques of catchment and are jealously managed and transported.

The places and the dates of the early domestication of palm trees are not easy to establish. The origins of this plant date back to the myths of the fortunate island, of the earth of the blessed souls and of the first paradise gardens. The Sumerians and the Egyptians called Dilmun the Edenic island where the first domestic palm tree was produced as the basis of the existence of each oasis. This mythical place has been identified with Bahrein, in the Arabian-Persian Gulf (Cleuziou, 1988). The island has been cultivated since the 6th millennium, and at the end of the 4th millennium it was organized around an accomplished economy typical of an oasis and involving the palm-grove agriculture as well as fishing and pastoralism (Cleuziou and Laureano, 1999). This would confirm the ancient myth of Eden being on an island and other plausible circumstances support the theory. On the shoreline, a large family group can at the same time cultivate a palm-grove, breed cattle, fish, and sail, exploiting the different possibilities of success of these practices. When different possibilities combine in one or more islands, it gives rise to a niche of intensification and the prodigious creation of a seashore oasis.

The Saharan civilization of Tassili of Ajjer could be pointed out as a further area of early domestication dating back to the same time as Bahrein. However the finding of prehistoric paintings representing date palms of an uncertain date is insufficient proof of this hypothesis. The process of dissemination of the cultivation of palm trees, which began in the 4th millennium in the well-watered areas of Mesopotamia, the Persian Gulf, and the Nile, can be more surely followed up. From these areas, in the 3rd millennium the palm-groves spread up to the Indo valley to the east and in the 2nd millennium up to Crete. The process of implantation of oases slowly proceeded from east to west in the innermost Sahara which has been cultivated since the 1st millennium, thanks to the employment of the technique of the drainage tunnels. In the first centuries of the Modern Age the palm-groves spread up to the Canary Islands, the Spanish and Sicilian coasts.

Depending on the hydraulic and geomorphologic system, it is possible to make a distinction between: the wadi oases which use the large river bed of a dried-up river; the erg oases situated in the very heart of the sandy desert; and the sebkha oasis created around the depression of a big salt lake.

FIGURE 5.2 The hole protects the palm tree and allows it to flourish. Each palm tree is carefully planted and cultivated. Without periodic cutting of the leaves and irrigation, it would be a sterile bush.

The wadi oases are located along the upper part of the hydrographical networks where the well-defined water courses carve deep canyons out of the sand sediments or the limestone rock. Because of their proximity to the mountain peaks or the highlands, the wadi oases sometimes benefit from water coming from slim perennial courses but more often they benefit from water in the form of underground flows or in the form of floods with annual rainfall. These oases appear as long ribbons of vegetation running between steep slippery cliffs. The palm groves wholly cover the river bed because the latter is tilled. Only in the deepest part of the bed does a narrow strip without vegetation, or crossed by a slim creek, prove the existence of run-off deep dams built perpendicular to the wadi bed stop the underground flow, retain the soil, and turn the water course into a succession of embankments where fields are tilled. Further farming lands can be obtained along the slopes of the two opposite riverbanks where they are organized into terraces that follow the water course. Since these lands are at a higher level than the wadi bed, they are irrigated by means of an ingenious technique that does not require any hoisting systems but it only exploits the force of gravity. At upstream of the fields to be irrigated, there are water intakes from where canals branch off following the slope of the land. However, they are higher than the river bed, thus enabling irrigation by the mere force of gravity and fields under cultivation at a higher level than the natural bottom. The water supply depends on the water capacity of the wadi. In some circumstances water is only available in the underground sediments. Consequently, surface run-off takes place, thanks to embankments that, using the water intakes located at the bottom, tap the water harvested on the deposits upstream of the dam. When this system does not work, water is extracted by means of wells that thanks to underground dams catching the humidity stored in the subsoil. The buckets are lifted up by a long rocker arm that is fixed with a balance weight and placed on two tall adobe uprights. This technique is known as khottara in the Algerian Sahara and is similar to the Arabian shaduf technique. It is illustrated in a tomb in Thebes dating back to the 14th century BC and in an Acadian cylinder dating back to the 3rd millennium.

FIGURE 5.3 Roufi (Algeria), a wadi oasis that uses the protection of the walls of the canyon and the wadi bed for the cultivations. The water supply comes from the underground flow and the sporadic floods.

FIGURE 5.4 Wadi Saoura (Algeria). The long rocker arms placed on tall adobe uprights, here called khottara and very similar to the ancient Egyptian and Arabian shaduf, enable water to be drawn from the wells dug out of the wadi's sediments.

The erg oases use the large sandy lands as a protective factor and as a resource. The dune desert called erg is the most implacable and the most difficult to cross. However, it gives hospitality and subsistence to those who know the ecological laws. The erg has a complex and rigorous geometrical shape that is determined by the direction of the wind and by the form of the rocky chains. Each grain of sand is impalpable and very fine because it is transported by the wind and therefore selected in very precise and homogeneous size. The grains of sand are in continuous movement but the formation of the dunes is not accidental, and their accumulation on the big parallel hard rocky surface that forms the erg is due to precise factors. The sand accumulation on long lines of dunes is an undulating arrangement that depends on the vertical result of the pressure exerted by the wind both at macroscopic and microscopic levels. Viewed from a satellite, the erg as a whole looks like each of its smallest particles where sand accumulates in subsequent waves. It can be assumed that the shape of the erg is the very visualization of the acting forces, like the model of a mathematical theorem. When an obstacle slows the power of the wind down, the grains of sand are released to the soil. The most corpulent grains run on and progressively bounce on the hard rocky surfaces. Thus, after a first deposit of sand grains, the accumulation grows steadily larger because the grains no longer bounce off the sand. Huge mountain ridges at a great distance from each other, or more microscopic obstacles to the sliding of the sands can therefore be the cause of the triggering of the dune formation and of the morphology of the erg.

The horizontal component of the wind's action controls the movement of the dunes. Not all of them move but only the isolated crescent-shaped dunes called barcane. The other ones have their single grains of sand that continuously move backwards and forwards, from one dune to another one, although the general shape keeps unchanged. For this reason you can find oases lying at the foot of a large dune that seems to be on the point of sweeping over them. Actually, the oasis has been living in safety together with the dune for ages. Like the sea for coastal settlements, the edge of the erg although undergoing continual change is not a peril except after catastrophic events or disturbing interventions.

Erg oases follow the laws regulating the formation of the great ocean of sand and use those laws to set up protective dune barriers. They are not based on a geomorphologic structure or on a well-defined hydrographical system because the ridge is covered with sands. In some cases erg oases depend on shallow underground water that the roots of the palm trees can directly reach in the subsoil. Therefore, these palm groves do not need to be irrigated and, in fact, they are called bur, which means not irrigated. The farmer has the harder task consisting of sweeping the sands from the isles of palm groves. The farmer starts to dig out a ditch enabling the palm trees to reach the humid area of the soil. Dried palm leaves are arranged around the circular cavity because they slow down the power of the wind and cause the sand to be released. Following the mechanism of successive and continuous accumulation, artificial protective dunes called afreg are thus created. Over time the afregs grow higher and the oasis takes on the shape of a sand crater with a tilled bottom. The leaves of the palms close off the top of these large funnels that maintain an ideal microclimate inside. In the region of the Souf of the Great eastern Erg, the excavation of these depressions out of the sand shapes an extraordinary landscape where the perpetual movement of the erg, which is composed of long dune lines, is modulated by hundreds of craters. The latter look as if they are floating on the sand, which could submerge them at any moment, whereas the destructive strength of the erg is actually turned in favour of the oasis, which absorbs moisture from the erg and thus can protect itself from the wind and the heat. Therefore, a titanic deed is accomplished: to live constantly in the continuous changing of the sea of dunes, control its movements, and shape its landscape.

The sebkha oases are situated along the edges of the low depressions. The latter have an elliptic shape with one side against the front of the erg and the other free of sands. The oases, like the coastal settlements of a lake, surround the sebkha, using strategies of both the erg oasis and the wadi oasis. Their specificity is due to the type of water supply that is based on huge hydraulic works with their own special characteristics. The oases exploit the particular morphology of the sebkha where the flows converge. The oases make it possible to survive deep inside the Sahara, which can be rendered fertile even though there is no running water at all on the surface and there is absolutely no rain.

5.2 The Water Mines

Water resources are collected by means of an extraordinary technique, which exploits the underground drainage tunnels locally called foggara. This method dates back thousands of years and is adopted over a very large area stretching from China to Spain, throughout Persia and as far as Latin America (Goblot, 1979). The foggara of the Sahara desert are

FIGURE 5.5 The erg oases (Algerian Sahara). The oasis is the result of human action which makes the arid areas of the sandy desert fertile.

FIGURE 5.6 The oasis of Taghit, in the Algerian Sahara, and the adobe fortified habitat. At the foot of the dunes, the oasis is supplied with the waters filtering through below the Great Western Erg.

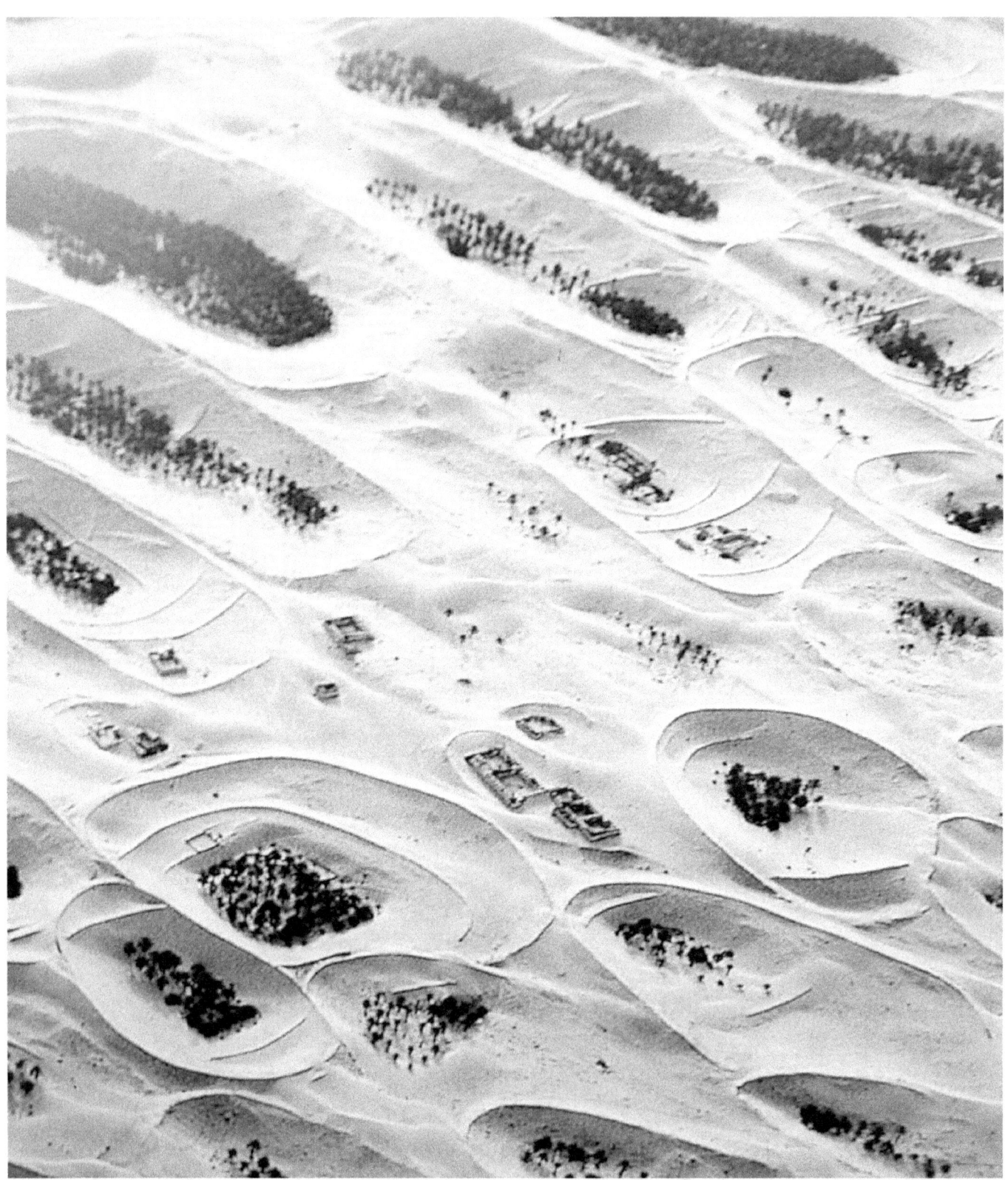

FIGURE 5.7 The erg oases in the Algerian Souf region with artificial craters (bur) dug out and protected by barriers of leaves, regulate the dune movements and shape the great sandy desert landscape.

FIGURES 5.8–5.9 The formation of artificial sand dunes called afreg in the Sahara Desert. The method exploits the natural principle of dune formation. The dunes originate from the sand transported by the wind that accumulates when it finds an obstacle or a deposit of sand, which stop the grains of sand from bouncing ahead. Figure 5.8 shows a raw earth cordon which creates the first accumulation of sand on the ground. Then dry palm leaves are progressively laid on the top as the sand dune rises. As time goes by, formations reaching up to 100 m in height generate beautiful pyramidal artificial dunes such as the one in Fig. 5.9.

FIGURE 5.10 Oasis of Ighzer at the margin of the Sebkha of Timimoun (Algeria). The cordon of artificial dunes (on the right) protects the palm-grove, which slopes down towards the deep depression of the sebkha, from the rock of the citadel, where the drainage tunnels running down from the highland come out.

very similar to the qanat or kariz of Persia, the falaj of Arabia, the khottara of Morocco, and the madjirat of Andalusia, although they have different characteristics. Very similar water systems have been found in Peru and in Mexico within pre-Columbian farm units called hoyas (Soldi, 1982). It is difficult to exactly establish if these systems come from knowledge dissemination or from reinventing processes in areas with the same physical characteristics. As a matter of fact, the construction of the most ancient towns was based on the building of these systems: the biblical town of Qana was probably named after the qanat that assured its existence; Jericho and Jerusalem had the same water systems; in the oasis of Megiddo the tunnels for water harvesting date back to the 16th century BC. The Arabian geographer al-Idrisi reported that the town of Marrakech developed thanks to the building of a drainage tunnel carried out under the leadership of an engineer from Andalusia. The name of Madrid itself is supposed to derive from the above-mentioned madjirat. In the subsoil of Palermo a network of drainage tunnels built during the Muslim age or dating back to the Punic-Phoenician period (Todaro, 1988) were found and analogous devices built during the Graeco-Roman or Arab ages are still working in the town of Taranto (Grassi et al, 1991) as well as in other Apulian towns such as Gravina and Laterza in southern Italy.

The first documentary inscriptions on the qanat date back to the 7th century BC when during a battle in Persia the Assyrian King Sargon II described the unearthing of underground water canals. It is said that Sennacherib, Sargon's son, learnt in Urartu, an ancient mining centre, the technique of using underground water canal systems to supply the town of Nineveh. Polybius, the Greek historian who lived in the 2nd century BC refers to so many underground wells and canals dug out in the desert of Asia Minor that "nowadays he who exploits those waters does not know whence they spring nor where they are conveyed" (Tales, X, 28). Vitruvius, a Roman architect and essay writer of the 1st century BC, describes, among "the techniques to find water", the one based on the airing wells connected to each other by underground pipes (De Architectura, VIII, I, 6) recalling the technique of the foggara. During the Muslim period several essays on the maintenance and the construction of drainage tunnels were written. In the early 11th century AD, The mathematician Hasan al-Hasib al-Karagi wrote "The art of making hidden waters spring".

These ancient methods of water production and the complex management procedures are still used in the regions of Gourara and of Touat in the Algerian Sahara desert. These systems are made up of about 1,000 foggara, half of which are still working. They extend for 3,000 km to 6,000 km. underground. The several wells on the surface, which can be recognized by their characteristic raised edge resulting from the excavation wastes, help to identify the tunnel. The wells are dug about 8–10 m apart in order to guarantee proper ventilation during the underground digging; they are also used for maintenance work but are not used for extracting water. The excavation of the foggara, unlike the Iranian qanat, starts from the settlement site and follows the edges of the alluvial cones of the fossil wadi. Unlike a feeder canal, the foggara do not convey water from the springs or underground pools to the place where it is used. However, thanks to their horizontal development, they tap the microflows seeping through the rocks and create free waters, thus acting as production systems or water mines. The tunnel that is dug parallel to the ground does not go down as far as the groundwater, but when it is possible it drains off the upper part. Thus, it prevents the aquifer from lowering and absorbs the right quantity of water for the replenishment of the aquifer itself. The subsoil area for water supply looks like a big rocky sponge rather than an underground basin. It is fed with microflows conveyed to the sebkha, the surfacing of deep aquifers made up of non-replenishing geological conditions and atmospheric supplies that can be classified into three types.

The first comes from the flows running under the sands of the erg that are due to the rainfall in the north, on the highlands and on the Sahara Atlas. These mountains are thousands of kilometres away, and it takes the microflows 5,000 years to cover this distance under the sands of the erg and to reach the oasis where prehistoric rainfall is harvested.

The second atmospheric supply comes from regular rainfall, which in these regions does not exceed 5–10 mm per year. Though it is quite a small water supply, because of the enormous size of the basins it can provide them with a significant contribution. As a matter of fact, if the rainfalls of Gourara look like a trifle both in temperate areas where rainfall reaches 3,000 mm and in dry areas, defined as such when the annual rainfall is less than 300 mm, it is necessary to take into account that even only 5 mm of rainfall on a 10 hectare surface means 50,000 litres of water to harvest.

The third source of supply is due to even more intangible and imponderable phenomena where water is produced by surface condensation. This is the phenomenon of hidden precipitations that is of primary importance in the ecology of the desert. Hidden precipitations allow gazelles to drink by licking the night dew off stones which are steeped in moisture; lizards and scarabs get the water ration they need to survive from the water contained in the air. Because of the temperature range from night to day that can exceed 60°, there is a lot of night condensation on the ground that wets the sand. This wet sand is dried by the sun's rays and creates a hard crust which typically creaks when trod upon. If the hidden precipitations are properly managed, then they can form sizeable water reserves. Hydraulic arrangements can then collect the water vapour from the air and preserve it the subsoil before it fades away at the first light of dawn. Under some circumstances, 4 cm^3 of water can be collected in the desert at night over a surface area of only 1 m^2. Some of the foggara networks, which are typical of Touat, are fed in this way. They are not deeply dug out of the ground and for this reason they are called surface foggara (Gauthier, 1928).

Research still has doubts about the way the air condensation drainage tunnels work and this is due to the fact that so far research has specially concerned Iranian qanat that receive a richer underground water supply. The differences in the kind of water supply would also explain the different ways of extraction between the qanat and the foggara. The simple needs of extraction do not justify the special characteristics of the huge quantity of wells built along the path. In fact, it would be cheaper to discharge waste along the horizontal pipe, as happens in common underground waterworks, rather than excavating numerous vertical shafts. Therefore, the latter must play an important role in the dynamics of the foggara system. Thanks to the presence of vertical shafts, the atmospheric pressure inside the tunnel is kept the same as the external pressure, thus favouring water flow even at minimum slopes. It is plausible that they are directly useful for absorbing moisture.

FIGURE 5.11 Oasis of Timimoun (Algerian Sahara), the interior of the drainage tunnel called foggara. The tunnel is dug out of the limestone rock, and thanks to its linear development it is able to catch the quantity of water contained in the porous ground.

5.12 Oasis of Timimoun (Algerian Sahara). The water sharing system at the surface outlet of the foggara.

FIGURES 5.13–5.14 The heaps of stone on the surface, resulting from the excavation wastes of the vertical air shafts, show the underground layout of the foggara. Figure 5.14 shows air shaft of the drainage tunnel which opens beneath the built-up area into large cavities for ablutions and cooling.

The whole foggara network, with its huge quantity of vertical shafts and drainage tunnels, is a maintenance system for the aquifer, keeping the soil humid by means of the exchange with atmospheric moisture. Al Karagi's essay lists three origins of qanat water supplies corresponding to the dynamics found in the foggara of the region of Gourara. As well as the primordial waters and rainwater, the medieval mathematician significantly highlighted the underground transformation of water into air. Thanks to the heat excursion during the night, humidity is released into the sand and flows down the underground canals until it reaches the fields. The foggara foster this process by acting as pumps which attract the vapour-loaded air and produce water coming from the atmosphere as air sources. During the night, cold air sinks to the ground and humidity seeps into the foggara. After sunrise, the process is reversed. As the ground heats up, the air in the foggara tends to rise as it is expelled through the air shafts, which are exposed to the burning temperatures of the desert. The air circulation in the underground tunnel operates by drawing the air from the lower part of the shady area of the palm grove. The humidity is thus sucked out and re-condensed on the walls and on the ground before the air escapes from the wells. Water is retained in the porous soil that becomes more and more steeped in water; gravity pulls the water down to the underground channel as far as the opening which feeds the oasis.

Prehistoric structures made up of barrows and underground rooms that the Sahara desert is rich in can also be described as moisture and dew harvesting systems. Underground rooms or mounds of stones favour the process of condensation and of water conservation. The so-called solar tombs of the Sahara desert, made out of concentric rings around a barrow, are linked to the ancient water harvesting methods and water cults. An explanation for the mysterious

FIGURE 5.15 Prehistoric mausoleum near the oasis of Janet (Tassili n'Ajjer, Algerian Sahara). These complex monuments, called solar tombs and made out of concentric rings, can be interpreted as dew harvesting systems.

Oases   **107**

FIGURE 5.16 Entrance to the underground chamber containing the hydraulic system of the Ghardaia oasis (Algeria). Underground tunnels convey floodwater to the different parts of the palm-grove.

FIGURES 5.17–5.18 In the Algerian Sahara a number of prehistoric traces of circular rings, rows, and mausoleums of stone proves a numerous human presence in the territory, now completely deserted. As in the Negev desert many of these structures can be identified as water devices or monuments related to them. The double ring structure with the entrance passage from Fig. 5.18 shows analogies with the complex in Fig. 5.17.

long lines of stones, which sometimes branch out from the ring-like long tentacles, thus making the monuments look like a curious space probe, is that they were water collectors. They are open to the slope and converge into the underground room. They were used to channel and convey the moisture harvested on the condensation surface that was enclosed between these two big shafts. The origin of the foggara is likely to have been due to the development of the condensation chamber technique. Even in the still marshy environment of Saharan prehistory, it was useful to produce drinking water through the percolation in the caves. As desertification developed and the water supplies of underground rooms were depleted, man probably tried to widen the excavation to follow the direction of the flows, thus creating a tunnel that made the condensation chamber longer and expanded the drainage area. This is actually the technique of the foggara whose peculiarity is the exploitation of all the principles of water production: catchment, percolation, and condensation.

5.3 The Structure of the Oasis

The excavation of a foggara must ensure that its layout reaches the fields under cultivation, which are the clear orographic outlet, otherwise the general runoff by gravity would not be possible. Therefore, the underground layout must be skilfully calculated and run on towards the highland with a very slight slope in order to ensure the runoff but also to prevent the bottom of the tunnel from eroding and waste and sand being carried away, which could lower the level or obstruct the passage. The layout maintains an almost horizontal route but gradually deepens because the ground above rises as the distance from the sebkha increases. The wells are dug about 4–8 meters apart to connect the tunnel with the surface and allow the excavation waste to be expelled. The latter are arranged around the entrance of the wells thus shaping the characteristic little craters, which make the pathway of the foggara evident from the ground above. As the length of the

FIGURE 5.19 Aerial photograph of an oasis showing the structural elements: the artificial dune, the path of the drainage tunnel in the depression of the dune, and the palm-grove extending according to a geometrical shape, following the gravitational line of flow and division of the water and depending on the quantity of water produced by the drainage tunnel.

FIGURE 5.20 Water is distributed to each owner by a series of channels on the surface and is temporarily collected in small basins called majen. The shade of the palm trees and the formation of algae on the water surface obstruct evaporation.

layout becomes longer, the wells can reach up to 150 metres in depth. They are used for going down the tunnel during maintenance works, but as we have said, they have a precise function in the particular water production systems of the drainage tunnels.

The structure of the oasis can be described as being made up of a 4–8 kilometre long foggara, which starts from the edge of the depression and goes upstream towards the highland, of a fortification situated along a rocky edge and of a strip of palm-grove extending downstream into the sebkha, as deep as the foggara's water capacity allows. The amount of the ploughing land that can be obtained from the desert depends on the water resources of the drainage tunnel. However, the possibility of extension towards the bottom of the sebkha encounters an insurmountable limit because here the salt concentration of the soil is higher. Therefore, the palm-grove is extended along the borders of the sebhka by excavating new foggara and building new villages.

The open-air channels called seguia, which flow through the tilled areas, follow the paths marked by the earth walls; they flow beneath the walls or flow along them. The irrigation by continuous runoff is necessary for a constant leaching of the soil since the concentration of salts is higher in the areas closest to the sebkha. However, this method is not suitable for growing vegetables and would require a large quantity of water. Therefore, the higher concentration of salts due to the strong evaporation on the soil surface is contrasted by maintaining a microclimate under the canopies of palm trees and irregular irrigation can be supplied by harvesting water in single small rectangular basins with rounded edges called majen. Like an arterial system, the total water capacity is meticulously divided up until it reaches these small final reservoirs, each with a minimum storage and distribution capacity, for each parcel of cultivated land.

The humidity in the desert ranges from a very low 0% to 5% but can increase up to a rate of 80% in the oases and these values are kept thanks to the runoff. The quantity of water that apparently evaporates is actually rendered by the overall oasis effect. The palm-grove both controls the phenomena of water dispersion caused by the evaporation and the transpiration of the biomass, and attracts and collects moisture.

The measurement of the water flow is carried out by the water masters kiel elma who block it in the main canal by means of a perforated copper sheet known as hallafa, whose tiny holes are closed with clay. The next step is to unstop the holes progressively until the water regularly flows. The set of holes which is thus obtained and which represents the overall flow is then subdivided according to each owner's share and is used to determine by the same method the size of the holes to be pierced in the kesria, the comb-shaped stone that is used to share out the water.

It is interesting to remark that the smallest hole, as large as the tip of the little finger, is called habba, which is a term also applied to the barley seed and which is used for the measure of the gold. It is not possible to say whether the diameter of the hole was made on the basis of the diameter of the barley seed; however, there is a clear correspondence between the barley seed and a precise quantity of gold. Therefore, a significant relationship between the measure of water and of cereals and gold is created. Since all the foggara have the same runoff speed which is controlled to avoid erosion and the lowering of course of the canal, the volume of a habba can be univocally established.

Actually, the foggara water supply is subject for several reasons to seasonal changes, and the habba is consequently a relative value whose variation affects the value of all the other commodities. As a result, it is not a fixed quantity, but a measure of value which represents the status of water production at any time, that is to say the status of the oasis economy. Since the water system automatically shares the variations in water production, it is a physical model of the devaluation and revaluation processes: the water in the oasis is the same general factor that circulates, is exchanged, and flows as money in the monetary system of contemporary economies.

5.4 Water Genealogy

Through the sharing of the inheritance, marriages, and the sale of possessions, the water quotas are continually parcelled out and restored. A complex system of kesria, junctions and little bridges – the latter are needed to prevent water from merging at the crossing of one or two canals – is the development on the ground through time of the ownership system. A water network is created, and it records the passing generations, the family ties, and possessions in a system of kinship that is physically made out of a network of canals (Marouf, 1980). Like a garden of memory, the oasis tracks its history by the precious water flow.

FIGURES 5.21–5.22 The majen (see Fig. 5.21) is the oasis farmer's fortune. It is periodically opened by lifting a stone which functions as a little sluice gate for the irrigation of the fields. In Figure 5.22, a water master from the Algerian oasis of Adrar showing the perforated sheet (hallafa) that is used for measuring the flows at the outlet of the big foggara.

FIGURE 5.23 Oasis of Timimoun (Algerian Sahara), kesria, a water quota sharing system.

Water is the life blood shared by the families: for this reason the jewel that is the symbol of fertility worn by Berber women around their necks features the stylisation in different shapes of the water distribution system. The Egyptian hieroglyphic mes that means "to be born" has the same shape, which confirms the very close connection between the oasis culture and the most ancient civilizations of the desert. The same drawing is reproduced on the pattern of the carpets, in women's hairstyles or it is tattooed on women's skin. The hairstyle marks the different phases of the women's growth closely linked to the agricultural practices and to the genesis of the oasis. At birth, the women's hairless head represents the original cosmic space. During childhood, girls have their heads shaven except for a single lock that is left in the middle of the head; the lock symbolizes the primordial land. During puberty, only a narrow shaved strip surrounds the hair growing in the middle of the head: it represents the salted and sterile ocean surrounding the land which is fertile but still untilled. As time passes, women keep their hair shaved around the circumference of the head, while the hair growing in the middle of the head is divided into locks by a median line reproducing the central canal of the irrigation systems. When a girl is ready for marriage her hair, no longer shaved off, is divided into lines and thin tresses, representing the tilled land where the water flows through the irrigation canals. Married women gather their long hair in thick tresses: woman is now as fertile as the oasis.

The different hairstyles reproduce in the individual the general events occurring, thus the personal history coincides with the story of the whole system. Water, which fertilizes the fields, is shared among the properties and is inherited. It is the vital sap of a fertile union that founds the family and perpetuates the community.

The correspondence between the ego and the world establishes a pact between culture and nature; the symbol and the tradition are witnesses and guardians of this pact, which ensures the maintenance of the universal harmony. Thanks to this solid relationship man can find consolation for the precariousness of his existence, and space becomes full of the holiness which is necessary for his safeguard and protection. The close link between actions and nature's harmony imposes a set of prohibitions, restraints, and precepts since even the simplest action can contribute to the maintenance of universal balance. Thus, in the oasis the constant relationship between the microcosm and the macrocosm is not a metaphysical conceit but rather an ethical principle based on precise material needs.

5.5 The Great Caravan Nomadism

The oasis system spread out and was perpetuated by the nomadic world, which is not the antithesis of the oasis system, rather it is its complement. However, in this phase nomadism was completely different from the social formation of the hunter-Gatherers, where the errant life was a migratory practice linked to the animals' movements, to seasonal and environmental changes, and to the maintenance of a low population density on the territory through a constant occupation of still uncontaminated lands. The nomadism of the desert differs from both the migratory practice typical of the Age of Metals, which was based on the use of carts, and from the organisation of the first transhumant pastoral communities. The latter is the best breeding method, taking advantage of the variability of climate and grazing, but it should not be confused with nomadism. In fact, cattle rearing is entrusted to specialised groups settled in a stable place. Desert nomadism is organized over very large areas and around all the families, in order to breed cattle rather than for game hunting or the conquest of new lands because of a demographical growth. In the desert, meat is produced at very low cost by means of camel and sheep farming, exploiting the scarce resources scattered over vast areas. In fact, it would be a waste to feed herds with the vegetables painstakingly grown in the oases. The breeding organized according to the great caravan nomadism allows the best use of the natural desert vegetation. This is the only practice achievable in weak ecosystems where a long-lasting demographic burden in the same place would be destructive for the environment. A reproposal of nomadism would be still today a solution to regenerate ecosystems which have been exhausted or where particular conditions prevail.

Nomadism develops a refined environmental knowledge for seeking out the pastures which can suddenly appear in an area thanks to imperceptible climatic factors, finding routes and discovering or organizing water resources. In particular, the knowledge relating to water techniques is the most widely spread. As a matter of fact, the name of the tuareg, the great Saharan nomadic caravaneers, derives from a Berber word which means water canalisation. This knowledge is applied for the practice of caravan trading over long distances. Nomadism holds the links among the oases. The latter, in fact, thanks to the phenomenon of nomadism, are never isolated communities but live in an international context of commercial and

FIGURE 5.24 The fruitful fields are arranged in small garden parcel's called jenna which means "garden" and "paradise". The geometrical shape of the cultivations corresponds to the order which underlies the close relationship in nature between microcosm and macrocosm typical of the notion of oasis.

FIGURE 5.25 Tassili n'Ajjer (Algeria). Painting of the late Metal Age which represents a march of nomads riding a dromedary and the characters of an archaic alphabet written from top to bottom like the Tuareg's writing, the tifinagh, into which the former evolved.

cultural exchanges. The nomadic groups represent the military force, guarantee mobility and rapidity of movement; they are the means both for conquest and trade. The nomadic people ensure contacts and disseminate information, but above all they guarantee the continuity of the cultures through catastrophes and exoduses.

Thus, the desert people's civilisation is passed on through intangible assets and minimal signs rather than through impressive architectural structures that eventually deteriorate. In fact, it is passed on through the learning of cultural values such as behaviour, literature, art, or artefacts which are easily transported such as the chisel, weaving, and decoration. It can be said that the organisation of a camp, the structure of a tent and an adobe building include and excel in planning, design, and technology of the ancient architectural constructions. The tuareg's hemispherical reed dwellings in their several evolutions from tents made of leather or wool and the temporary and rapidly assembled furnishings present, in already defined shapes, the structural characteristics and development potential of a variety of architectural shapes such as domes, exedras, and enclosures. The srefe in Mesopotamia and the reed huts of the rasciaida population in Eritrea are made, by binding together bundles of vegetation, barrel-vaulted structures, ornamented with the architectural elements of columns, gables, and sloping roofs with eaves. Rushes are used to make light boats that are easy to carry in the desert. They are used as practical moveable roofs, ready for nautical use in the case of watercourses in flood. Light papyrus pirogues similar to Neolithic drawings sail still now across Lake Tana in Ethiopia, on the upper Nile and in Sardinia.

FIGURE 5.26 Tuareg of the human grouping Kel Ajjer of the Algerian Sahara. The Tuareg are one of the best-known great nomadic groupings of the Sahara. They are called "the blue men" because of the stains of indigo left by the traditional clothing over their body. The veil that covers their faces is useful as a protection against sand storms and to recover the humidity released in breathing.

FIGURE 5.27 Organisation of a Tuareg camp with the typical structure of a circular tent made of camel hide and reed finishings.

The nomadic culture perpetuates knowledge and technologies through these shapes. In the history of the desert people, phases of stability and sedentariness continually alternated with phases of collapse and dispersion. During periods of crisis, people moved away and started a nomadic life again. The knowledge heritage was guarded and passed on by oral tradition or was taken on by transportable means. Thus, weaving, ornaments, jewels, and decorations, worn or painted on the human body, are the vehicles for memory and knowledge. This explains the agricultural and hydraulic signs that can be found on a piece of embroidery or on a carpet, just as female makeup recalls the decorative motifs of a dwelling, or a ring brings to mind complex architectural structures. Over the long periods passed in the desert, these drawings and the objects gain a symbolic value and an imaginary and fabulous meaning. Sometimes the original functional meaning is utterly lost and the shape alone is obsessively reproduced with figurative redundancy. Other times, nostalgia and a desire for the lost land and the promised house turn memories into hallucinatory fantasies. The native town corresponds to the final destination and the material pathway becomes the metaphor of a spiritual path. This is why both the Arabic architectural constructions and the towns often take the shape of fabulous and dreaming creations. They arise up suddenly after a long intimate elaboration. Like a recurrent dream, whose real context is no longer distinguishable from the mental elaboration, these constructions are the result of a memory continually and collectively enriched by the tales narrated during the long watches of the caravans.

Urban Ecosystems

6

FIGURE 6.1 Matera, Civita, and the glacis of the Sasso Barisano. An urban ecosystem is an oasis model which evolves into a town. It gains complexity and stratification, but retains its organic relationship with the environment and a sustainable use of resources. The aesthetic qualities we appreciate in the Sassi di Matera are due to the rules and restraints imposed on the settlement by the water and energy requirements and the need to protect the soil. The adoption of the same principles in similar environmental situations explains the similarities arising even with distant urban ecosystems such as Ghardaia in Fig. 6.2.

6.1 Complexity and Stratification

Oases are not just tilled areas nor a type of landscape but rather the sum of all the environmental and architectural elements that are the result of a wise organisation of space. It is a typical pattern of the dry areas of the Saharan, Arabian, or Eastern deserts, but it can be applied to all those situations where the symbiosis of factors and the careful management of resources create ecosystems which are in harmony with the environment. Therefore, the urban ecosystem is the result of larger dimensions, higher levels of social specialisation and construction that are obtained while maintaining these characteristics. This is the oasis model extended to a wide range of settlements based on autopoiesis, homeostasis, and self-maintenance, but they improve their quality by exploiting the commercial standing or the wealth provided by a specific resource and make use of their enhanced potential. The urban ecosystem is the sum of the local knowledge built up over time and in the cultures. It no longer has a village dimension, but presents stratifications, social complexities, external connections through trade and cultural exchanges and architectural features typical of a town.

Some of these situations directly depend on arid conditions and others on diversified climatic areas and environments where the human presence and the use of resources are in perfect harmony even if urbanisation develops. Each of the following examples shows the main geographic area where the stratification of social groupings developed from the Palaeolithic, through the Neolithic and the Age of Metals up to the establishment of oasis communities. The case of Ghardaia shows that the application of the knowledge about oases in the most arid areas of the Sahara desert increases the local resources until a system of towns is created, and can be continuously generated without destroying the environment. The water society of Ghardaia is based on solid community principles resulting from a strong cohesion and on spiritual and religious concepts. In the south of Arabia, the town of Shibam shows the levels of complexity and of integration of resources to which the Neolithic techniques used in the adobe villages can evolve. Furthermore, they can completely control the organisation of the landscape and soil fertility depending on the existence of the town itself that takes on specific shapes and typologies. Petra is the synthesis of very ancient traditional knowledge in the Near East. It was the place where Neolithic development occurred as is shown by several villages including the town of Beida. Petra was the main centre of the Hedomites in the Age of Metals and of the Nabateans. The capital of the hidden waters of the desert during the Hellenic age, it was crossed by thirsty caravans on the Incense Road to the south and of the Silk Road to the east, using its outstanding monumental façades carved out of the rock and the incredible playing fountains to draw the attention of rich merchants. Matera boasts the Sassi, a primeval ancient site where the Neolithic ditches and the agro-pastoral terracing systems attest to the ways of inhabiting the caves and managing the soils. It is an example of the techniques and knowledge widespread in southern Europe and in the Mediterranean isles and peninsulas that crystallize in the stone town (Laureano, 1993).

6.2 The Society of Waters

The town of Ghardaia built on the limestone highlands of the Algerian Sahara desert is an example of an oasis which developed into a town system. Ghardaia gives its name to a pentapolis composed of five settlements rising up on high pinnacles along the sinuous M'zab valley. Whitewashed stone houses are clustered on the five hills in narrow concentric circles up to the top of the pinnacles, towered by a lone minaret. The low houses, each one with its own courtyard, seem to climb the rocky slopes thus carving clusters of terraces, yards, and narrow streets out of the hillside in a way that completely blends the city into the geomorphologic background. The architecture of the landscape shows a harmony not found elsewhere, a unique ability to use and enhance the characteristics of the site without damaging them. The lime walls of the houses stand out against the blue of the sky in stark contrast with the reddish brown colour of the desert soil, yet they also blend perfectly into the setting. The cities of the M'zab valley that cascade from a central mosque, set at the top of the highland, down the bottom of the valley, exploit the topography of the hills, thus becoming an integral part of them: it is an example of how architecture can decode nature. The mausoleums and the places for the cults with their organic shapes and anthropomorphic entrances have terraces and surfaces necessary for the catchment of the smallest quantity of moisture.

The Ibadite community that founded the M'zab pentapolis was banished from its original capitals, Tahert on the Atlas Mountains, Sigilmasa and Sedrata at the outskirts of the desert. In the 11th century AD, it settled in an area detached from any route, completely barren and weakened by natural conditions. The way this sunny stony ground was turned into a

FIGURE 6.2 Ghardaia (Algerian Sahara). The mosque had to accommodate all the inhabitants. When this was no longer possible, a new settlement was built in a similar context. The habitat, therefore, maintained its clustered shape which was in harmony with the environment.

green valley surrounded by harmonious cities is an outstanding example of how the Saharan desert can be made habitable. The perfect harmony of the landscape is due to a good understanding of the building techniques and of a valid ecosystem management policy. The appreciable aesthetic qualities and harmony are the result of a necessary rigour and the constant application of rules, which would have overwhelmed everyone if disregarded. Therefore, a harmonious pattern where architecture and community, shape and symbol, technique and spirit blend with each other was perpetuated over time. The single, central mosque representing the unity of faith has a prayer hall that must be able to hold the whole assembly of the town. When the mosque is no longer able to contain the growing population, a new one must be built and as a consequence a new town must be founded. This rule has determined a constant control over the size of towns. When the population increases, the settlement does not sprawl; but rather the original pattern is reproduced by building a new urban centre, in a similar geomorphologic situation and presenting the same characteristics as the older one. This method has brought about the progressive development of settlements on high and unproductive cliffs, which can be easily defended, thus protecting the bottom of the valley where the palm groves form a long green ribbon extending for about 1,000 hectares. Fruit trees grow in the shade of the palms and plots of vegetables and cereals lie under the trees. Water is drawn up from the wells but the replenishment of groundwater is not due to natural conditions. Sunken dams intercepting the underground microflows were built to preserve the humidity of the soil. The main water resource comes from the flooding of the wadi M'zab that

FIGURES 6.3–6.4 Ghardaia. The mausoleum of the holy founder with a terrace and a courtyard for harvesting humidity (Fig. 6.3). Below figure, the overbuilding of the settlements on the rocky summits along the palm-grove forms the so-called pentapolis of the M'zab valley (Fig. 6.4).

Urban ecosystems

FIGURE 6.5 The dam of Beni Isguen, one of the settlements of the pentapolis of Ghardaia. The dam is not used to create a water basin but rather it retains the flows in the subsoil, and water is drawn up from the wells like that above on the right in figure.

occurs every 3 or 10 years, and the whole valley is organised on the basis of this event. Large water intakes intercept the flow and distribute it to the tilled fields. The narrow streets enclosed between the high walls, which surround the gardens, become torrents that convey the precious water. Apertures are made in the walls to draw in the quantity of water needed for each garden where a further series of little channels, bridges, and basins ensure the irrigation of fruit and vegetable gardens. This water harvesting system of the torrent streets is still working in the Wadi Dhahr at 15 km from the town of San'a in Yemen, where during the rainfalls the small walled streets convey the water to the gardens that are arranged on a slightly lower level, by means of sluice gates situated in the enclosures.

The distribution of water and the exploitation of lands to till or build on are regulated by specific rules which constitute a proper legal system. In fact, Ghardaia's social system can be defined as a system regulated by the hydraulic law, which is made up of a series of rules partly written down and partly reported by the oral tradition through a series of verdicts and proverbs that represent a sacred natural law. One of these maxims says "When the wadi arrives it comes holding its laws in its hands". The wadi is a fossil river, which is generally dry and can suddenly flood, with beneficial but impetuous consequences. According to popular wisdom nothing can stop the wadi, because it follows its own law and will claim its flooding and passage rights without any possibility to raise objections. Therefore, people are forbidden to build in those specific areas that traditional knowledge has designated over time, thanks to the experience accumulated by many generations. The assembly of Elders dictates the rules of behaviour, thus helping the youngest to build a house like all the others and to start productive activity.

FIGURE 6.6 The dam of Beni Isguen in one of its sporadic moments of flood that even occur every 10 years, when the water intakes channel the flows towards the single parts of the palm-grove and replenish the water table.

FIGURE 6.7 Ghardaia. A big water sharing device used to distribute and channel the precious floods according to the different oases.

Similar social associations based on hydraulic rules still exist in Spain, in the region of Andalusia, where they are called alquerie, in Eritrea where they are called maihabar and in eastern Ethiopia where they are called afocha. The birth of these associations is due to the fact that the collection and use of poor and fragmented water resources, often coming from apparently negligible supplies of moisture, dew or hidden rainfalls need a complex and fragile organization of space. The latter must be commonly accepted because even the least deviation can cause the whole system to collapse.

In Andalusia the alquerie are either the result of the Berber-Arabian migrations or of a reuse of the oldest local habits by these social groups. They organize whole water basins on which the property of several families depends. The water supply of each parcel derives from a network of canalisations and cisterns that intercept the upstream resources and spread them out in the valley, thus widening the irrigated area at the margins of the natural riverbed. The layout and the slope of the valley must be perfectly calculated to equally supply all the families, since each of them depends on the water systems crossing the other properties. Therefore, common agreements regulating every activity are necessary: the location of the fields, the time of irrigation, the choice and rotation of the species planted, which need different quantities of water, the time of private or collective work, and the periods of rest as well. Also the area for settlements is chosen on the basis of precise rules, since it has to take into account the areas to be left free for use as water basins and farming spaces to be carefully saved.

FIGURE 6.8 Ghardaia, a torrent-street. When floods occur, the street directs water to the gardens beyond the lateral walls. On the right, figure shows the water intake which intercepts the liquid in the torrent-street and directs it to the gardens.

Urban ecosystems

FIGURE 6.9 Wadi Dhahr (Yemen). The landscape of roads, gardens, and cultivations created thanks to the water distribution technique of the torrent-streets. The water intakes open into the gardens situated between the walls of the narrow streets. The whole system works by gravity and determines a rigorous organization which fully functions only when of the sporadic floods occur and the pathways turn into watercourses.

The maihabars, which literally means "water cooperatives", are organizations based on an agreement drawn up between different family clans dealing with the construction of hydraulic systems and the fight against land degradation. If the soil were not enclosed with an embankment, if it were not made arable by water repartition systems, and were not protected by the shade of the plant, it would undergo the destructive action of erosion. Surface salinity would increase, the soil would be demolished and transformed into sand and dispersed by the wind's action. Whereas the soil is stabilised by agricultural work, it is fertilized with manure, protected with embankments and terracing systems built by the community. Everyone lends a hand in building the house of every person who is continuously supported and protected by the common agreement.

FIGURE 6.10 Ibiza (Spain), the entrance to an underground cistern. On the isle there are water-harvesting devices dating back to the Phoenicians, and hydraulic systems spread by Islam and typical of the Andalusian civilisation.

FIGURE 6.11 Ibiza (Spain), cistern and cistern-jar. The system of the cistern-jars, underground water reservoirs, is spread throughout the islands and along the arid Mediterranean coasts, providing a reserve known to travellers who used it during their journeys.

The Ethiopian associations, the afocha, are still working in the town of Harar, on the eastern side of the Rift Valley, near the Dankali desert. Harar, the town where Arthur Rimbaud spent the last years of his life, was defined as the only urban realization in western Africa. As a matter of fact, in the Middle Ages, after the fall of Axum and the decline of Lalibela, the Ethiopian sovereigns carried out a sort of nomadic urbanism, extreme and destructive development of the resources of the archaic practices of the migratory settlements. The capital periodically moved when the wood, water, and agricultural resources of a place were exhausted. Thus, the sovereign could control several regions of the country and maintain his power over the court, in order to prevent the formation of a stable feudal system, which could oppose him, and to reduce the authority of the traditional cooperative corporations that were based on an egalitarian and stable management of the places. Thanks to the Muslim expansion in Africa, Harar became a city-state set on a promontory between two wadis tapping a large basin. The latter was the crossroads of the caravan routes joining the Red Sea to the Ethiopian plateau and with a strong economic, spiritual, and cultural influence over the whole continent. In the 16th century, a massive boundary wall was built which enclosed the urban perimeter stretching over a 42 hectare area. The town was equipped with imposing water systems, which branched out over the surrounding country, and the terraced gardens allowed the cultivation of the mountain slopes of the basin up to a height of 3,000 metres. Harar is still now a walled town that has retained its original characteristics. It is a synthesis of an urbanism spread by Islam, on one hand; and the archaic traditions of the African villages, on the other hand.

FIGURE 6.12 Ethiopia, a slope organization system functioning by means of enclosures and progressive water-harvesting reservoirs.

FIGURE 6.13 An irrigation system in the valley of Gindah (Eritrea). The area situated between the arid coast and the highland receives the humidity of the thermal currents coming up from the Red Sea.

Harar has an arid climate but during the rainy season, in summer time, up to 700 mm of rain can fall in a single month so that the torrents widen and water is conveyed to the town by sluices and ditches to replenish the underground aquifers extracted from the wells set inside the courtyards of the houses. Agricultural irrigation is carried out by means of the so-called kurii, which are basins dug out of the torrent beds. Each kurii supplies about 20 farmhouses. The water use is managed by the malaak who are water authorities chosen by the farmers associated in mutual solidarity corporations called arsch, toya, and afocha. The latter helps the associates to build their houses and organise wedding and funeral ceremonies. It is also responsible for cleaning the routes and for the sewage and debris disposal system.

In Harar sewage disposal is done using a practice which recalls the prehistoric methods of totemic association and symbiosis with animals. Certain particular individuals are charged with feeding the hyenas and establishing with them singular empathetic relationships. The night scene at the entrance to the town of these hyena-men holding pieces of meat in their mouth offered directly to the beast mouth appears now to be a mere tourist attraction. Actually, it is essential for the complex urban ecological cycle: the hyenas are attracted into the tunnels where the debris and the sewage from the town are collected, and as skilful and voluntary scavengers they keep them clean. The forms of animal nourishment, semi-domestication, totemism, and possession are typical of the African tradition. In the town of Harar, the red ants that fight the termites, harmful for wood and fields under cultivation, are attracted and nourished with animal bones and carcasses left on the ground. Specific raised shelters are built in the fields for the wild birds, which are protected from the predators

FIGURE 6.14 The Hadramaut valley and the ancient walled town of Shibam surrounded by the embankments and the channels of the traditional system of flood sharing and cultivation of the fields, most of which are now abandoned.

and provide agriculture with fertile guano. The birds are very also useful for discovering the therapeutic properties of the plants, which are largely used to disinfect water and keep away diseases and pestilences.

There are also traditional practices that adopt the modern form of the ancient solidarity principles. In Botswana, the motswelo is a traditional form of cooperative bank, which usually gathers together between 15 and 20 people who join the group voluntarily and bring what they can provide: money, produce of the land or work. Thanks to this ancient system, it is possible to save money, to obtain interest-free loans and funds to start important activities. For instance, it is possible to organize the production and the sale of traditional beer, the cultivation of new lands or the restoration of villages. Production and trade are considered as the equivalent of money deposits. All the profits are given, in turn, to the members of the motswelo who use them to fund one of their activities or other social needs such as feasts, marriages, or the purchase of a house.

The rules of tradition are accepted because they are written in nature. They have been established thanks to the stubbornness of those who were able to find harmony with the strict laws of the desert, to obtain the resources necessary for life without spoiling them but continually renewing them. These include especially water and every other means of sustenance, the material to build the houses and the humus to grow the gardens, but also spiritual strength, collective wisdom, and common solidarity.

6.3 Flood Management Communities

Shibam, a town situated in the Hadramaut Valley, in Yemen, is the synthesis of the hydraulic and architectural knowledge of the human groups which inhabited the dry plains made out of mud and clay and were devastated by occasional floods. Shibam lies completely on the wadi, a dry riverbed. It is a precise quadrangle perfectly surrounded by massive city walls. Inside the walls, the urban layout is neat and regular with well-proportioned squares, buildings, and public areas in an orderly arrangement. Yet, the overall geometry of the city is never monotonous and is devoid of the cold rational rigour of a city plan imposed by the public authorities. Each building is an independent unit and contributes to the harmony and diversity of the overall conception. They are multi-storey tower-houses, which rise up to height of about 30 metres and are made of raw earth, the plain mud carried down by the occasional floods. These constructions look like modern skyscrapers, but they are actually 500 years old and only one family lives in each. The imposing and windowless ground floor is used as a storehouse, while the rooms at the upper levels are ornamented with fret-worked wooden windows. The highest floor is a terrace surrounded by the external walls and waterproofed with lime. The blending into the urban fabric of the religious architecture such as the mosques, the regular height of the buildings and their whitewashed roofs draw a compact and harmonious shape, thus giving the idea of equality and of the community through architecture.

Shibam was built with the accumulated knowledge of a population that because of its need for cooperation in order to ensure its water supply expressed a strong social unity and a planned control of space. Since the most ancient times, in the Hadramaut valley, the communities sharing an interest in irrigation have been using the highlands and the steep slopes, opportunely shaped and insulated as an impluvium to harvest rainfall in a system of basins and cisterns. Thanks to this constant work and to knowledge handed on by specific organizations, rushing torrents that come down the slopes after rainfall are controlled. Since no other water source is available but this, the regions of the slope exist thanks to the preservation of valuable flows and to the careful terracing system that creates the plots of land among which water is carefully shared out. Widespread social cooperation is even more necessary on the large plains of the wadi bed. Each tilled area depends on the construction of long stone, mud or adobe dams whose purpose is not the creation of open-air water basins. This would produce a decrease of the farming lands and considerable water evaporation. They are used to preserve water in the subsoil and protect the soil: sporadic rainfall and even the smallest floods are exploited by saturating the soil with humidity by means of the dams that block the underground flow and hold the humus; the violent rainfall and the devastating floods are controlled and shared over a larger area by means of dams and embankments. Thanks to the construction of wells and canals, water is then used to irrigate palm groves and fields cultivated in the dry but fertile loess. During dry seasons the water preserved in the sediments is taken from wells. They are built by means of a typical Yemenite technique that ensures maximum saving of the energy used by the dromedary to pull the rope with the bucket full of water. The well is raised several metres above ground level and the top can be reached by means of a long ramp. The dromedary follows this steep path without wasting any energy while the empty bucket goes down. Subsequently, when

FIGURE 6.15 The dwellings of Shibam are tall tower-houses made of raw earth. Each house is inhabited by a single family which is able to build the massive construction, thanks to the low cost of the material.

Urban ecosystems

FIGURES 6.16–6.17 In Yemen mausoleums and holy places are almost always related to water harvesting. The Hadramaut valley: the sanctuary above channels the runoff along the slope into the room of ablutions and prayer below (Fig. 6.16). Northern Yemen: the rainfalls collected in the courtyard for prayer fill up the open-air cistern (Fig. 6.17).

FIGURE 6.18 Yemen, underground cavities used for ablutions. All mosques always have hypogeal rooms which gather water. They are often devices which existed before and were built for the Sabean temples.

FIGURE 6.19 Yemen, terracing system for the protection and cultivation of the slope. The water intakes deviate the flows from their natural course and direct them along the walls on the terraces. Towers and stone buildings are placed to defend the cultivations.

FIGURES 6.20–6.21 Shibam (Yemen). The ancient dam was not used to create an open-air basin but rather to direct the floods (Fig. 6.21) to the embankments, the channels, and the depressions in the gardens.

the dromedary lifts the full bucket by pulling the rope keeping itself far from the well, it is favoured by the downward path of the ramp.

No archaeological remains prove the date of foundation of Shibam, although historians agree in stating that in the 2nd century AD it was already a prosperous and well-known town. According to the legend, the population that fled during the Himyarite wars were determined to reproduce, in Shibam, the plan of their ancient capital, Shabwa, the archaeological surveys of which show a regular plan and layout.

A close connection between history and tradition can still be seen in the building methods. In fact, according to a proud habit people must live in very high places, in palaces, and in castles, for prestige and protection reasons, like in Medieval European tower houses, but also for more specifically symbolic, social, and technical reasons. All the members of an enlarged family prefer to occupy the same ancestral ground and live in a common house unfolding in height. Thus, it saves farming ground and optimises the building factors related to techniques and climatic conditions. It is said that an adobe house must have both a good hat and boots in order to be protected from rain on the top and from moisture at the bottom. The upward development of the houses limits the size of the roof and foundations, which would require more careful and expensive maintenance. As time goes by, the high adobe houses undergoing decomposition and disintegration are rebuilt on their ruins using the same materials and reproducing their former appearance and size. The mud for the bricks is gathered in gardens shaping small craters separated by embankments and canals, which surround the town and protect it against devastating floods.

Upstream of the watercourse of the wadi, a system of dams distributing the waters widens the area subject to floods and dissipates the force of the water out over a larger area. The circular depressions of the gardens around the town gather and absorb water. In this system of artificial sandy craters, the fields under cultivation are protected by the boundary embankments of the landfill and shaded by the leafage of the palm grove. The organic waste of the town is deposited in these artificial craters and together with water it turns the sterile sands of the loess into fertile soil. Thus, it is the very existence of the town of Shibam, with its supply of biological matter, which allows the growth of the palm trees and agricultural production. A continuously interacting cycle starts. Not only do foodstuffs feed the population and return to the soil as fertilizer, but the entire city, with its forms and architecture, is founded upon the eternal principle of the complete reuse of the resources. As a matter of fact, the material to build the city is obtained by excavations in the garden. This is the only kind of soil suitable for building because of its richness in humus that gives it binding properties. In fact, the sediments of the wadi would be sterile and unusable without the biological components produced by agriculture and the organic fertilizer deriving from human excrement.

The latter is collected in the town thanks to a toilet that carefully separates the liquid waste, which is dangerous for adobe structures, from the solid waste that is essential for agriculture. This ingenious toilet has been in use for centuries in Yemen, since before the water closet was introduced in our society. The toilet allows the separation between liquid and solid excrement right at the beginning, by means of two outlets: a front outlet for liquid waste and a back one for solid waste that is carried by gravity down to the collection baskets on the streets. This device and the necessity of collecting droppings explain the complex urban plan composed of squares, streets, and blind alleys. As a matter of fact, each house is equipped with sewage shafts running along the fronts to discharge droppings into fitting baskets that will be carried away to the fields. These service fronts overlook secondary or boundary streets whose path defines the urban plan. Thus, an indissoluble circuit joins together the built-up area, its hygienic maintenance, and the organic waste of the inhabitants used in the fertilization of the gardens and the progressive reconstruction of the buildings. Like a biological organism, the town of Shibam renovates its single components but keeps unaltered its shape and identity. This secret alchemy fulfils a harmonious integration of the urban and agricultural exigencies and the preservation from the floods, in a virtuous cycle of disposal and reuse.

6.4 The Mother of the Cisterns

All the water knowledge of the ancient northern Arabian civilizations crystallizes in the single town of Petra, the ancient capital of the Nabateans. Today Petra features as a wholly bare place whose impressive and monumental architecture carved out of the rock attracts tourists. However, the town was very different in the past: it was an extraordinary ecosystem

FIGURE 6.22 Shibam. The dams conveyed the flows down the small watersheds where the soil saturated with humidity could be cultivated all the year round.

FIGURE 6.23 The harvesting systems of the floods in small depressions and gardens separated by land embankments are still in use in al-Hajarain, in the homonymous wadi, one of the numerous tributaries of the Hadramaut.

Urban ecosystems   **141**

where water rushed down and the gardens smelled of fruit and vegetables. At the end of the 1st century BC, the geographer Strabo described Petra as ornamented with fountains and basins, flourishing trees and tilled fields (Geography, XVI, 4, 21). Diodorus the Sicilian precisely described the natural citadels of the Nabateans. He said about the Arabs "they love freedom more than anyone else and if a strong enemy army approaches they disperse in the desert, which is their fortress. As a matter of fact, the lack of water makes the desert inaccessible to the foreigners. Only the Nabateans can survive thanks to the excavation of whitewashed underground tunnels. Since earth is partially composed of clay and partially of soft stone, the Nabateans smoothly dig out large cavities, with a narrow entrance at the top. They gradually enlarge toward the bottom till each side reaches a size of one plethron (about 30 metres).

After having filled these reservoirs with rainwater, they block the entrances by levelling them to the surrounding ground and leave marks that only they can recognise" (Historical Library, XIX, 94).

These techniques are still used by the nomadic people who always have a water reserve hidden along the most deserted routes and that only they know. The most imposing rock in Petra is Umm al-Biyara, the Arabian name of which means "mother of the cisterns". Archaeological evidence and an environmental analysis demonstrate that the mountain basin surrounding the wadi Musa valley has been wholly arranged over time in order to control water resources and convey them to the Nabatean town. Petra, which supplies all the waters, organizes the desert through every kind of water

FIGURE 6.24 Petra (Jordan). The reservoir in the foreground conveys rainwater to the cavity underneath. The garden carved out of the rock protects the soil and the plants from the wind and the heat.

FIGURE 6.25 Petra synthesises Hedomite and Nabatean hydraulic knowledge. The whole rocky landscape is carved and organized in order not to lose a single drop of water condensation on the mountains, runoff along the slopes or sporadic but possible flooding of the wadi.

and drainage system: the arrangement of tanks, cisterns, and gutters for the harvesting of rainwater and microflows dripping down the sandstone walls; the protection and the support along both the slopes and the wadi water courses in order to produce soil and farming land; the diversion of the rare but rushing and devastating floods and the canalisation of the spring water.

Rainwater harvesting on the high places and on the bare sandstone walls is the most archaic device and is used in many different ways. There are numerous types of cisterns carved out of the rock and waterproofed with chalk. They range from small pools for the harvesting of runoff on the highlands to the square or rectangular cisterns at the bottom of the natural drips, up to the cavities, which are similar to large rooms carved out of the vertical walls into which complex canals and pipe networks flow. Each slope or surface became a useful watershed to harvest rainfall and every form of water supply, from a few drops to big floods was stored. On the top of the Jebel Harun, the only water supply for the guardian of the mausoleum and for the pilgrims is still now a large underground cistern with arches covered with stone slabs fed by rock infiltration. Behind the theatre of Sabra, carved out of the rock, there are pipes coming down from the mountain conveying the rainwater into a large basin.

The smallest traces of moisture and the supply of night condensation of fog and dew were used. Along the steep Deir, the khottara are structures which provide water all the year round: the weak exudations from the walls, as a result of the condensation at high altitudes, are harvested by dripping into tanks and cisterns. This kind of device is probably the origin of the biblical episode in which Moses made water spring forth by means of his rod. By hitting the wall, the superficial coating is removed and there is a greater water flow. There are also underground hydraulic systems similar to the qanat, the drainage tunnels. Such an imposing system equipped with ventilation wells, carried the water from the highest altitudes of Bedebdeh passing under the present Umm Sahyun and descended towards the Turkmaniyah as far as the centre of Petra.

Along the route towards Sabra, at the bottom of Ras as-Slimane, a cistern called Bir Huweimel works as a trap for floods. A huge room having a depth of 9 m has been excavated under the riverbed. When the water passes, a series of small water intakes and decanting basins convey it to the cistern that stores it even when the higher watercourse is dry.

The excavation of a tunnel protected the central area of Petra from devastating floods of the wadi Musa. The riverbeds of the wadi al-Mudhlim and of the wadi Sadd al-Ma'-jan, used for this diversion, were arranged with a system of dams and sluices in order to act as big water reserves to irrigate the fields organized in artificial terracing systems along the banks of the wadi al-Mataha.

Along the line of the spring waters, a system of large rectangular reservoirs made out of blocks of limestone was used to harvest drinking water and distribute it by gravity to the residential area of Petra by means of a network of long canals carved out of the sandstone wall, of suspended ramps, of aqueducts, and of ceramic pipes, which are the result of extensive hydraulic knowledge. Two aqueducts branched off from the big reservoir Zurraba, situated just outside the area of Petra, at a height of 1,050 m. The aqueduct leading towards the south fed the Siq pipes, the other one, which followed a long path surrounding the Jebel el-Khubtha, entered Petra through the wadi al-Mataha. Once the canal had reached half of the height of the rocky wall, it fed the cisterns and the private houses carved out of the lower part of the rock. In some particularly impressive and isolated places, characterized by elevated passages or natural small streets in the canyon, the presence of a large number of worshipping niches, cubic stones, and seats carved out of the rock show that the path followed by the water was also used as a holy itinerary for mysterious ceremonies.

Each structure in Petra is always something more than a mere spectacular room with a monumental façade. On the so-called Turkmaniyah tomb there is an important inscription with the words: "the courtyard before the tomb, the porticoes, and the houses inside the gardens and the triclinium, the water cisterns, the terraces, and the walls". In the so-called Triclinium of the Garden, the cistern, closed by a massive retaining wall, is 18.2 m long, 6 m wide, and 3.6 m deep. Using the water harvested by means of an elaborate system of embankments, canals, and reservoirs, it fed a garden arranged on terraces with dry stone walling. A huge relief depicts a 4.5 m long lion after which all this canyon was named Farasah, meaning fierce beast. It was actually a monumental fountain pouring water from the mouth of the wild beast. The hydraulic system starts from the top of the Jebel al-Madhbah, which can be reached through the comfortable stairs and ramps that characterise all the rocks of Petra with a huge carving work of the rocky walls. Madhbah means "raised place". This name designates the holy sites which were common to all the Semitic populations mentioned in the Bible. The arrangement of these flat rocky peaks with reservoirs and basins leaves no doubt as to their use, which was certainly

FIGURE 6.26 Petra, entrance to an underground cistern. The most ancient water harvesting devices are small pools carved out of the highland which evolved into the so-called "bell-shaped cisterns" because of their bulb shape.

FIGURE 6.27 Petra, big open-air cistern. The structures built in the classic era present a regular geometrical shape and large excavated volumes. In some cases they have arches covered with stone slabs.

FIGURES 6.28–6.29 Petra. The interior of a cistern (Fig. 6.28). A device for harvesting humidity along the slope, here called khottara, that works by means of channels that catch water on the walls and convey it to the pools underneath (Fig. 6.29).

FIGURE 6.30 Petra, a trap for floods at Bir Huweimel. Stone embankments convey the floods of the wadi to the water-harvesting system. The latter is made of many basins for water decantation and cleaning by means of spillways.

FIGURE 6.31 Petra, a tunnel excavated by the Nabateans to deviate flood water from their natural water course across the canyon at the entrance of the town, called Siq.

FIGURE 6.32 Petra, the path along the famous Siq. Once protected from the danger of inundation, the Siq was transformed into the way leading to the town. Water channels were carved out of both the edges of the pathway to supply the caravans with water. (Right) The channel is supplied by the upstream cisterns by means of long aqueducts.

as worshipping places, but they also served the practical purpose of not allowing a single drop of rain or moisture to be wasted. It is not by chance that the same name indicates the mounds of stones for water condensation in the desert.

The need to create very important worshipping monuments can explain the meaning of the most mysterious and imposing monumental complex in Petra, the Palace Tomb. It is made up of a carved façade ending with an architectural cornice, which makes it look like a palace. The monument is situated just at the end of the long aqueduct. On the top of it a huge cistern was built. It formed a cascade, as long as the whole monument wall, which fed the big pools. The complex evidently did not have a solely functional purpose. As with the big Palace Tomb, the Fountain of the Lion, the monumental nymphaeum situated at the beginning of the road with the colonnade and each familiar triclinium, the use of water in Petra took on at the same time aesthetical, spiritual, and practical values.

The gardens of Petra were used both as fruitful fields and as spaces for feasts and funeral rites, and they were even something more. Qasr el-Abd is a monumental complex, the vestiges of which can be found near Amman. It bears many architectural similarities with the town of Petra. It was built by Tobias, the governor of the region between Amman and the valley of the Jordan. Flavius Joseph related that Tobias sent rare domestic animals to Ptolemy II Philadelphus in Alexandria, who gathered them in suitable structures, such as zoological gardens that were used at the same time as places for the magnification of the dynasty and for natural studies as well as worshipping places. At Qasr el-Abd an

FIGURE 6.33 Petra, natural systems of runoff and formation of water-harvesting cavities. Starting from these forms of erosion and the spontaneous water channels, the complex system of water harvesting and of water organisation for holy purposes, which characterises Petra, is created.

FIGURE 6.34 Petra. Over time the natural water channels were organised in an amazing water catchment system on which the town was built. The water collection places were made sacred with the addition of votive niches and became part of the mystical itineraries and Dionysian ceremonies.

entire valley was transformed into an artificial lake where a temple-like palace decorated with lion-shaped fountains rose up in the middle. The whole perimeter of the natural amphitheatre is dug with hypogeal structures, rocky dwellings, caves for water harvesting, and sepulchral chambers. The water harvested down the valley fed gardens and tilled lands, according to the pattern of the pairidaeza, the protected parks full of rare animals and every species of trees and plants belonging to the Persian kings with whom the dynasty of Tobias had dealt, since the 5th century BC. The botanic research carried out in Persia and in the East by Alexander the Great stimulated the organization of these places as research and harvesting centres as well as centres for the study of plant essences and animal species. This research triggered a real agricultural revolution in Europe. As a matter of fact, the practice spread out from Alexandria, the capital of Hellenism during the Ptolemaic dynasty, to the whole Mediterranean area and Europe. However, in Egypt the tradition was even more ancient and dated back to the Thebes of the Pharaohs. When the first translation of the Bible from the Aramaic was drawn up in Alexandria, the expression used to indicate the garden of the origins was pairidaeza that became our paradise. Thus, the centre where knowledge accumulated by tradition was gathered, the technical centre of farming and hydraulic experiments, was mixed up with the Garden of Eden. From a garden on earth, the source of sustaining and life, it became a celestial place, a distant and lost paradise.

FIGURES 6.35–6.36 The upper part of Petra is the holy summit where the first rains and the night dew are harvested in a double circle pool. Later, water is conveyed downstream to the cisterns (Fig. 6.36).

FIGURE 6.37 The famous monuments of Petra, wrongly defined as tombs, were the representative places, deposits of goods and places for family rituals. All the excavations were also in connection with water. The figure shows the so-called Palace Tomb, a monumental complex situated at the end of the long aqueduct of wadi al-Mataha which formed a big cascade (see fig. 344-45).

6.5 Water and Urban Shape

The Sassi of Matera and similar settlements found in the plateau of the Murgia extending up to the town of Taranto are a prime example of how archaic societies lived and managed resources in the karst areas of Lucania, Apulia, and Sicily regions. The towns were built on the edge of deep gorges, the gravine, having a highly irregular water flow. But inhabitants are settled along the highland and the steep slopes rather than at the bottom of the canyon as one would expect if it were the real water resource. In the event, water from the sky, rain, and dew, harvested in the drainage devices and the caves, is the resource of these maze-like troglodyte complexes typical of the Sassi of Matera as well as of the other stone towns of the gravine. They are the synthesis of the organization of space carried out by the different socio-cultural groupings that have inhabited these areas. The hunter-gatherers left evidence of their presence in the natural caves that open in the hardest rock of the Gravine. During the Neolithic age the limestone highland was populated as is testified by the presence of a large number of villages bound by ditches. During the Age of Metals, the agro-pastoralists did not come into conflict with the previous Neolithic settlement because they settled on the slope. Therefore, there is the physical synthesis of different cultures and of three geographic environments: the plain, the slope, and the caves. By developing

FIGURE 6.38 The gravina of Matera. Gravine are deep gorges having a highly irregular water flow which characterise the edge of the Murge highland along the Ionian ridge. The gravine have favoured human presence since prehistory, thanks to its microclimate and the natural caves. Water is provided by intercepting the runoff along the slopes on the edge of the highland where the settlements concentrate.

FIGURE 6.39 Grottaglie (Taranto, the gravina of Fullonese). The figure shows the channel system conveying water to the terraced gardens along the slope.

FIGURE 6.40 Conversano (Bari), water-harvesting system called lago. Karstic depressions and natural dolinas function by means of cisterns which intercept the water flows.

the original prehistoric techniques, an adapted system of built-up area is created in the Sassi of Matera, a stone oasis that enables to inhabit a sterile and arid area by combining the different principles of water production.

The traditional use of space to build houses saves the argillaceous hills upstream of the canyon which are left to woods and orchards. The water absorbed during the rainfall, which naturally pours down the gravina, also comes from these hills. This water is impounded on the edges of the gravina by sinkholes and dolinas typical of the karstic and limestone areas. These are the so-called laghi (lakes) that characterise the toponymy of the Apulian and Lucanian highlands of the Murge. These pools, which are completely dried up for most of the year and are able to receive quantities of overflowing water during the rainy season, have been equipped with systems of cisterns and used through time to store water before it disperses into the karst meanders. Around the region of Alber-obello these depressions are organized as water catchment systems very similar to the lakes of Conversano and are called cisternali. On the promontory of Gargano the same walled and waterproofed karstic formations are called cutini.

In the Sassi of Matera and in other very similar habitats of the gravine, the process of urbanisation started from the lakes on the upper edge of the canyon downwards. The place where the water leaps down from the edge of the gorge is a symbolic place: it is the threshold between the upper plain and the abyss, the life and the afterlife. In the Metal Age, these edges were endowed with buildings, temples, and grain stores belonging to individual family clans which used them to practise purificatory rites and to dedicate the first fruits, offering them to the precipice below. The cave-tombs were dug

FIGURE 6.41 The Bronze Age site of Pantalica in Sicily, situated along the gorges of the Hyblaean mountains, locally called caves, is made up of about 5,000 hypogeal cavities carved out of the slope.

out of the ridge along the slope. In the Sicilian Hyblaean region, the site of Pantalica was abandoned during the classic era and did not undergo subsequent superpositions; therefore it is a valid example of that period. On the highland of Pantalica the Cyclopean masonry of the anaktoron, the shepherd-prince's palace dating back to the Bronze Age, are still visible. The complex overlooks about 5,000 tombs carved out of the rocky sides of the cliff; the most archaic ones were small circular single room caves with an entry passage. Later, false domed caves dug out of the rock like the tholos appeared. Tombs with several square chambers with a common entrance and vestibule date back to more recent times. The artefacts dating back to the most ancient phase, from the 13th century BC to the 10th century BC, are shaped according to the local tradition, with strong Mycenaean and Aegean connotations. It is significant that, in the same region, the historical centres of Ragusa Ibla, Scicli, and Modica, which developed from a water matrix like that of Pantalica, present strong morphologic similarities with the habitat systems of the Sassi of Matera and the Apulian gravine.

In Gravina in Puglia, the edge of the canyon of Botromagno, the "big bothros" (gorge or holy well in Greek) bears evidence of an ancient water use and a ritual function. Prehistoric engravings and graffiti follow one another and among them there are the notorious potholes and the mysterious pairs of holes documented from the Sahara to Malta, in Greece and even in Yucatan, in the corner of the stone wall of the Maya temple of Uxmal (Mori, 2000). The potholes are pools of water probably used for lustral purposes; however, they surely derive from the rainwater harvesting pits dug out on the highlands for the cattle. The holes were used for lowering the offerings and the depositions, or they were used for the excavation activity that, as in Petra, was carried out, from the top to the bottom, on footbridges hanging from ropes fastened to the holes. It is also possible that by using the same technique they were useful for lifting water bags. The bases of the many monumental complexes carved out of the limestone, similar to the anaktoron of Pantalica, are very evident. In the Age of Metals, every large family clan would have its place for ceremonies and representations on the edge of the deep abyss. The built-up area was composed of huts, of which the holes left by the poles can still be seen in the ground, and scattered cave-dwellings.

With the passage of time, massive works to prevent earth movement and to control the water flow, to protect this area from the erosion of the hill behind, show the formation of larger social communities with a proto-urban character. The slope below was used for dwellings and agro-pastoral activities, thanks to the excavation of caves provided with bell-shaped cisterns which extended downwards the network of water and of garden threshing-floors. When in 700 BC the Greek colonisers had only just founded the town of Taranto, the indigenous populations of the town of Gravina, probably triggered by that external presence, carried out massive works for soil preservation and for the harvesting and distribution of the precious water resource. On the hill of Botromagno, beyond the massive building works and the canalisations, which are the result of hard work and a community effort, the remains of agricultural slope terracing like those still now in use were found. During the Greek civilisation, the area on the edge of the gravina was confirmed as a place of worship where a great necropolis was established, with monumental hypogeal chamber-tombs cutting through the previous anaktoron. Water was still the most important element in these works. A recent excavation has brought to light votive spaces hewn out of the rock-like little sacred isles, separated by canals where the water of the drainage ditches flowed (Petrassi and Pracchia, 2000). In this area, the long drainage tunnel resembling the Saharan foggaras reaches a cave which was transformed into a church in the Middle Ages. Hydraulic works continued up to more recent times: canals and pits prolonged the tunnel along the edge of the gravina up to a magnificent stone arcade aqueduct-bridge built in the 18th century AD, which supplies the town on the opposite side of the canyon.

In the classic age, Matera did not have the same importance as Gravina in Puglia. The present situation of the Sassi of Matera is the result of the evolution and the urban saturation of the archaic agro-pastoral structure, and the development of an urban ecosystem. The dolina lake on the edge of the gravina turned into the hypogeal pit courtyard or the well courtyard from which radial tunnels branched out. The family communities had the imposing underground rooms as places to worship their ancestors and as the places for their collective rites. Tufa barrel-vaulted structures were built with the same blocks of limestone dug out from the caves. They are called lamioni and represent the outward projection of the underground rooms. The lateral caves were extended forward and closed up in a horseshoe shape round a terraced clearing which created a central protected area. The original irrigated vegetable garden and the threshing floors became a place for family meetings and for social and community exchanges called vicinato. The big collective cistern for harvesting water off the roofs was excavated in the courtyard. In order to accomplish this task the pitches of the roof never protrude from the houses. The roof is built within the walls that do not allow a single

FIGURE 6.42 Ragusa Ibla (Sicily). The town was built along the gorges arranged by means of terracing systems, water-harvesting systems, embankments, and channels like those of the Apulian and Lucanian gravine. The altitude and the stateliness of these canyons, called caves in Sicily, enable a humid microclimate to be maintained, favouring a flourishing vegetation as well as a rich biodiversity.

Urban ecosystems

FIGURES 6.43–6.44 The old centres of the Hyblaean region (Sicily). Scicli and the built façades overlapping the network of underground structures (Fig. 6.43). Modica organised in concentric circles along the slope. The similarities with the Sassi of Matera and the ecosystems of the gravine are evident because of their common origin in the hydro-agricultural layout (Fig. 6.44).

FIGURE 6.45 Gravina in Apulia, tombs, water cisterns, and hydraulic systems at the bottom of the hill of Botromagno. The aqueduct-bridge still connects both the edges of the canyon to each other.

Urban ecosystems 161

FIGURE 6.46 Sasso Barisano, one of the two large depressions forming the ancient town of Matera. The houses, terraces, and gardens develop in successive circles and surround the riverbed of the narrow drainage stream, the "grabiglione", now paved. The high spur of the Civita, where the Cathedral stands on a rise, overlooks the urban landscape. The dwellings envelop the limestone bed by stretching out into the rock with deep underground cavities whose entrances may be observed where the buildings become fewer and leave the rock matrix bare.

FIGURE 6.47 Matera, the Ofra valley. The excavation and the closure of the apertures by means of a tufa wall and the construction of a barrel-vaulted structure, called lamione, are the different types of construction which can be observed.

FIGURES 6.48–6.49 The hydro-agricultural origin is important to understand the urban layout of the Sassi of Matera. The Sasso Barisano is a basin into which water coming down from the plain above conveyed (Fig. 6.48). An overhanging garden resulting from the threshing-floors, the agropastoral matrix on which the process of urbanisation was implanted (Fig. 6.49).

FIGURES 6.50–6.51 The Sassi of Matera. Hypogeal barn and transformation of a cavity into a rocky church. The agropastoral devices such as the silos and the cisterns are previous to the process of urban densification during which they lost their original practical function and were turned into cave-dwellings or places of worship.

raindrop to be wasted, conveying it to the cistern by means of earthenware gutters. The overlapping step becomes an overhanging garden. The lateral water channels became the stairs and vertical connections of the urban complex. The whole network of small streets and paths was formed by following the canal system which explains why the streets are so intricate and only apparently inexplicable.

Medieval monasticism contributed to this archaic fabric. The hermitages, parish churches, and farmhouses located at the checkpoints of hydraulic works represent the poles of the urban growth process. There are two main drainage systems called grabiglioni that provide land and humus by means of sewage collection, for two urban divisions called Sasso Caveoso and Sasso Barisano. In the middle there is the Civita, the fortified acropolis, the ancient shelter in which to take refuge in case of danger and where the cathedral was built. Along the boundaries of the highland where there are the large cisterns and the ditches, the cave silos for grain storage, and the craftsmen's workshops. The vertical arrangement of the town enables gravity to be used for water distribution and protects from wind blowing on the highland. Matera is embellished with hundreds of rock-hewn churches painted with beautiful Byzantine frescoes or built on the flat and bearing monumental façades carved out of the tufa, according to the architectural style of the period of construction: medieval, classic, or baroque. However, the maze of small streets, stairs, and underground passageways continues to follow the ancient hydraulic structure. Thus, it is still possible to understand the urban layout of the Sassi of Matera only by starting from the original matrix of the underground spaces, the cisterns, and the terraced gardens, making use of the process of accumulating traditional knowledge and a concentrated use of resources which dates back to prehistory.

Water Techniques and Landscape Building

7

FIGURE 7.1 The crusade castle of Shaubak (Jordan) is one of the numerous fortifications overlooking the long depression which connect the Gulf of Aqaba with Lebanon across wadi Araba, the Dead Sea, and the valley of the River Jordan. One of the most ancient historical communication routes, which was controlled by the Nabateans who sent iron ores to the east during the Age of Metals. Later it was met by the Silk Road from China, and the question of the control over it triggered the ensuing conflicts. The landscape of this arid valley has been organised and shaped by means of terracing and water systems. From the inside of Shaubak, a tunnel of 375 steps leads to an underground water-harvesting system.

7.1 Permanency of Traditional Techniques in the Mediterranean Area

The process of organising space in the Mediterranean is carried out, thanks to the exploitation of the slopes and the practice of the techniques for fertilising those inaccessible areas disregarded by the previous colonisers. The iron ploughshare, which had been used since the start of the 1st millennium BC in the Near East, spread over Europe at the end of the millennium. The use of metal tools determined a more aggressive approach to the environment with the phenomenon of deforestation as well as of the productive exploitation of the marginal areas. In that same period the system of three-fields rotation was introduced: cereals, oats, and legumes. From then onward, agriculture in the temperate Europe was able to support levels of population and urbanisation comparable with those based on irrigation of the hot and sunny areas of the Middle East. There were no other major inventions in the following periods, only the development into more sophisticated systems of already existing techniques and knowledge. The grapevine and the olive tree were grown on the terraced systems by that time. Drainage systems, canals as well as irrigation and reclamation methods allowed the plains to be used for agriculture. The practice of leaving land fallow and manuring the soil made agriculture more productive.

The organisation of the land in the Roman Age did not undermine that arrangement of the landscape. As a matter of fact, the imposing Roman hydraulic works did not change the lie of the agricultural land, which was based on the large variety of technical solutions widely used on a small scale by the local communities. Thus, the building of the countryside around Rome as a hydroagricultural monument was continued. Today, it is being carefully studied by the most advanced archaeological research (Petrassi, 2001; Pracchia, 2001). The Roman civilisation cannot therefore be defined as a hydraulic society based on the magnificence of its works and on state despotism, because of the physical nature of the Mediterranean territory featuring inaccessible places, small parcels of countryside lacking large river basins and land areas typical of hydraulic gigantism. Moreover, in the institutions of Roman society the municipality granted autonomy to the local communities which counter-balanced the state power. However, the complex organisation of the fields under cultivation and of the built-up areas closely connected with ritual and spiritual occasions, which underlies both the arrangement and the maintenance of the ancient Italian and Mediterranean landscape and its permanency up to our time, was confirmed in the Roman Age.

FIGURE 7.2 Terraced glacises of the Apulian Murgia highlands on the Adriatic side organised by means of dry stone walls.

The Mediterranean lies between two climatic systems: the continental and the African zone. This boundary condition called ecotone makes the Mediterranean climate unique. It can be found in only a few other situations all over the world. The threshold line is never stable and its fluctuation through time causes the typical variability of the Mediterranean climate. Although these fluctuations do not have a significant influence on a worldwide scale, they are decisive on a local scale. It is supposed that the period of greatest expansion of the Roman civilisation was connected with the northward shifting of the optimum Mediterranean climate line, whereas the following period when the barbarian invasions occurred coincided with the southwards spread of the northern climate. Until 300 AD the Mediterranean ecotone reached the British northern coasts and carried the Roman model of soil usage based on cereal production, supporting large settlements. After 300 AD the ecotone started shifting southwards thus favouring, from 500 AD, the supremacy of northern populations organized in pastoral economic systems and scattered settlements suitable for a climate that was becoming colder and colder. In that period, temperatures fell so much that in 829 AD the Nile froze (Crumley, 1994). Those slight historical fluctuations are today replaced by a process of constant global warming caused by the greenhouse effect, which determines the so-called "tropicalization of the Mediterranean". This condition accentuates the typical characteristics of this area, making it extreme.

We generally think of the Mediterranean as an environment in which nature is favourable and with pleasant spots gratified by a mild climate. These are thought to be the reasons why it is one of the first areas all over the world for the growth of different cultures and societies. The truth is the opposite: the Mediterranean has three sides touching areas where humanity has always dealt with the phenomenon of aridity; it also has islands and peninsulas lacking in both ground and surface water; its orography is impenetrable and uneven, and even in the north the seasons alternate with an irregular and catastrophic range of climatic conditions. The traditional Mediterranean knowledge system that was able to shape and characterize the territory over time, developed by dealing with these geographical conditions. The Mediterranean coasts, islands, and peninsulas are all inaccessible, and hostile areas where the culture that developed was triggered by difficult living conditions. In these bare, scattered areas where communications were impossible, the human communities could neither gather together in large systems nor found empires similar to those that rose up in the large continental lands or in the large river basins with huge water flows. The Mediterranean coasts and hinterland are not fed with big perennial rivers. The water arrives suddenly, with catastrophic results. The flow may be infrequent and poor in some periods and on the contrary, violent and ruinous in other periods. Therefore, small communities have organized the management and the protection of space on the oasis model based on the control and the harvesting of scarce quantities of humidity in order to trigger vital processes.

The Cretan buildings, the Apulian puli, the Palestinian cultivations, the stone towns of the gravine, the Tunisian neighbourhoods built around wells, the fences, and the ditches in Attica and Boetia, the underground settlements in Anatolia, the cave complexes in Malta, Jordan, Spain, and Algeria are examples of oases. The latter are systems for the collection of the precious rainwater and for its best usage both in case of excess and shortage so that it cannot be destructive for the slopes and the soil, and the rainwater can be saved and distributed. These simple structures are carved out of and camouflaged by the landscape. The organisation of space in the Mediterranean is the result of constant work to preserve the soil and of the proper use of resources, and of mistakes for which a high price has been paid in terms of erosion and desertification phenomena. Civilisation is born of a continuous struggle against nature that never spared the populations' hard trials and all sorts of cataclysms: earthquakes, floods, and drought; migrations and diasporas; as well as fights, fratricidal wars, and undying hatreds, as recent events teach us.

In spite of this, the populations have been able to perpetuate their culture, save traditions and guard art over time. Nomads, transhumant people, and dispossessed landowners have saved the ancient memory in transportable goods: in their handcraft, carpets, gestures, human pride, and song. They have kept the ancient memory in places elected by myth, epics, and poetry and crystallised it in the mausoleums, in the rural buildings, in the names given to the mountain ridges and in the tales that permeate the river valleys. The communities established a set of rules, customs, ways of acting and living by means of this cultural process that underlay their identity. They took possession of the places and shaped the landscape. The building and the maintenance of the landscape are closely connected with a process of knowledge and identification: all that is understood and felt as one's own is safeguarded. Today, the main risks for people derive from the loss of this balance. The sensation of losing every point of reference is purposely called "disorientation" which means being without landmarks. The essential knowledge for making space suitable for human living is disregarded with the migrations and the agricultural crisis. The ancient structures are attacked by such highly deteriorated contexts that their original function of territory maintenance is difficult to recognise. The Mediterranean environment bears the signs of the destruction and the degradation caused by natural phenomena or by bad interaction between human beings and space, but also of the communities' commitment to learn from the disappearance of the early paradises to recreate harmony and culture. The traditional knowledge which was formed within this process periodically emerges in the great store of popular wisdom: the landscape.

In the Mediterranean there are most of the traditional techniques related to water management for harvesting, storage, and channelling as well as the systems for the protection of the slopes and for soil production with their characteristics emphasized differently according to the environmental background. The former were introduced by the sailors who created water reservoirs, known only to them, in the cistern-jars in the islands along the arid coasts; the latter were spread by the nomads and the transhumants who were the guardians and the disseminators of knowledge related to landscape organization. Devices such as the underground drainage tunnels, showing features of more specifically North African or eastern oases, have also been found in the south of Italy, in the region of the Mont d'Or near Lion in France (Garnier and Renault, 1993) and in Spain, where they have an ancient origin or were introduced by the Islamic civilisation.

The several techniques of water saving typical of the Nabatean agriculture – the caves and the condensation wells, the rows of stones for rainwater harvesting, and the underground dams – are to be found in the Negev and all over the Mediterranean area. These techniques developed into an urban ecosystem in the town of Petra in Jordan but they exist in Tunisia, in Libya, in southern Italy and particularly in the islands transmitted by the ancient prehistoric tradition or introduced with the most recent communication flows. The Andalusian agricultural techniques in Spain showed a great intensification of these techniques connected to the Islamic civilisation. This kind of particularly ingenious irrigation practice called feixe persists in the isle of Ibiza.

Feixes are a system of cultivation based on a typical hydraulic organization. The fields are divided into long, narrow rectangular parcels separated by a network of channels for draining away excess water, water harvesting and saving and as field irrigation systems in periods of drought. As a matter of fact, without this organisation of space, the area would be marshy in some seasons and arid or inundated by the salty seawater in other seasons. The technique has a capacity of self-regulation that enables both the marshy and arid environments to be intensively cultivated. The open-air channels are about 1 m in depth and flow at a lower level than the plots of land so that it is kept dry. The ground dug out to build channels is used to raise the level of the tilled land. In hot periods when there is high evaporation from the soil, the necessary quantity of moisture is absorbed into the subsoil by osmosis and capillary action directly from the sides of the channels.

This process is supported by further underground channels dug out within the plots. These underground channels are made of porous stones and pine branches covered with a layer of Posidonia seaweed gathered on the coast. The method ensures both the functioning of the water feeder pipes and sufficient permeability of the ground to release enough water to maintain humidity. Thus the plant roots are irrigated directly from underground. This technique saves water that would otherwise evaporate using open-air irrigation methods. A similar procedure is adopted by the Aztecs in the Mexican floating gardens, the chinampa, where the fields are arranged on rafts in freshwater lakes, absorbing their water supply straight from them.

Traditional techniques can be found not only on southern Mediterranean shores and in southern areas of Europe but also in northern France and even in the Swiss mountains, where specific geomorphologic conditions cause aridity. This situation depends on the position of the mountain slopes compared with the direction of the dominant winds, which release all their moisture as they rise up the sides. Once they have reached the top, they lash against the slopes below with high pressure dry wind currents that dissolve the clouds. This is the phenomenon of the foothill deserts that in Switzerland creates dry, arid conditions in the valleys. In the region of Valais and the province of Sion on the contrary, there are green pastures and plentiful vineyards. The landscape is not the outcome of natural conditions but rather of a skilful use of a traditional local technique called bisse. This consists of a series of channels made of wood or carved out of the rock, which extends up into the mountains as far as the sources of the brooks and the perennial glaciers, running for many kilometres. They slope very gently down the steep edges, remaining at a high altitude to convey the water along above the natural course of the bed river and use the force of gravity alone to irrigate distant valleys. Otherwise, they would completely

FIGURE 7.3 Gravina in Puglia. The underground tunnel of the water system, very similar to the Saharan drainage tunnels, supplies the fountains in the historical centre of the town, situated on the opposite side of the canyon, by means of an aqueduct bridge which is, in its turn, supplied with water tapped on the hill of Botromagno.

FIGURE 7.4 Based on the Nabatean and Sabean agriculture, the Yemenite farmers arrange stones near each new bush planted. Stone soaks up humidity and allows it to be retained in the soil.

Water techniques and landscape building

FIGURE 7.5 Gravina of Laterza (Apulia). Techniques of humus production, plant protection, and moisture harvesting, commonly used all over the Mediterranean since the beginnings of agriculture.

FIGURE 7.6 Ibiza (Spain), typical landscape of feixe with the characteristic portals marking the crossing point of the channels before they enter the fields.

FIGURE 7.7 Red Sea. Pool of fresh water in the salt deposits on the Red Sea coast. Since the most ancient times along the arid coasts of the Arabian desert, water reservoirs were created in pools or buried jars, known only to the organisers of the sea or caravan routes.

Water techniques and landscape building

lack water. This system is supported by social cohesion, by water boards and companies similar to those that manage Andalusian agriculture or the Saharan drainage tunnels. Just as in northern Africa and in Spain, this system generates a particular landscape where the location of the settlements is determined by the layout and the outlets of the bisses.

The most widespread system that can be defined as one of the typical features of the Mediterranean area is the terracing which can be found from the Middle East to Greece and from Italy to Portugal. Terracing associated with olive and wine growing actually contributes to shaping the landscape. The slopes and hills in the northern Mediterranean have stood up to erosion over time and their present shape is the result of that long-lasting titanic action. Along with the dry stone walls, the stone barrows (specchie) and the tholos constructions (trulli), terracing is typical of the Apulian region in the south of Italy. Here, the terraced slopes of Amalfi and in the north of Italy, the Cinque Terre in Liguria, create fascinating and traditional urban ecosystems. In Sardinia and in the isle of Ibiza, there are systems of fields surrounded by dry stone walls called tanka, which is a term deriving from an ancient Mediterranean toponym.

The dry stone walls impound the moisture and help supply the soil with water. The fact that this technique has spread over northern Europe, northern Scotland, Ireland and the Orkney Islands, would make one think of a spread linked to cultural reasons, as a heritage of the prehistoric megalithic culture and of pastoral practices. However, it is necessary to consider that in cold climate conditions, the walls and the heaps of stones prevent the water in the soil from freezing. Therefore, acting as thermoregulators, they provide the plants with an adequate water supply. In the region of the Burren, in Ireland, in spite of a humid and rainy climate, the pastoral needs and the karstification have caused the spread of pools and of the rainwater catchment systems. Some of them date back to the age of the dolmens, the cromlecks, and the prehistoric fences present in the area. Certain devices that are still in use could help to explain how the Apulian specchie work. Heaps of oblong stones very similar to the specchie have their tops covered with plaster for the harvesting of rainwater that pours down into side tanks. For want of rainfall the stone barrow itself attracts the moisture and provides the water supply.

The building of most of the ancient Mediterranean centres followed the layout of the terracing and the water systems network. As a matter of fact, the rainwater-harvesting techniques, the areas with the walled gardens, the use of organic remains for the production of humus, the passive architecture methods, and climate control for food conservation and for energy saving and the practices of recycling production and food residues have been integrated and perpetuated in the very structure of the ancient Mediterranean centres. The aesthetic components that we appreciate in ancient towns, the beauty of the natural materials, the comfort of the buildings and spaces, the organic relationship with the landscape are due to the intrinsic qualities of the traditional techniques and to the search for the symbiosis and the harmony embedded in the local knowledge. All over the Mediterranean, the archaic societies that developed in economies with scarce means based their survival on the careful and parsimonious management of the natural resources. The close relation between the ancient agricultural technique and the settlements makes the traditional historical centres fundamental for the preservation of the environment. Throughout the Mediterranean area, which is characterized by an intense and historical anthropic process, there is no totally natural environment. The Mediterranean is a cultural landscape where the historical centres are the crystallization of knowledge suitable for a correct management and maintenance of the environment.

7.2 Hydraulic Structures of the Indian Subcontinent

Water and the ablution rites connected to water are the main elements of Indian spirituality. The sacred nature of water is connected to its functional use and to the practices related to it, which were passed on, kept, and disseminated through religion. In southern India the temples still have a central role in irrigation since they are associated with cisterns and canal networks. Near the holy city of Allahabad, at the point of confluence of the sacred rivers Ganges and Jumna, in the place where Ramah crossed the Ganges during his exile, Sringaverapura was founded in the 12th century BC, according to the epic poem Ramayana. The excavation of this town highlighted a striking hydraulic system where the worshipping, aesthetic, symbolic, and practical aspects are directly linked with each other. The structure dating back to the 1st century BC is composed of a series of basins and tanks extending 250 m along the River Ganges. The river's flood water is conveyed into the first two square tanks that retain the sediments and expel the waste by decantation. Thus, only clean water flows into the third tank used for water needs. The last circular basin, accessible from a flight of stairs with large stone steps, was used for ablutions and holy ceremonies. An elaborate system of filters comprising a dam for the waste

FIGURES 7.8–7.9 Valais (Switzerland). Channels called bisse collect water coming from the glaciers melting along the long pathways carved out of the sides of the mountains and use this water to irrigate the otherwise completely arid valleys.

Water techniques and landscape building

FIGURE 7.10 Sion (Valais). Landscape created by the bisse technique, with terraced slopes where high quality grapevines are grown, thanks to an irrigation system carried out by means of hydraulic devices. The outlet of the latter determines the location of the historical settlements.

FIGURE 7.11 Santo Stefano Belvo (Langhe-Piedmont). Hillsides organized and protected by terraced fields.

FIGURE 7.12 Cortemilia (Langhe). Particular types of terracing systems made out of a series of stone arches. The arcade enables to save building material and create some openings useful to the water drainage and catchment.

FIGURE 7.13 Ibiza (Spain), terraced fields called tanka.

and seven further chambers for cleaning the water by means of spillways allows the perfectly purified excess water to return from the last basin to the river.

The most ancient Indian document, the Rig Veda, whose oral tradition dates back to about the 1st millennium BC, contains numerous references to the agricultural irrigation techniques, watercourses, embankments, cisterns, wells, and structures for lifting water. The Vedic hymns are transcribed into Sanskrit, the Aryan language that arrived in India in the 14th century BC from the territories of Afghanistan and Iran, although elements of the more ancient Dravidian culture converge in them. This name is shared by languages spoken by the first Indian inhabitants such as the Tamil, who have kept very ancient traditions intact, the Ghat and the Toda, which are isolated populations living in the highlands. The Dravidian languages are still spoken today by 170 million people who guard their customs and keep alive all over the subcontinent a huge heritage of knowledge and techniques relating to water collection and irrigation. The first great civilisations developed in the valley of the River Indo between 3000 and 1500 BC. The excavations at Harappa in eastern Pakistan and at Mohenjodaro in India have revealed water supply systems in the houses, techniques for the disposal of used waters, and irrigation practices similar to those which were used in Rome 2,000 years later. The invention of wells is attributed to the civilisation of Harappa. In Mohenjodaro alone there are about 700 wells built starting from 2600 BC. The location of the wells in the middle and in the upper part of the site and their very small diameter, allowing an almost Artesian flow of water, show their irrigation purpose on the fields located at lower levels. Therefore, the city would have been the archetype of the circular urban settlements which appeared during the Bronze Age, proving the hydrological genesis of this model that develops radially from the central core of water production and follows the path of the water running along the narrow streets, which function as irrigation channels.

FIGURES 7.14–7.15 Ireland, natural park of Burren. In this cool karstic region Mediterranean water-conservation techniques and practices are frequent. A prehistoric cromleck with dry stone walls which preserve the hydromorphic qualities of the soil and preventing it from freezing in winter (Fig. 7.14). Water harvesting system based on a heap of stones similar to the Apulian specchie (Fig. 7.15).

FIGURE 7.16 Alberobello (Bari) is the historical centre where the megalithic technique of the trullo evolves into an urban ecosystem.

Some extraordinary devices found mostly in the arid regions of the Baluchistan, called gabarband, are older than the civilisation of Harappa itself. Their dating comes from the ceramics found in these devices at the end of the 4th millennium. The gabarband are stone structures over 1 m in length similar to dams. The latter are made of a series of about 60–120 cm high platforms overlapping each other in steps up to the top. In the past, the gabarband were probably used for controlling the floods and alluvium coming down the hills. In fact, they are diversion dams similar to those still in use in the Hadramaut Valley in Yemen. The fact that these constructions are never isolated along the course of an arid river basin but rather follow one another in a series of terraces, makes one think of their use to retain the fertile soil and the floods in the wadi, like the underground dams. The gabarband together with the gobrikarez, the local name for the qanat, the underground drainage tunnels also found in Baluchistan, are described in the works of Zoroaster, dating back to around the 7th and the 6th centuries BC, and have been ascribed to him. However, it is more likely that the Zoroastrians contributed to the reuse of older practices. As a matter of fact, the tradition of the Indian water techniques has been kept alive over time with the help of manuals and continual reconstruction. Kautilya, a minister of the first Indian emperor, Chandragupta, who reigned from 321 to 297 BC, described several irrigation and water-harvesting techniques in the Arthasastra, a political and administrative treatise that is often compared with Machiavelli's The Prince. He mentioned the help that the government provided for the inhabitants of new villages who undertook irrigation but also the punishment given to those people who disregarded maintenance. In that period, a class of administrators who supervised the rivers also had to measure the soils and control the sluices that conveyed the water into the canals. Dedicatory inscriptions on the repairing of the banks and the dams date back to the 2nd century AD. In the 11th century AD the lake of Bhopal was built. It is the largest Indian basin for irrigation, which impounds springs and watercourses over an area of 65,000 ha. In western Bengal the irrigation system by inundation worked perfectly till the start of British colonialism (17th century). That system had not only guaranteed soil replenishment but also kept malaria under control.

A number of traditional techniques are still used to this day. In the north-eastern regions and in the Nicobar Islands bamboo trunks are very widely used as gutters arranged along the slopes to capture each single drop of water and convey it in the wells. In Rajasthan, the kundis are structures for rainwater collection featuring a circular surface for harvesting and a depressed dome in the middle covering the entrance to the cistern. Both the harvesting systems by surface infiltration called kuis and by underground capillarity called jheel were widespread among the maldhari nomads of the desert of Thar, in Gujarat. A construction very similar to the air wells of the islands of the Red Sea called surangam lies along the northern coast of Malabar overlooking the Arabian Sea. This construction consists of a tunnel dug out of a laterite hillock and the water produced by the moisture and the dew drains from it. A third of the territory of the state of Tamil Nadu, in the far south of India, is still irrigated, thanks to an extensive system of cisterns called eris, which play a central role in the ecological balance by keeping the floods under control, preventing soil erosion, reducing the abrasive action of the brooks and replenishing the groundwater. The traditional techniques are also adopted in the trans-Himalayan areas where there are cold deserts, and where rain never falls because of frost, and only snow is possible. Therefore, water is only available as ice on the high peaks. In Ladakh human action allows fertile areas to produce vegetation and the crops appear as unexpected green spots in the sunny but cold stony ground. A network of channels stretches up to the glaciers, which release small quantities of water during the day due to the sun's heat that partly melts the surface snows. The channels slowly feed the cisterns of the villages, which fill up late in the evening. The water course is protected as a precious and inviolable asset and a feeling of great spirituality permeates and perpetuates the cultural landscape of these oases in the frozen desert on the roof of the world.

7.3 Water Pyramids of the Ancient Mayas

"In the 6th Ahau the Itzá discovered the place called Chichén. Forty years later they built the town called Chichén Itzá. Two hundred years later they abandoned it". This quotation has been taken from the Chilam Balam of the maya chumayel, the manuscripts reporting the chronicles of the ancient Mayas (Roys, 1993). Chichén Itzá is one of the largest and most striking pre-Columbian towns in Yucatan, the Mexican region inhabited by the Mayas. By comparing the Maya calendar with our calendar it emerges that the town was founded in 495 AD, 40 years after the discovery of the site by a Maya group called Itzá. In 692 AD it was apparently abandoned. Chronicles and archaeological research say that the town was resettled in 987 by the Itzá under the leadership of the mythical Quetzalcoatl, the "plumed serpent" called Kukulkan in the Maya language. Around 1200 the Itzá were driven out of the town that was once more abandoned in the middle of the 15th century.

Chichén Itzá was a holy town attended by hundreds of pilgrims who practiced religious ceremonies in the large squares ornamented with beautiful stone-terraced pyramids and harmonious temple constructions surrounded by colonnades. The climax of the rites was the offering to the holy well, the cenote, which was considered to be the residence of the gods and of the ancestors' souls. The cenote are natural sinkholes deriving from the depression in the limestone crust on a level with underground cavities. The openings expose the ground water fed by the rainfall through the fissures and the porosity of the rock. The cenote are essential in the ecology of the region of Yucatan, a karst area where in spite of the abundant precipitations that provide a dense vegetation cover, the fertile soil is thin and the surface waters are inexistent. Without the latter and the karst cavities (such as the cave called Loltun) where since prehistory drinking water collected under the stalactites, life would not be possible. By analysing the water resources, it is possible to understand the vicissitudes of the town. The name Chichén derives from two Maya words: chi that means "mouth" and chen that means "well". The ancient chronicle narrates the discovery of a place called "the mouth of the wells". These explain why the town was founded. The alternate abandonment and reuse leading to its final collapse is explained by the constant need for water supplies and by the establishment of the supremacy of the nuclei that possessed the necessary knowledge.

FIGURE 7.17 Chichén Itzá (Yucatan), the holy cenote of the town. The natural sinkhole is used for water harvesting and the monumental architecture for the periodical votive offerings.

FIGURE 7.18 Yucatan, the cenote that still supplies a village in the jungle and a Mayan guide.

FIGURE 7.19 Reconstruction of the ancient Mexico City, Tenochtitlán, situated in the middle of the lagoon cultivated by means of the technique of floating gardens, the chinampa, (National Museum of Mexico City).

Historical and archaeological research has confirmed that the group of Itzá spread quite late in Yucatan, when a considerable number of sites were already occupied. The Itzá arrived in the town, which was not yet known as Chichén Itzá, only after the first abandonment, in 987, at the time of the dissemination of the religion of the god Quetzalcoatl who was personified by warrior-priests who adopted his name. Therefore it is likely that they took credit a posteriori for the first foundation but that they actually developed the town in the post-classic age (Piña Chan, 1992).

In the pre-Columbian civilisations the practices of landscape modification to build rainwater-harvesting systems on a large scale by creating water intakes along the slopes, dams, and watersheds, predate the monumental architecture and date back to the 1st millennium BC (Scarborough and Isaac, 1993). The most ancient site where the hydraulic works explain the same architectural development which was to lead to the building of the pyramids is Saint Lorenz, dating back to the pre-classic age and accomplished by the Olmec people. In Saint Lorenz and later in La Venta the problem was the excess water transported by sudden floods. Since 1200 BC the Olmec had built up a wide artificial platform made out of earth and coloured clay, on the top of which other elongated hillocks were built. The overall appearance is that of a natural hillock with sloping glacis dug out by erosion channels. Actually, the channels are perfectly symmetric and the complex as a whole is an architectural work which anticipates the step pyramids. A sophisticated drainage system provided pure water, which was filtered through a series of basins and collected in reservoirs by a network of channels made out of well-shaped and perfectly connected stones.

Among the pre-Columbian techniques for using humid areas, the floating gardens called chinampa were disseminated by the Toltec population after the fall of Tula in 1165 AD. The water of the marshlands irrigates the soil where the plants grow, directly from below, supported by wooden bases that in some cases may actually float. Nowadays, at Xochimilco, a town 30 km from Mexico City and whose name means "place of the fields of flowers", the chinampa are arranged in chequered cultivations. Like islands in the freshwater lagoon, they are separated by a regular layout of canals, which can be navigated by flat-bottomed boats. Today, the situation is closer to the feixe than to gardens on floating rafts.

In the inland areas of Yucatan, the Mayas had instead to solve the problem of finding sufficient water resources in all seasons in order to meet the needs of the massive urban areas and of agriculture. These needs could not be satisfied by the natural cave reservoirs or by the cenote pools alone. Moreover the latter were subject to the seasonal changes in level, to salinity due to the link with the underground passages down to the sea or to desiccation by obstruction of the tunnels. Bell-shaped cisterns called chultun were dug out of the stone to obtain drinking water supplies. In the classic age, from the 3rd century AD, the development of important towns was organized around natural depressions called aguada, into which the water collected by the dams and cisterns along the slopes flowed. The surfaces of the aguada were paved with flat stones whose joins were waterproofed by means of red and brown clay. Wells and chultun were dug at the bottom to keep the water when the aguada dried up. The system is very similar to the technique of the cisternali typical of the Apulian karst areas in the south of Italy. At the end of the classic age, around the 9th century AD, driven by defensive purposes or under the pressure of the need to irrigate by the force of gravity larger and larger areas of farmland, the Maya hydraulic technology developed so much that it exploited the highest peaks as harvesting systems. Thus the town itself with its numerous step pyramids, the monumental architecture, the paved squares, and the large courtyards became a big rainwater-harvesting system.

These techniques that the Itzá developed under the pressure of the environment and of the ecological catastrophes, which had triggered the previous exoduses, made the resettlement and the monumental development of their town possible. Quetzalcoatl was the rain god and his priests were wise hydraulic technicians. According to the Maya language the name Itzá is itself composed of itz that means "proud man" and of há or a that means "water". Therefore, the name of the town Chichén Itzá stands for: "the place of the wells of the proud men of the waters".

7.4 Local Knowledge in the Hydraulic Societies: China

Unlike the Mediterranean societies, the Indian and Maya ones can be defined as hydraulic societies because they are characterized by agricultural economies based on irrigation and on water control on a large scale. These economies are usually managed by a despotic central authority. The Egyptian and Chinese civilisations also belong to this model. However, the overall condition does not exclude the coexistence within these areas of different situations based on

FIGURE 7.20 Chultun of Uxmal (Yucatan), a cistern dug out of the limestone to harvest and store water.

FIGURE 7.21 Reconstruction of the natural karstic system of the aguada and cenotes (National Museum of Mexico City).

FIGURE 7.22 Chichén Itzá (Yucatan), the statue of Chac Mool, the rain and water god, identified with Quetzalcoatl, the plumed serpent. The spiritual chiefs who possessed water knowledge personified the divinity and led the installation of new centres.

small-scale, family-run farming in communities able to keep their independence and to pass on ancient knowledge. Thus, the local knowledge is perpetuated in societies that in contraposition to the hydraulic ones are hydroagricultural, hydrogenetic, or autopoietic communities. These social forms continue to exist, thanks to their isolation and to the harsh geographical conditions or for specific reasons of economic supremacy due to trading or growing a rare species or else for cultural reasons linked with religion or a strong social cohesion.

These societies often use the same knowledge that is the basis of the hydraulic societies. Egyptian irrigation techniques are based on nomadic cultivation practices, the use of flood flows, and all the knowledge useful in the desert to obtain the maximum benefit from moisture and fertility. Both the Incas and the Mayas carried out small-scale irrigation before building their hydraulic empires. Mohammed, the founder of Islam, a basically hydraulic civilisation, always referred during his teaching to the easy systems of water harvesting and distribution and to the oasis community. However the most evident case is that of Chinese society. In fact, it is the example of eastern hydraulic despotism par excellence whose origins lay in a tradition based on temperance and the small-scale practice of hydroagriculture, an activity that lasted throughout its history.

Confucius relates that Yü, the legendary founder of the protohistoric dynasty Xia (2200 BC) whom Confucius himself thought to be the real hero of the introduction of the agricultural practices, ate ordinary meals, wore poor clothes, lived in a modest house, and concentrated all his energies on the technique of the small irrigation channels. That period dated back to the early Chinese society that was born along the silk caravan routes and developed in the north of the country on the borders with Mongolia across the depression of Turpan, the desert of Taklimakan, the Gobi desert, and the Loess highlands. The latter region is made of deep layers of thin mud cut away by high gorges, deep valleys, and cones of erosion sloping down the Chinese lowland. The area is drained by the Huang Ho, the Yellow River whose name derives from the sands dissolved in it. Over time the territory was turned into farmland by making terraced fields along the steep slopes and growing crops that were irrigated by means of an intricate network of channels on the fertile lowland plains.

The original situation changed during the imperial phase when the economic power was transferred to the river basin of the Yangtze, the Blue River, and the Chinese Grand Canal was built. It is the longest canal system in the world, which developed approximately north-southwards for about 1700 km. Its geographic stateliness and its environmental impact have caused it to be considered an artificial Nile. The completion of the Grand Canal gave China a structure and followed the transformations in the land, in society, and in the administration, from small-scale communities to a hydraulic society. The most ancient canal dates back to the 4th and the 5th century BC and links the two big Chinese rivers, the Huang Ho and the Yangtze. At the beginning of the 6th century AD, this part was rebuilt and new canals were added. During the 13th century the hydraulic system was extended northwards up to Peking when this city became the Yuan dynasty capital. Late in the imperial period the hydrobureaucratic system developed more and more impressively to the point that it needed for its civil service alone about 40,000 officials who had at their disposal 1,200,000 employees and over 5,00,000 messengers.

However, the primordial condition of the small hydroagricultural communities is still present in Chinese society where the most archaic excavation practices for the organization of shelters, the digging out of water harvesting pits, the creation of drainage systems, and even the building of great hypogeal pit courtyard complexes, which were also pointed out by Marco Polo, may be recognized. About 40 million Chinese people still live in the underground habitat of the Huang Ho region on the arid loess platforms. These villages have always been refuge areas far from the central authority and in 1934 Mao Zedong ended his long march here. After having established his headquarters in the hypogeal, he lived for 14 years as a troglodyte. The Huang Ho basin is essential for the most archaic development of the water practices on a small scale starting from prehistoric times. In the region of Shaanxi along the river Wei, the main tributary of the Huang Ho, are located the Neolithic villages of Banpo dating back to between 5,000 and 3,000 BC. With their elliptic ditches for drainage and water harvesting, the pools and the channels between the huts feature some analogies with the Neolithic complexes in the south of Italy. It is particularly significant that a large circular structure (called hwai yuen lo), which gives shelter to the whole community of the village, with a pitch roof and an impluvium in the middle of the courtyard is still in use. This structure brings to mind the stone rings and the megalithic complexes of the European Bronze Age.

The traditional water techniques and knowledge about energy saving and soil protection are still largely used in China. The Chinese government is currently fostering on a large scale the ancient systems of terracing, deep ditches or banks, and little dry stone lunettes. These practices that exploit the slope are typical of the Loess highland. In the Gobi

FIGURE 7.23 Gorzegno (Langhe). Stone-terracing systems.

FIGURE 7.24 Riomaggiore (The Cinque Terre – Liguria). The use of terracing systems becomes an identity mark which is celebrated on wall paintings by an ancient master at the station place of the little town.

FIGURE 7.25 China, the ancient settlements along the Silk Road undergoing the phenomenon of desertification and the invasion of the sands.

desert the formation of artificial dunes is encouraged by means of windbreak barriers to stop the sand that is progressively submerging the ancient oasis settlements along the silk road. The same result is attained by combining mechanical with biological works. The vegetal networks extending over large areas of land enable vegetation to grow as a definitive barrier against desertification.

The silk road has been a means of dissemination of the oases where every typical technique of water catchment was used, from underground drainage tunnels to buried dams, reservoirs, and cisterns set in the subsoil to prevent water evaporation. The ancient agricultural region of Turpan was made inhabitable over time, thanks to the excavation of drainage tunnels that converge towards the bottom of the depression.

They thus allow irrigation by the force of gravity and the optimisation of the water supply by avoiding evaporation that would otherwise be considerable in the case of open-air run off. This practice is adopted today for the establishment of new oases. Both the traditional use of solar energy, constructing greenhouses surrounded by raw earth walls, often painted on the inside with black mud so as to trap more heat, and the exploitation of wind power are widely used in order to save energy. Irrigation methods that do not involve watering the fields have been attentively studied. As a matter of fact, sprinkling water on the soil, and droplet irrigation, with the evaporation and the release of salts, eventually makes the soil sterile, and this is supposed to be one of the reasons for the crisis and the sudden collapse of stable hydraulic societies such as Mesopotamia. The traditional practices, instead, used either a system of irrigation channels, which allows continual

FIGURES 7.26–7.27 China, soil protection system on a large scale. Vegetable fibre barriers to stop the sand (Fig. 7.26). Dry stone lunettes for the creation of soil and the protection of the slopes (Fig. 7.27).

leaching of the soils and keeps the degree of humidity unaltered, preventing evaporation, or an irrigation system without watering, which increases and protects the hydromorphic qualities of the soil. Traditional logic is currently being used to investigate the possibility of irrigating the plant roots directly from the soil by using jars buried underground, injector pipes, and techniques similar to the Andalusian feixe (China National Committee, 1999).

These simple precautions, reproduced on a scale of millions of communities, constitute a titanic job of shaping, building, and maintaining the landscape. However, the transformation of the land may be accomplished by means of hydraulic practices that have never been abandoned. Indeed, an impressive series of dams and basins are continually being built. The completion of the project for the Yangtze dam, called the Three Gorges Dam, will spoil areas of great cultural worth and force millions of people to migrate thus exposing the environment to an ecological risk and even more populations to the threat of floods. Therefore, this building will have a disastrous effect on the territory like that produced by the Aswan dam on the ecosystem of the Nile valley. In its current choices China seems to keep the historical dichotomy between local water knowledge and hydraulic planning personified by the role played by the two big Chinese rivers – the Huang Ho and the Yangtze: the spread of successful practices of traditional knowledge which are locally run and symbolized by the Yellow River of the desert and the imposition of giant hydraulic power projects represented by the Blue River of modernism.

The Water Crisis and the Decline of the Civilisations

8

FIGURE 8.1 Amman (Jordan). The Roman theatre surrounded by the modern buildings is an emblematic image of the physical and cultural process of desertification due to the spread of concrete and the destruction of the historical heritage that protected and managed the environment.

8.1 Water Distribution and Climate Changes

Water is a resource unequally shared all over the planet mostly because of the different climatic conditions. Ninety-eight percent of the available water is present in the temperate, the tropical humid, and the arctic regions, and only the remaining 2% is present in the arid and semiarid regions. The total of the approximately 1,385 million km3 of water is divided into five big groups linked to each other: the oceans (97.4%); the glaciers (2%); the terrestrial fresh waters: lakes, rivers, underground waters, and moisture of the soils (0.6%); the atmospheric water vapour (less than 0.001%); all the living cells (only 0.00001% of the total water but in absolute terms this quantity is a significant 1,100 km3). These five stores of water continually exchange water with one another in a never-ending cycle. The initial phase consists of evaporation over the oceans and the continents. One thousand billion tons of water is released every day into the atmosphere. Only a small quantity of water falls on the continents and is in its turn divided into two parts: one evaporates again, a certain percentage of it after passing through living beings as perspiration, and the other part is drained towards the oceans. In the second case the flow provides the so-called renewable resources which are divided up in three ways according to the permeability of the soils: flowing in streams which feed the rivers and the torrents; drainage by surface infiltration which replenishes the groundwater; underground drainage which replenishes the deepest aquifers.

The oceans act within the water cycle as huge systems of purification by distillation: they purge water of its impurities, salts, toxins, and bacteria and produce fresh water. The sun provides the necessary energy and maintains on earth the temperature which allows water to keep its liquid state, a vital condition for every form of life. The sun is the engine that drives all physical processes. The oceans catch and discharge solar energy that, in its turn, is intercepted by the plants, where it is stored in their trunks and in fossil fuels. Wind, in its turn, is the great mediator in climatic processes. The water cycle depends on these two elements exactly as stated in the inscription of the emerald tablet "Its father is the Sun, […], the Wind carries it in its lap".

The sun, the wind currents, and water establish a particular energy balance within which water plays a fundamental role: in the atmosphere, in the form of clouds, which cover more than 60% of the earth's surface and affect the shielding from radiation flows on earth as well as those reflected by the earth itself; and on the ground, through the precipitations which modify the local heat balance. In the last 50 years, rapid changes have occurred both on a global and local scale. In the atmosphere the greenhouse gas emissions have caused the average temperature to rise, producing catastrophic effects on the climatic trends. The global warming that has been registered in recent years and is bound to increase, produces more total energy that, in its turn, causes greater evaporation and water circulation in the atmosphere, also thanks to the supply coming from the melting of the glaciers. When the climatic phenomena intensify, they may cause catastrophic occurrences such as cyclones, droughts, and floods. The extent of the damage is worsened by the local circumstances, which with the development of the civilisations, have suffered a continuous and growing assault on the forests and, starting from the industrial revolution, a massive process that has made the soils impermeable in urban areas.

The effects of the rains depend on the soil conditions. Generally, 60% of the rainfall returns to the atmosphere, though this process undergoes strong variability due to the soil morphology and the plant cover. The latter has the role of balancing the water situation. As a homeostatic reservoir, it stores the water excesses and mitigates aridity, prevents soil erosion and reproduces it by using the vegetal waste. So vegetation is a fundamental element of hydrogeologic regulation. By deforestation, the wind and the sun dismantle the soil and make the humus disappear. As a consequence of this, the beneficial waters turn into destructive waters, which erode the soils on the slopes or stagnate in the plains. Since there are no plants to provide shade, the waters evaporate and salts collect in the topsoil. Vegetation can no longer grow again and an unstoppable cycle of degradation is set in motion. Without forests the rain disappears even in humid areas. As a matter of fact, the wind is charged with water evaporating from the seas and the lakes but also with the humidity given off by the woods and every other form of plant cover. One hectare of birch wood transpires 47,000 litres of water in a single day; during the good season an oak gives off more than 100,000 kg of water which is equivalent to 225 times its weight; a maple emits a quantity of water equivalent to 445 times its weight; and 1 ha of beech wood discharges into the atmosphere between 3,500 and 5,000 tons of water vapour. At the same time, the fertile substance from which all that is alive on earth derives is produced through that process of degradation undergone by the organic matter from which life originates. Over an area covered with trees 100 mm of rain are able to produce 1,000 kg of vegetal substance which turns into humus. Without water and vegetation, a centimetre of lost fertile soil is estimated to take 100 years to reproduce.

A plant has to be able to transpire from 3 to 8 litres of water to produce 1 g of dry matter. The production of 1 kg of grain demands 1,500 litres of water, whereas 4,500 litres of water are needed for 1 kg of rice. About 1,000 litres of water have been estimated as necessary to produce a hen's egg by industrial methods. When we eat oranges, 85% of what we eat is water, thus, in exporting them we are also trading water whose real value has not yet been realized.

About 3 litres of drinking water a day is the minimum quantity necessary for the survival of a human being. Yet, water is also an indispensable item to each human activity such as agriculture, industry, personal hygiene, and household cleaning. The per capita consumption in western countries has increased from 10 to 300 litres of water per inhabitant over the last two centuries. On a world scale, consumption varies enormously. It ranges from 5 litres a day per inhabitant in Madagascar to 500 litres in the Unites States. Though more than a quarter of humankind still lacks drinking water, consumption is rising in all countries by proceeding at the same rate as urbanisation and the disappearance of the traditional ways of life. At present the real average water demand on a world scale stands at about 500 m3 per capita a year and can reach over 1,000 m3 in western countries. These figures are bound to double during the 21st century. Estimating that throughout that same period the human population will grow from the present over 6 billion people to 20 billion expected by the end of the 21st century, more than 20,000 km3 of water will be needed to meet the essential needs. And if the consumption level of the western countries becomes generalised on a world scale, it will be impossible to meet the water demand.

8.2 The Desert and Desertification

The formation of arid areas results from the combination of different phenomena, which in turn enter a more and more extensive interactive mechanism. On a world scale, the big processes, the thermal factors and the general atmospheric circulation and the geographical components on a local scale act and reciprocally integrate each other in specific areas as the sum of many elementary conditions. The overall system works as a big amplification mechanism within which the micro factors can also spread and produce lasting effects with a series of consequences over a long period. The desert regenerates itself and once small areas of degradation have started they spread and extend by accumulation.

Thus, one can understand that the theory of the advance of the desert has often been used to explain the causes of desertification. However, desert and desertification differ from each other. The latter has assumed the look of a real calamity in the Sahel regions in the southern Sahara. The disastrous effects it produces on the soil may be ascribed to different causes: wind erosion creates vast bare areas and the accumulation of dunes; water erosion gives rise to sterile sand and mud concretions or limestone crusts; the strong evaporation contributes to the salination and alkalization because of a high concentration of salts in the waters, insufficient drainage, and a water shortage. Therefore, the spread of physical or chemical–physical degradation is driven by biological or physical mechanisms, which reduce the plant cover and the original bio-productivity of the soil and make the environment impossible to use.

In the Sahel these processes start in a climatic area that receives more than 200 mm of precipitation per year and also in a deeper strip in the south where the rains may reach 800 mm per year, i.e. areas that cannot be properly defined as a desert. It is estimated that in these countries one million hectares of tropical forests are destroyed and 100,000 hectares of soil are irremediably covered every year with the advance of the sands produced by wind erosion. In Africa, altogether more than one billion hectares have been damaged by this phenomenon. Millions of people have been forced to emigrate elsewhere. In Mali and in Burkina Faso one-sixth of the inhabitants have been forced to abandon their villages. In Senegal two-fifth of the population of the upper valley of the homonymous river has been forced to emigrate. Mauritania is disappearing under the sands. Here, the population established in the capital, Nouakchott, has increased from 9 to 41 per cent in 20 years, while the nomadic groups have fallen from 73 to 7 per cent. All this is apart from the cyclical climatic fluctuations and from the climatic changes in recent years. Therefore, non-natural factors trigger an environmental mechanism of degradation which must therefore be ascribed to a single factor: human intervention.

The demographic growth, the abandoning of archaic techniques and social habits even though they were in harmony with the environmental potentialities, as well as the imposition of new crops according to the requirements coming from the world market and the dissemination of the monoculture are only some of the causes of a state of degradation. Above all, the settlement of people gathered in small areas according to the necessity of the modern economies gives

FIGURE 8.2 Senegal. In the Sahel, where the tall baobabs soak up rain water during the summer, the phenomenon of desertification advances because of the impoverishment of plant species and soil quality due to the crisis of the traditional knowledge and the overexploitation of resources.

rise to a large energy demand which is satisfied with a massive devastation of the arboreal and forest heritage. The wounds inflicted on the woods trigger processes of continual and substantial collapse of the biological variety, quality, and productivity. Animals and plants are decreasing and the number of species is falling so much that they have no potential to provide a genetic answer to the altered circumstances and for that reason they are irremediably destined to disappear. The soil becomes sterile and its physical and chemical features are altered, so it is impossible for the soil to retain water. The triggering of both the processes of wind and water erosion and the mechanisms of sand accumulation is a consequence of this situation.

The misuse and the overexploitation of the resources are the main causes of desertification which in the United Nations Convention is so defined: "deterioration of the lands in the arid, semiarid, and semi-humid dry areas due to different factors including climate changes and human activity". This process starts right around the main centres of human activity and irremediably spreads over the whole territory. It is incorrect, therefore, to speak of the advance of the desert. There is a precise environmental model that occurs in a specific climatic context with its own laws, biological activities, and an appropriate human use, whereas desertification produces an environment in full decay and totally devoid of ecological balance. In these circumstances as in the other ones originated by human intervention such as climate change, the difference lies in a specific variable: time. The natural establishment of the desert has followed the very long geologic times enabling the species to follow the changes with a process of transformation and evolution and therefore allowing the creation of environments that in spite of the harsh climate are rich in adaptations and in the biodiversity of the species. On the contrary the processes of desertification and the climate changes triggered by human intervention are rapid. The biological and physical structure of the planet has not had time to adapt to them, resulting in desolation and decay.

Thus, it may be asserted that even the desert can undergo a process of desertification. Precisely in the environments with a more critical and difficult balance, characterized by a strong interaction between the processes, each intervention from the smallest to the most macroscopic one may produce lasting devastating effects. In the Sahara the traces left by the vehicles during the Second World War are still evident on the characteristic microvegetation of the soil that 40 years later has still not recovered. In the Sahel the environment reacted to the roughness of the seasonal differences and to the cyclical climatic alterations by properly diversifying and varying each situation. Once the period of crisis had passed the environment had the potentiality to return to its initial situation. Because of the overexploitation due to human action, which intensifies its destructive activity against the species and the residual varieties just when the resources are becoming rarefied, any capability of recovery disappears even when the favourable conditions have been re-established.

This mechanism is operating today all over the world and consequently 30% of the lands have been estimated as undergoing a risk of decay. In the Amazon, the process of deforestation exposes the soils to the climate's violence. The waters take away the thin layer of fertile soil which is no longer able to be reproduced. The plants do not grow again and in time the rain itself fails. The result is a desert where there was previously a pluvial forest. The deepest forms of desertification affect over 100 countries, menacing the survival of more than one billion people. 24 billion tons of topsoil disappears each year all over the world. The world loss in the last two decades was equivalent to the total arable land in the United States. The situation is particularly dramatic in the arid zones where about 70% of the areas corresponding to a quarter of the total earth's area are threatened. However, this problem is largely present also in the temperate areas (Brandt and Thornes, 1996; Mairota, Thornes and Geeson, 1998). In the United States the proportion of the arid zones undergoing desertification is the highest in the world and reaches 74%. In Asia, desertification has spread over 1.4 billion hectares and the worst threatened lands are in the area of the former soviet bloc. In Italy, according to European Union estimates 27% of the territory is exposed to a high risk of erosion (European Commission, 2000ab). The regions of Apulia, Basilicata, Calabria, Sicily, and Sardinia show an already advanced process of desertification. On the basis of the evaluation of the United Nations Programme for the Environment (UNEP), desertification costs the world 42 billion dollars per year (9 in Africa alone). More than 135 million people risk losing their lands in a very short time. Desertification concerns both the agricultural contexts and the urbanized areas.

In the agricultural environment the process manifests itself through the following phenomena: water erosion; loss of fertility of the soil; salination of the soil; destruction of the humus; disappearance of the plant cover; exhaustion of the aquifers and drought; decay of the slopes and landslides. The urban areas contribute both directly and indirectly to the process of desertification. Directly the massive urbanisation may be considered in itself as a form of desertification

FIGURE 8.3 Sahara. Even the desert can undergo a process of desertification because of the lack of management of the oases and the water resources along the caravan routes. The abandonment of traditional techniques because of leaching and the use of modern irrigation techniques increase the salinity of the soils.

due to the spread of concrete over large natural surfaces; but also indirectly through the absorption from the soil of the natural resources and their destruction in the areas with a high demographic concentration. A close relationship between urbanization and desertification may be found both in the non-industrialised countries and in the most developed ones. In the first case, the process of decay is triggered and extends starting right from the areas undergoing a modern and accelerated urbanisation which by their necessity impoverish the surrounding territory. In the advanced economies, and in particular in Italy, whose territory is strongly characterised by human settlement, the spread of the process of desertification is directly linked to the crisis of the historic city centres which replaces the traditional arrangement of the landscape made out of building systems that have a strong natural component and low consumption of resources with a model based on massive building operations that waste energy and pollute the environment. The exodus of the population from the ancient centres and the consequent disappearance of the local systems that were able to properly manage the landscape are the result of the urbanization of new areas. Thus, a process of physical and social desertification begins. The impoverishment of the human resources corresponds to the architectural decay and to the erosion of the mountain, hilltop, and slope systems. Emigration, the loss of identity and values are the sociocultural aspects of desertification. The extreme situations of the Sahara and the Sahel are the test-bed and the alarm signal of a peril involving everyone: desertification caused by man's negative interaction with the environment is today a menace in any climate and in every region.

FIGURE 8.4 Sahara. The desert is an ecosystem full of specific living but fragile organisms which adapt to the environmental conditions over the millenniums. It will be difficult to recover the microvegetation and the biodiversity demolished by the passage of vehicles.

FIGURES 8.5–8.6 Mali, the watercourse of the River Niger. An aerial photograph taken in two different moments showing the extremes of floods alternating with phases of aridity. The traditional techniques used in the circular village (see Fig. 8.6) tend to balance the environmental variability. Modern techniques intensively exploit and exhaust the resources, preventing their periodical reconstitution.

FIGURE 8.7 Brazil, the remains of the Atlantic Mata, the original rainforest on the coast has already almost disappeared. The demolition of the plant cover leaves the soil without humus and exposed to the agents of dissolution and unable to recover.

8.3 Calamities, Cultural Shock, and Urban Exoduses

Chichén Itzá and the great pre-Colombian capitals, Marib and Shabwa with the numerous ancient caravan centres, still submerged under the Arabian sands and Petra in the Jordan desert are all towns which were periodically and suddenly deserted by their inhabitants. These civilisations inexplicably disappeared because of mysterious exotic and remote events. However, beyond the historical, cultural, and geographic differences, the delicate environmental balances ruled by a series of techniques, knowledge, and spiritual values on which the existence of these centres was based, allow us to understand the urban crisis and of the exoduses that are still among the inscrutable curiosities of history. The anthropologic, economic, and climatic reasons for the urban collapses can thus be explained, and it is possible to reflect on the destiny of civilisations subjected to environmental and cultural pressures.

The case of the Sassi of Matera is exemplary: from 1950 to 1960 about 15,000 inhabitants left the ancient centre and moved to new purposely built-up suburbs. This expulsion of the population is one of the most recent large urban desertions in history. In a few years a town that had been until then a living inhabited centre was evacuated by all its inhabitants. The phenomenon may be compared to the sudden desertion of the great pre-Colombian capitals or of the caravan centres of the Arabian desert. In Matera, the population evacuation was a planned action fostered by hygienic

FIGURES 8.8–8.9 Basilicata, desertification and degradation of the soils. The calanchi (cones of erosion) in Pisticci (Fig. 8.8). The arid valley of the River Basento (Fig. 8.9).

and health reasons. This operation was possible only with the pressure exerted by a violent cultural shock, due to the impossibility for the civilisation and the traditional habitat of the Sassi of Matera to compare with the building process powerfully conducted during the post-war period in Italy and by the economic and cultural values system of modernity. The definition of "national shame" which was attributed to the Sassi of Matera and the transfer of its inhabitants are part of the large exodus from the countryside, the dissolution of the peasant world and the emigration from the south of Italy aiming at industrialisation and the affirmation of the consumer model.

The triumph of the paradigm of shame with the consequent defeat of the archaic society of Matera would not have been possible if at that moment it had not already been deeply undermined by structural causes which had threatened the complex social, environmental, and architectural organisation of the Sassi. The 18th century saw the last great public works for the restoration of the water-harvesting system of the ancient Dolina on the edge at the top of the grabiglione of the Sasso Barisano. By re-joining and digging out the previous caves and tunnels equipped with plenty of bell-like cisterns of ancient origins, a colossal cistern was made with massive pillars hewn out of the rock and with over 15 m high vaults, the walls of which were perfectly insulated by means of plaster made out of lime and shards. The fogge, cisterns, and pits for grain storage, the tanks and the installations for wool milling and treating skins, the market and the economic heart of the town were placed inside the numerous well neighbourhoods which were dug out along the Gravina. However, with the industrial revolution the new strategies of the world wool market, driven by England, determined the crisis of the economy of the Sassi which was based on the manufacture of the raw materials of the yarns, on the tanneries, on the breeding, and on agricultural food production. Transhumance and the agro-pastoral society begin to inexorably decline, triggering the abandonment of the practises of drainage, maintenance of the soils and caves, and of water catchment and distribution which had enabled the Sassi to be inhabited. The great religious and administrative complexes moved from the deep valley of the Gravina to the plain, right between the hills and the water-harvesting systems, interrupting the water channels. In the middle of the 18th century, the whole system of the well neighbourhoods, the Doline and the cisterns on the edge of the Gravina was filled with earth and the central square of Matera was built over it in the 19th century. During Fascism the grabiglioni, the natural little drainage channels of the Sassi, were also asphalted and a ring road was built. It cut the lower border of the habitat and separated it from the bottom of the ravine. When the inhabitants moved, the ecosystem of the Sassi was then completely spoilt. The water crisis, the abandonment of the practices, and of the knowledge by means of which the community had built its space made the Sassi fragile in comparison to modernity, leading inevitably to their desertion.

The vicissitudes of Matera enable us to re-interpret the history of Petra in Jordan. According to the modern world Petra is considered as an archaeological town which had undergone desertification already at the end of the classic age and was completely abandoned from the Middle Ages at least. Starting from this point of view, in 1980 the population and the nomadic groups living in Petra were all transferred; in the name of restoring to international culture, the vestiges of a Petra interpreted according to the classic feeling. However, nothing allows Petra to be defined as a necropolis and identified only with its large Hellenic monumental façades. The town is generally supposed to have been destroyed by an earthquake in 365 AD, but then in 447 the impressive monumental complex of the Byzantine church called Urn Tomb was built using the older hypogea. Another earthquake, which occurred in 746, would explain the final abandonment of the site. The crusaders occupied it in the Middle Ages and in 1276, on the occasion of the journey of the sultan Baibars fleeing from Cairo towards Kerak, the Arab historian an-Nuwairi (1279–1332) described the many dwellings in Petra "carved out of the mountain, marvellously shaped, ornamented with columns and provided with doors, the façades decorated with sculptures hewn out of the stone by means of blades and all engraved with images and decorations". The excavation of the crusade settlement of Petra, which was conducted by Guido Vannini and Roberto Franchi, has revealed a regular frequentation of the site by Arab nomadic people (Vannini, personal statement made to the author). The moments of stately growth, which were characterized by episodes of generally appreciated monumental building, were limited in time in comparison with the long-term frequentation that conserves the ways and the techniques that ensure a human presence. This knowledge also underlies the moments of cultural and economic renewal.

Petra, Marib, Shabwa, and Chichén Itzá are towns which have all undergone both periods of decay and rebirth. Recent studies on the climatic cycles of the planet tend to relate the disappearance of ancient civilizations to exceptional catastrophic events caused by volcanic eruptions (Keys, 2000) or recurring cyclonic phenomena such as the so-called Niño (Fagan, 1999). The end of the Mayan civilization was explained as the result of a series of devastating droughts which occurred between the 9th and the 10th centuries and which left the populations without food, and especially without water (Gill, 2000). Each of these interpretations is, however, limited. Only an understanding of these places as ecosystems created, thanks to a wise use of the local resources in difficult natural conditions may provide an exhaustive answer. A commitment to water management and to urban and territorial maintenance requires a constant effort. Social cohesion is guaranteed by environmental and economic success and by a strong spiritual adhesion. A close interrelationship of these elements within the traditional practices makes the system weak. If sudden changes simultaneously occur in each one these aspects, collapse is inevitable. This is the principle of the concomitant cause, the combined action of the natural catastrophes with human intervention and cultural traumas, which explains the urban exodus to be interpreted in the framework of the desertification and water crisis phenomena.

A town left without food may resist for months but a human being left without water for only a day is reduced to a serious condition. The second day everybody is obliged to leave in search of the vital liquid. The third day is the end. The method of interpreting towns based on the hydrogenesis and on the management of the local resources is an important means of understanding the settlements and expresses a meaning able to go beyond the aim of simple historical research. Events involving exoduses and urban collapses are a warning, alluding to possible worrying destinies but also indicating scenarios for alternative futures. They make us aware that the gaze scrutinizing the town and the discourse describing it have been deviated, in certain moments, from the environmental customs and the cultural biases of that time. Whereas, taking the complex urban ecology as a synthesis of millenary stratifications, some of them more evident and others submerged and forgotten, brings to light knowledge from which new paradigms can be drawn.

Traditional Knowledge for A New Technological Paradigm

9

FIGURE 9.1 Sahara, an ancient shaduf moved by means of photovoltaic cells. The use of the solar energy is an example of an ancient traditional form of energy which can be largely exploited today, thanks to appropriate advanced technologies.

9.1 Interest and Studies on Traditional Knowledge

The validity of traditional knowledge and the use of practices derived from it, variously named as endogenous knowledge, appropriate technologies, local knowledge, indigenous techniques, nature-based knowledge, sustainable knowledge, folk knowledge, and cultural knowledge, have been asserted for many years now on various levels. In the scientific field, research on traditional knowledge has continued for more than 20 years within a specific line of research aiming at tackling the problem of overcoming a top-down approach to the transfer of technologies as well as the problem of achieving a participatory relationship able to foster sustainability (Brokensha et al, 1980). Many international bodies such as the International Labour Organisation (ILO) (Bhalla, 1977; ILO 1985), the Organisation for Economic Co-operation and Development (OECD) (Jequier and Blanc, 1983), the Food and Agriculture Organization (FAO) (Saouma, 1993), the United Nations Educational, Scientific and Cultural Organization (UNESCO, 1994ab), the United Nations Environment Programme (UNEP) (Dowdeswell, 1993), and the World Bank (Vernon, 1989; Davis, 1995) have declared its validity in research and documents. The interest of the United Nations' conventions is clearly highlighted in the report entitled "Building Linkage between Environmental Conventions and Initiatives" (UNCCD, 1999a).

In June 1999, UNESCO and ICSU (International Council for Science) agreed upon the following statement: "The local and traditional knowledge system, as the dynamic expression of perceiving and understanding the world, can give, and historically has given, a valuable contribution to science and technology. For this reason, there is a need to preserve, protect, research, and promote this cultural heritage and empirical knowledge".

Numerous research centres and Websites now deal with these issues. Indeed, they globally reach a number of over 40 research centres and some of them have very good Websites that offer valuable bibliographies and research on this topic. In particular, the UNEP's International Environmental Technology Centre (IETC) in Japan is planning to publish an International Source Book on Environmentally Sound Technologies for Wastewater and Stormwater Management. The IETC uses the term "endogenous sound technologies" to point out the technologies described in chapter 34 of Agenda 21 as technologies that have produced positive results on the environment compared to other technologies. Broadly speaking, these protect the environment, are less polluting, use resources in a sustainable way, recycle most of their refuse and products, and dispose of all residues in an environmentally acceptable way, better than those technologies they substitute. These do not properly constitute "individual technologies but a whole system that includes know-how, procedures, goods and services and equipment, as well as organisation and management procedures" (Sakaguchi, 2000).

The FAO is currently carrying out research for the creation of a training course on Water Harvesting for Crop Production (Prinz et al., not yet published). The large majority of the NGOs promote traditional knowledge as a new approach to the international development and cooperation problem after observing negative results of technological decisions taken in the West, in particular, because of the assumption that we could adopt the same system in different contexts and societies as well as the disastrous conviction that everything that is technically possible should be done.

Despite this full commitment and interest, the fields of application and the innovative dissemination of traditional knowledge are still below their real potential. This is not due to the lack of achievements and experience since these are now numerous and significant, promoted by an efficient network of operators. Indeed, a cultural and operative movement now exists, supported by economic and productive interests, which bears traditional knowledge as well as its dissemination and re-use. However, despite the ever-increasing environmental damage produced in all countries, this movement has been unable to oppose the central role of modern techniques in the process of territorial development and organisation. Therefore, it is necessary to wonder why traditional knowledge still plays only a minor role within the nations' technological policies and practices.

The answer can be summarised as follows:
- The lack of awareness that environmental damage, soil degradation, and desertification mostly result from the loss of traditional knowledge;
- The lack of information as to the validity and benefits of traditional knowledge from the experts responsible for national planning;
- The limited understanding of the role to be assigned to traditional techniques and their way of operating;
- The lack of communication and exchange of successful experiences;

- The unawareness of the innovative use of traditional knowledge;
- The dissemination of a series of biases and critiques regarding traditional knowledge.
- This latter point requires an exact estimation of the prejudice and the wrong ideas about traditional knowledge.

9.2 Critiques and Biases Against Traditional Knowledge

1. **They constitute a specific and limited series of technical solutions**

   The concept is contradicted by the very same definition of traditional knowledge as an integrated learning organisation, a complex system with multifunctional characteristics, and an integral part of the construction process of the collective identity as well as of social cohesion. Taking it as a series of expedients to solve specific problems is reductive and deceptive. Each traditional practice responds to a specific necessity but is highly integrated with the environmental and social context, is part of a complex set of social, ecological but also symbolic and aesthetic values. This makes it difficult to classify traditional knowledge in terms of technical solutions, but brings it much closer to the contemporary problem of sustainability.

   For instance, the rice cultivations in the Philippines and Indonesia which cover the mountain sides with an extensive system of terraces constitute a wonderful landscape created by the people. The beauty of these terraces does not result from aesthetic choices but depends on the harmonious application of the traditional techniques of engineering the environment in order to organise catchment areas, gather flowing waters and rainfalls, create terraces on which flows are channelled, and preserve the ground from washing away or eroding.

   Traditional techniques relating to water management in the Ladakh region in India are another example. These enable fertile mountain oases to be created in otherwise arid lands. The techniques for using the water resources provided by seasonal snow melting are based on a system of rights and rules closely linked to the social structure, to the norms regulating the traditional division of work between sex and age groups, as well as to the ecological situation of each oasis-village. The great social cohesion and spiritual motivation has enabled these people to apply modern techniques such as methods for using solar energy, considered in harmony with their ideals, and to reject others such as chemical fertilizers regarded as harmful for the soils (Wacker, 1997ab).

2. **They are not technologically competitive, are technologically inefficient and less productive than modern technologies**

   This critique is not justified since there is no reason to hold traditional technologies as less competitive, inefficient, and unproductive. Traditional technology achieves results differently and considers a series of contextual factors omitted by modern techniques. The procedure is sometimes less immediate and needs more work. However, this is not a negative feature in many countries that face the problem of unemployment. In order to assess the efficiency of a process, both internal and external aspects are considered. Indeed, the application of a technique determines effects both before and after the use of the necessary resources and has more general consequences on the entire economic, social, and environmental model. These interactions are not taken into account in the application of a modern technique based on specific and immediate yield criteria. On the contrary, traditional techniques are selected and accepted through a process of environmental, historical, and social considerations. Their efficiency is appraised according to their validity in the long term, their contextual benefits and their overall sustainability.

   Failure to evaluate these aspects has led to unsuccessful projects for development cooperation which have not taken into account the necessity of proposing the technologies that could be managed through the local knowledge system and the social categories, mainly women. Within this framework, the case of the irrigated perimeter of Ras Djebel in the north-eastern part of Tunisia, 30 km from Biserta, is a significant example. Here a traditional kind of cultivation is applied, following the oasis model and to the Maghrebian and Andalusian models of arboriculture and vegetable-gardens. Fields are formed of small parcels divided according to complicated procedures of inheritance and marriages that continuously divide and re-compose the properties. In this way, 2,000 ha of land can be divided into 4,500 parcels. Traditional irrigation is carried out through harvesting subterranean waters by means of family-managed wells or irrigation, thanks to superficial channels running all over the agricultural area. A project aiming at modernizing the system created a 15,000 m3 tank, fed by a lake located on the hill. The agricultural perimeter was then subdivided into larger parts; each supplied by a modern water drawing system that irrigates large areas by sprinkling. Such a perimeter involved the removal of small property boundaries. The peasants distinctly rejected the new division of the parcels as well as new methods of irrigation resulting from social, productive, and symbolical reasons which can be summarised as follows:

- The use of family wells enables each owner to manage his own water independently. Such water was previously free whereas there is a charge for the one provided by the project.
- The division of small land parcels responds to ancestral structures which extend the domestic space into the agricultural one. In this way, women can work in the fields and at the same time feel at home.
- Irrigation through sprinkling is considered negative since it "favours the burning of the leaves and the appearance of new diseases".
- Ground water is commonly considered as "alive since it originates from the earth and feeds the plants", in opposition to the water of the project which is held as "a dead water coming from a stagnant basin and thus harmful to agriculture".

Despite these oppositions, the project was carried out with disastrous consequences. Indeed, after the project was implemented, a 20 m lowering of the water table as well as a 3 g/l increase of salinity were verified (Bouayard-Agha, 1997).

The unsuccessful outcome was actually due to the incapacity to take into account the fact that there was an unwillingness to give up traditional techniques, even if relating to symbolical reasons, resulting from a better productivity in addition to a better ecological and social compatibility. The oasis, Mediterranean garden, or Andalusian agriculture uses techniques of irrigation through superficial canals fed by wells, systems of water collection through flood diversions or subterranean drainage tunnels (foggara, guettara, qanat, etc.) and are the most suitable for optimising the water use. Traditional irrigation allows continuous leaching of the soil and prevents the accumulation of salts on the surface, whereas sprinkling irrigation favours evaporation and salt deposits. The building of large dams and water basins generates an accumulation of uncovered water which, stocked in this way, evaporates much more. Moreover, the basin is very easily filled up by the wadi's sediments, whereas the upstream subterranean water table of the dam is no longer fed nor renewed.

In the Ziz wadi region in Morocco, the construction of the ar-Rachidiya dam brought about the abandonment of the nomadic life and of the people's traditional agriculture in order to earn wages from the new activities. A city was created which required new building work and attracted more and more people. The earnings reports thus register wage increases and urban expansion while, on the contrary, we are facing a precarious success which relies on wasting resources. The water from the dam is now used to quench the thirst of the city whereas, because the water table has been exhausted, the oases can no longer use traditional supply methods and depend on the State's networks of pipes and meters which have a cost. However, if during one season the supply from the water basin is not sufficient to cover the new urban requirements and agriculture, a new catastrophe will then be bound to happen. This situation has already occurred in the region of Béchar in Algeria, where the whole agricultural area of Abad-la, fed from the Kenadsa dam created with long and impressive efforts rapidly became deserted waste land.

These examples constitute an additional justification to the vast movement of opposition against the construction of great dams that were developed in Asia, Latin America, and Mediterranean Europe. The achievement of these projects over the last 50 years brought about the transfer of millions of people, overwhelmed hundreds of thousands of hectares of forests, and nearly destroyed the way of living for entire communities without generating the expected water benefits in the long term. Furthermore, the realisation of great dams also constitutes a reason of conflict between States since, very often, the big rivers originate in different countries.

Nowadays, the international financing bodies advise against building big dams and prefer to take care of the integrated organisation of water basins bearing in mind the historical local techniques (Richter et al, 1997). In this way, traditional knowledge is adopted to bring about numerous successful experiences.

In Morocco, interesting experiments are being carried out in landscape restoration and rehabilitation of the old foggara technique. The foggaras are draining tunnels left in a state of abandonment, and which, in the medieval period enabled the irrigation of hundreds of kilometres of palm trees. A modern well deeply dug out and able to reach the water by means of a motor-pump produces immediate results; however, in the long term, it lowers and depletes the water table. The traditional system of the foggara drains the superficial part of the water table by drawing quantities always proportional

FIGURES 9.2–9.3 Tunisia. Application of traditional plant protection techniques and intensive palm-grove planting programme. The programmes to combat desertification promote both local forms of agricultural organisation and new modern practices. In this case (Fig. 9.3), the new irrigation systems form a palm-grove layout alien to the oasis tradition.

FIGURES 9.4–9.5 Morocco. Vegetable fibre barriers to stop soil erosion and provide protection from sandstorms (Fig. 9.4). Restoration of the drainage tunnels and the air shafts (Fig. 9.5). The Moroccan foggara system allowed the building of the complex urban layout of the medieval capitals. When the foggaras were abandoned, entire towns completely disappeared.

to its capacity of renewal. At the same time, it feeds the water table with the supplies coming from the capillary drainage of the micro-flows in the sand and with the water produced by hidden rainfall. This determines the oasis effect, a self-catalytic system in which the water from the foggaras irrigates the palm-grove whose existence favours moisture and water production. Furthermore, the necessities of irrigation by gravity decide the precise location of the settlement and of the cultivated areas in relation to where the foggara network has been dug. The territory is therefore subject to an imperative general canon which gives it a pattern with great aesthetic qualities. As a matter of fact, the specific benefits of the traditional techniques lie in the fact that they constitute a system of self-regulation able to produce the best results in harsh ecological contexts, prevent long-term risks, and respond to environmental modifications, by shaping landscapes with an extraordinary aesthetic value. Industrialisation, urbanisation, and agricultural mechanization cause the loss of traditional technologies and decrease the quality of the environment and the landscape.

3. **They particularly concern the southern part of the world and are marginal compared to the major economic and technological processes**

The critique is contradicted by the fact that situations in which traditional technologies persist, and their role in the economy and society is consolidated and stabilised, can be proved specifically in the more advanced countries. The values of tradition, manufacturing practices, and the craftsmen's skills are the basis on which is founded the great added value of productions of enormous economic importance for many advanced countries. In particular the typical food production (oil, cheese, wine, etc.) safeguards both the aesthetic and environmental quality of the landscape, since the old production systems are available, thanks to the maintenance of traditional techniques of soil management. In this same field, the growing dissemination of organically controlled agricultural productions and meats shows even more interest in traditional techniques of husbandry and breeding. These considerations are true even in other sectors from quality articles and haute couture to real estate and the building market. The most refined production houses are proud to be able to list the traditional techniques they use in their manufacturing methods and the success of so many companies is actually due to the capacity to incorporate tradition into their processes or to be located in traditional environments or historical town centres.

On this subject, it is useful to consider the regions of Valais in Switzerland, the Loire valley in France, and Tuscany in Italy. Here, the maintenance of traditional techniques in agriculture has ensured the stability of high quality landscapes. The major difficulties and burdens due to the use of more expensive labour techniques can be overcome, thanks to the great value of the product that can be obtained with these techniques, and in these cases, the wines. In Valais, the water catchment systems from the sources of springs and from glaciers which, through little surface canals called bisse, allow mountain slopes to be irrigated by gravity on a higher level than the stream's natural course. In the Loire valley, the traditional technique of the cave-dwellings and of the excavation of subterranean caves is maintained in order to preserve each single metre of surface area, precious for the production of champagne and, in order to organise wine cellars with a perfect microclimate for wine production. In Tuscany, the Chianti production provides the economic resources necessary to preserve from destructive transformations one of the most wonderful agrarian landscapes, consolidated and affirmed over the centuries.

Thus, it is wrong to consider traditional knowledge as marginal compared to the great economic and technological processes under way. Even from a quantitative point of view, their use still supports most of humankind which is distributed throughout the less industrialized countries. Paradoxically, in these places where traditional techniques are still used in a massive way, these are considered by the modernist thought as a phenomenon of backwardness, whereas, in advanced countries, they create an image and provide added value. Modernization, the industrial sector's higher profitability, the processes of domination and of economic and cultural dependency, together with the phenomena of agricultural and productive transformation related to them constitute the pressures of dissolution acting on traditional knowledge.

4. **They are proposed because of an ideological anti-technological vision**

The fourth critique is to be rejected since, even if in the traditional knowledge movement there are some anti-technological components, as a whole it is not true at all. Traditional knowledge is proposed not because it contains less technology compared to conventional knowledge, but because it is more technologically suited to the specific environmental and social context. Sometimes, it is the bearer of most refined technologies; some other times, it is very

FIGURES 9.6–9.7 Valais (Switzerland). The practice of the channels (bisse) is still used and supported by community interests and rules. Diversion of the bisse by means of a traditional irrigation device (Fig. 9.6). Sluice gate and water sharing system (Fig. 9.7).

simple but still more appropriate, that is ecologically compatible and locally manageable. Furthermore, traditional knowledge is re-proposed through every possible innovative use that is in conjunction with modern technologies, which can operate within the same logic. As a matter of fact, it is the principle of traditional knowledge that is useful to spread and reproduce, not the technique itself. This is possible actually thanks to the use of the most advanced technologies in the field of eco-energies, recycling, zero emission production, maintenance of old procedures, thanks to low impact processes of mechanization that are self-manageable.

As an example, the use of sewage waters or excrements in order to improve the soil fertility is a very old practice used in many traditional societies which became obsolete with the modern sewage network. To use sewage waters as a resource is a way to specifically work with traditional technologies which can be re-proposed today together with modern techniques able to solve hygienic problems that may arise.

Calcutta's wetlands case is a good example within this framework. In the moist areas of west of Calcutta, the traditional fishing and agricultural practices cover approx. 10,000 ha of the territory. Here the world's largest network of urban sewage water reuse is in use. Thousands of peasants convey millions of litres of sewage water from Calcutta towards their land. They consider these waters as an advantageous nutrient supply and not as something harmful they should get rid of. At the same time, they provide an extraordinary contribution to the waste water drainage system of Calcutta completely free of charge. The Ganga Action Plan, the biggest initiative in the field of environmental improvement planning in the southern Indian continent has enabled this traditional knowledge to be standardised and spread over several municipalities. In this project, methods of appropriate use are taken from traditional knowledge and methods of health safety are covered by new technologies. In this way, sewage waters become a matter of conservation, as for pure water, instead of a problem of treatment. To consider sewage waters as an asset that provides valid support to existence, constitutes a new way of thinking for the modern productive logic, but is actually the principle according to which traditional knowledge operates. It is a principle that the supporters of traditional knowledge re-propose even in a technologically advanced perspective.

9.3 Tradition as a Dynamic System Able to Incorporate Innovation

The logic with which traditional knowledge operates can be summed up in the following principle: to turn a problem into a resource in such a way as to enable places of major environmental difficulty to become also the ones where appropriate techniques are applied. Within this process, the traditional knowledge system does not refuse innovation but continuously develops it or absorbs it from other situations. What we recognize as tradition is not a static and immutable condition but a dynamic system which evolved by making innovative aspects so much an integral part of itself that sometimes it becomes difficult to interpret. For instance, nowadays, everyone considers the Mediterranean traditional space as one which cannot be separated from olive and tomato cultivation; however, both of them were introduced: the olive in ancient times and the tomato after the 16th century. In the same way, it is commonly thought that American native peoples are associated with the use of horses. However, the latter arrived on the continent only after the Europeans' arrival. American nomadic people used them immediately and, during the period of colonisation of the American Far West, the horse was already an indissoluble component of the local tradition.

All over the world and during each period, there are societies which rejected innovation owing to cultural preferences or because of their social system. In general, a society socially less stratified and governed by authoritarian principles is more resistant to innovation. Well-known examples are the abandonment of the technology of oceanic navigation by ancient China or of firearms technology by the Japanese during the 17th century. The latter case was due to the dominant Samurai group's resistance to firearms, considering the upsetting of military practices as an attack on their caste. In both situations, in order to prevent the spread of innovation, it was necessary to have strong State powers, which precisely because of their impossibility to evolve, were bound to collapse in the long term.

In general, in history, in the presence of diversified social groups, there is always one able to accept the innovative process which gives an advantage over the others and the power to spread. The appropriate technology develops in vast areas with differentiated resources, inhabited by numerous populations, and subsequently divided into competitive groups where potential innovators or spreaders of innovation are created. Local knowledge progresses through the accumulation of experiences, and tradition is perpetuated specifically when it is constantly capable of incorporating innovation.

FIGURES 9.8–9.9 The Cinque Terre (Liguria). The figures show conditions of slope degradation due to the constructions and the abandonment of the terracing system, in 1940 (Fig. 9.8) and today (Fig. 9.9). In the Cinque Terre Park which is on the UNESCO World Heritage list, innovative practices for the rehabilitation of traditional techniques and systems are currently being carried out.

Thus, we can speak about an ongoing construction of tradition. The process operates by selecting, filtering, and accepting innovations through the whole series of values and conceptions of the social structure. When the latter is culturally, socially, and economically steady, the process is then possible. Only a great cultural steadiness and independence make it possible to guide the tough process of incorporating innovation without being overwhelmed by it. Instead when the system of social values is destabilized by cultural and economic dependence, it is then no longer able to make a critical selection nor to adopt transformations necessary to make progress within its own system of knowledge. Local knowledge becomes fossilised and is bound to disappear under the burden of destructive modernisation. In this process, the economic conditions play a determining role. The system of traditional knowledge constitutes the cultural and technological mediation through which a vision of the world becomes a social practice, environmental management as well as guarantee of food and production. When economic conditions or expectations are not guaranteed any longer, the traditional cognitive system is then exposed to dissolute pressures. An entire conception of the world as well as family ties, the decisive role of social categories, and bearers of traditions, such as the elders and women, is threatened. With emigration and the transfer from traditional habitats into new urban agglomerations and the rapid abandonment agriculture by large sectors of the population, the process of conservation and dissemination of knowledge is interrupted. Thus, these phenomena are socio-economic indicators useful for the valuation of the loss of traditional knowledge. On the contrary, the good welfare conditions of the people favour social cohesion, confidence within cultural identity, and enable the safeguarding of traditional systems through the guarantee of a high remuneration of the work necessary to maintain them. It explains the apparent paradox of rich countries such as Switzerland which, as in the Valais region, were able to maintain high levels of traditional techniques, and succeeded in paying for the necessary efforts with a great increase in product value. Thus, we can state that tradition is a feature of "successful modernity", capable of recovering benefits and values from it.

In geographical situations similar to the ones in Switzerland, such as in Mediterranean countries, the same practices were abandoned due to the fact that these societies felt the cultural effects of modernity very strongly. It is the case of Piedmont, in the Aosta valley and of Alto Adige in Italy or in mountain regions of France where techniques similar to the bisse, called ru, are completely forgotten bringing about environmental degradation and the loss of the landscape's aesthetical qualities. This is the fate of a great part of the rural environment, as we have said for Tuscany, the Loire, and other regions, which was safeguarded only thanks to the strong presence of historical and cultural qualities and to the high remuneration reached by agricultural produce.

In Liguria where in the Cinque Terre region there is one of the largest systems of terraced slopes in the Mediterranean, this traditional practice that protects the soils, catches, and channels the waters, has been perpetuated through innovative agricultural mechanization. Agricultural work on terraces is hard due to tiring transport systems which are operational only on foot. Traditionally there were techniques of transport by means of sledges drawn up the hill by ropes. Already at the beginning of the century these were substituted with mechanical funicular systems on rails. The same techniques are re-proposed today with innovative systems that enable the ascent of the slope without disturbing the landscape or the ecosystem. This solution safeguarded the extraordinary environment of the Cinque Terre, but did not spread to analogous situations, especially in Southern Italy where the abandonment of terraced slopes because of the difficulty of working, this millennial heritage, has caused landslides and soil degradation.

As a whole in the Mediterranean, only in the sectors where a great cultural investment has been achieved, has the traditional knowledge successfully persisted by combining with successful technological and economic innovation. While in Switzerland, this commitment was taken in rural areas, in the remaining European countries it has mostly concerned the historical and monumental urban heritage. Medieval historical houses persisted in Europe, thanks to the fact that this architecture was restored and adapted, with the hygienic facilities necessary to modern life. The more this operation is done with respect for tradition and authenticity, the more it requires advanced innovative capacities and creates added value as well as economic effects. The same consideration is true for entire historical centres which are doomed to perish and be abandoned when they are unable to incorporate the innovations they need in order to function. This is the case of the traditional historical centres in southern Italy and the Maghreb. They constitute an intensive and concentrated model of settlement typical of the Mediterranean organisation system that works in a close relationship with the agrarian landscape and which acts for the latter as a grain store, trade emporium, and as a service organisation centre. The crisis of traditional agriculture coincided with the exodus from these centres, generally located in inaccessible mountain areas that

FIGURE 9.10 The Cinque Terre (Liguria). With the traditional technique of agricultural transport along the slopes by means of sledges, substituted with appropriate modern funicular systems, it is possible to continue the activities necessary to perpetuate the cultural landscape of terracing.

constituted territorial entities able to tackle soil degradation with their traditional architecture, water collection systems, and soil protection techniques.

The systems of hills and slopes are an essential element of the traditional European and Mediterranean environment. Over time, they were managed with techniques of appropriate space organisation, i.e. terraces, irrigation, water catchment, rainwater collection and conservation, and saving areas for forests and pastures. Modernity determined the abandonment of these places and of the old ridge ways, preferring huge plains and coasts. Powerful mechanical means enabled the transformation of ecological systems considered as marginal, but essential for the bio-system (such as marshes, karstic places, coastal dunes), and made it possible to attack the same slopes with agricultural transformations unable to guarantee soil conservation and renewal. The result is the exodus from inland areas with desertification, loss of cultural quality and of biodiversity.

The same processes which have accelerated over the last 50 years in Europe and the Mediterranean are now under way all over the world with the industrialization process. African, Asian, and Southern-American countries constitute important reserves of local knowledge because of their size, environmental and geographical variability, cultural and ecological diversity, and the persistence of their traditional communities. However, the degree of steadiness of traditional techniques varies a lot. In the less-industrialized countries, the main cause of the disappearance of traditional techniques is poverty. It is poverty created by the sudden development of new needs and models which have impoverished local resources. Populations become completely dependent on solutions and assistance which make them deny their past, take ways opposed to their own culture, thus worsening their poverty (Tirfe Mammo, 1999). The latter in its turn brings about a further abandonment of traditional techniques, and thus further environmental degradation. For instance, cooking practiced with traditional fuels is indicated as the only cause of the deforestation and the destruction of the plant cover in many regions of the Sahel. However, traditionally, in a situation of non-poverty fuels made from animal dung were used, or only the dry parts and branches of trees were cut in order to respect and protect them in the name of sacred symbolism. These practices were abandoned only in situations of economic shortage, the decline of cultural values with massive urbanisation, and the disappearance of the integrated cycle of cultivation and breeding. Extreme poverty determined the attack on and the impoverishment of the previously wisely managed resources and worsened soil degradation in an ever-increasing negative spiral. For this reason, the most significant loss of traditional knowledge occurs specifically in the poorest countries; whereas still in Asia, Africa, and Southern America, the areas with better welfare conditions are those with the highest quality and persistence of tradition. Consequently, traditional residential roofing techniques such as roofs made of straw, appropriate to energy saving, continue to be used in Holland, England, and Ireland, whereas in Africa the traditional hut is abandoned for concrete-made constructions and corrugated iron roofs. In the same way, in California, valuable adobe houses are built and in Southern Italy and in the Loire in France, the houses in the caves are the most appreciated and costly.

However, significant successful uses of traditional techniques are under way specifically in less industrialized countries. In China, a fight against the invasion of sands in the soils has been carried out on a very large scale by using traditional techniques of withholding the sands by means of vegetable barriers. In Madagascar, Peru and Indonesia, there have been successful experiences in the re-organisation of the terracing systems. In Namibia and Israel, traditional techniques for creating soil in the desert and condensing atmospheric water have been applied. In Brazil and Sri Lanka, innovative water-harvesting techniques are successfully used.

Social co-operation practices are gaining a new vitality. They have traditionally involved the common management of entire territories, voluntary actions to achieve works of common interest during the festivities, or mutual assistance to help families or individuals in specific critical moments (building a house, extra agricultural work, etc.), recover a new vitality. In Mauritania, successful experiences have involved women in water distribution co-operatives. There is a proliferation of cases of self-managed, interest-free loan companies, or innovative forms of mutual solidarity, such as time banks (voluntary loan of services), collective help for those who want to undertake an activity, or social solidarity organisations for building homes like Habitat for Humanity in the United States.

The case of the Hadramaut valley in southern Yemen is a significant example of the persistence of an integrated traditional cycle. The old knowledge is perpetuated in order to build a complex adobe city system along the arid course of the wadi, transformed into a rich valley full of life and cultivations. The Hadramaut is now fertile thanks to the organic

FIGURE 9.11 Ireland, traditional houses with thatched roofs used for warmth and as elements of distinctiveness and prestige.

waste of the inhabitants themselves and is irrigated through an elaborate system of diversion and conservation of the flood water. Each family can inhabit elaborate buildings since the low cost of the materials and the social cooperation enable everyone to erect beautiful constructions. Houses and the entire urban plan are wisely organised in order to be functional to the collection of the human excrement necessary to fertilize the gardens. For this purpose, a two-outlet toilet which separates the solids from the liquids has been in use since the more remote past together with the careful organisation of the buildings and streets for a correct control and collection of the waste. Today this kind of toilet is made of modern ceramics in Sweden in order to equip new neighbourhoods based on sustainability.

In the Hadramaut, the whole system still maintains vitality and quality but is fragile compared to modernity. The introduction of new materials such as cement increases costs and creates new needs and poverty. The integrated cycle which links adobe cities, achieved with the same humus created by irrigation, urban excrement and cultivated fields, collapses. The transformations of the agricultural practices determine the abandonment of cultivation techniques on small plots and threaten the water collection and distribution system. The old system of flood diversion and mud conveyance towards the gardens, storing the water within the same subterranean sediments is at risk of being replaced by modern water networks which impose the use of open-air dams and basins as well as of chemical soil fertilisation. The valley, no longer maintained as in the past millennia, risks reverting to a sterile desert. Only by safeguarding the housing and agricultural traditions can the Hadramaut wadi be saved. To this end, it is necessary to give dignity and value to local knowledge, but also to proceed with innovations essential to obtain the maximum remuneration from products recovered through this authentic ecological, urban, and rural cycle. In this case, the occasions offered by e-commerce can provide new opportunities for increased value and presence on international markets of the highly organic products of the Hadramaut. By incorporating the new economy, traditional knowledge can enable the territories to overcome the industrial economy phase, which harms the environment, and to enter the dimension of sustainable human development directly.

9.4 The Future of Tradition

The examples mentioned above contrast with the commonly accepted notion according to which the cultures based on collection and distribution techniques in accordance with the hydraulic society model elaborated by Karl August Wittfogel in the 50s had to be marked by state despotism and control (Wittfogel, 1957). This is true for the great empires that rose up around massive water resources like the Chinese, Indian, and Egyptian rivers. There, the great works for channelling and managing water courses determined the creation of an administrative and military system run by an authoritarian power. The characteristics of the hydraulic model consist of centralised sovereignty, the large territorial dimensions structured by a large hydrographical basin, and the existence of a numerous population. In architecture, this hydraulic model corresponds to the building of colossal constructions, which are based on a symmetrical conception, clarity in building, a strong expressiveness, and the employment of a mass of workers led and organized by the central authority. In city planning, a planned system with Hippodamian-type intersecting axes, typical of the towns founded by a sovereign or resulting from a colonial decision. All the houses feature a very similar exterior concealing their real economic wealth from the envy of the central power. They hide their luxury and decorations inside and the dominant palace always towers over them. The socio-economic model is that of a growing expansion supported by a massive population growth triggered by the agricultural potential and supported by a policy of imperial conquest, the income coming from the exploitation of a vast quantity of workers and by spending resources on monuments or wars. The long-term results of this are the hypertrophy of the population and of the territory, authoritarianism, state centralisation, and the increasing destruction of the environment leading to an ecological catastrophe.

The societies which have chosen the impenetrable and unpleasant areas, giving them a self-supporting existence, survive on the fringe of the great empires. These autopoietic societies use the gathered experience of traditional knowledge and become centres of innovation for the amplification and the proper use of the local resources. The agricultural economy based on a small-scale irrigation system and on the subsequent works for the organisation of space such as terracing systems, dry stone walling, and levelling the ground produces a core group of small landowners who own animals and production tools. The architecture is based on the synthesis of the structured environments from the inside to the outside similar to the organisation of a system of caves. Their notion of the world is based on the combination of technique, art, and symbolism for the creation of a global space, dense and full of meanings, where man and society, nature and history are unified.

The prehistoric art of the caves is the demonstration of this way of perceiving and living in space. Paintings give a global view in which the dimensions of surface, volume and time are not separated. They are uninterruptedly spread over the wall where all the characteristics, the gibbosities, and the anomalies of the substratum are integrated into the representation. Paintings were added onto each other and different shapes and styles overlapped over very long periods. Their use was at once aesthetic, symbolic, and practical. Through art, symbol, and initiation, the identity and the cohesion of the group are created and knowledge is passed on.

This nomadic and multidirectional logic underlies the small-scale urban organisation of the societies that is based on the equivalence of the directions: not univocal but multipurpose, not planned but spontaneous, not imposed but stratified over time. The enveloping and maze-like space disorients and gives chaotic sensations, though it is supported by specific principles. The whole cannot be overlooked from a dominant position, such as a monument or the sovereign's gaze, but it has to be gradually discovered and is usable from the inside of the single independent cells.

In its turn, the social organization is composed of self-governed communities based on the use of the rare means locally available that are ruled by family, religious, and consuetudinary authorities and led by the peers' assembly. This is the way the Berber populations in Cabilia, many traditional societies and the communities based on water agreements were ruled. The technologies use the archaic practices controlling water on a small-scale, such as the structures of capillary percolation in the caves, the ditches and the cisterns and develop into larger scale hydraulic works of flow catchment and flood repartition but always ruled by the cooperation of the whole community. The technologies employ the methods of harvesting on the slopes and the watersheds and create devices, though sometimes difficult to distinguish, drawing humidity from the atmosphere both to produce drinking water and to water the plants. Real artificial aerial springs supply the habitat systems which result from the environmental knowledge based on hydrogenesis, or water production.

These societies evolve into more complex ecosystems based on the use of the local resources, but which assume a larger dimensional scale by exploiting their position to control the trade roads and convey huge economic incomes. In Petra, in Marib, in the Saharan oasis-towns such as Ghardaia, as well as in the ancient capitals dating back to the Bronze Age, the ever increasing effort to organise space depended on the economic benefits ensured by the role undertaken within an international exchange economy: the caravan gold routes in the Sahara, the incense route in Arabia, the silk route in Palestine and in the East.

The community's acceptance of the necessary tasks for preserving the geographic positions depends on delicate environmental, economic, and cultural equilibriums. The whole determines a unified conception of the world and its values according to which even when one single link is broken the whole system is bound to collapse. If the equilibrium between the resources, their productive use, and the conception of the world maintained with difficulty over the ages, fails, the urban ecosystem collapses, starting the land degradation of whole territories. In the Mediterranean basin, in its isles and peninsulas, in Syria, Lebanon, Mesopotamia, Palestine, Arabia, and Northern Africa, the places of the most ancient civilisations, where archaeological excavations have brought to light towns once surrounded by abundant nature, rich in flourishing fields and gardens, are now abandoned and lie under the sand. The water crisis due to the abandonment of the appropriate water and soil management techniques triggers a process of land degradation and desertification which has progressed over the last 3,000 years; this process was accelerated during the industrial era but attained catastrophic dimensions only in the last 50 years. In this period, new immediately efficacious values and the huge capacity of changing nature threatened the equilibriums based on a timorous respect for the environment. As a matter of fact, the degradation is not due to natural and climatic causes but rather to the indiscriminate pressure exerted on the natural resources. The models of existence, production, and consumption which have replaced the traditional arrangements in the advanced countries, cause the total depletion of the local resources by fostering the hypertrophic growth of the developed areas by means of a massive recourse to energies obtained outside, firstly from the hinterland and then from progressively remoter areas. Thus, the destruction of the plant and landscape heritage is extended and the millenary chain of the proper environmental knowledge passed on down the generations is interrupted. The disappearance of that knowledge causes the loss of the skills of maintenance and of management of space on which the harmonious arrangement of certain ideal territories such as the landscapes created by the work and the culture depends.

However, the knowledge is not completely lost. It survives among the populations living in the apparently undeveloped areas or the interstices of the advanced society and the places protected for their cultural value. Knowledge is a great potential because the local know-how, which improves under the harshest environmental conditions, and the existence of intact ancient structures are a valuable heritage on which new models of sustainability have to be based. The historical settlements, the traditional landscapes, and the local knowledge provide solutions to be safeguarded and which can be re-proposed, adapted, and renewed by means of the modern technology. It is not a question of reapplying or transforming the single procedures but rather of understanding the logic of those models which have allowed societies to positively advance their status and to make technical, artistic, and architectural implementations, fundamental in the history of the civilizations. Knowledge about the most distant past can lead to the founding of new technological paradigms: the capability of enhancing the inside resources and managing them at a local level; the versatility and the interpenetration of technical, ethical, and aesthetic values; the production not per se but for the good of the community and based on the principle according to which each activity has to start up another one without waste; and energy use based on cycles in constant renewal.

In southern Italy, traditional sites like Matera were completely abandoned in the 50s and 60s because they were considered as outmoded places. Nowadays, they have been restored and repopulated reusing the traditional architecture built up by means of local materials aiming to save energy, harvest rainfall in cisterns, and recycle waste. The enhancement process has started with the creation of a new paradigm: to use places that were once symbols of poverty and famine as congenial areas and models for the future. Along the gravine, the abandoned slopes that were affected by erosion and soil degradation have been reinstated with dry walls and terracing systems. The works that are being carried out by employing a large labour force are recovering the ancient knowledge and consolidating the slopes by creating, at the same time, leisure gardens for the population and areas of cultural interest. Therefore, these projects have become tourist attractions, thus bringing additional benefits to the population. As a matter of fact, the traditional systems are archaeologically, historically, and anthropologically interesting, thus adding a cultural value that allows further economies to be made. This process can be extended throughout the Mediterranean, from the kasbahs and the medinas of Northern Africa to the traditional systems of the Middle East.

The logic of traditional knowledge and urban ecosystems indicates a new model of environmental management to combat desertification and soil degradation, a model based on autopoiesis, homeostasis, and self-sustainable development. The current model of industrial agriculture and breeding have reached a condition of paradoxical unsustainability which causes damage and imbalance both in Western and undeveloped countries. The overproduction of the rich countries, sustained by substantial economic incentives, swamps the markets with goods which are highly competitive in comparison with the traditional goods. In the West the production techniques spoil the agricultural landscape and cause a progressive worsening in quality, with ever-increasing risks and consequences on the food chain, as the recurrent epidemics demonstrate. In the less-developed countries, where a chicken reared with the traditional methods is more expensive than a chicken reared in a battery in only 40 days with hormones and medicaments, the invasion of imported goods pushes the local production out of the market. Thus, the local production is abandoned and the country becomes dependent on food aid. It would be beneficial for everybody to lessen western productivity in favour of traditional quality and to enable other countries to maintain their local agriculture and breeding.

The following guidelines should be developed: (a) in the rural areas to conceive agriculture as an action necessary for the maintenance of the territory and not as a mere production system; (b) in the urban areas to integrate the environment and the towns and to implement action plans for the realization of self-sustainable human settlements and for the management of the town as an ecosystem. The programmes must involve innovative actions for the management of the soil, water, and energy. In particular it is necessary to: direct elsewhere the funds which cause the loss of the local knowledge, fires, soil degradation, and the damaging transformations of the landscape; foster and promote the traditional systems for the production, harvesting, and distribution of water; foster the traditional practices for the organisation of production within integrated cycles; boost the programmes of autopoiesis and sustainability of the urban system; promote the integration systems within the segments of the urban cycle (production, consumption, and waste); foster the participation of the populations by reappraising especially the role of the old people, the women, the children, and the marginal groups and by organising territorial networks among the municipalities, territorial pacts, river basin communities, and parks.

Local knowledge and the traditional territorial arrangement must be re-proposed for the safeguard and the conservation of the typical landscape quality in new forms and with new solutions in order to implement:

- A new global role of the traditional rural systems able to be re-proposed with the aim of conserving the soil and saving resources, all activities that have been made sustainable also thanks to the integration of different markets, such as cultural and discovery tourism, archaeology and the fruition of the environment, with the consequent proposal to reconvert the agricultural methods that have been factors of desertification and to re-naturalise areas spoilt by industrial agriculture;
- New integrated cycles of production, consumption, and recycling in urban areas, by enhancing the ancient centres and reusing traditional materials and building techniques in the new constructions, proposing new areas based on the saving and the proper use of resources and environmental re-naturalisation and transformation of areas exposed to urban or industrial desertification;
- New generation territorial management programmes taking into account the aesthetic, cultural, and economic values of the landscape, conceived as specific qualities which have developed within the millenary relationship between humankind and nature, and aiming at strengthening the landscape aspect by typifying its characteristics and by re-proposing the traditional logic in an innovative way by replenishing the soils and the aquifers and saving resources.

Guaranteeing the future of tradition does not mean erasing the creative and innovative capability. Today's appropriate innovation is tomorrow's tradition. The present study deals with questions relating to historical and anthropological knowledge, such as the recurring motives which are common in outlying and different societies. The origins of the techniques have been investigated, giving priority to functionality in order to explain physical and social structures without denying the role of the spirit than cannot be disregarded in the affirmation, permanence, memorisation, and transmission of forms. It has been seen that the environment affects the constant process of elaboration and dissemination and that the value of art, symbols and the mythic and poetic construction as a vehicle and specific way of knowledge has emerged from the never-ending transhumance of forms throughout history and geography.

Creativity for pleasure, imitative observation, and symbolic and aesthetic elaboration are specific human characteristics. Devotion to activities not directly related to subsistence has given results that, in new and changed conditions, have later become concretely useful. The way how time is used in works with no practical purpose is important for an understanding of how culture originates. The common use of apparently unproductive energies determines the belonging to a group, social cohesion, and identity. This is how the great separation between humankind and nature took place. The propensity towards what we call art is probably typical also of other animals, and the germ must have existed in previous hominids. However, it fully developed only with Homo sapiens, and the human species evolved more than the other species. From a biological point of view, the most amazing aspect is not the diversification of the human groupings but rather their uniformity. The study of the genetic heritage has demonstrated only the slightest differences at a world level. As a matter of fact homogeneity and common origins can be noticed among people belonging to different continents and also have different morphologic characteristics more frequently than people from the same country. This fact is even more impressive in the relationship between man and the mammals that are closest to him and between man and all the other animals: we have got almost all the chimpanzees' genes and 90% of the genes of a species of fishes. Therefore, we are part of the common biosphere of the living beings. The long process of evolution has been a co-evolution of the environment and animal and plant species whose destinies we share, although we take heavier responsibilities.

If there is very little biological difference, then the distinction between the human groups and their capacity for success depends on cultural factors rather than on biological differences. The capacity to process knowledge, but above all to share and pass it on – this is culture – has been the decisive factor. It is this aptitude that gives rise to the variety of the societies which will thus be able to tackle the environmental differences and the contingencies of history. The recovery of traditional knowledge is, therefore, a commitment to safeguard the rare and precious asset that is cultural diversity. However, the purpose of the research is its proposing force. Making an inventory of knowledge means not to leave it in a museum of lost knowledge but to take new lymph from it, a renewed propulsive force for human progress. The logic within knowledge is typical of the most advanced technological experiments which are engaged at the furthest frontiers of the human cognitive adventure such as the conquest of the universe. A space station produces its own energy, the necessary water, and it recycles waste. The same logic will also allow the colonization of the planets according to a model of self-sustainability indispensable to the subsistence of the earth itself.

Analogous considerations are also true in a social context. Desertification, as we have said, is a physical and mainly social phenomenon. The loss of knowledge is due to an accelerated and forced dispersion of the populations under the pressure of needs, wars, and ecological catastrophes. However, in the past these processes mainly depended on natural causes, while today they are driven by the development of the logic of expansion and increasing incomes, the hoarding and exploitation of resources, and the upsetting of the ecosystems and the local ways of living. Paradoxically, the places we consider unique from a natural and cultural point of view are also the most affected by the migration phenomena. The inadequacy of these places to guarantee people's subsistence with the local resources implies that the universally imposed model of usage of these resources has to be debated.

The limitations of the pretension of the West to oblige the world to develop in terms of continuous expansion to be accomplished by damaging the natural resources were denounced long ago (Mit Club of Rome, 1972). They form the basis of taken of the conclusions of the Rio Conference and reported in Agenda 21 (Unced, 1992); they are discussed by economic, sociological, and environmental researchers (Sen, 1999; Latouche, 1989; Cassano, 2001; Brown, 1991); and they have been the debated subject in Rio Conference and Johannesburg world conference. The pretension of the West is based on one hand on a dominion realised by absorbing cultures and knowledge which would have been able to go forward in different directions, and on the other hand on the technical–scientific superiority resulting from the ancient material and cultural appropriations. Jared Diamond (1997) reconstructed the western expansion and hegemony process accomplished by the supremacy of weapons and the bomb of infections spread to other populations, thanks to the European bacterial charge. Both these records, in war and in immune capacities are the consequence of the competitiveness and of the demographic and urban density achieved because of geographical, environmental, and territorial specificities. Martin Bernal (1987–1991) demonstrated that the paradigm of the Hellenistic values, which underlies the western identity, is the outcome of an 18th–19th century system and that classical thought originated from the Eastern and African world. Giovanni Semerano (2001) demolished the cliché of the Indo-European derivation of many etyma of the European idioms by demonstrating that the foundations of western philosophy lay in a misunderstanding.

Apeiron, the term on which Anaximander's thought was based, was used by Plato and Aristotle with the meaning of "infinity". And it is from this notion that the western thought started out. Since human destiny tends towards infinity, Luther's religious reform justified earthly sacrifices, the upsetting of nature, and the supremacy over other living beings, providing an ethical justification for the capitalistic accumulation of the industrial revolution (Weber, 1905). Semerano explains that the term apeiron stands for "mud" and derives from Acadian, the language spoken by the ancient Mesopotamian civilisations in their trade exchanges with the Egyptians and which had spread up to the Dravidic communities. Therefore, agreeing with both Tales who referred to water and the other philosophers of the Ionian school, Anaximander made the origin of everything derive from a material principle, mud, i.e. a mixture of water and earth. The most famous reflection of Anaximander, a Phoenician from Asia Minor, was thus translated: "Man generates from infinity and comes back to infinity". But if you mean apeiron through the Acadian term eperu, corresponding to the Semitic apar meaning "dust", "mud", you get a version confirming the humble conception guarded in Egyptian esoterism, typical of the Indo civilisations, spread over the Mesopotamian adobe towns and transmitted to the Bible itself: "Man is generated from mud and to mud returns". Thus, western pride is based on a conceptual mistake which needs to be reversed in order to bring back human self-respect on the earth, into that mud, the slime, humus or manure from which the civilisations derive and to trace it back from a superb pretension of infinity to a simple materiality depending on the fundamental elements of nature. Humankind has struggled against its fellow men to get resources and energy. The first hostilities occurred because of fire that Palaeolithic human groupings were able to store, but not to light. As a matter of fact, in the case of a spontaneous fire they took it away, which was guarded and carried as ferociously defended embers. Armed conflicts took place later to tear land away from other people. Today, wars are already breaking out over water; indeed water will be one of the main causes of conflict in future centuries. However, one day somebody taught his fellow men how to light fire. Since then, everybody knew that fire is not a substance over which ownership can be claimed but rather a process. It is just the same for all the resources of the earth. In our relationship with the planet's ecosystem we are still in the phase of unconsciousness preceding the great Palaeolithic discovery. But the answer is before everybody in the narration of the extraordinary journey made by a little drop of water, diffuse and rare, clear and multiform, simple and responsible for world equilibriums, inorganic and vital for all living beings. Hoarding is useless, hostility is unjustified, and shortage can disappear if we understand that the resources are part of the continuous flowing of nature which continuously changes and reproduces everything: water, earth, air, and fire are all linked to each other in the cycle of life.

APPENDICES

APPENDIX 1: HUNTER-GATHERERS

The hunter-gatherers' mobility is possible, thanks to a deep knowledge of the territory and the nature and in particular of the methods of water discovery and supply. This knowledge, the result of experiences verified over a long period, is consolidated by the success of its bearers, memorized through symbolic thought and art and passed on to the new generations through the tales. Starting from the most archaic places of origin in Africa, this knowledge spreads all over the world together with the expanding of the human groupings. The hunter-gatherers' knowledge system is a substratum shared by all the populations, a changing substratum which evolves or vanishes according to the environmental and social conditions. And sometimes it emerges again. So this explains the analogies that were often noticed in the myths, the techniques and the forms found among distant people and places.

A1.1 From the Embankments to the Hydraulic Labyrinths

The embankments and the areas for water harvesting were built since the first hominids. This fact should not be surprising. Animals such as beavers build dams to regulate water and in the desert different species of mammals dig out cavities in which water collects naturally. The Palaeolithic people harvested drinking water in the cave-dwellings and on the stone paving. Dams and ditches were created to favour spontaneous vegetation and the practice of fishing. In the steppes, the savannas and the deserts along the karstic plateaux or the inter-fluvial plains, human groups exploited favourable areas at

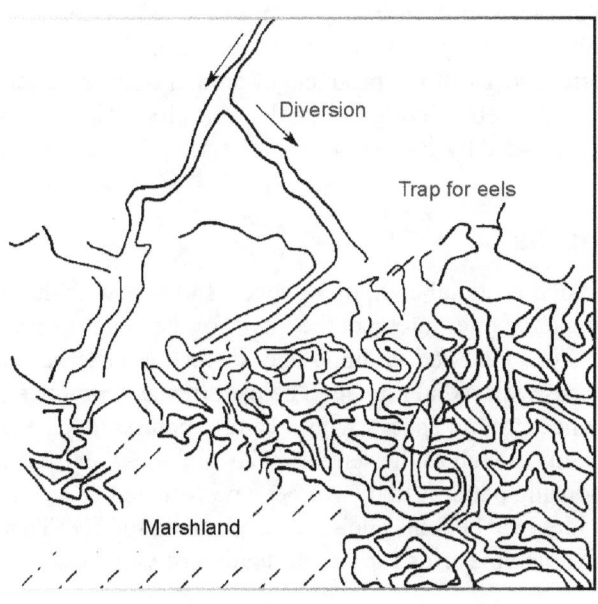

FIGURE A1.1 Eel trap on Mount William (Australia), Palaeolithic Age [Adapted from a drawing by Lourandos, 1980].

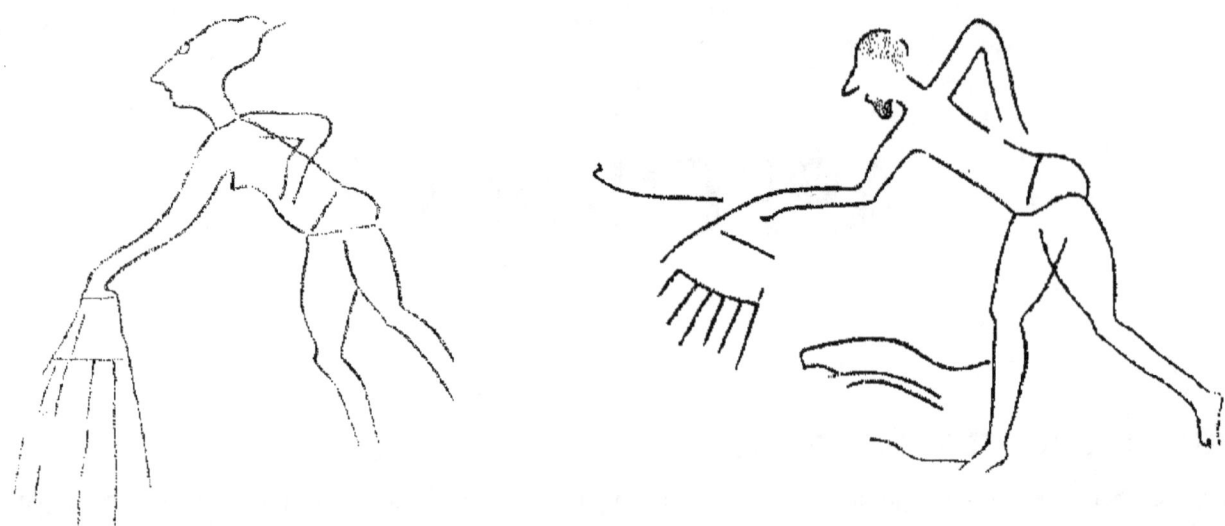

FIGURE A1.2 Wadi Jerat (Algeria), cave engraving, Saharan Palaeolithic Age. The subjects are a woman and a man with an enigmatic tool in one hand, probably a structure made out of vegetable fibres to intercept prey in the water labyrinths. The graffito shows how fish are caught: the left arm holds the tool used to block the fishes' way through the channel, while the right arm is ready to seize the prey. The feet are not represented because they are submerged in the water [Adapted from a drawing by Lhote, 1976].

the borders of the areas undergoing the alternate swamping and drought by using flow-regulation techniques. The latter evolved into imposing systems of traps used for fishing. The maze-like forms reproduced in the symbolic rock graffiti are the same used in the fences where the first forms of domestication were experimented. Water harvesting is connected to the origin of spirituality and art as the drawings in the caves and the barrow of El Guettar in Tunisia prove.

APPENDIX 2: FARMER-BREEDERS

A sedentary life presupposes the regulation of water supplies. This exigency becomes essential with the increase of farming and breeding and implies the use of techniques for water production and management. The different areas of neolithisation draw knowledge suitable to their environment, which spreads over the territory, thanks to social success and demographic growth. Knowledge is transferred not only through invasions and population movements but also through changes, communication, and cultural hybridisations. The innovations consist of the products of animal domestication and plant cultivation as the outcome of a selection operated in the places where the original wild species live. Therefore, products and management techniques are passed on to the areas not separated by geographical barriers.

A2.1 From the Natural Cavity to Underground Rooms

The enlargement of natural cavities is the first form of appropriation and artificial creation of space. In the caves where the natural dripping of water takes place, people dig in order to follow and better intercept the flows, or they enlarge and dig out the natural sinkholes more deeply, making apertures on the slope side and draining and harvesting cisterns. In the Neolithic age, the flint mining activity created the first pit courtyards with radial tunnels. The pattern was reproduced in devices for water harvesting and housing systems composed of underground spaces with a central courtyard. These techniques spread over the arid karstic areas and the limestone highlands as well as the semiarid clay and loess plains. In the latter the ease of excavation allows very large settlements with housing patterns that have been perpetuated up to our time such as in China in the Loess zone. The underground house provides heat benefits and saves land on the surface. That is why it persists in the Loire valley, in France, where the highly valuable vineyards for the production of vintage wines explains the digging out of caves, cellars, and underground houses.

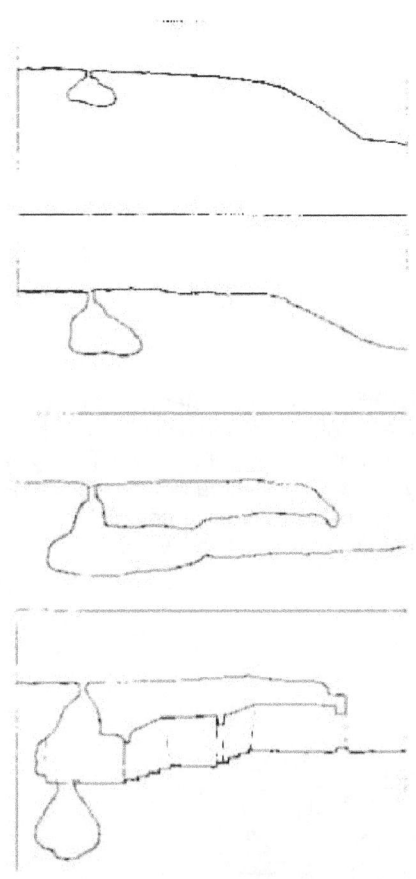

FIGURE A2.1 From the natural cavity to an artificial cave with a bell-shaped cistern.

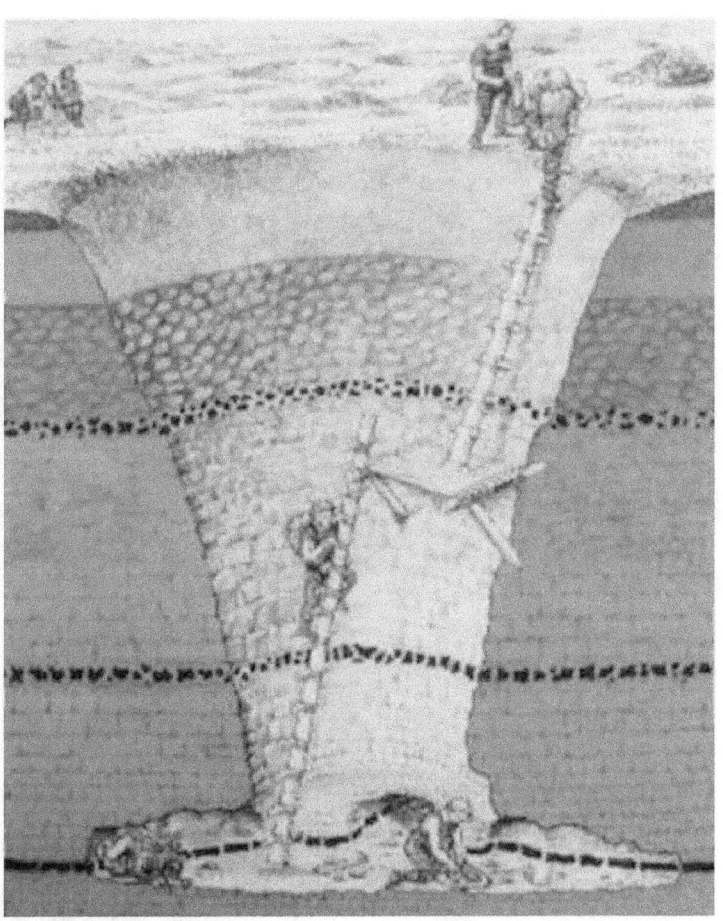

FIGURE A2.2 Reconstruction of a Neolithic mine from which the bell-shaped cisterns and the pit courtyards originated.

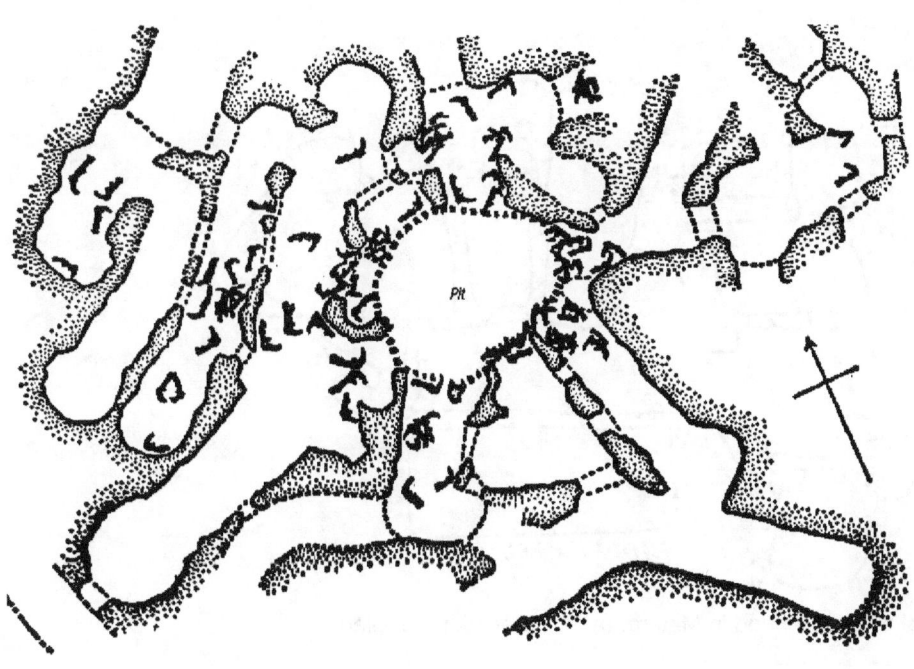

FIGURE A2.3 Map of a Neolithic mine. Underground passages branch off from the open-air pit in the middle.

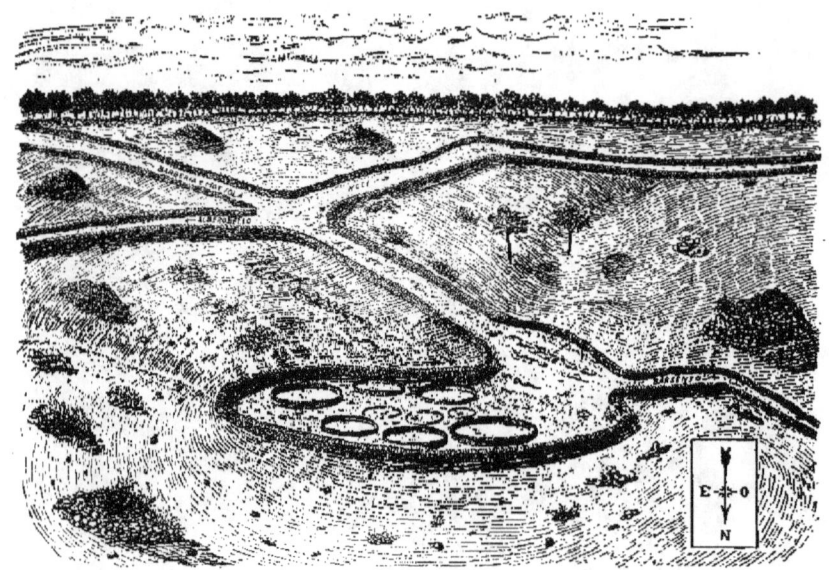

FIGURE A2.4 The cisternale of Traversa near Alberobello: a whole view dating back to the beginning of the 20th century. This system, very similar to the "laghi" of Conversano, consists of a depression containing cisterns dug out to impound flood waters.

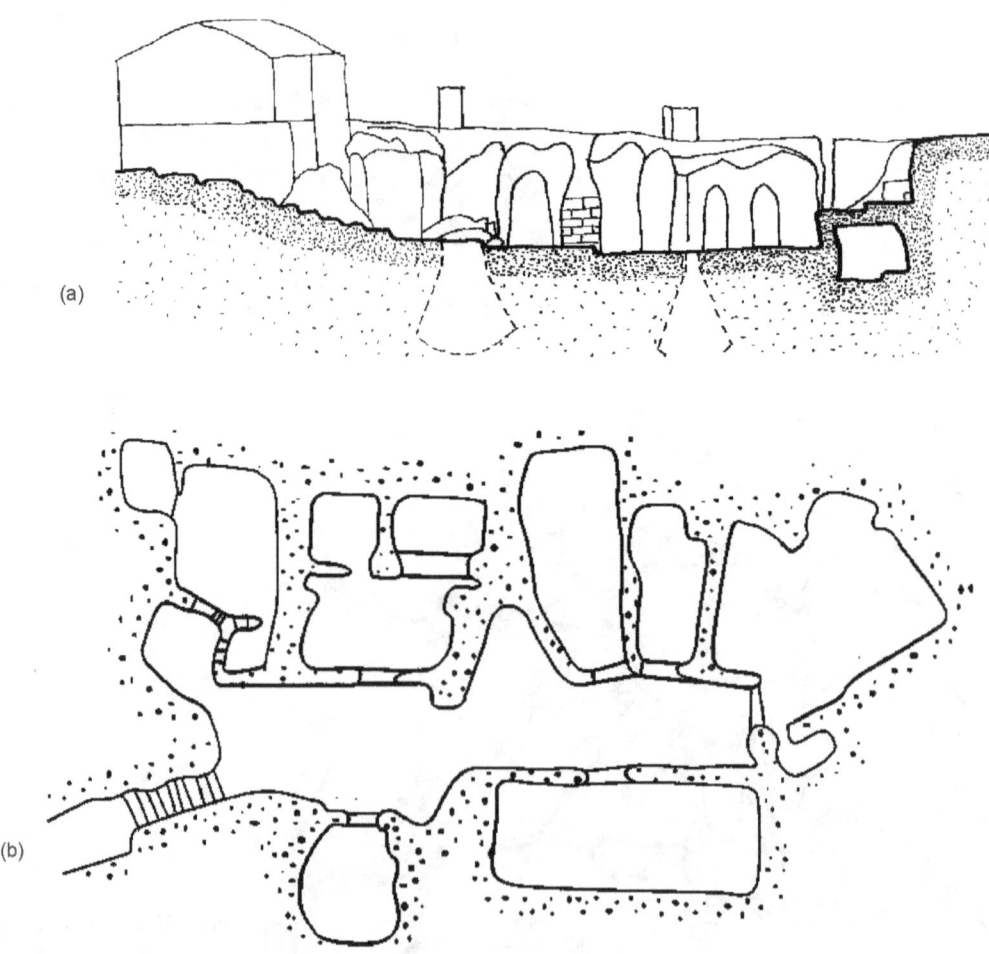

FIGURE A2.5 Hypogeal neighbourhood in Matera: (a) cross section, (b) plan.

A2.2 The Stable Settlement: From the Circular Dwelling to the Village

The circular shape is the simplest architectural structure to build. The curtain wall forms a single unbroken structure which closes and supports itself without forming corners, which need special solutions of chain and prop solutions. The base is generally semi-hypogeal and the massive masonry, with its lobes and meanders, recalls the shapes and the thermal inertia of the carved out works. The first stable settlements had a semi-circular base and were founded in conditions of climate range in which the ditches of the villages performed multipurpose functions related to the water balance: water drainage systems during the rainy season and water stores during the dry season; drinking troughs and ditches to collect the sewage and waste used as soil fertilizers; symbolic demarcation lines of places and elements strengthening social cohesion, group identity, and the propensity to a sedentary life which emerged during the hard building work. The settlement was composed of hut-like structures scattered also outside the perimeter, equipped with cisterns and ditches for grain storage. With the propagation of the model the settlement multiplied. Therefore, the building of the settlement was understood also as building of the territory. The organisation of the village coincided both materially and symbolically with the organisation of the space intended for production as well as with the image, the functioning, and the order of the world.

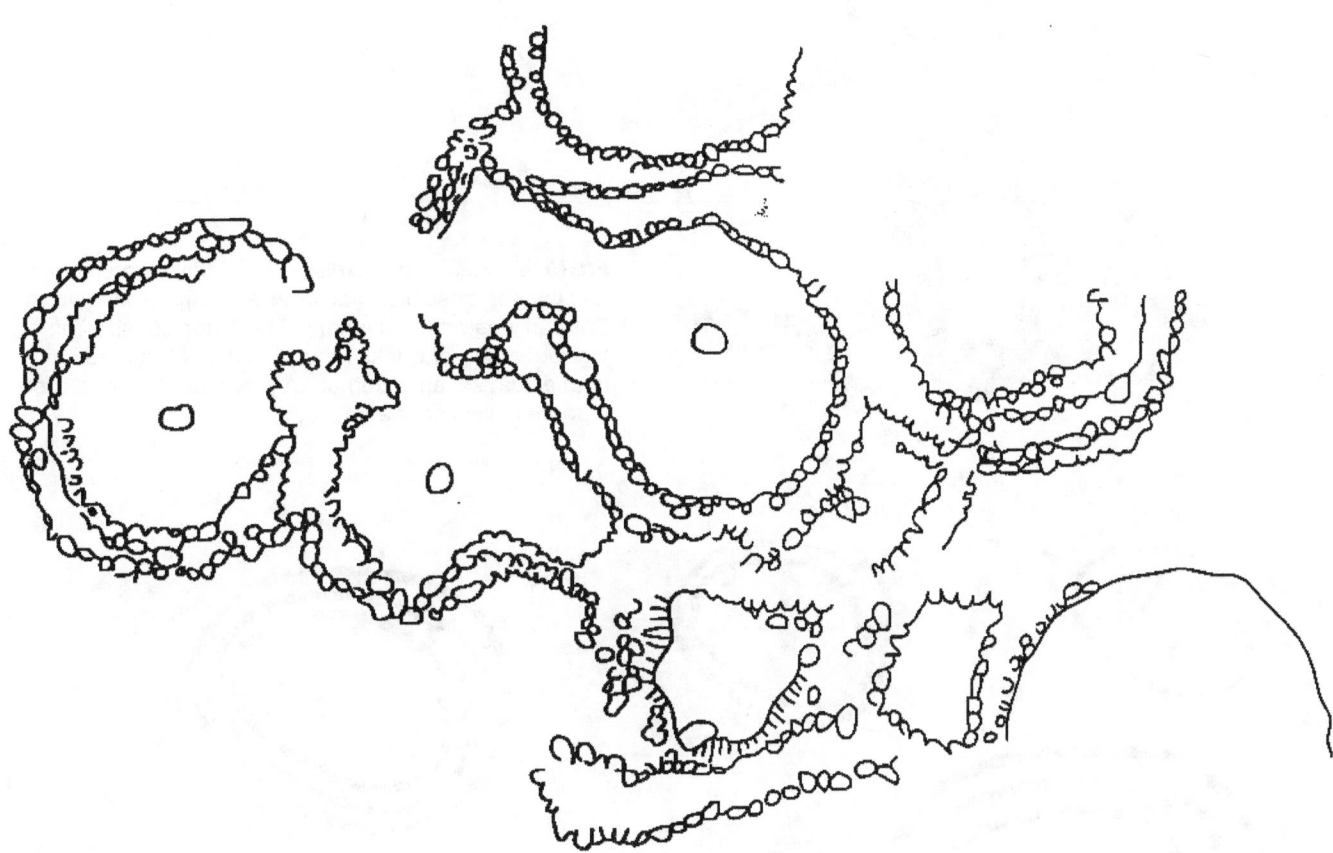

FIGURE A2.6 Pre-ceramic Neolithic site of Beida (Jordan). Stone circular dwelling.

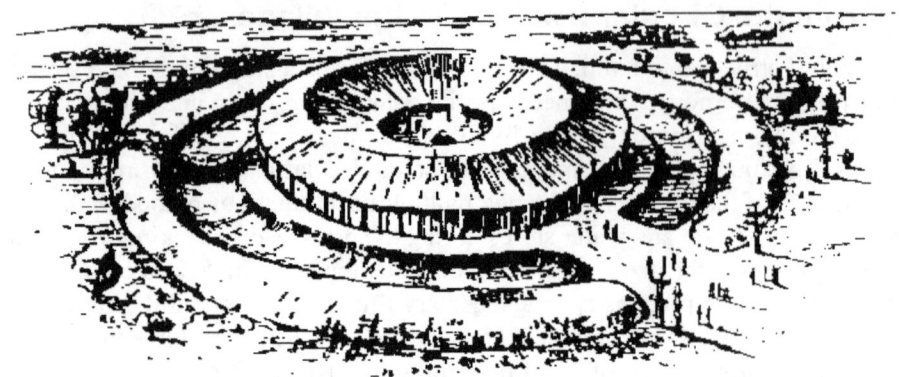

FIGURE A2.7 Woodhenge in Great Britain is a prehistoric site characterised by a big circular wooden house surrounding a central courtyard.

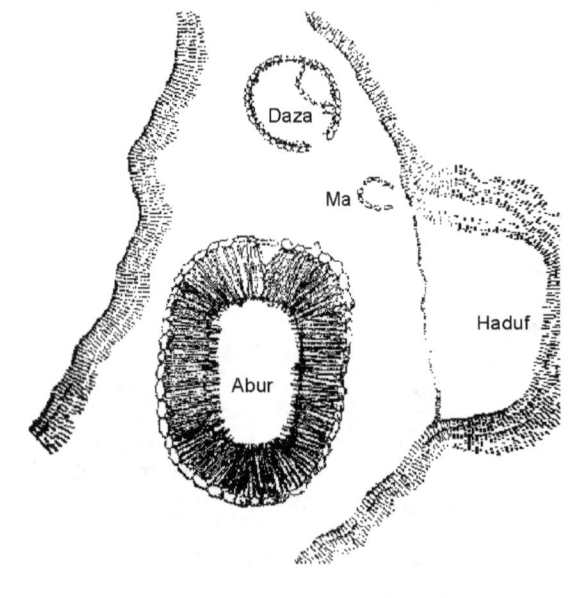

FIGURE A2.8 An explanation of Woodhenge's functions is possible, thanks to a comparison with an Eritrean pastoral settlement. The latter consists of: a big roof made of trunks (abur) to shelter the herds; the house (daza); an external fireplace (ma); a ditch for manure collection (haduf).

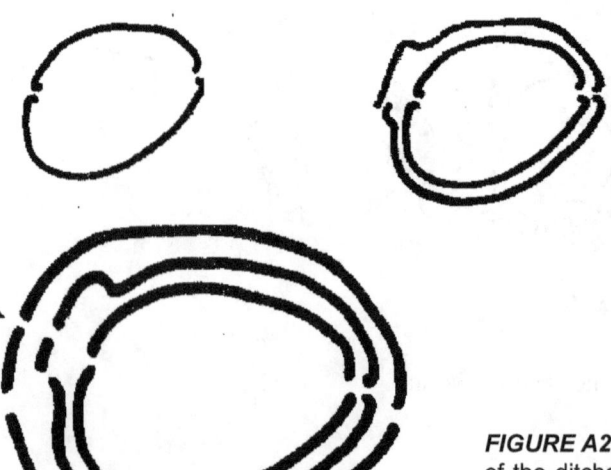
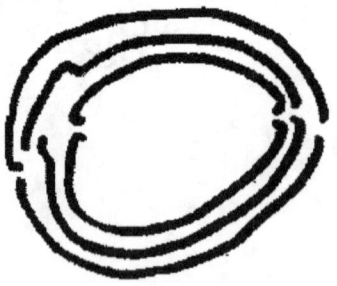

FIGURE A2.9 Types of Neolithic villages. The layout shows the perimeter of the ditches. The entrances always face east-west. The perimeters are often open and have a semi-circular shape or ramifications. This proves their water function rather than a defensive purpose.

A2.3 Proto-Urban Settlements: From the Square House to Clustered Villages

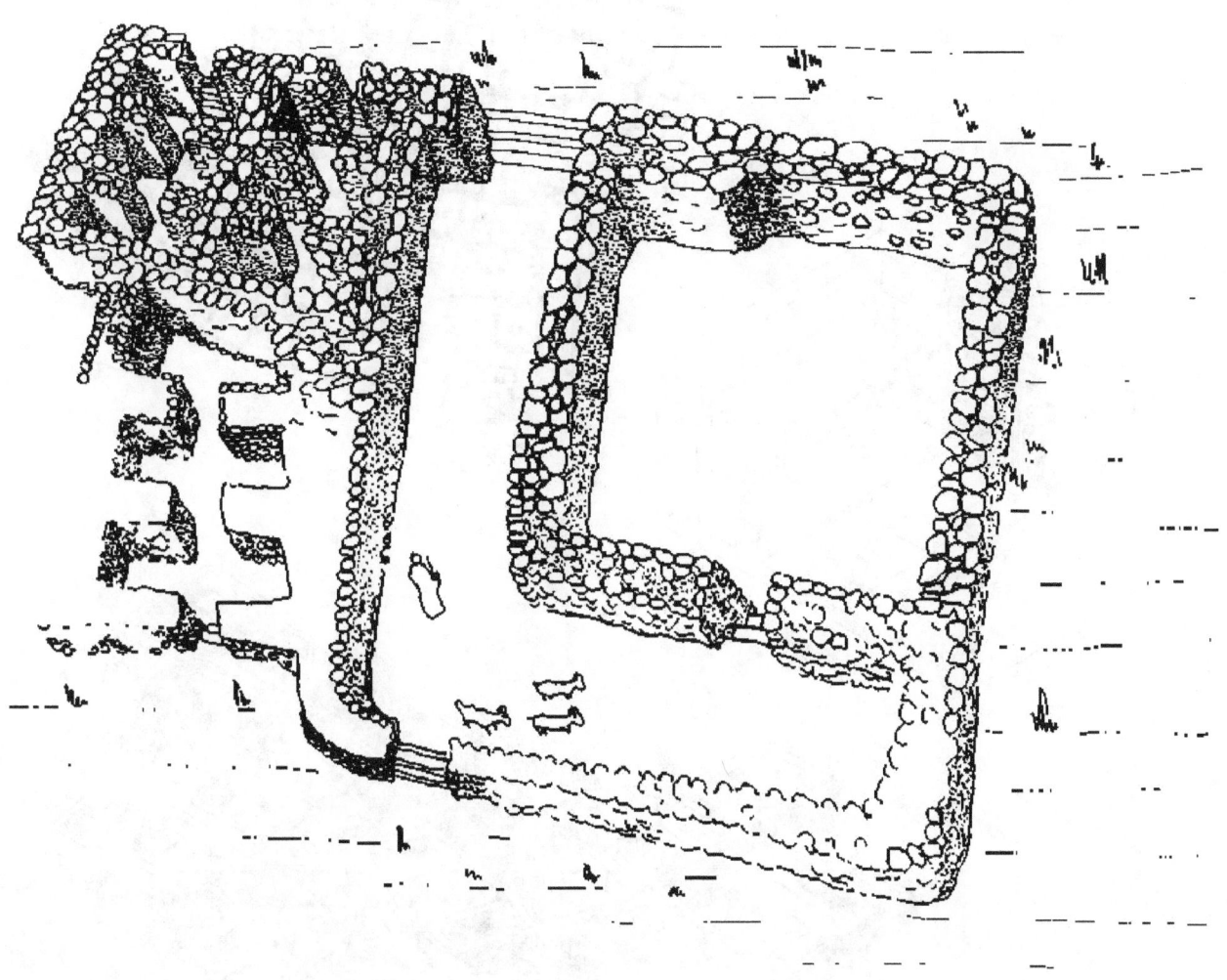

FIGURE A2.10 Pre-ceramic Neolithic site of Beida (Jordan). Corridor-dwellings and construction with an L-shaped courtyard. The structures resembling a "b" were probably used for handcraft and pastoral purposes.

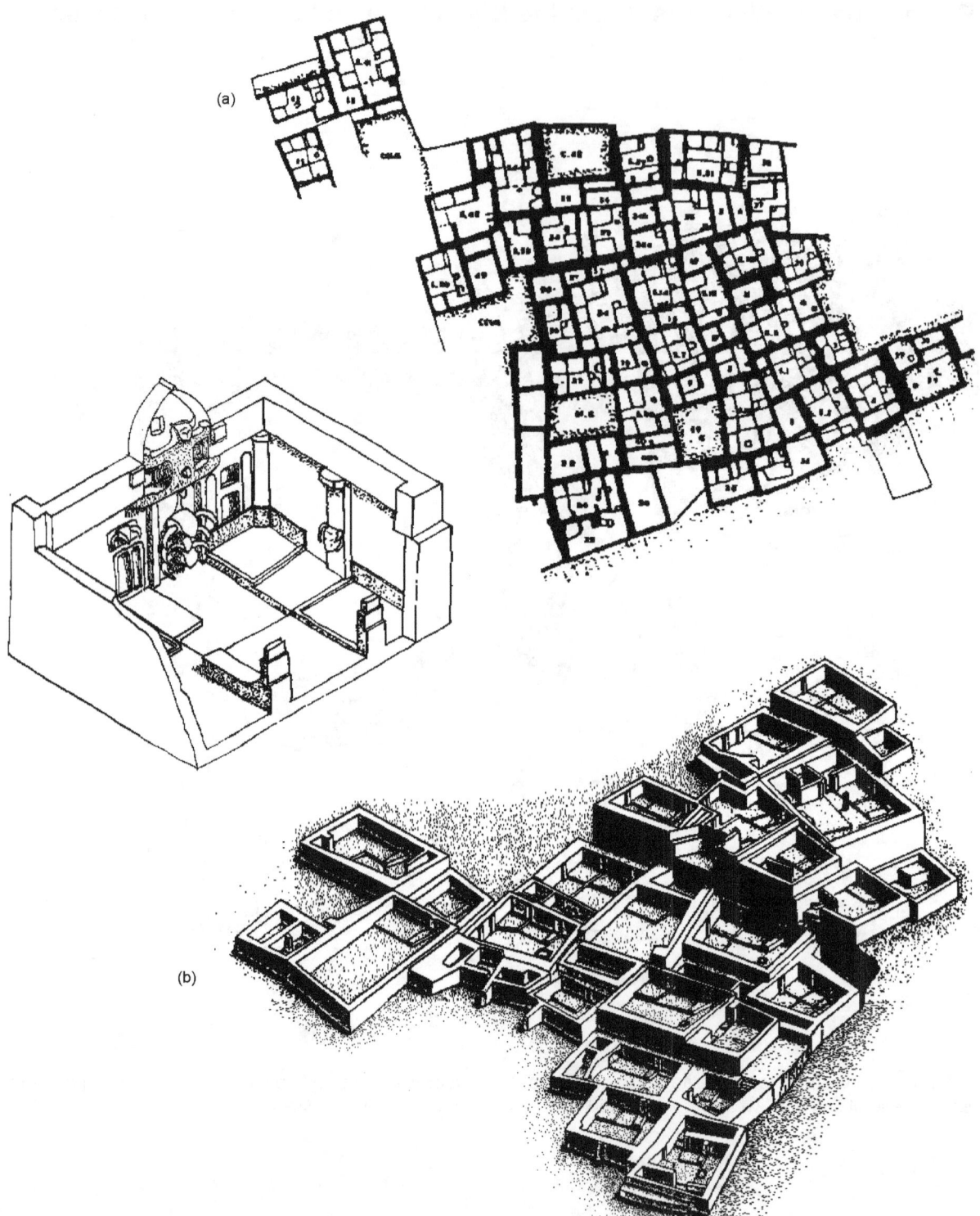

FIGURE A2.11 Neolithic site of Çatal Hüyük (Anatolia): (a, b) planimetry and axonometric projection of the settlement; (c) axonometric projection of the domestic sanctuary of the Mother Earth. In the archaeological reconstruction of the habitat, the absence of entrances to the dwellings is supposed (access would be down the stairs from the terraces). A comparison with the oasis settlements (see Fig. A2.14) shows the possibility of entering from narrow covered streets [Adapted from a drawing by Mellaart, 1967].

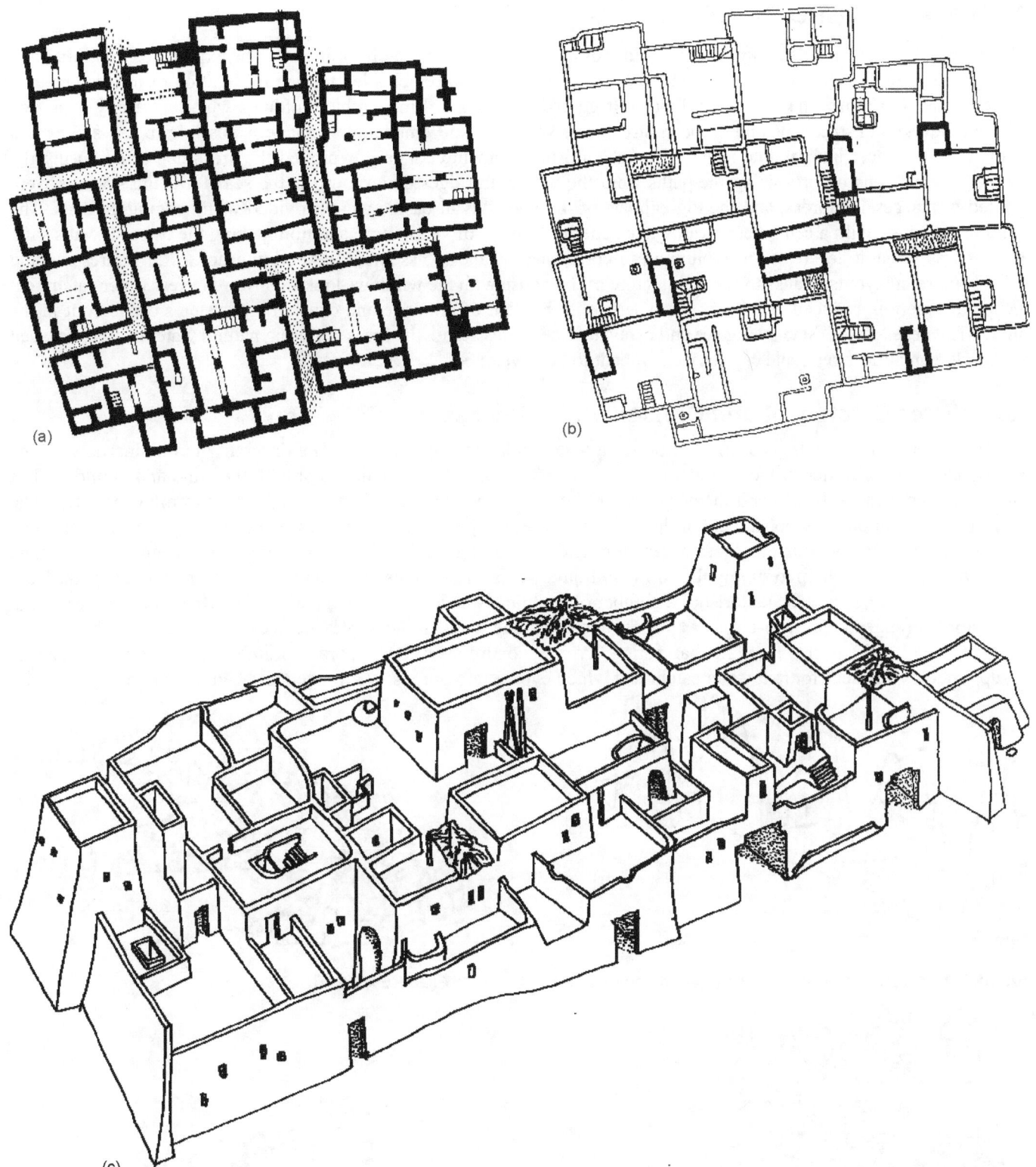

FIGURE A2.12 Oasis settlement: (a, b) planimetry at the level of the plain and the terraces; (c) axonometric projection. The surface of the terraces extends forward on the covered narrow streets which are inserted as a tunnel in the built-up area.

APPENDIX 3: AGRO-PASTORALISTS

The mounts and the carts determined a renewed mobility driven by the search for metals. The experience in mining and the new metal tools facilitated the hypogeal practices. Defence requirements led to the proliferation of fortified centres while the need to affirm the status and the clan triggered the spread of megalithic buildings which generally consisted of stone hutlike constructions and wooden structures. Walls for soil embankment made it possible to use slopes and to organise the most inaccessible ridges. The pastoral transhumant economy exploited the areas neglected during the previous expansions by organising the paths from the mountain ridges down towards the sea. Terracing systems were created in inaccessible areas, and the big capitals of the inter-fluvial basins were provided with hanging gardens. The building typology with a central courtyard gave benefits in terms of ventilation: aeration making the external walls safe. Thus it was possible to create an impluvium to collect water, and to assemble the outlying houses in impressive and unbroken urban layouts, thanks to the architecture of the house with the windows looking inwards. New water catchment techniques were introduced, thanks to the expertise in the field of drainage and channelling systems carried out in the mines. The necessity of establishing sea and caravan trade routes across the areas suffering natural water shortage caused knowledge on atmospheric and capillary catchment to be developed.

A3.1 Water Catchment and Conservation Devices

Every rock or building mass is used for producing water and protecting the soil. The different thermic inertia with the atmosphere creates colder surfaces which originate condensation. The walls intercept both the wind and humidity. The interstices between the blocks and the porosities of the rock impound water. The shade protects from evaporation. The heaps of stones stop the demolishment of the soils and foster the production of humus. They preserve the hydromorphic qualities of the soil by acting as thermoregulators and controlling the humidity both in arid and deeply cold climate conditions. Thus, they help to supply the soil with liquid water that is be used by the plants and prevent the water from freezing. Because of these characteristics a number of techniques have developed in arid areas where they evolved from mere stone arrangements, semi-circular barrows and dry stone walls into complex devices made out of double curtain walls provided with cisterns for water harvesting. Even in conditions of only sporadic rainfall, the use of these devices is supported by surfaces for rain water catchment which evolve into purposely arranged terraced or courtyard structures.

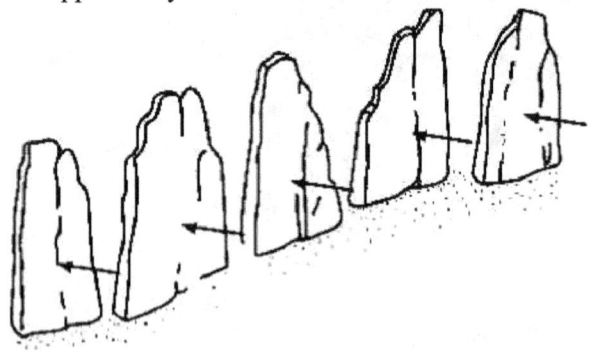

FIGURE A3.1 Arrangement of stones (marbid and manhal)

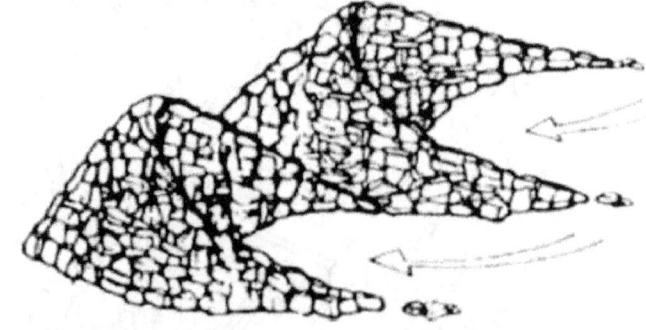

FIGURE A3.2 Tu'rat

FIGURE A3.3 Harrah

FIGURE A3.4 Barrow and specchia

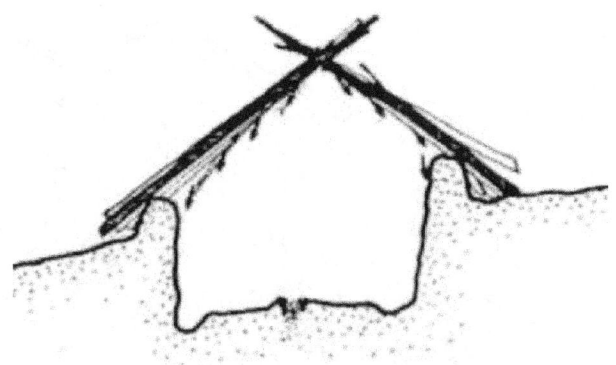

FIGURE A3.5 Boina

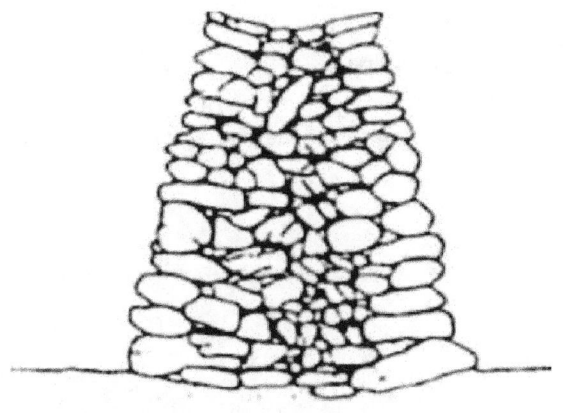

FIGURE A3.6 Dry stone wall

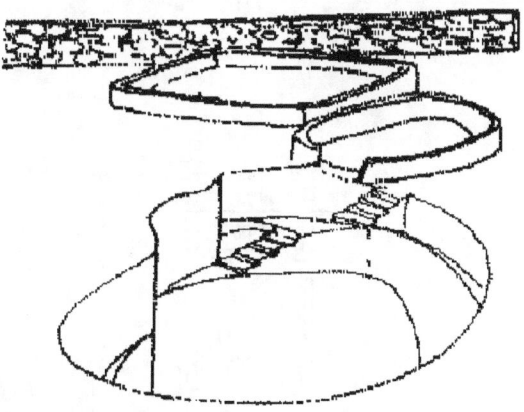

FIGURE A3.7 Resaf

FIGURE A3.8 Mahfid

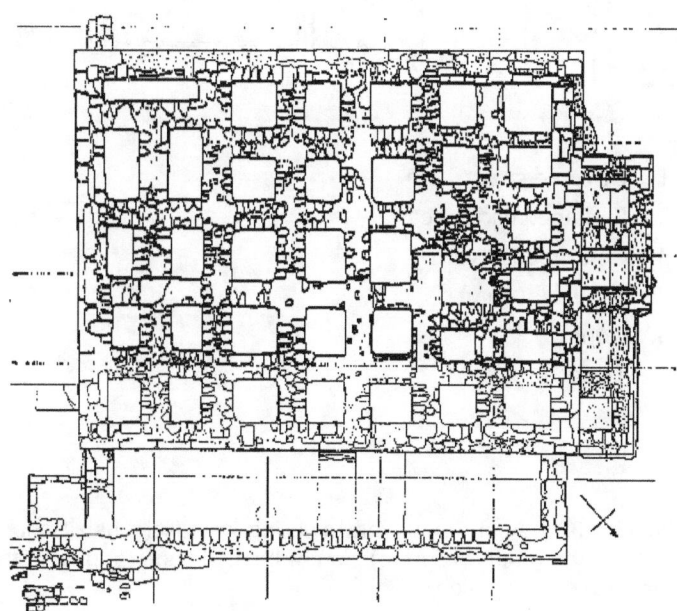

FIGURE A3.9 Plan of the structure dug out in the archaeological site of Shabwa (Yemen) by means of the mahfid device, the 3rd and 2nd millennium BC [Adapted from a drawing by Pirenne, 1977].

Appendices

1. Rainfall catchment terrace
2. Drainpipes
3. Harvesting channel of the underground cistern and stairs leading to the ma'had, the room for ablutions

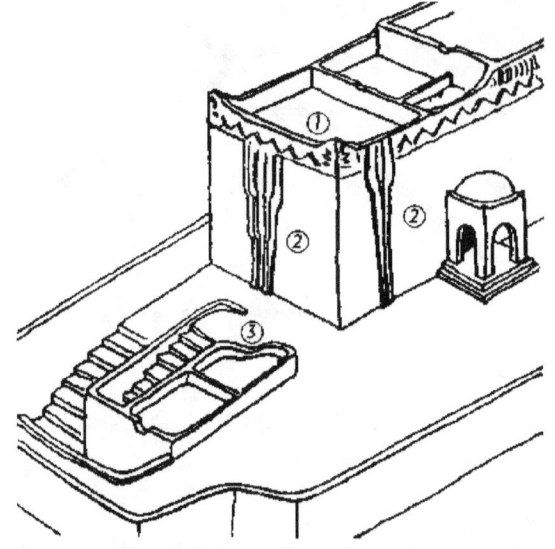

FIGURE A3.10 Small mosque in Yemen.

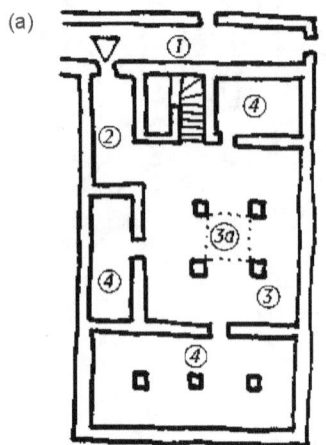

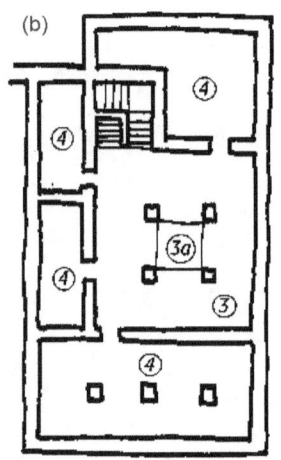

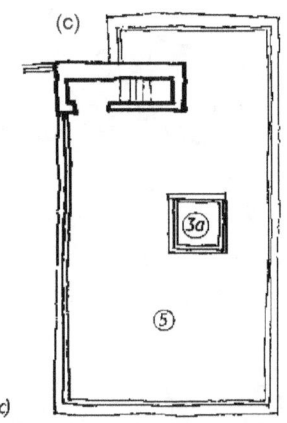

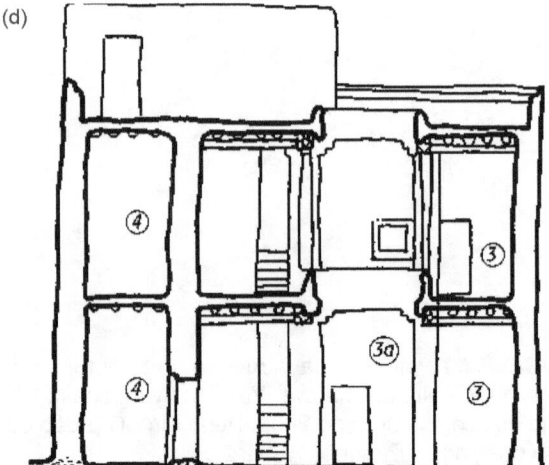

1. Covered street
2. L-shaped entrance
3. Central courtyard
   3a. Light shaft
4. Room
5. Terrace

FIGURE A3.11 Adobe courtyard dwelling in the Algerian Sahara: (a) plan of the ground floor, (b) plan of the first floor, (c) plan of the terrace, (d) cross section.

A3.2 From the African Hut to Condensation Systems and Megalithic Monuments

The African hut anticipated circular-shaped architecture and pseudo conical-shaped vaults. The variety of the shapes and the quality of the constructions still existing in Africa synthesize, with sobriety and purity, knowledge adapted to the places and social needs. This proves that the term hut is a very limited description for these buildings. In spite of the plainness of their shape, they give the idea of the multiplicity and complexity of the architecture. The materials used vary from the well-known wooden and straw structures to the constructions wholly made of reeds, which anticipate the modern tensile structures, or of massive stone curtains more similar to tower dwellings than to huts. The bases are ornamented with projecting porches or cubic volumes inside which create a complex division of the space between the rooms and the circular perimeter. These constructions achieved their utmost evolution in the Ethiopian Coptic churches which were real basilica-huts. The basic pattern has been widespread since the most ancient ages as is proved by the circular-shaped dwelling of Mari with a central square space. This pattern is the basis of the megalithic structures, built up as stone huts, and of their derivations, from the cistern-wells and the water condensers to the tholos, trulli, and nuraghi which represent the utmost evolution of the round shape and its aggregating potential on the territory.

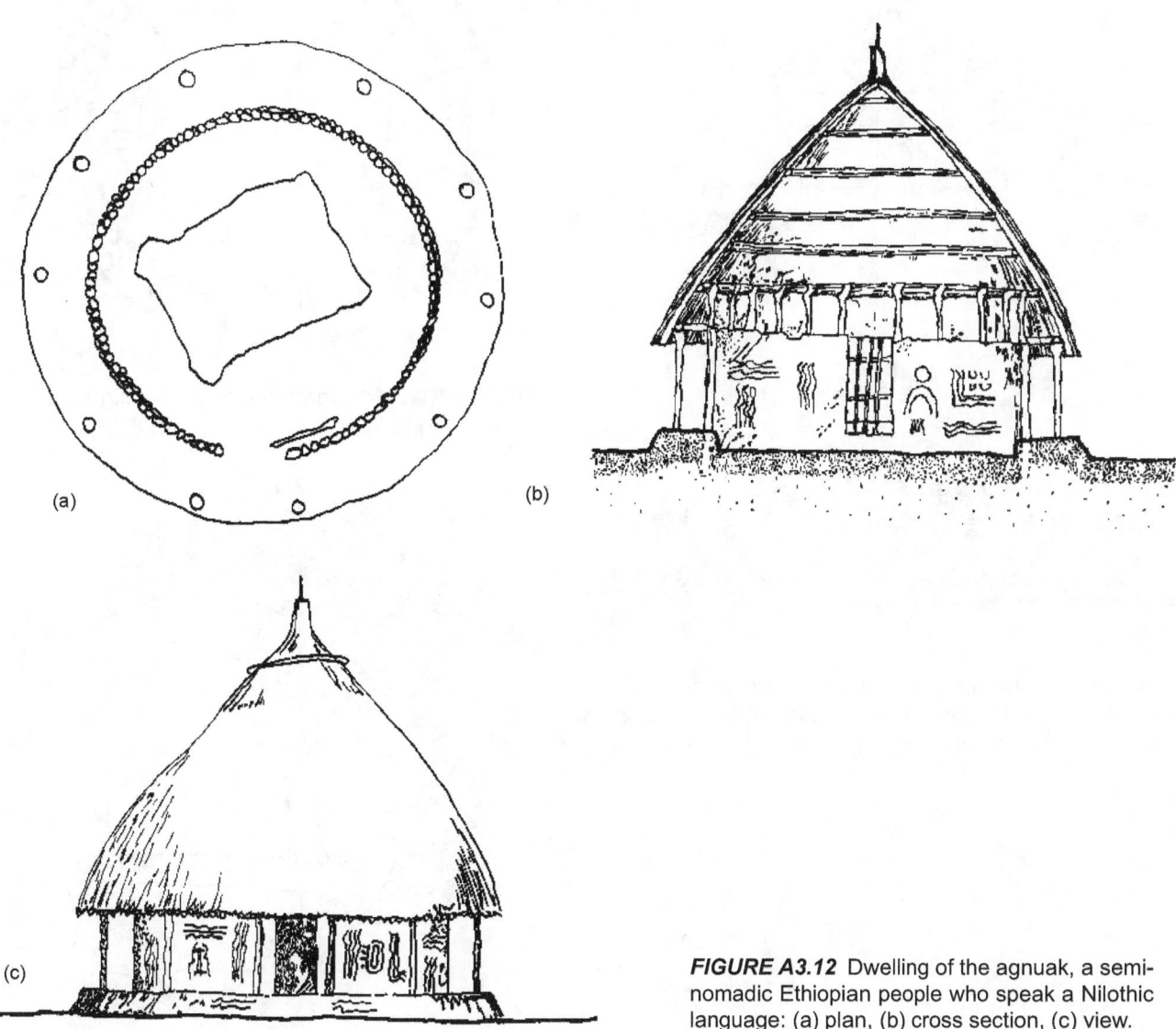

FIGURE A3.12 Dwelling of the agnuak, a semi-nomadic Ethiopian people who speak a Nilothic language: (a) plan, (b) cross section, (c) view.

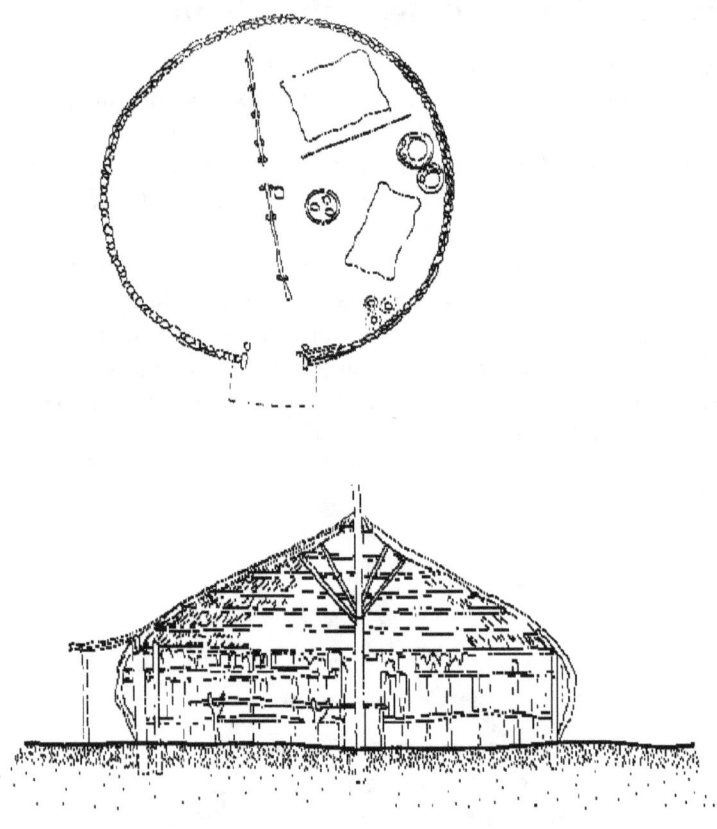

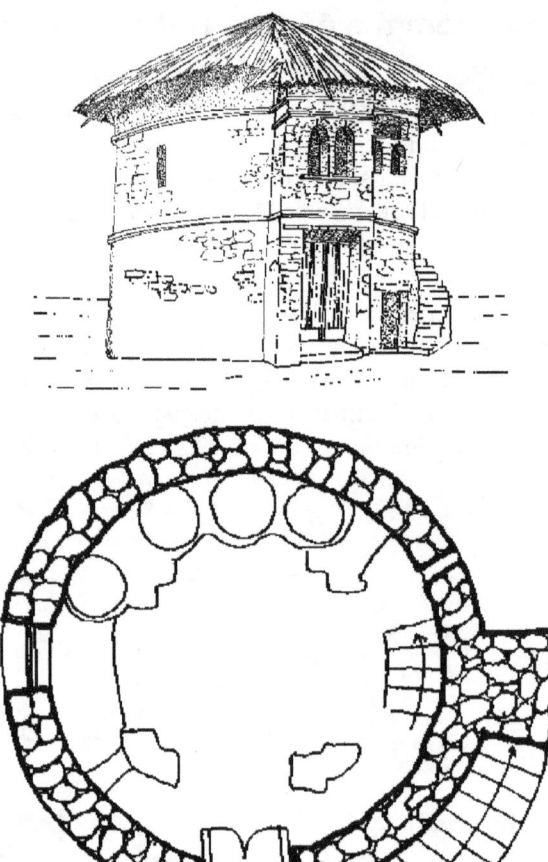

FIGURE A3.14 A double-storey dwelling of Lalibela (Ethiopia) built in masonry: (a) view, (b) plan.

FIGURE A3.13 Dwellings of the dorze and sidama groups of southern Ethiopia made of vegetable fibre: (a) plan, (b) cross section, (c) view.

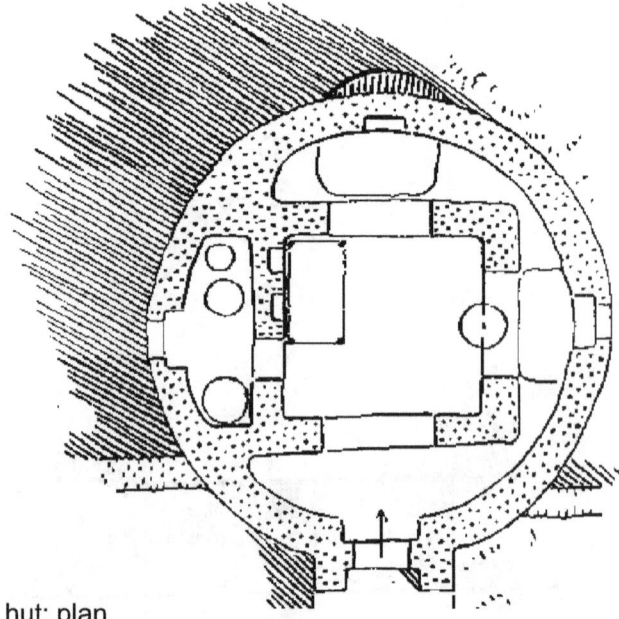

FIGURE A3.15 African hut: plan.

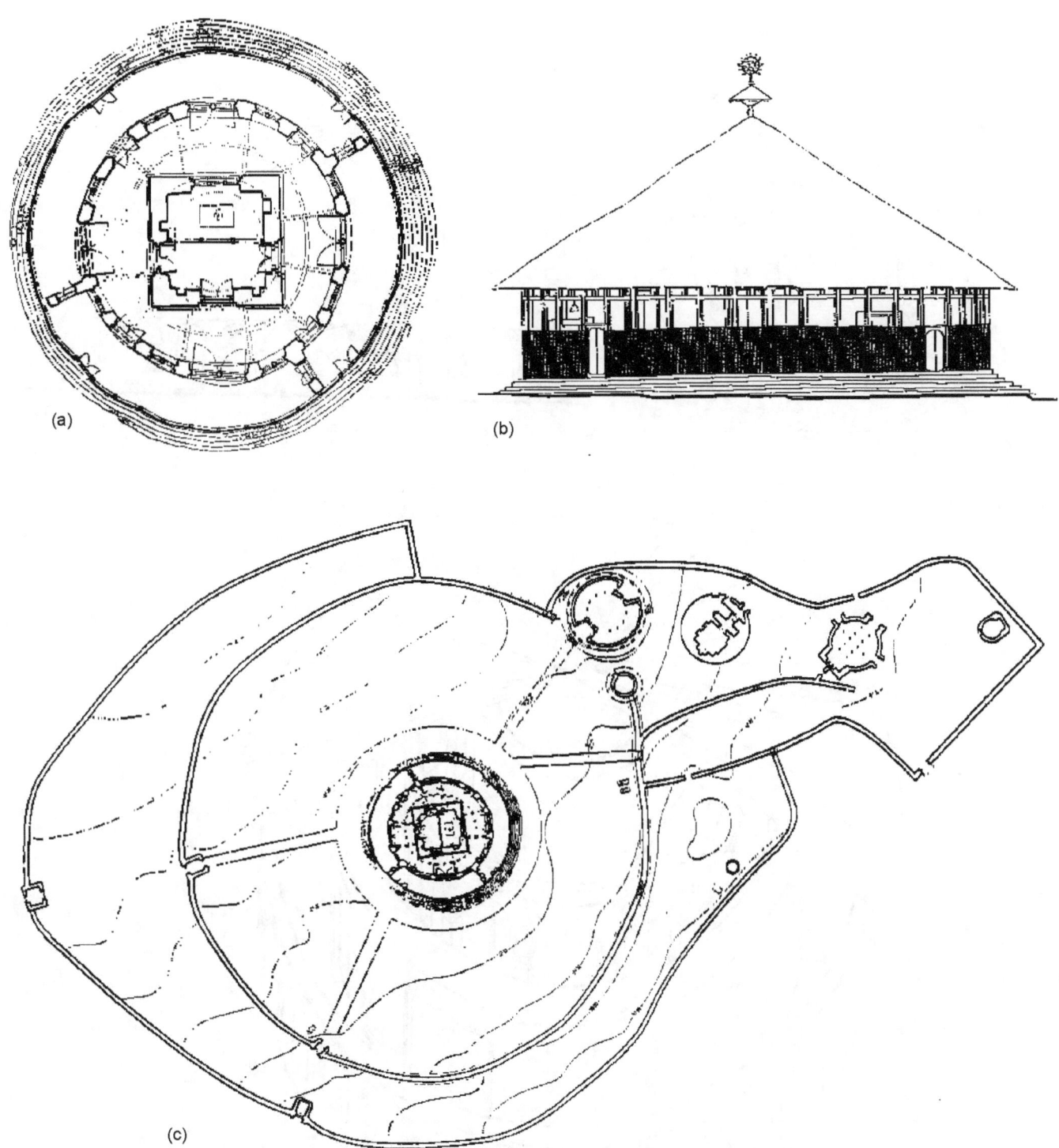

FIGURE A3.16 Church of Ura Kidana Merhat on Lake Tana (Ethiopia), 18th century AD: (a) plan, (b) view, (c) planimetry of the structure [Adapted from a drawing by Di Salvo, 1999].

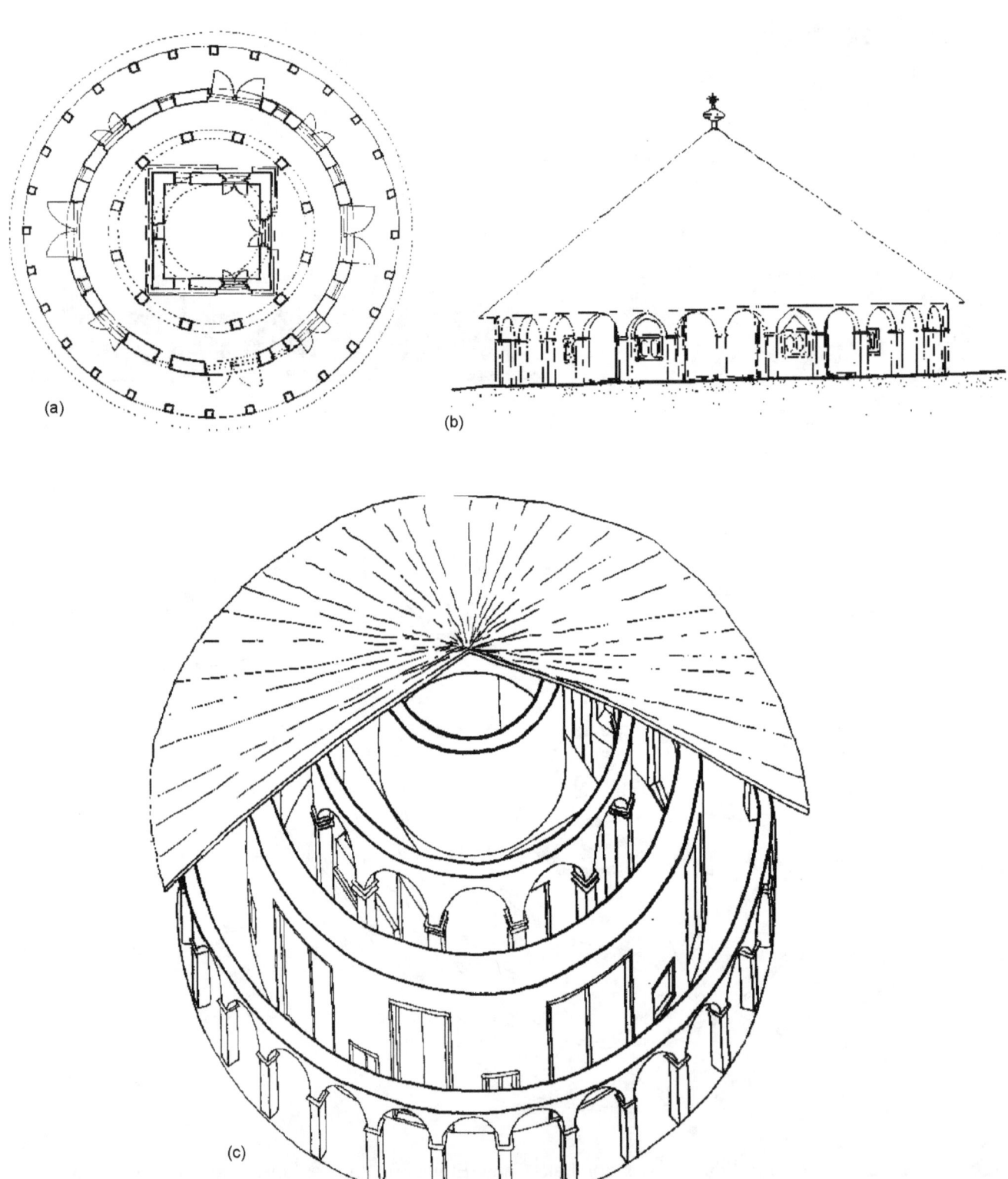

FIGURE A3.17 Church of Kebran Gabriel on Lake Tana (Ethiopia), 17th century AD: (a) plan, (b) view, (c) axonometric view [Adapted from a drawing by Di Salvo, 1999].

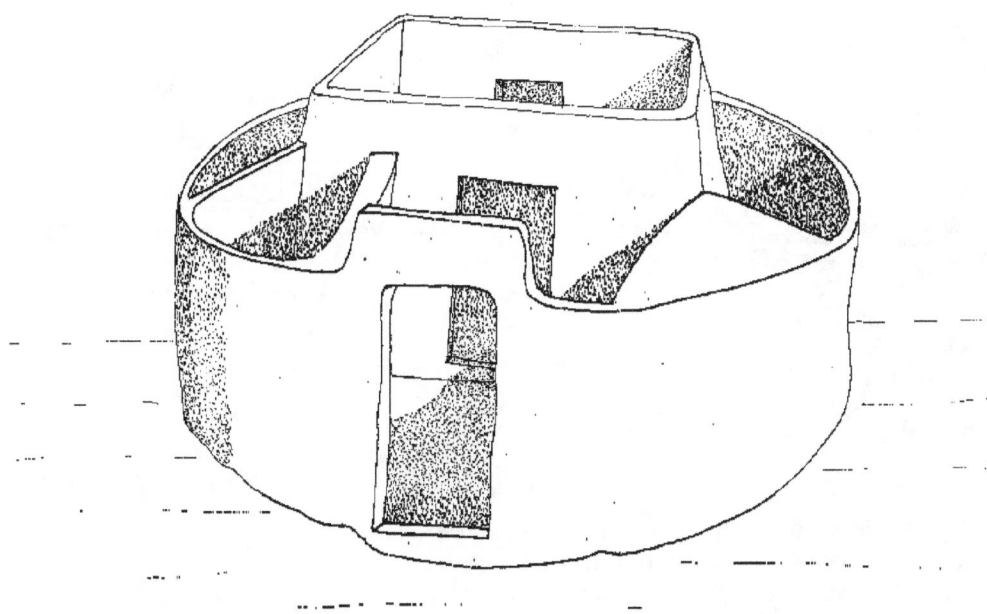

FIGURE A3.18 Circular dwelling of Mari, middle of the 3rd millennium BC. It is subdivided into four groups of two rooms around a square space in the middle, with a horseshoe-shaped fireplace and corner seats.

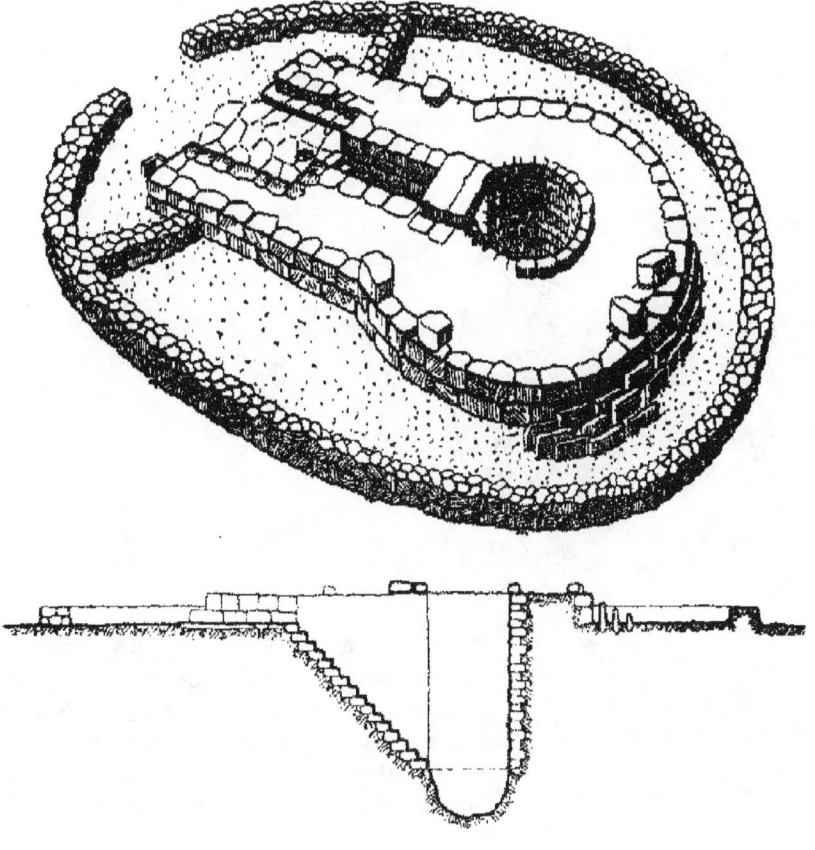

FIGURE A3.19 Enclosure and holy well of the complex of the nuraghi of Santa Cristina (Oristano). The shape of the double circle with a corridor and the stairs carved from the inside, leading down to the water-harvesting hypogeum, is similar to the Murgia Timone complex in Matera (Fig. 4.26) and to the Saharan solar monuments (Figs. 5.15, 5.17–5.18).

Appendices

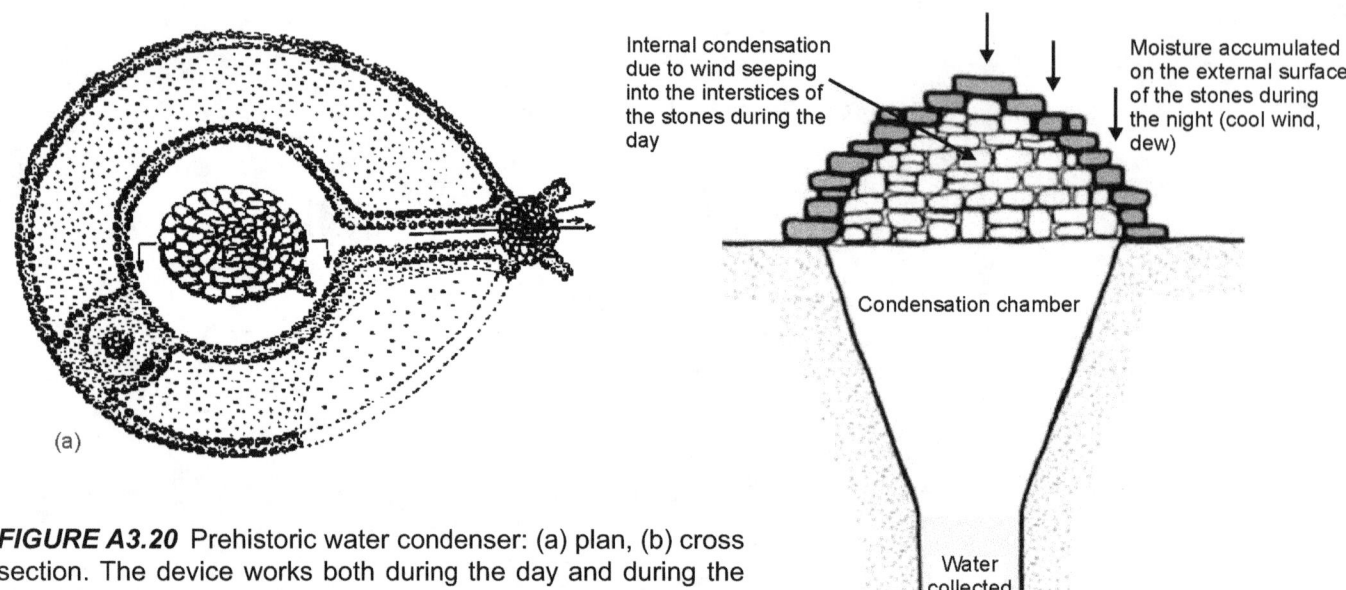

FIGURE A3.20 Prehistoric water condenser: (a) plan, (b) cross section. The device works both during the day and during the night. During the day, the wind seeps into the stones where it finds the internal temperature lower than the outside temperature and the moisture of the wind condenses. During the night the condensation process occurs outside on the surface of the cooler stones.

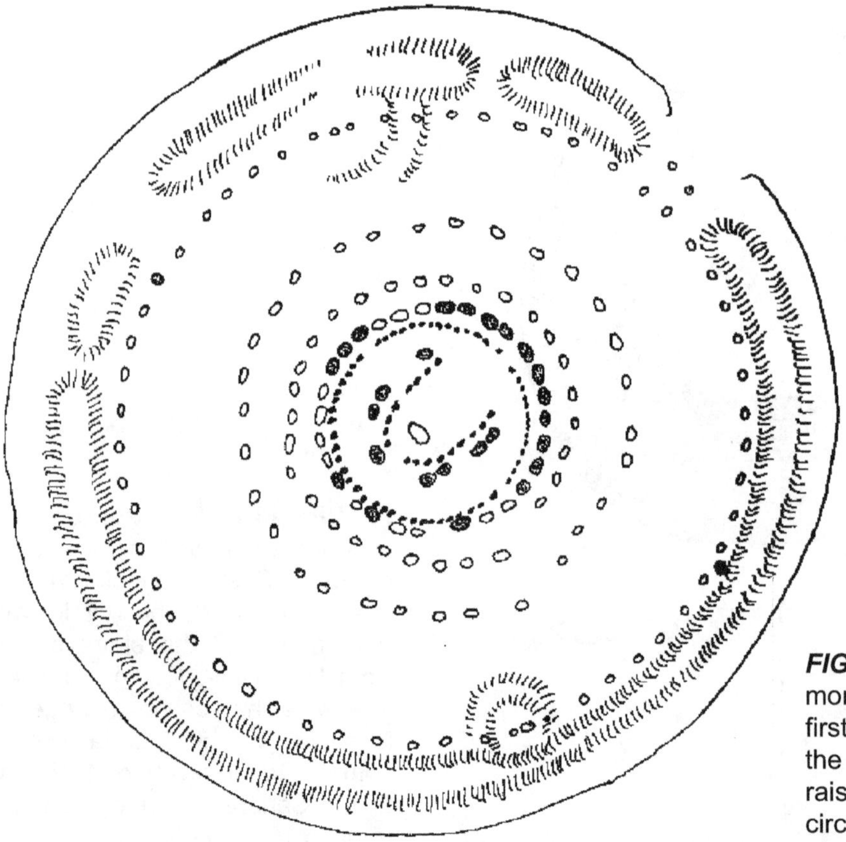

FIGURE A3.21 Plan of the megalithic monument of Stonehenge (England). In the first phase of building around 3000 BC, when the stones in the middle had not yet been raised, the monument already featured the circular ditch with a 93 m diameter.

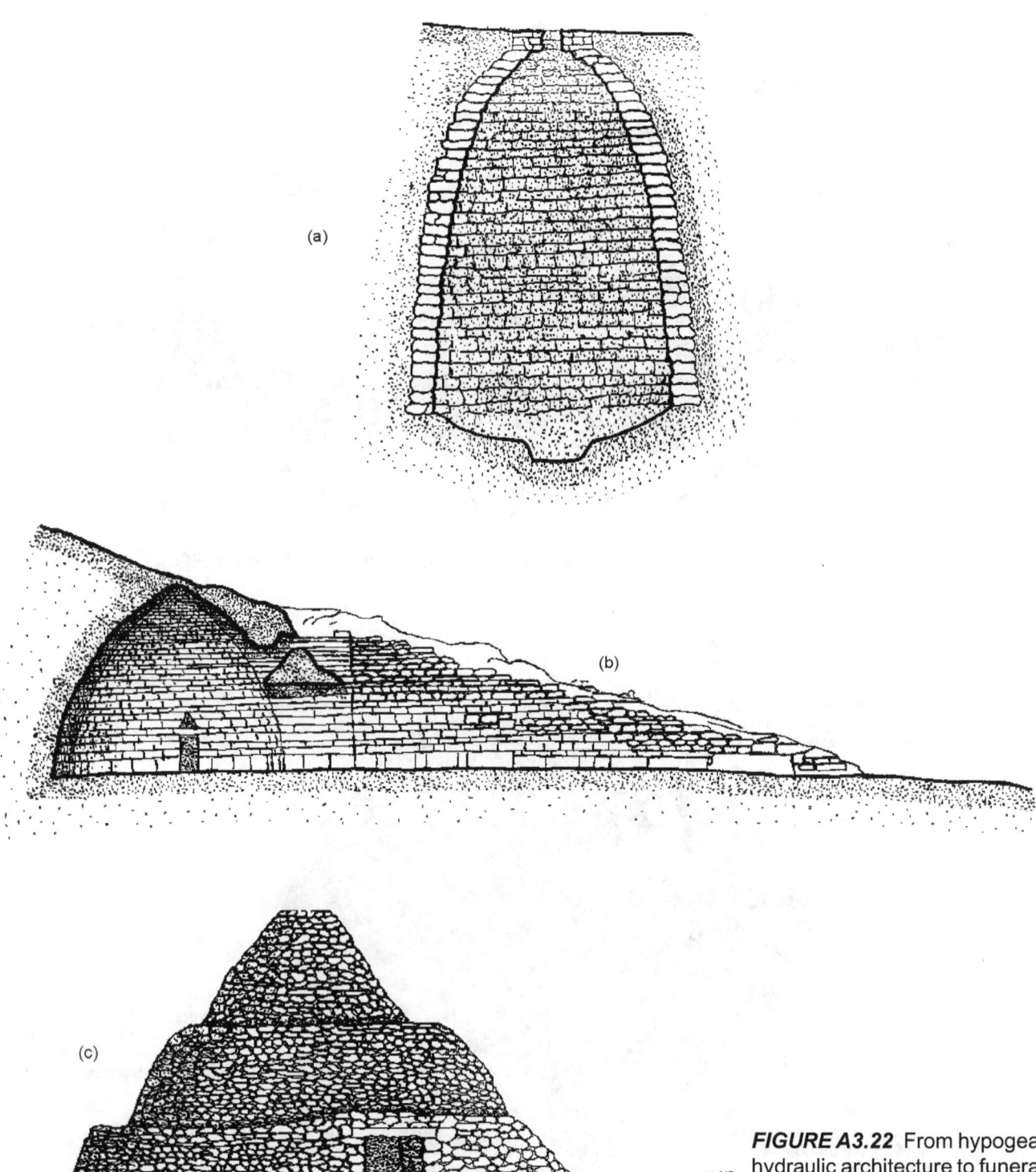

FIGURE A3.22 From hypogeal hydraulic architecture to funeral architecture and the false-dome on the surface: (a) cistern; (b) tholos called the Treasure of Atreus in Mycenae (1500 BC); (c) Apulian trullo.

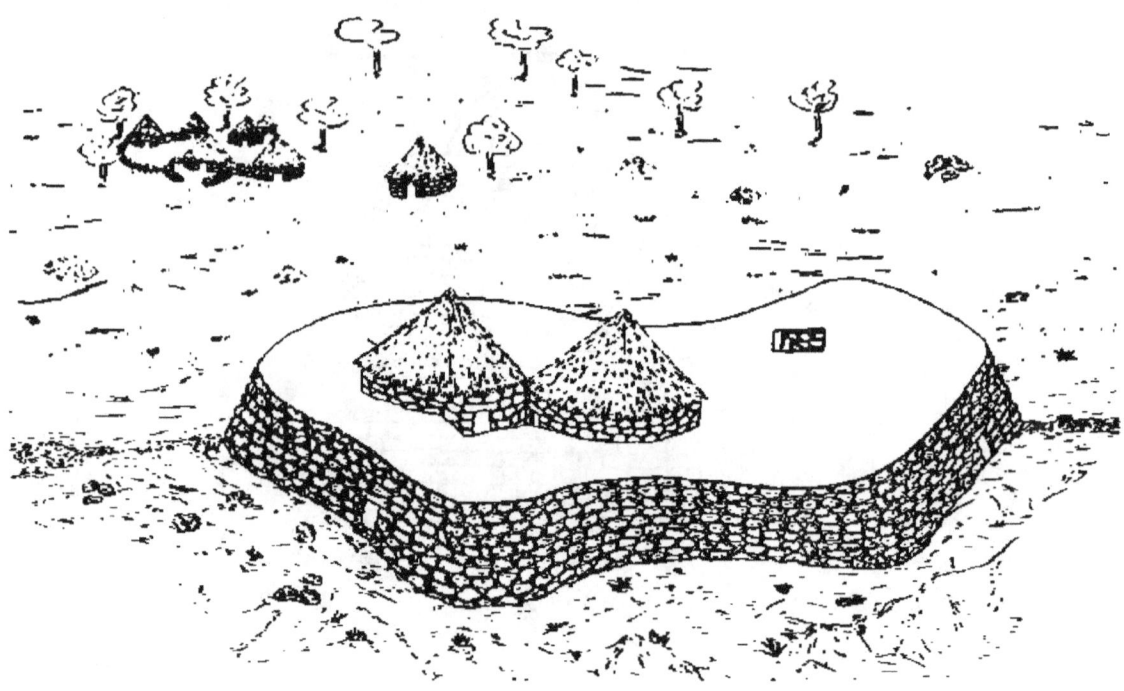

FIGURE A3.23 Reconstruction of a Sardinian nuraghi dated back to the 2nd millennium BC.

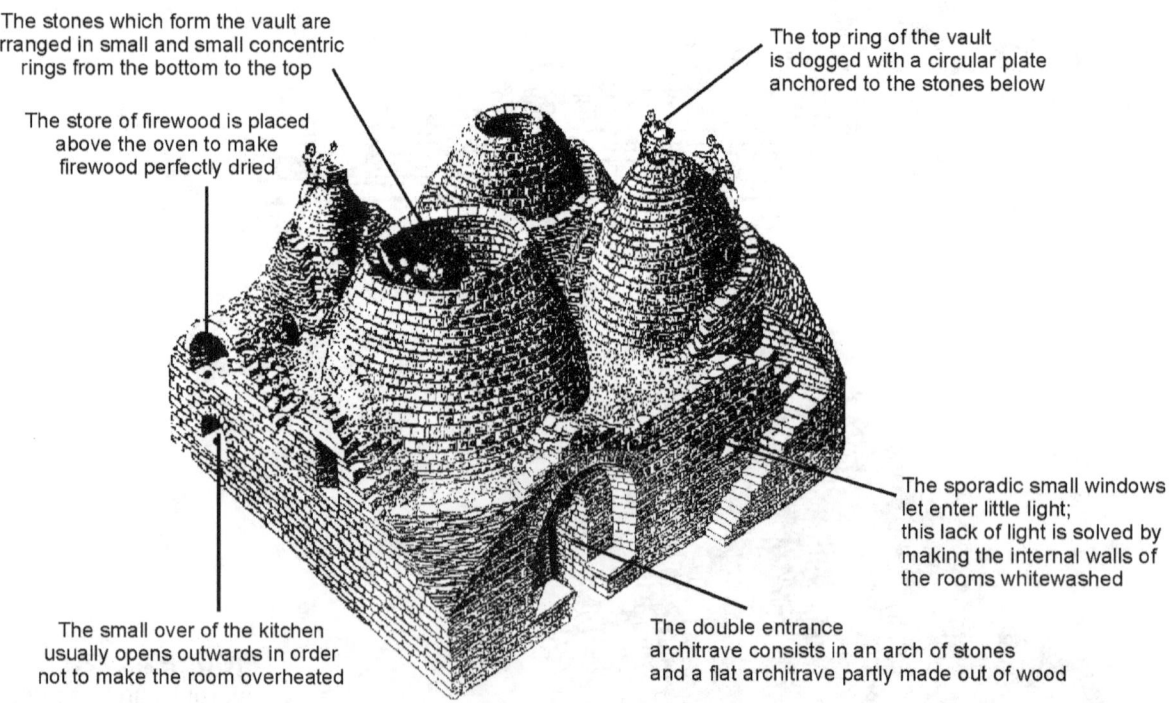

FIGURE A3.24 The town of Alberobello, a UNESCO World Heritage site, has the densest concentration of trulli, creating an urban ecosystem. The layout dates back to the Middle Ages but the building typology originated from the tholos-huts and the dwellings of the ancient Italic people, as can be noticed in the preservation of traditional knowledge as in the pagghiari and the rural buildings.

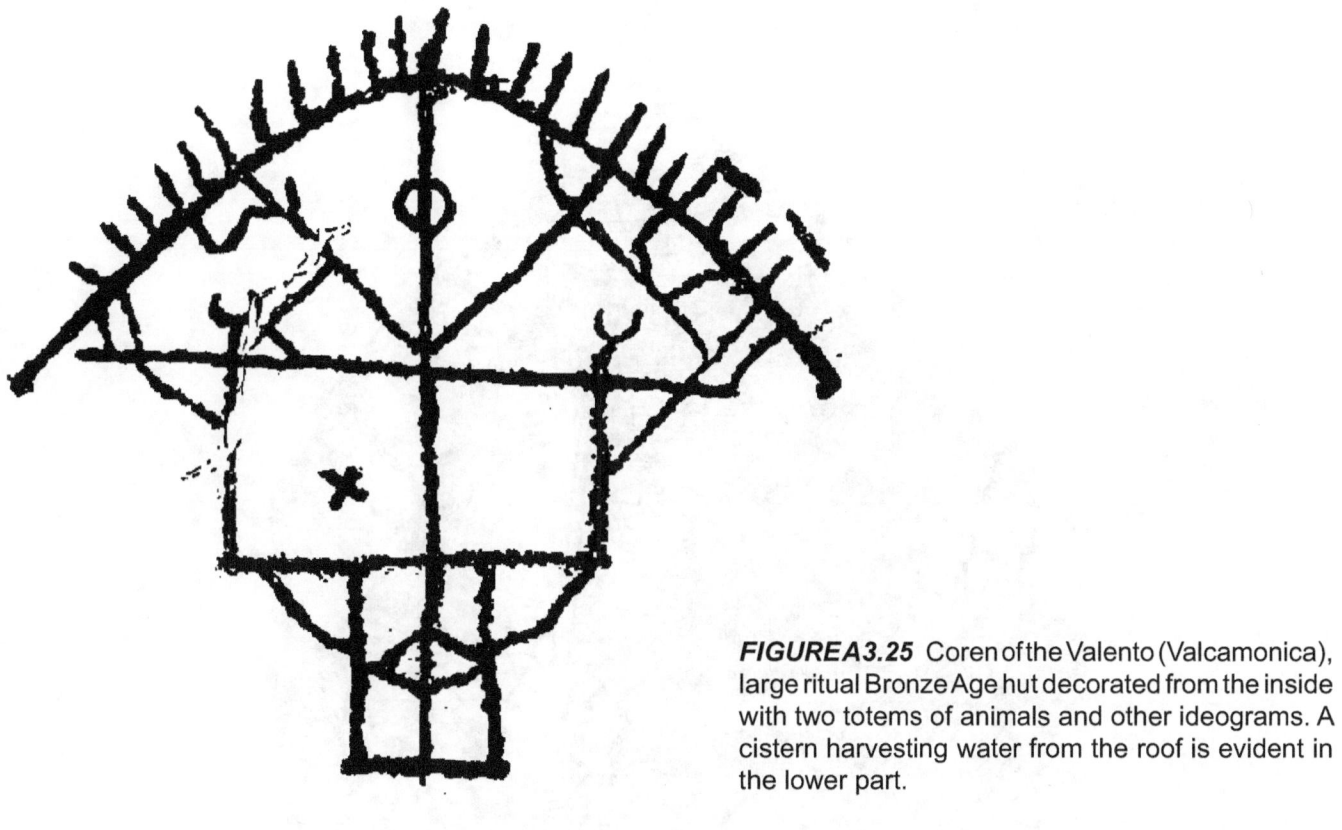

FIGURE A3.25 Coren of the Valento (Valcamonica), large ritual Bronze Age hut decorated from the inside with two totems of animals and other ideograms. A cistern harvesting water from the roof is evident in the lower part.

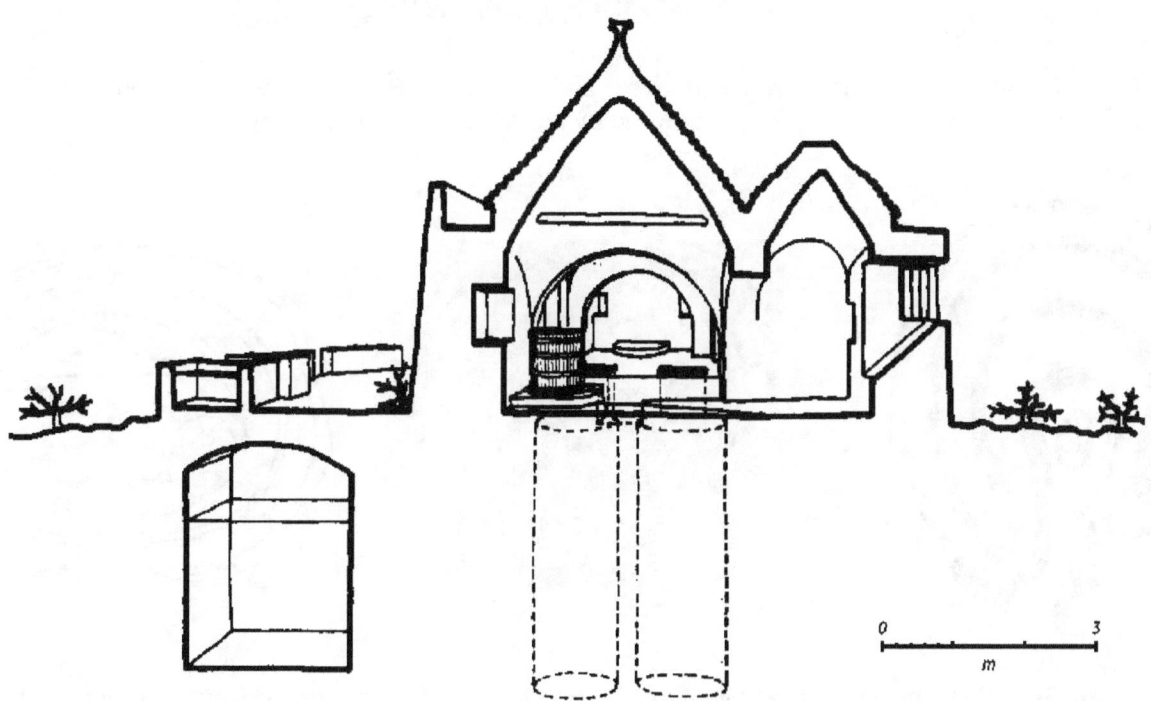

FIGURE A3.26 A trullo in Alberobello with the water-harvesting cistern situated beneath the courtyard.

FIGURE A3.27 Palmavera (Sassari) nuraghi complex, 2nd millennium BC; Ideal reconstruction of the village hut with the furniture found inside [Adapted from a drawing by Moravetti and Tozzi, 1995].

FIGURE A3.28 Sexual symbolism and architecture: (a) prehistoric Saharan graffito which represents the female sex organ; (b) Cretan labyrinth of seven circumvolutions representing a coin from Cnossus (180 degrees rotated); (c) planimetry of a trullo.

A3.3 Models of Urbanization of the Hydroagricultural Morphology

In the inaccessible, karstic and mountain areas or in the slope systems such as those typical of northern Yemen, the agricultural pattern structured by the water systems is the key to understanding the models of urbanization. The agricultural pattern depends on the knowledge accumulated in the arrangement and maintenance of the agropastoral space. The force of gravity used to harvest and channel the water reserves, and the techniques of water intakes, and diversions to irrigate the slopes along the sides of the natural watercourses create the main lines of the built up landscape. Urbanization progresses according to this hydroagricultural pattern by saturating the sloping terraces with constructions or turning the fields in the valleys irrigated by stream-roads into squares surrounded by buildings. The areas subject to periodic floods were reserved for temporary activities such as the weekly or seasonal market which became established over time and became itself a structure of the town, built up by transforming the tilled areas into stone gardens.

FIGURE A3.29 Hydroagricultural morphology before the urbanisation process: (1) systems of descending terraced slopes; (2) plain with fields irrigated by torrent-streets; (3) depression; (4) volcanic craters used as rainwater reservoirs.

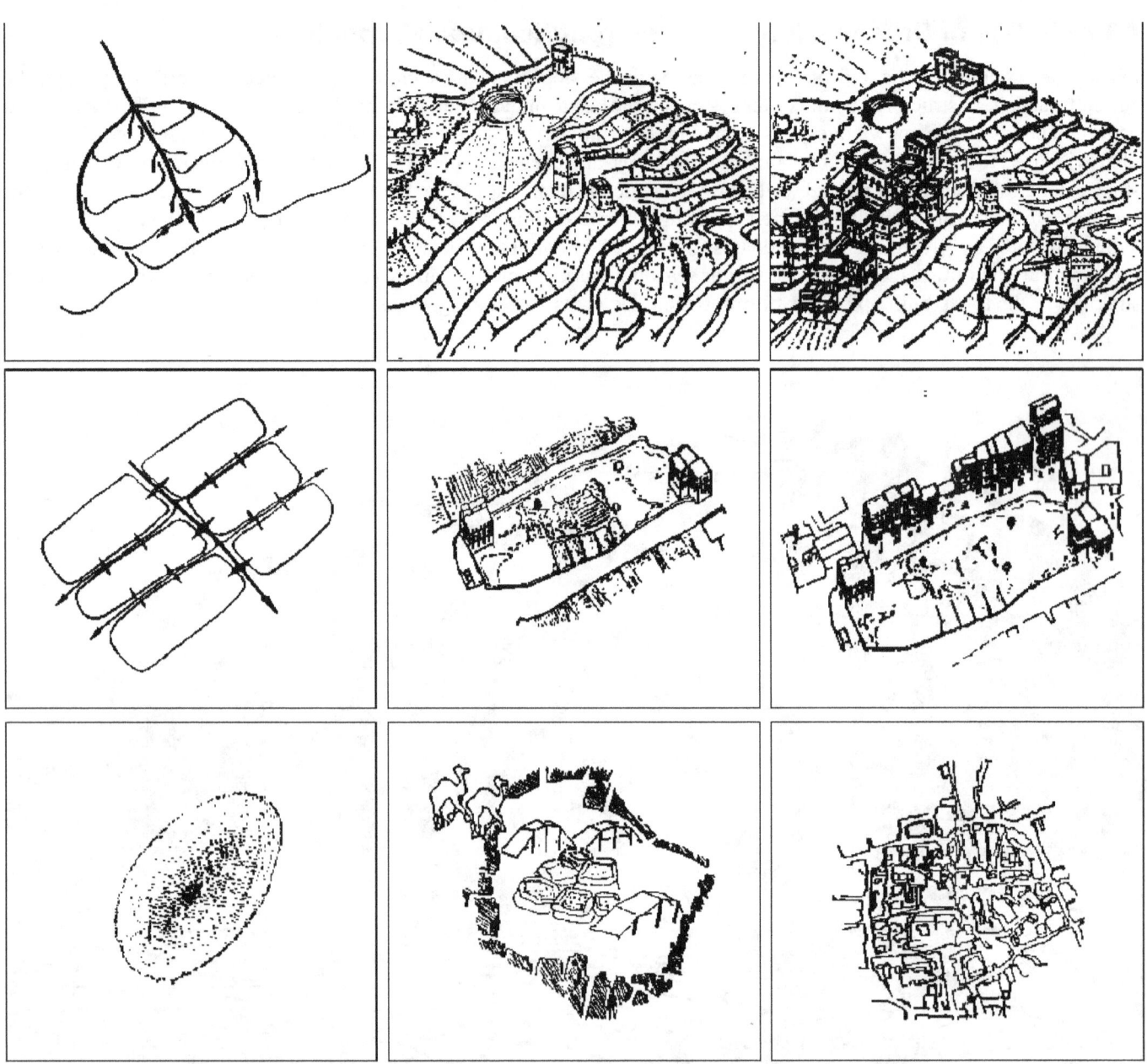

FIGURE A3.30 Evolution of the hydraulic layout into the urban layout: above, urbanisation of the terraced slope; middle, urbanisation of fields on the plain; below, use of a semicircular depression subject to floods as a market area and subsequently as a building area.

A3.4 Urban Settlements Founded on the Organisation of Water

Since the 3rd millennium the human settlements set on fortified hilltops spread over the Middle East, the Mediterranean islands and peninsulas and the coastal promontories of arid areas. Towns, citadels and acropolises had to withstand sieges and find drinking water. The area inside the walls acted as a harvesting surface to feed cisterns in the open air or deeply dug ones which could be reached by means of tunnels and stairs. Water pipes supplied the land under cultivation or any urban developments in the foothills, or in the case of coastal agglomerates, supplied water for harbour activities and for the ships. In the event of a siege, the canals were cut and the defenders, barricaded on the summit, continue producing the water resource denied to their attackers. This is the urban pattern of Troy, celebrated by Homer, the predecessors of which are the Mesopotamian towns, such as Ur, the first town of the Chaldeans and Sumerians, and the organisation of the water devices that can be found in the urban plans of Arad, Jawa, Qana, and Aden.

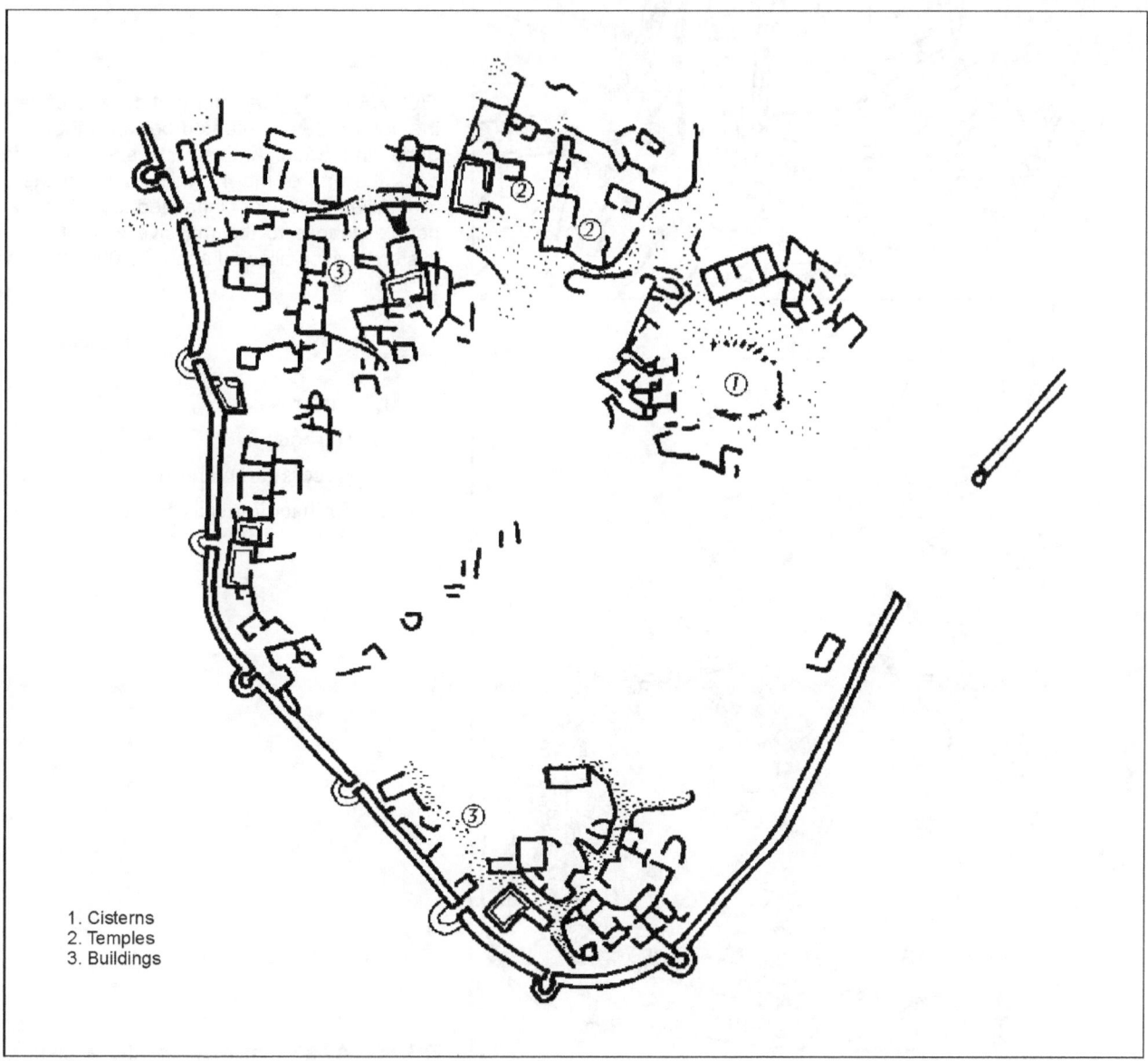

1. Cisterns
2. Temples
3. Buildings

FIGURE A3.31 Planimetry of the site of Arad in the Negev desert. The early Bronze Age settlement is situated on the hollow top of a hill which acts as an impluvium to collect water for the cisterns surrounded by the built-up area.

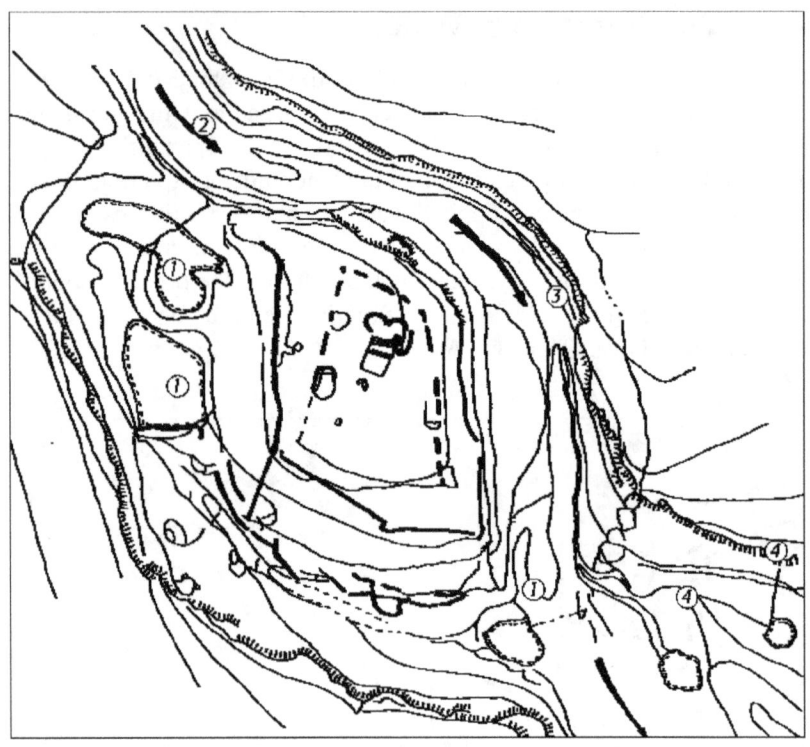

1. Big cisterns filled with rainwater
2. Wadi Rajil
3. Flood diversion intake
4. Cisterns supplied with floodwater

FIGURE A3.32 Planimetry of the site of Jawa in the Jordan desert situated between the south of Syria and Saudi Arabia. The settlement dating back the end of the 4th millennium or the early 3rd millennium was inhabited by about 2,000 people, thanks to the massive water-harvesting systems which allowed about 50,000 m3 of water to be stored.

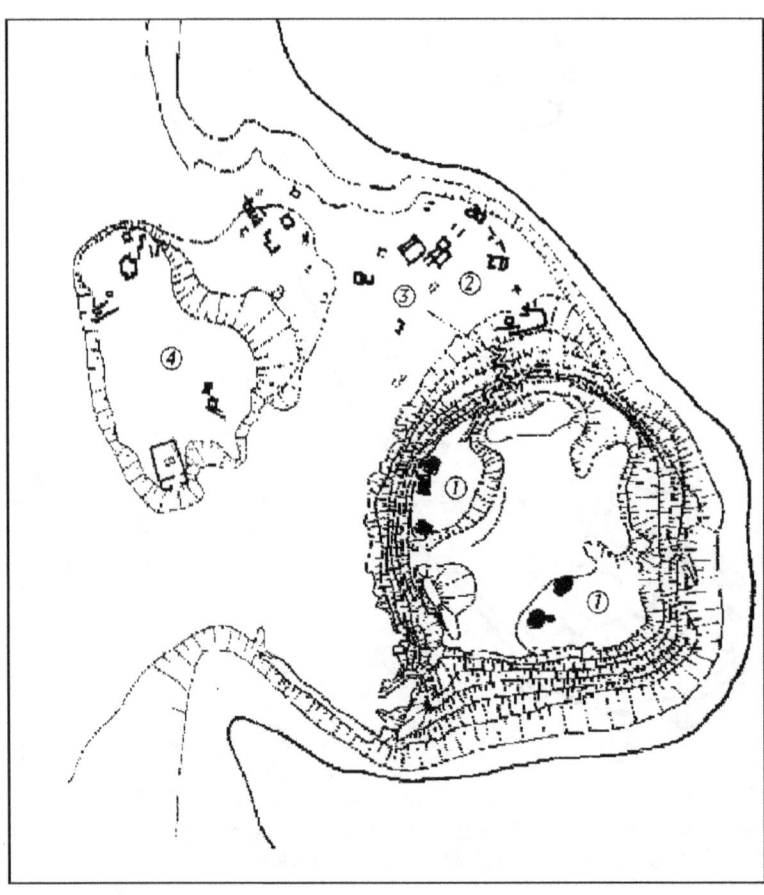

1. Cisterns
2. Harbour
3. Access ramp and run-off
4. Archaeological vestiges

FIGURE A3.33 Planimetry of the ancient Qana (Yemen). The archaeological vestiges along the coast are surmounted by a high cliff equipped with rainwater-harvesting cisterns.

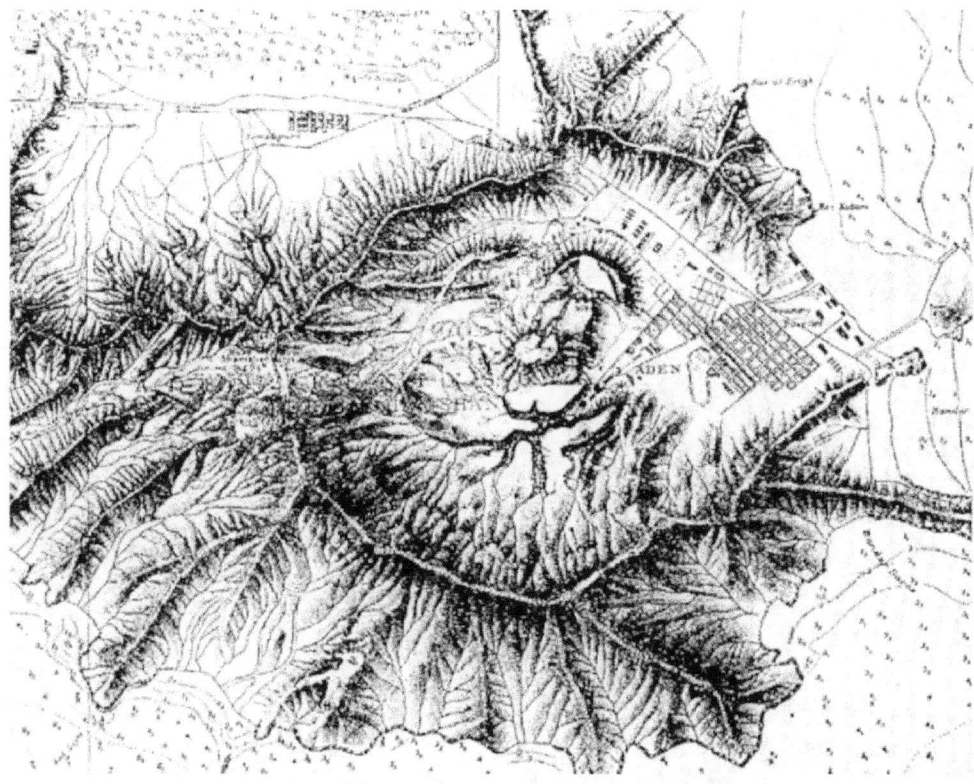

FIGURE A3.34 Aden (Yemen), situated at the outlet of the crater. Water harvested in the volcanic cone was put in storage in a series of deep cisterns in order to be sold to the ships bound for India.

APPENDIX 4: OASES

The domestication of the date palm, foenix dactilifera, is a precondition for the establishment of desert oases. From the principal Neolithic centres, palm groves spread out across the Sahara and the other deserts, with the development of knowledge capable of creating the oasis effect: determining autopoietic cycles of water production and the management of resources. These techniques also spread to the northern Mediterranean and to the southern edges of the desert, in places in which the date palm does not reach maturity. In these situations other plants – such as the olive in the Mediterranean and the papaia in the Sahel and in southern Arabia – are used in association with horticulture to provide a widely used commodity and to ensure maintenance of the soil and provision of shade. An extended oasis model is created in terms of its capacity to create the conditions for living in difficult and hostile environments, thanks to the use of hydroagricultural knowledge.

A4.1 Creating Fertility in An Arid Environment

In deserts and arid zones, knowledge of water management techniques is used to preserve soil humidity and to collect underground water. Since evaporation is considerable, any water stored above ground would be quickly lost. So the properties that sediments have of creating a barrier against high temperatures are exploited, safeguarding the floodwater or occult precipitation reserves and the capacity of the hypogea to absorb and condense capillary humidity. A series of devices have been created on the basis of these principles, from the underground barrier technique to the creation of oases by organising depressions protected by artificial dunes or based on drainage tunnels (foggara, qanat, madjirat, kariz). The latter are conventionally held to be of Iranian origin, but the difference in their functioning from the Saharan ones allows us to suppose that they originated autonomously in this area. In this regard they are remarkably similar to the Egyptian hypogea in the Valley of Kings, which like the foggara were built right along the wadi courses.

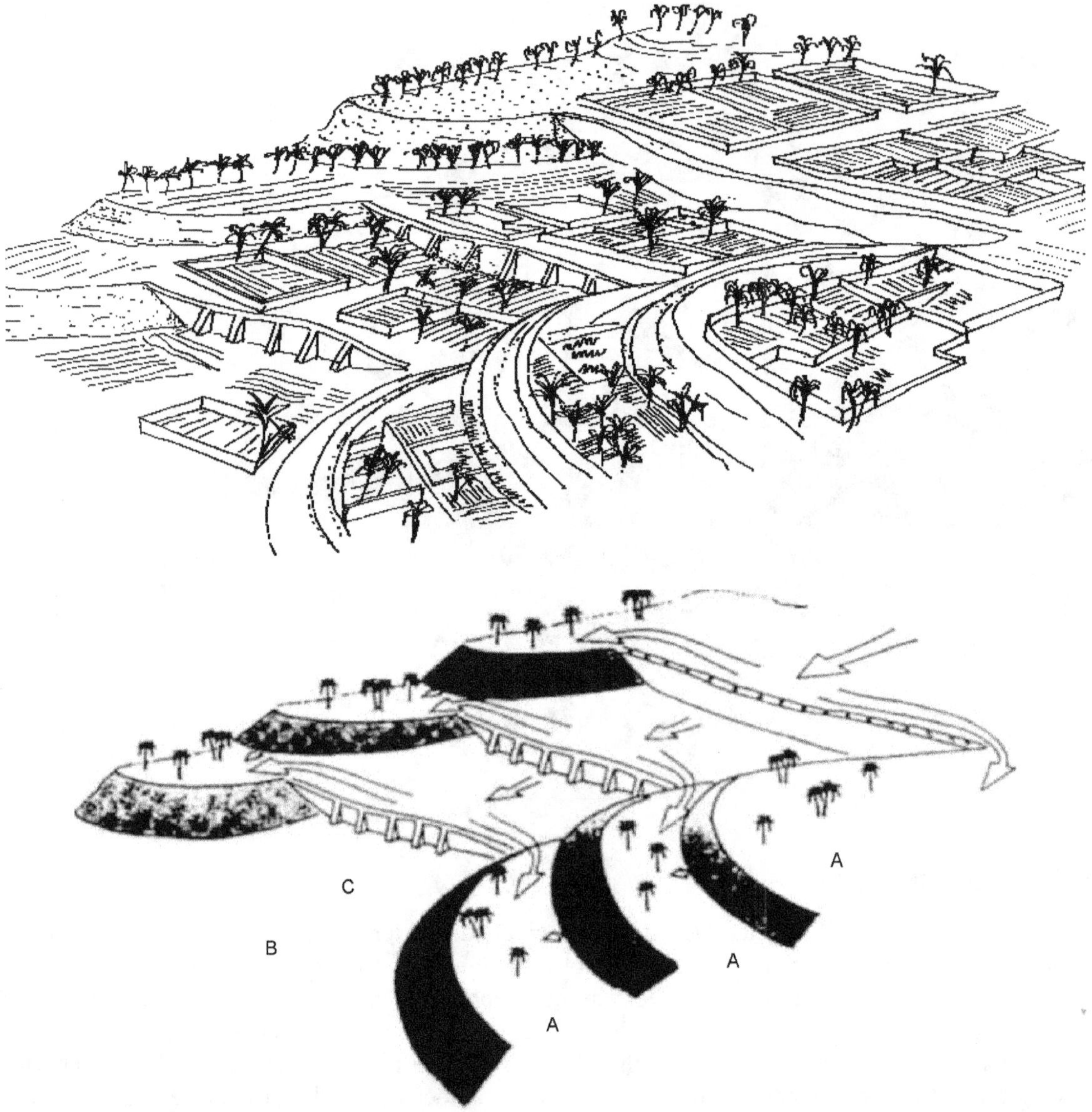

FIGURE A4.1 Along the upper course of wadi Saoura (Algeria), the dams stop the underground flow and produce surface water for the crops planted along both sides of the riverbed. When floods occur and form water courses flowing on the ground, the latter are conveyed to the lateral terraces (A) in order to allow irrigation by gravity at a higher level than the natural run-off (B). In periods of aridity, humidity is retained in the subsoil and water is drawn up from an outlet situated at the foot of the dams (C).

FIGURE A4.2 Erg oases situated in artificial sandy craters (bur) typical of the Algerian Souf region. The dunes protect the oases at the perimeter, and the palm trees, which directly soak up water from the subsoil, create a microclimate suitable for horticulture.

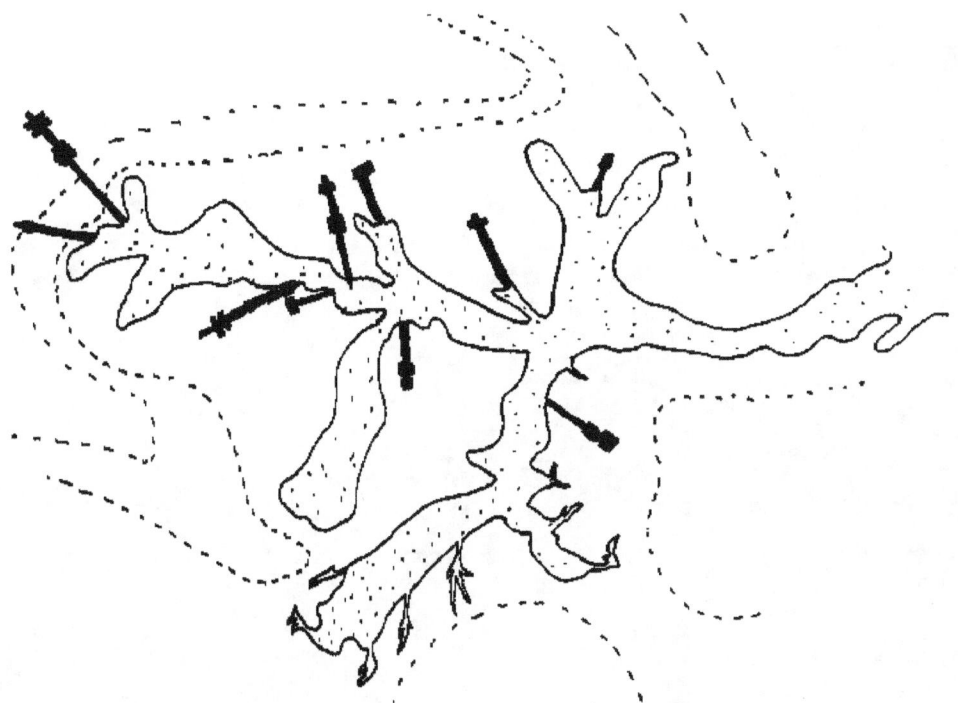

FIGURE A4.3 Thebes (Valley of the Kings). Topographic plan of the "hypogeums in the wadi" that Pharaoh Thutmosis I had dug out in the middle of the 2nd millennium BC.

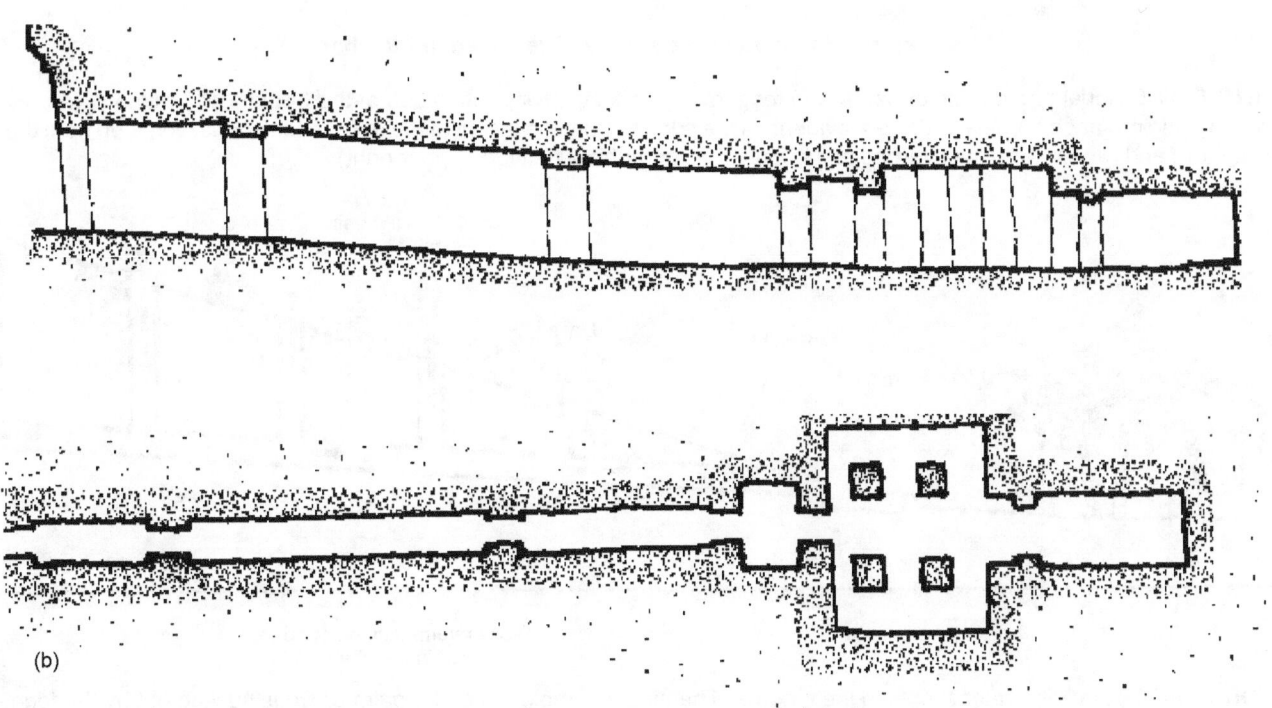

FIGURE A4.4 Thebes (Valley of the Kings). The plan of a hypogeum: (a) cross section, (b) plan.

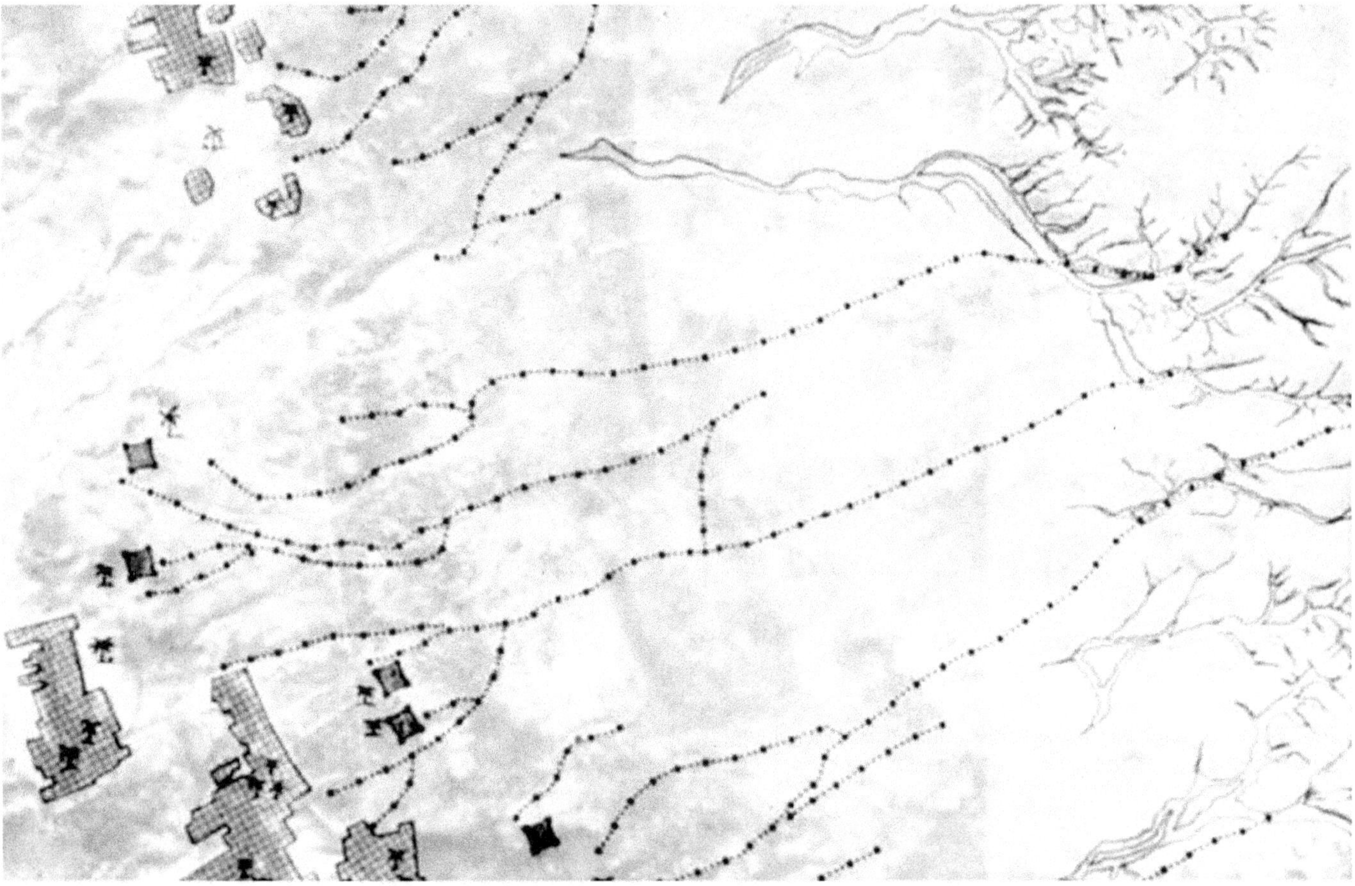

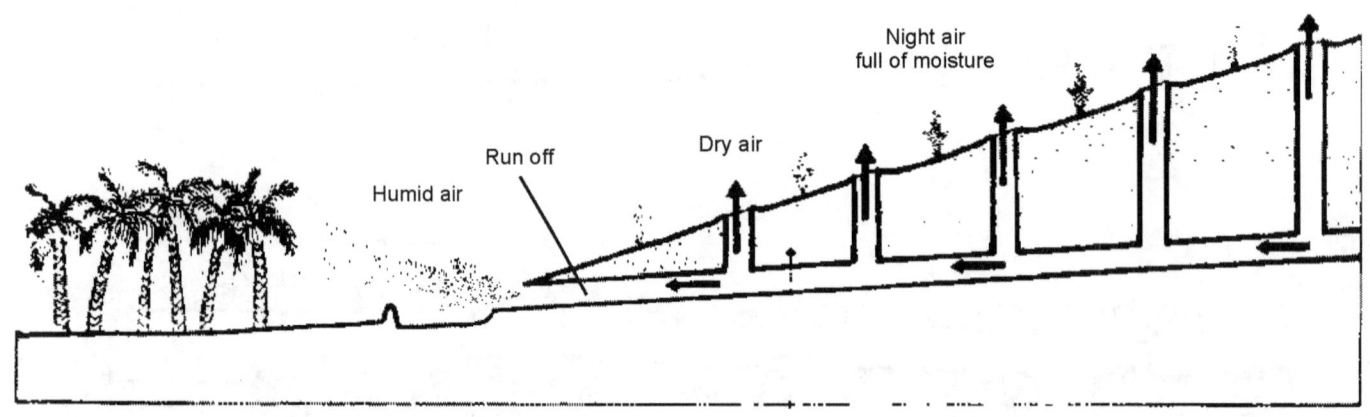

Humidity retained in the sand and released in the channel

FIGURE A4.5 Aerial photograph of part of the foggara network supplying the oases of the Sebkha of Timimoun (Algeria). The underground drainage tunnels, which are evident on the surface from the layout of the excavation shafts, come up from the oases (lower left) and run towards the riverbed of the fossil hydrographical network (upper right).

Humidity retained in the sand
and released in the channel

FIGURE A4.6 Humidity water supply to the foggara. The air full of moisture of the palm grove is sucked out by the foggara in the opposite direction to the water run-off; it condenses in the tunnel and comes out of the shafts as dry air. During the night the temperature decreases and determines a further moisture condensation on the soil surface that is absorbed by the shafts and the tunnel.

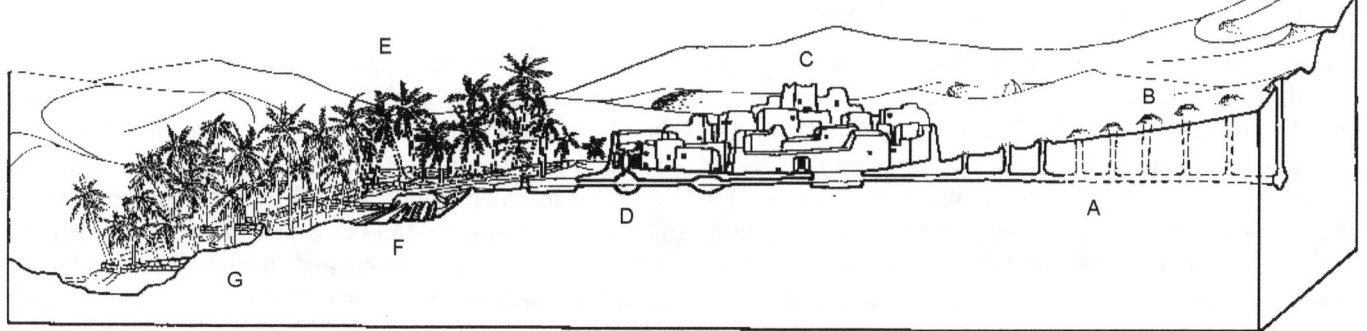

FIGURE A4.7 Structure of the oasis. Water produced in the underground tunnel of the foggara (A), which is visible thanks to the excavation shafts on the surface (B), runs beneath the adobe habitat (C) and gathers further along in decantation tanks (D), useful for drinking water, ablutions and for cooling the dwellings. Once conveyed in open-air channels by means of the kesria (F), which serve to measure and distribute the water flow, water irrigates the palm groove (E) subdivided into tilled parcels by low mud walls (G).

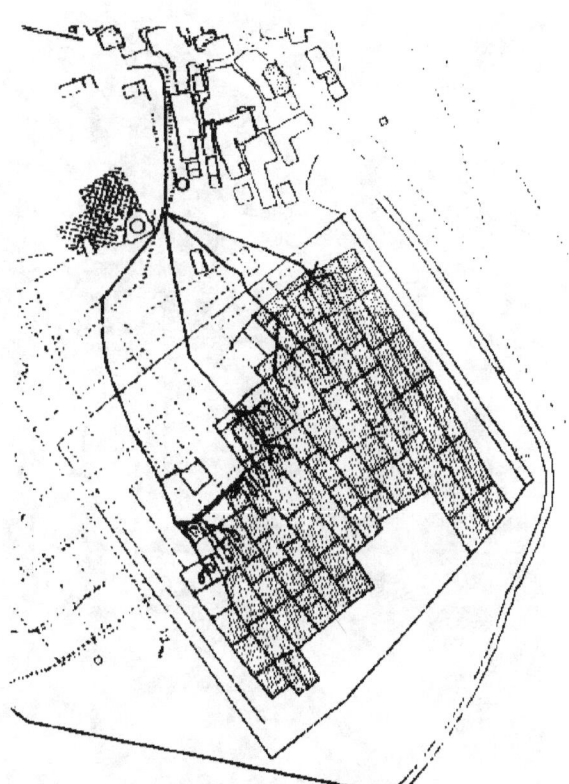

FIGURE A4.8 The foggara network of an Algerian Saharan oasis.

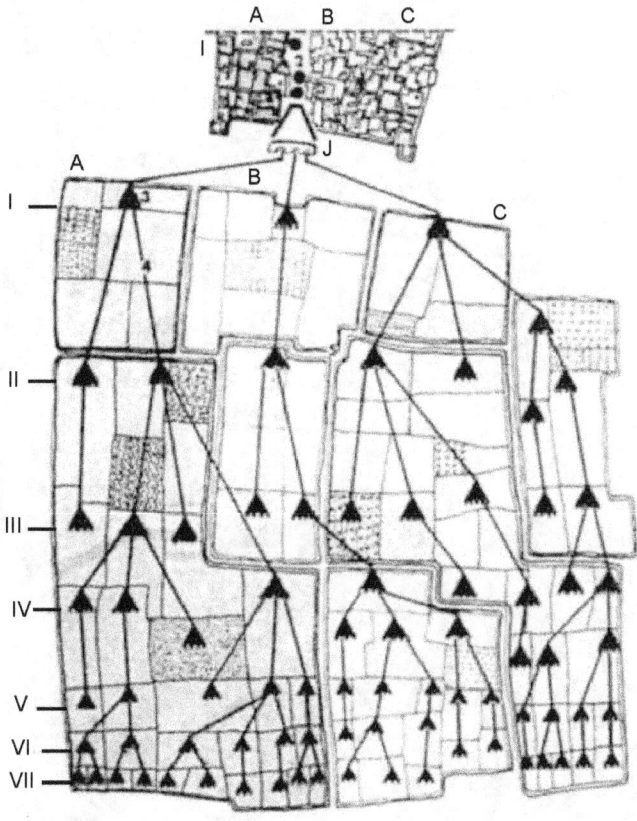

FIGURE A4.9 Graphical representation of the water distribution in the oasis. The three families (A, B, C) in the village (1) shared the water supply of the foggara (2) by means of the kesria (3). As time went by, water was distributed to the generations (I–VII) by creating an intricate layout of channels, water-sharing devices, and tilled parcels.

A4.2 Systems for Organising Water

When there are particular geographic conditions, specific water technologies form the basis of the entire landscape organisation. This is the case of the high mountains in the Valais region in Switzerland. Here the winds sweep the slopes after having released all their humidity in the ascending phase along the opposite slopes, and in areas that should be humid at this latitude, they give rise to piedmont deserts, chasing away the clouds, creating high pressures and arid conditions. The fields would not look green and fertile if they were not irrigated by the bisse, which draw water from the glaciers or from the head-waters of streams and carry it through the mountain ridges and down the arid valleys, creating settlements, pastures, and crop fields at the bottom. The same practice, called ru, is present in Valle d'Aosta. Under different geomorphologic conditions, the water system known as feixe is used on the island of Ibiza to control alternating situations of excess water and of aridity. Marsh water is drained into a network of channels and then conveyed along porous pipes beneath the fields. Thus the crops can tap the water they need directly through their roots, by means of the feixe system that regulates winter excesses and saves water during summer droughts.

FIGURES A4.10–14 The technique of the bisse consists of carrying water from the glaciers to the valleys of the region of Sion (Switzerland). Figure A4.10 shows suspended wooden ramps for channelling water along the edge of the mountains.

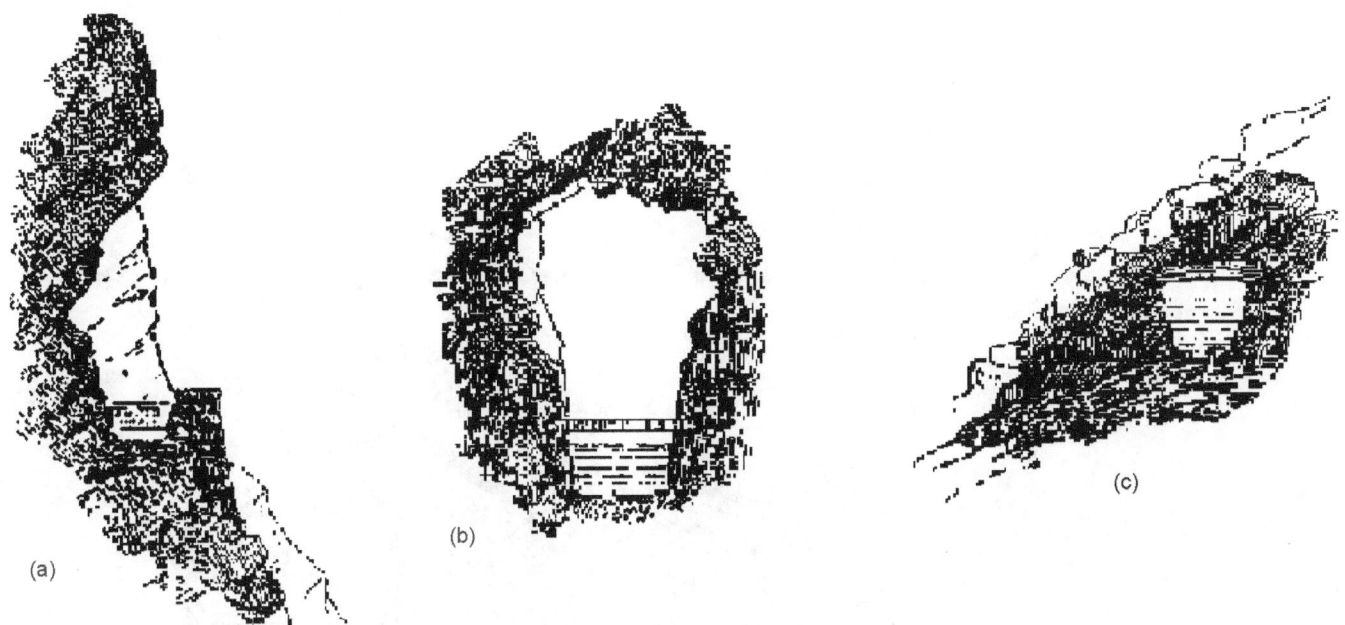

FIGURE A4.11 (a) Rock channel, (b) practicable tunnel, (c) underground channel.

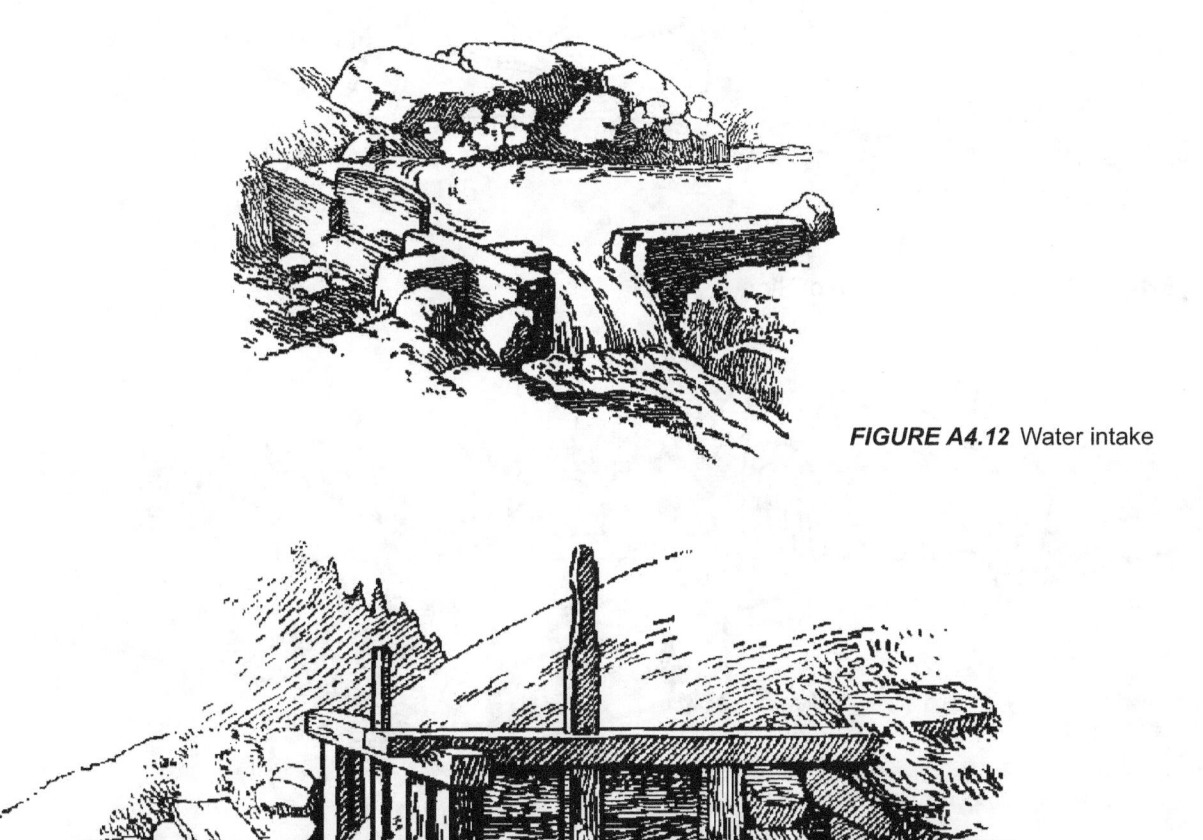

FIGURE A4.12 Water intake

FIGURE A4.13 Sluice

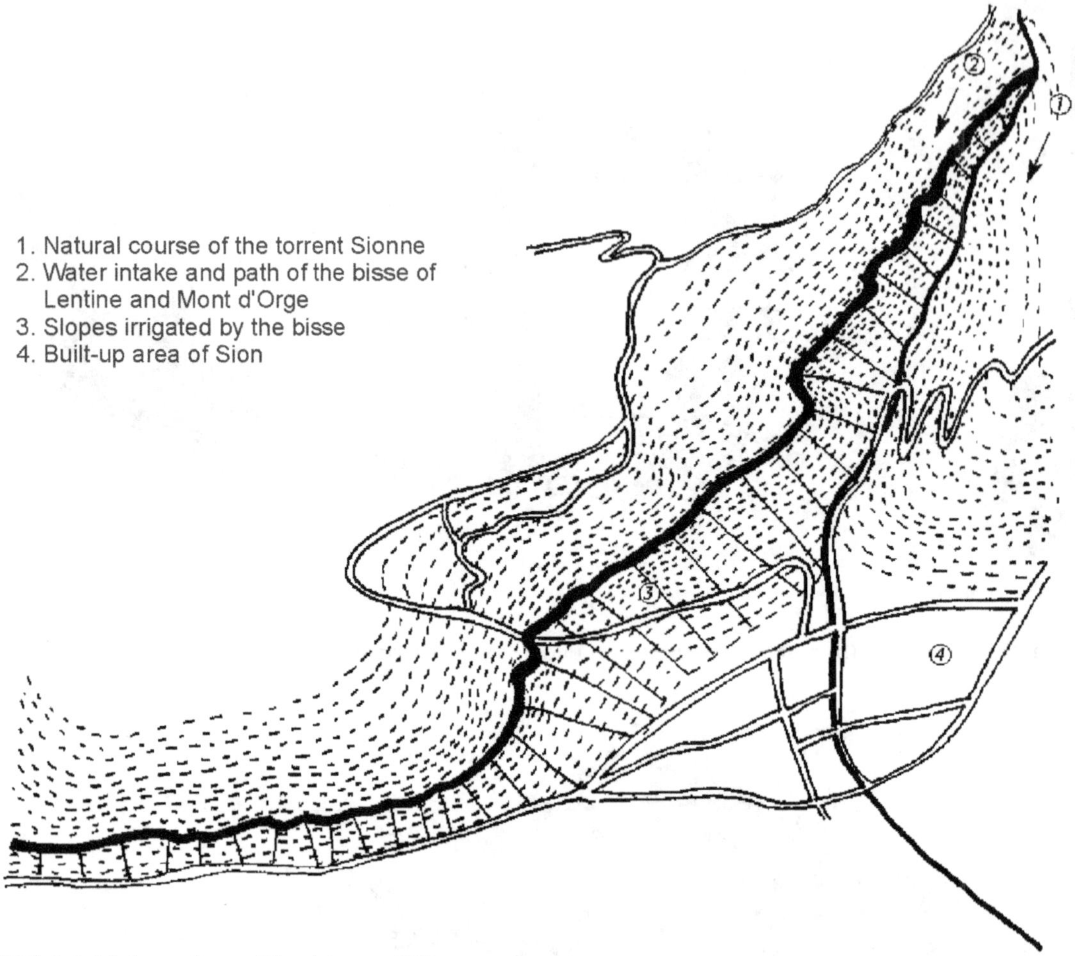

1. Natural course of the torrent Sionne
2. Water intake and path of the bisse of Lentine and Mont d'Orge
3. Slopes irrigated by the bisse
4. Built-up area of Sion

FIGURE A4.14 Location of the bisse of Sion.

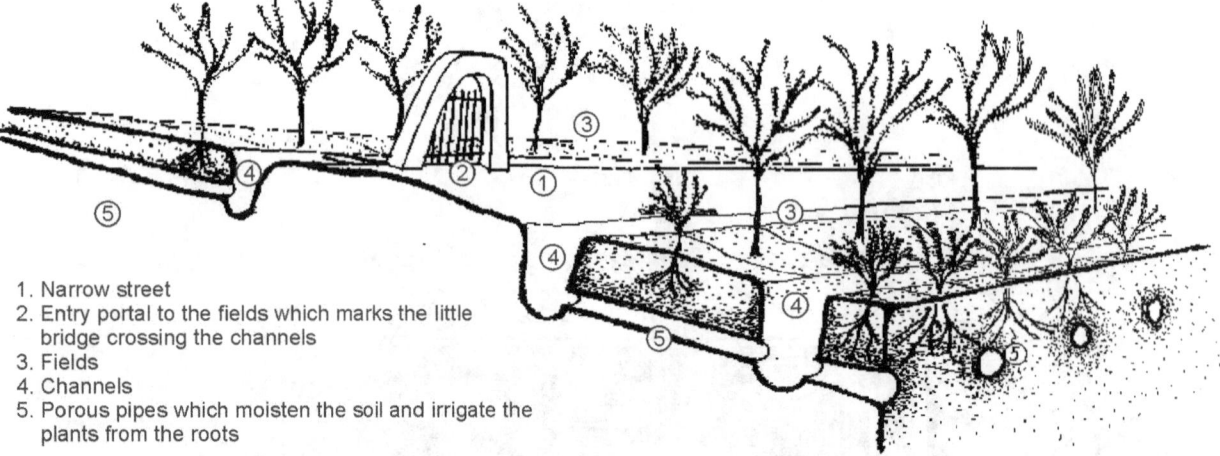

1. Narrow street
2. Entry portal to the fields which marks the little bridge crossing the channels
3. Fields
4. Channels
5. Porous pipes which moisten the soil and irrigate the plants from the roots

FIGURE A4.15 Ibiza (Spain). Feixe, system of intensive cultivation in marshy or arid environments, based on a particular hydraulic organisation. [p. 210]

APPENDIX 5: URBAN ECOSYSTEMS

The urban ecosystem is the sum of local knowledge accumulated and stabilised in a dimension that is no longer that of a village but of a town. Irrigated areas are created utilising geomorphologically favourable situations in specific geographic systems. A capital dominates each unit of landscape: isolated basins in the middle of a desert; great plains among mountain peaks; strips of oases along watercourses; crossroads of far-reaching, international or intercontinental routes. Even small habitat systems, fully exploiting the available resources, become the historical towns of regional importance and with urban characteristics. A variety of situations will be encountered in different geographical areas: adobe city oases, such as in the Sahara or the Yemen, use the inhabitants' organic waste to fertilise the sterile sands and make them suitable for audacious architectural exploits. Stone oases, carved since prehistory in the south of Italy and the Middle East, are capable of condensing the necessary water in the caves and dry stone constructions. Religious oases, carved out of the eroded valleys of Cappadocia, Palestine, the Thebaid and Ethiopia or installed along the silk road as far as China, are organised as walled hermitages and gardens, irrigated by means of drainage tunnels, cisterns, and channels. Sea oases, disseminated over the arid islands of the Mediterranean and the Red Sea, are supplied by air sources.

A5.1 The Hypogeal System

There are such a wide variety of hypogeal techniques developed for reasons of climate, water collection, passive, sepulchral and monumental architecture, that they constitute a system that can be classified according to the morphological matrix on which the excavation is made. Rocky wall hypogea are those that exploit an existing slope to make a horizontal excavation in it. Residential complexes, tombs, and monuments are organised using this technique: from simple shelters under the rock to the complexes with several storeys above one another in Matera and Cappadocia, and the monumental façades of Petra and Abu Simbel. A particular variant of this type is the architecture of the hypogea, formed of constructions built inside the caves. Pit hypogea are excavated vertically in the flat surface and include simple cave tombs and even imposing underground churches and many chambers. Monolithic hypogea are made by isolating a rocky monolith on the surface, carving out the inside to make simple shapes or elaborate monuments. Courtyard hypogea combine the digging of a vertical, central shaft with tunnels or rooms developed horizontally and arranged radially. In complex systems such as those of piazza Vittorio Veneto in Matera, these hypogea have an opening in the wall overlooking the slope. Finally a particular type is the artificial hypogeum. Like the dolmens that were originally buried underground, and the megalithic complexes in Malta, these structures are built with walls that reproduce the forms and characteristics of the hypogeal habitats.

Rocky wall hypogea

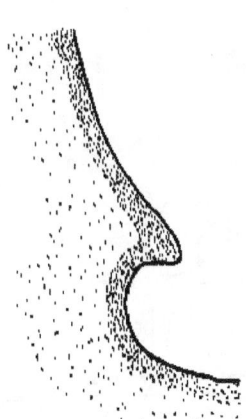
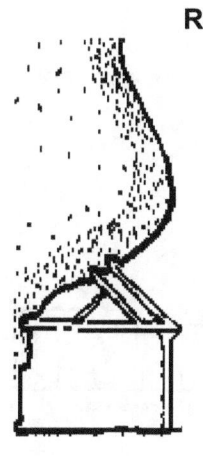
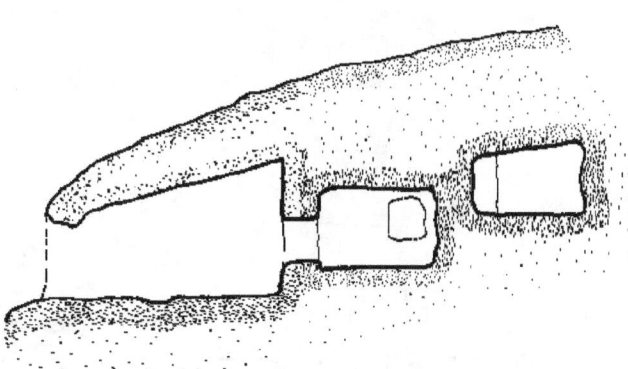

FIGURE A5.1 Natural rock shelter.

FIGURE A5.2 Dwelling in a rock shelter.

FIGURE A5.3 Tomb of the necropolis of Sas Concas (Nuoro), Aeneolithic – Early Bronze Age [Adapted from a drawing by Moravetti and Tozzi, 1995].

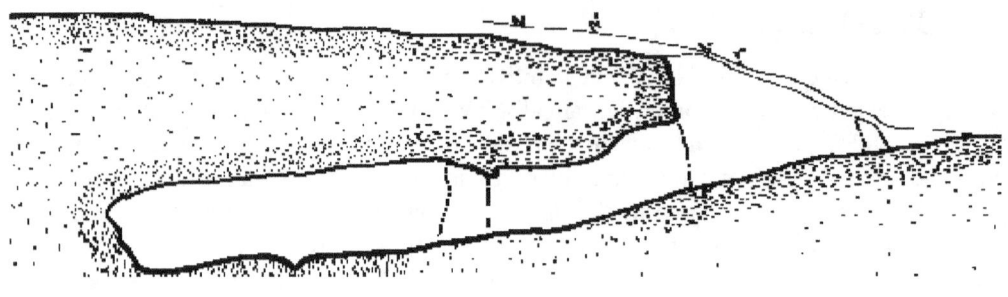

FIGURE A5.4 Tomb of the necropolis of Toppo Daguzzo (Potenza), Middle Bronze Age [Adapted from a drawing by Cipolloni Sampò, 1986].

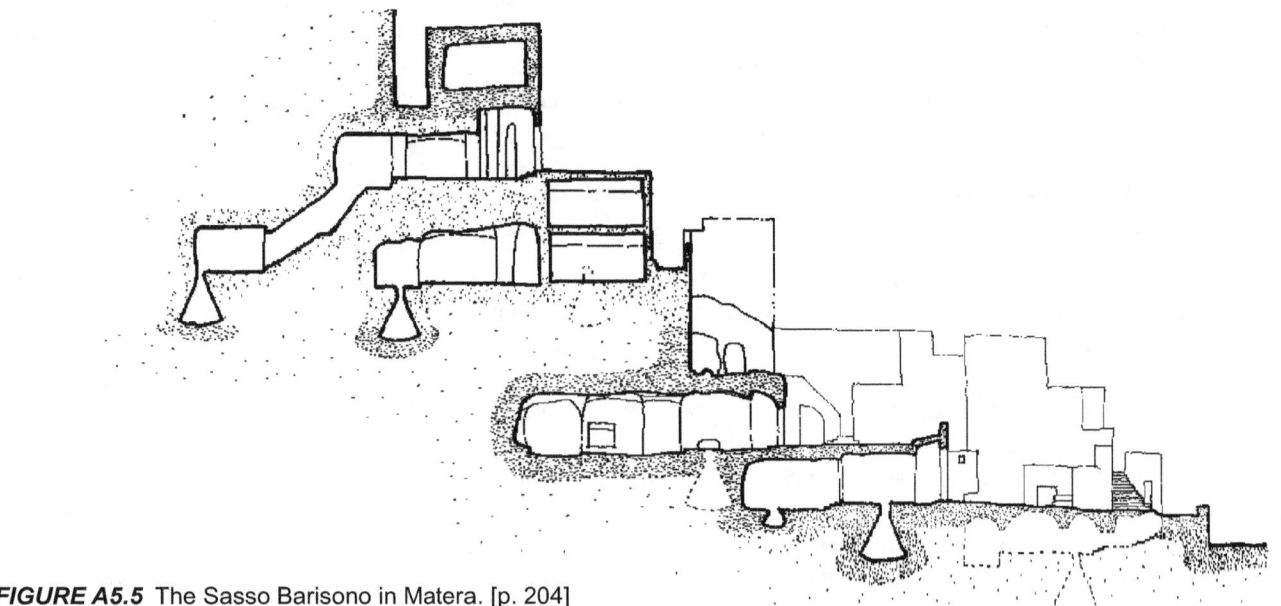

FIGURE A5.5 The Sasso Barisono in Matera. [p. 204]

FIGURE A5.6 The Khazneh (or Treasure) of Petra (Jordan), 1st century BC.

FIGURE A5.7 Rock-hewn temple of Ramses II at Abu Simbel (Egypt), 13th century BC.

FIGURE A5.8 Church of San Pietro Barisano in Matera, 13th–17th century AD.

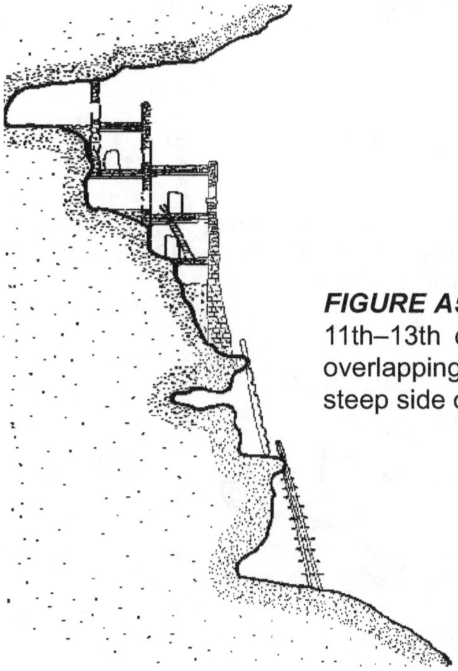

FIGURE A5.9 Anasazi Indian pueblo of Montezuma Castle (Mesa Verde, Colorado), 11th–13th century AD. This type of village structure consisting of different storeys overlapping each other was built inside the large hollows or the rock shelters in the steep side of the canyons.

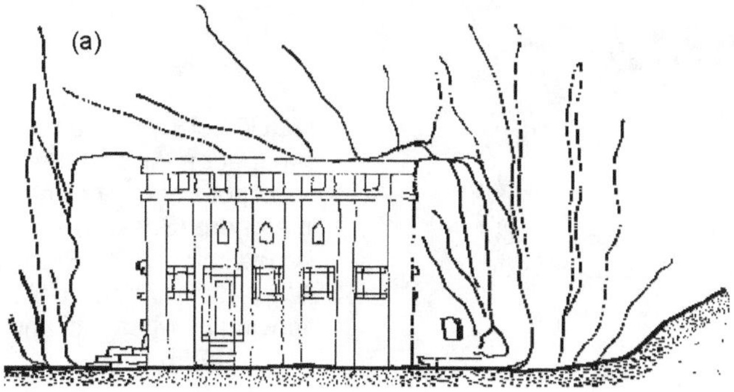

FIGURE A5.10 Church of Abba Libanos in Lalibela (Ethiopia), 12th century AD: (a) view, (b) cross section.

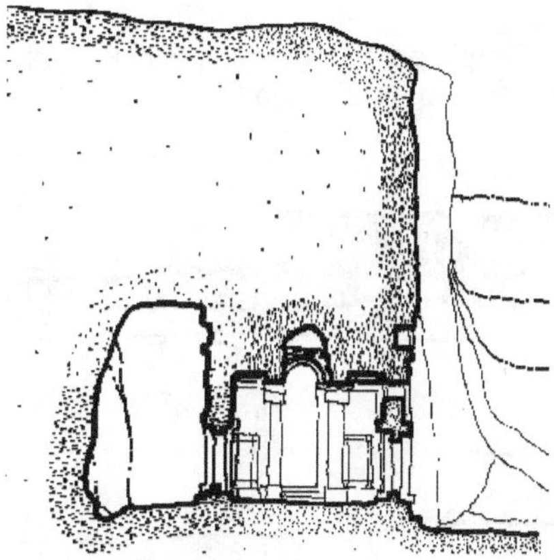

Appendices 259

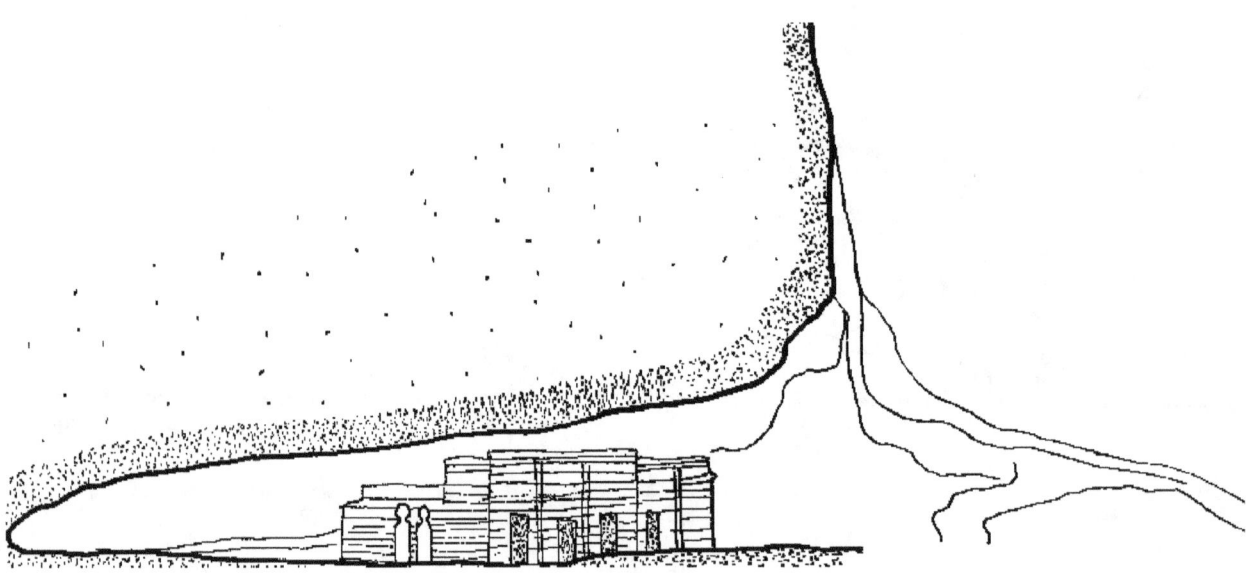

FIGURE A5.11 Church inside the cave of Imrahanna Kristos near Lalibela (Ethiopia), 12th century AD.

Pit hypogea

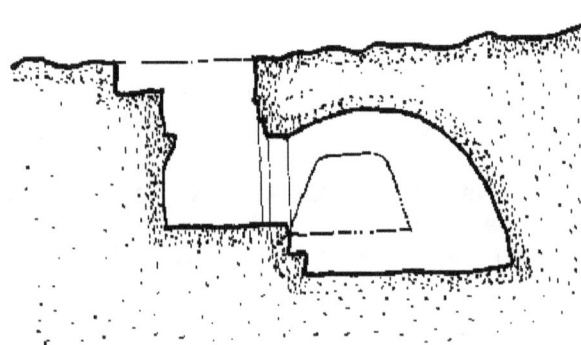

FIGURE A5.12 Cave hypogeum: tomb of the necropolis of Thapsos (Sicily), Middle Bronze Age – 15th–13th century BC [Adapted from a drawing by Bietti Sestieri, Lentini and Vozza, 1996].

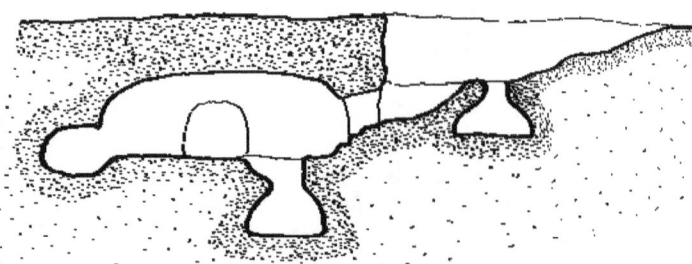

FIGURE A5.13 Simple pit hypogeum: dwelling of Bersabea (Israel), 4th millennium BC.

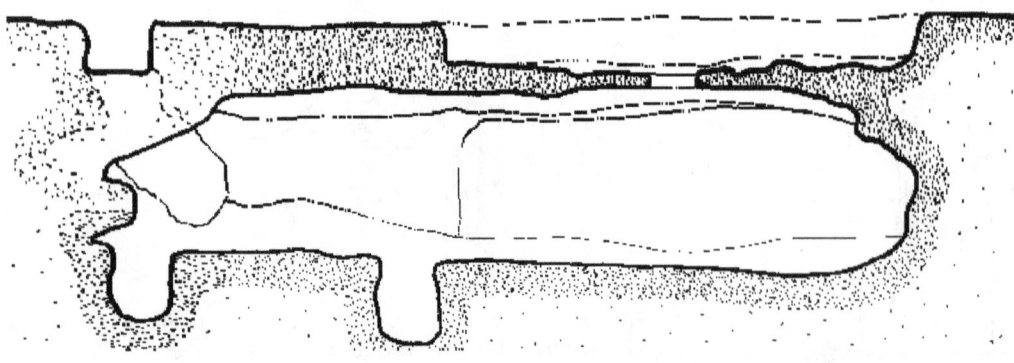

FIGURE A5.14 Chamber hypogeum: tomb of the necropolis of Santu Petru in Alghero (Sassari), Aeneolithic – Early Bronze Age [Adapted from a drawing by Moravetti and Tozzi, 1995].

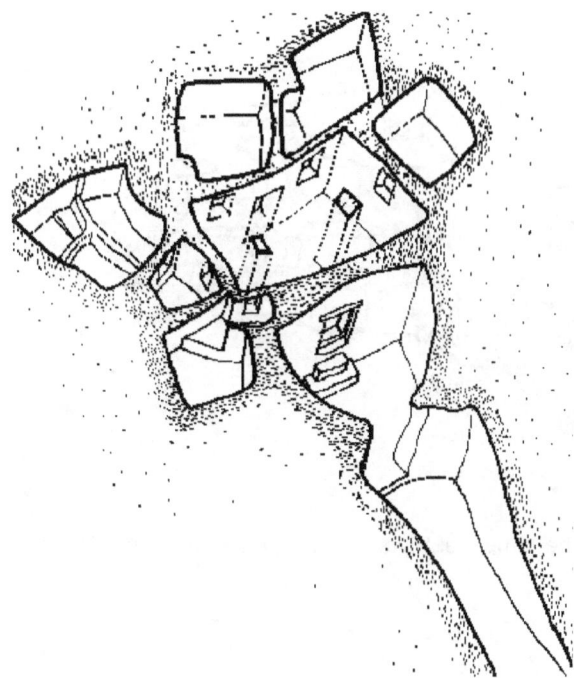

FIGURE A5.15 Pit hypogeum: tomb of the necropolis of Santu Petru in Alghero (Sassari), Aeneolithic – Early Bronze Age [Adapted from a drawing by Moravetti and Tozzi, 1995].

FIGURE A5.16 Complex pit hypogeum: domed church of the rupestrian monastery of Gegard (Armenia), 13th century AD [Adapted from a drawing by Rewerski, 1999].

Monolithic hypogea

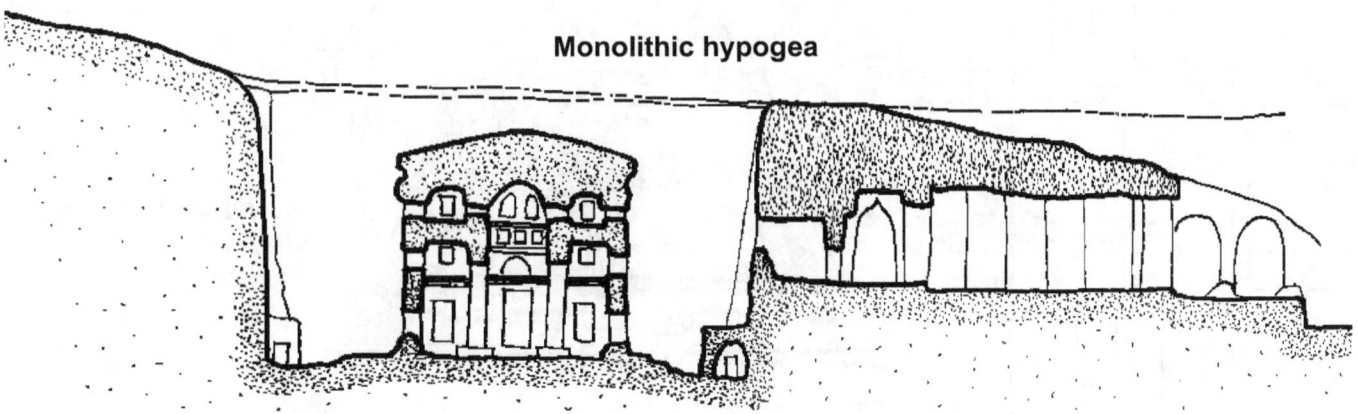

FIGURE A5.17 Simple monolithic hypogea: Church of Biet Emmanuel in Lalibela (Ethiopia), the 12th century AD.

FIGURE A5.18 Complex monolithic hypogea: Kailasha (or Rang Mahall), the temple of Siva at Ellora (India), the end of the 8th century AD.

Courtyard hypogea

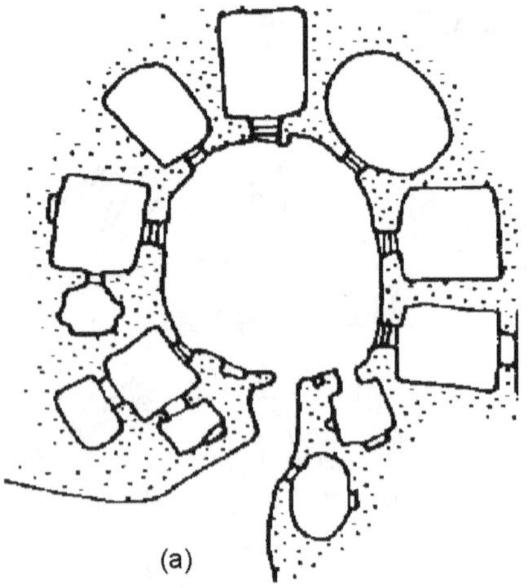

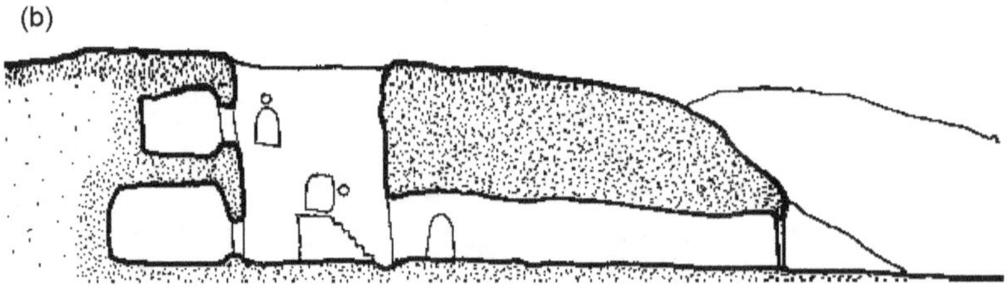

FIGURE A5.19 Courtyard hypogeum of Matmata (Tunisia): (a) plan, (b) cross section.

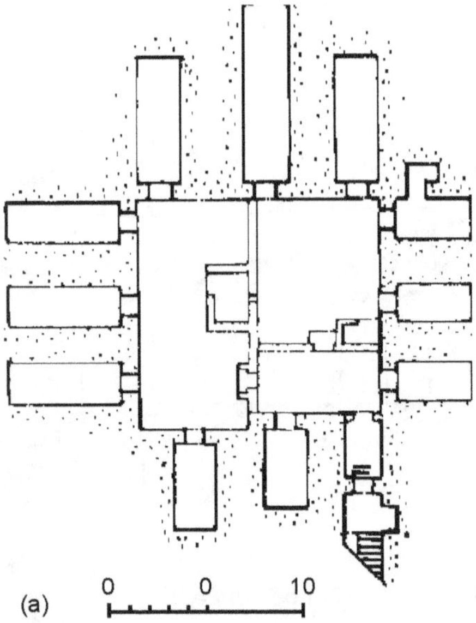

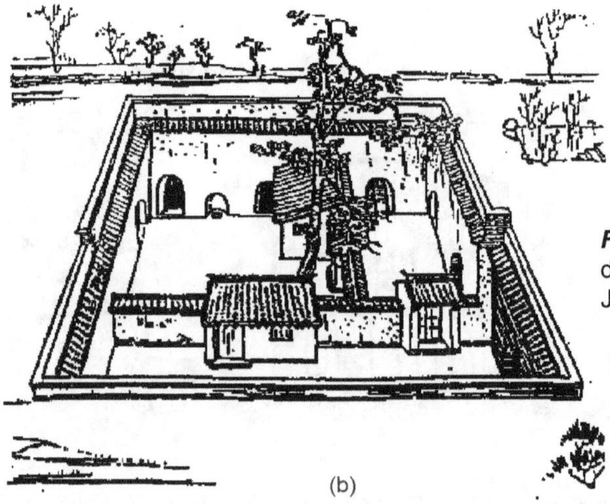

FIGURE A5.21 Troglodyte dwelling of Salillas de Jalon (Spain).

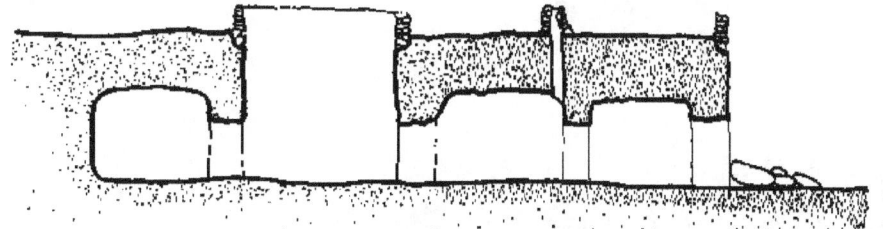

FIGURE A5.21 Troglodyte dwelling of Salillas de Jalon (Spain).

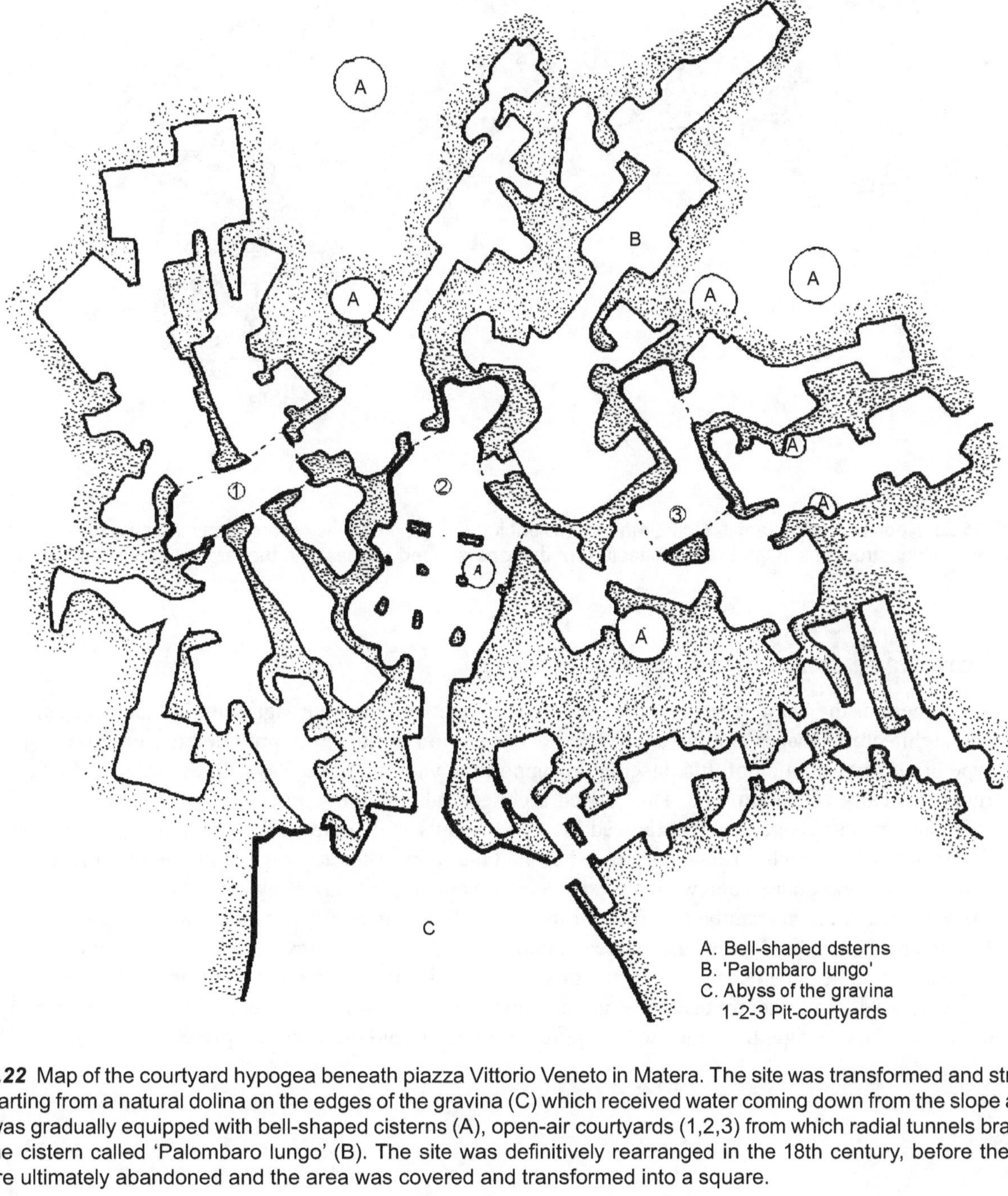

A. Bell-shaped dsterns
B. 'Palombaro lungo'
C. Abyss of the gravina
1-2-3 Pit-courtyards

FIGURE A5.22 Map of the courtyard hypogea beneath piazza Vittorio Veneto in Matera. The site was transformed and stratified over time, starting from a natural dolina on the edges of the gravina (C) which received water coming down from the slope above. The dolina was gradually equipped with bell-shaped cisterns (A), open-air courtyards (1,2,3) from which radial tunnels branched out, up to the cistern called 'Palombaro lungo' (B). The site was definitively rearranged in the 18th century, before the water systems were ultimately abandoned and the area was covered and transformed into a square.

Appendices 263

Artificial hypogea

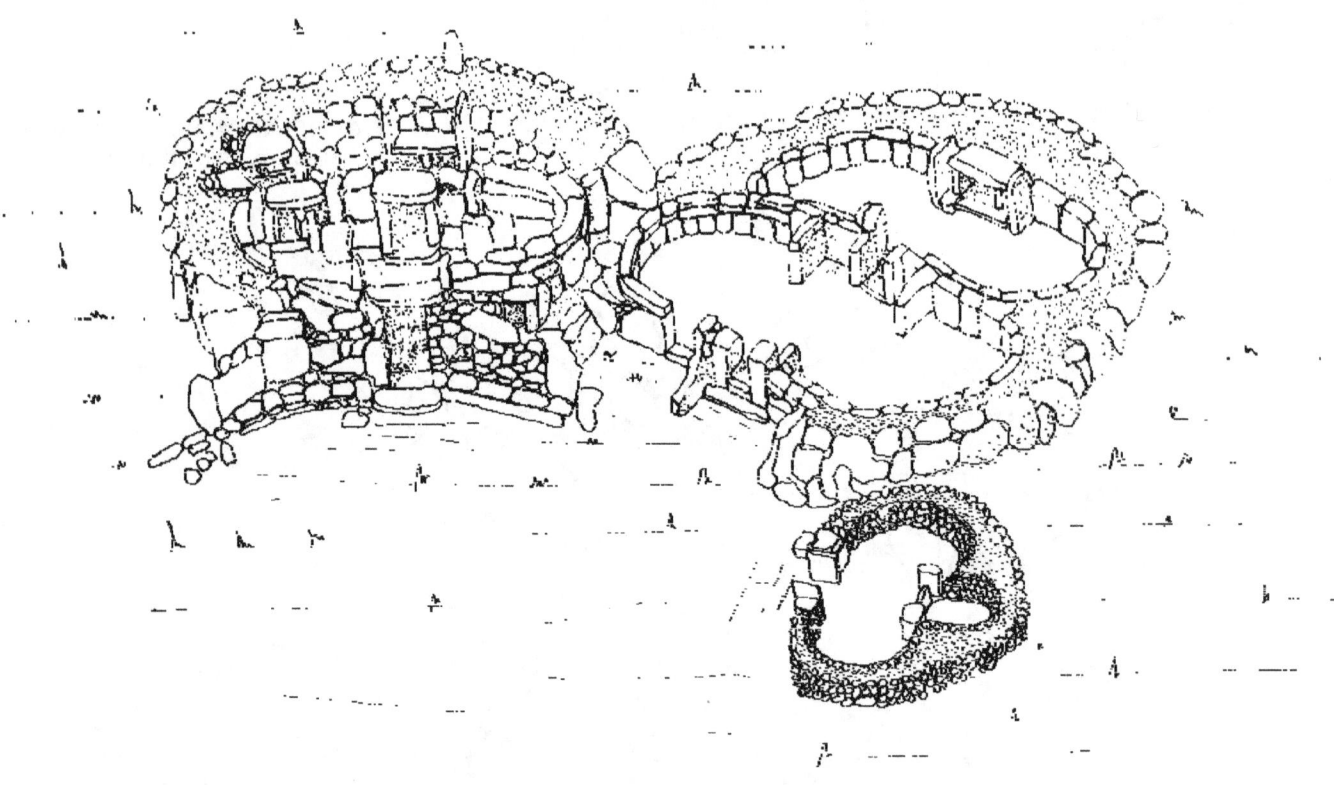

FIGURE A5.23 Neolithic monument in Malta, 4th–3rd millennium BC. The complex reproduces the structure and the heat inertia of the hypogeal constructions in the built architecture of the lobe-shaped spaces and the large masonry structure.

A5.2 From Cave to Architectures

In the development of the Sassi of Matera, the troglodyte habitat and the hydroagricultural matrix of cultivated terraces dictated the architectural shapes and the urban layout. Excavation of the caves provided the limestone blocks to create the first type of closure. A lining of tufa, inserted to support the vaulting of the cave, foreshadowed the barrel vault type of construction, locally called lamione. This gained architectural autonomy, but was still linked with the underground network of cisterns and hypogea that guaranteed the water supply and control of the microclimate. The original layout consisted of caves with an arch formation arranged around a threshing-floor garden, with the water reserves replenished from the plain above, and drained below by the excavated rock or condensed by capturing humidity in the caves. With the building of the barrel-vaulted chambers in front of the caves, the plain above became a hanging garden. The water was collected on the roofs, whose sloping sides were set into the walls for this purpose, and it was conveyed into the cistern well in the courtyard. The latter became the centre of social organisation for the neighbourhood. This urban courtyard, the home of the extended family, centre of family and neighbourhood relations, the scene of the dramas, and joys of private and public life, draws its origin from the meeting points created around the watering places.

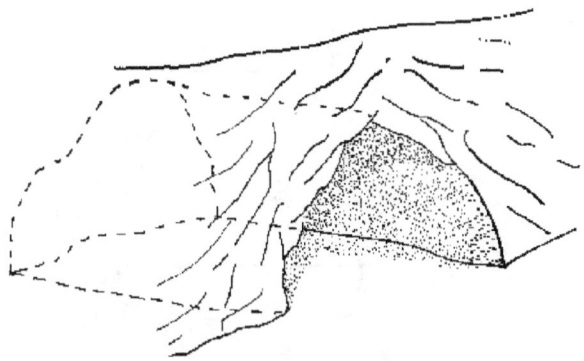

FIGURE A5.24 Cave.

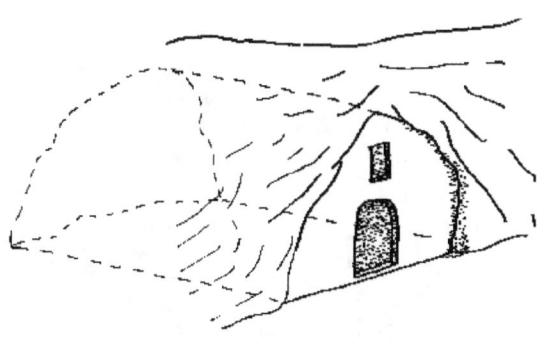

FIGURE A5.25 Cave with front curtain wall.

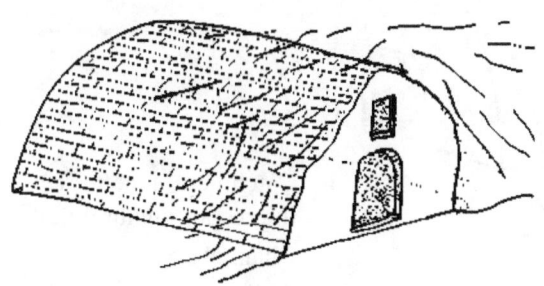

FIGURE A5.26 Barrel-vaulted cave.

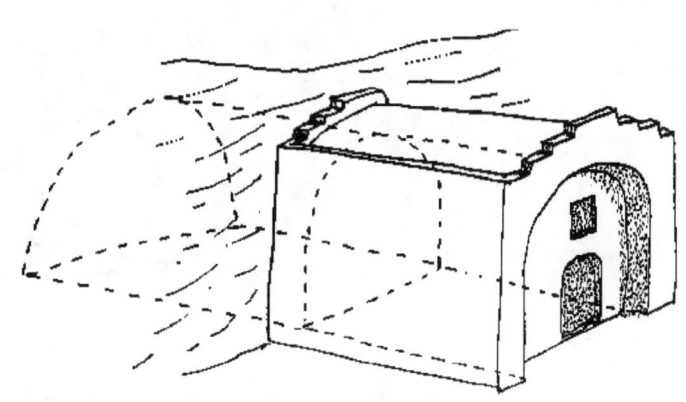

FIGURE A5.27 Lamione, barrel-vaulted architecture before the cave

FIGURES A5.28–30 Types of cisterns in the Sassi of Matera.

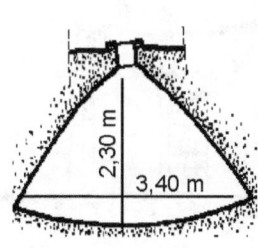
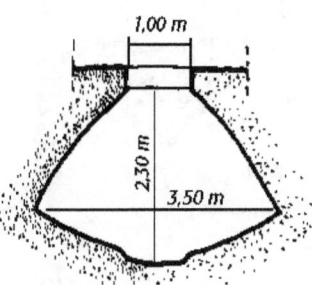

FIGURE A5.28 Bell-shaped cisterns.

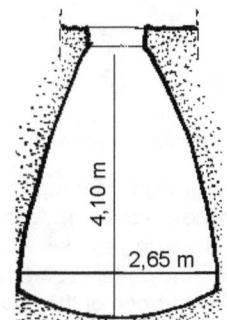
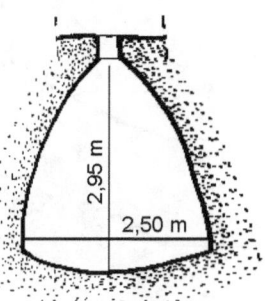

FIGURE A5.29 Tholos cisterns.

Appendices 265

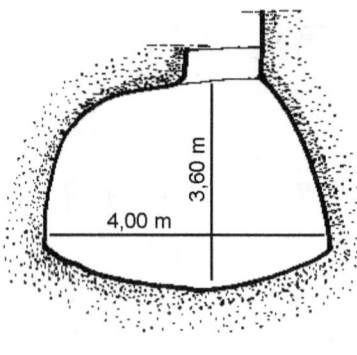 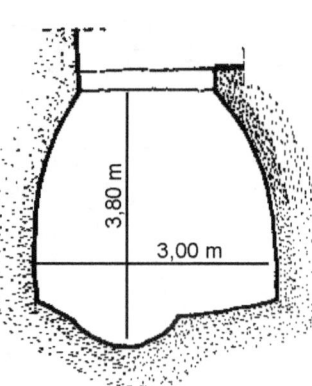

FIGURE A5.30 Pit cisterns.

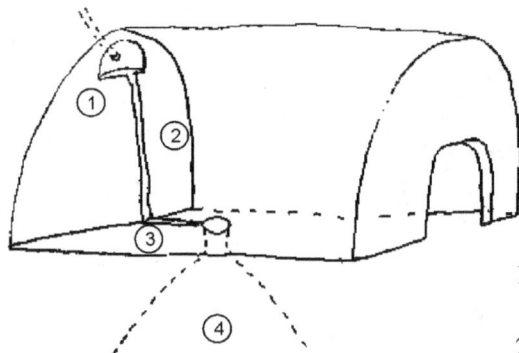

FIGURE A5.31 Catchment cave with sedimentation floor and bell-shaped cistern.

1. Catchment lunette which intercepts a natural fault
2. Channel
3. Sedimentation floor
4. Cistern

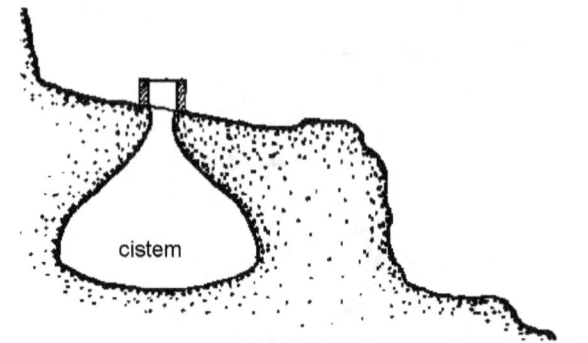

FIGURE A5.32 Transformation of a cistern into a dwelling.

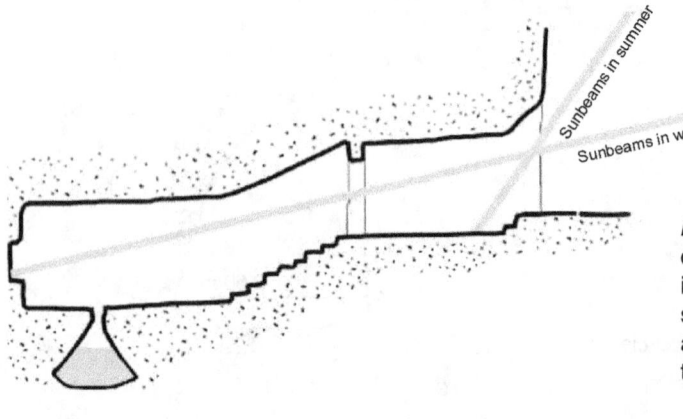

FIGURE A5.33 The sun's height through the seasons determines the inclination of the excavation. A double objective is pursued: in winter, when the sun reaches a certain height, sunbeams strike the bottom of the cave; in summer, sunbeams are only allowed to reach the entrance of the cave, because of the heat and to help moisture condense in the cistern.

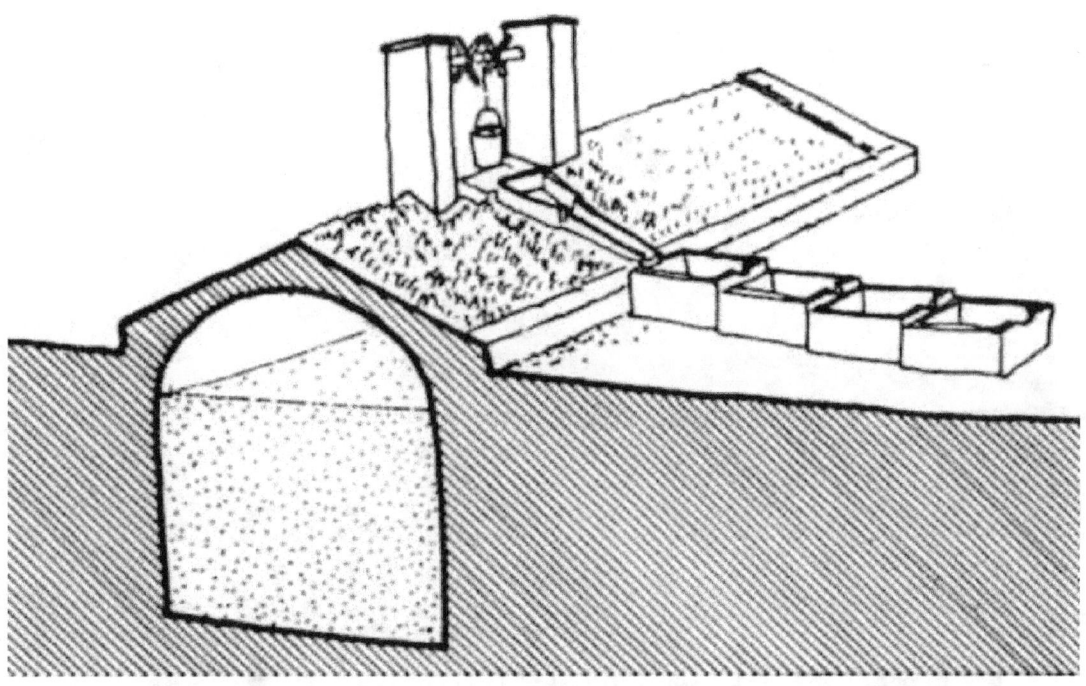

FIGURE A5.34 Roofed cistern, a water-production device typical of the Murgia highland.

FIGURE A5.35 The hypogea along the terraced slope arranged in a horseshoe shape round tilled terraces.

Appendices

FIGURE A5.36 Jazzo, sheepfold typical of southern Italy: (a) cross section, (b) plan.

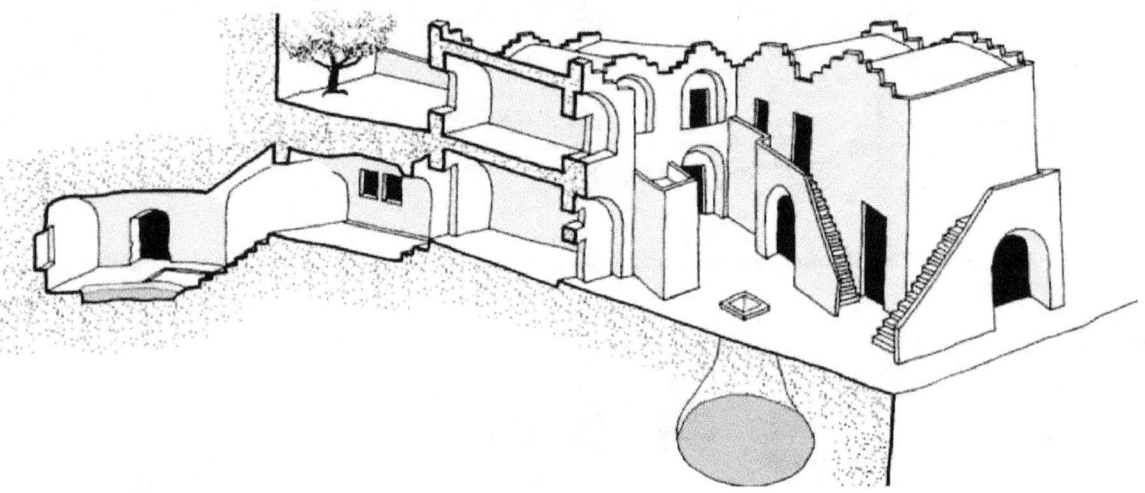

FIGURE A5.37 Vicinato of the Sassi of Matera: (a) cross section, (b) plan.

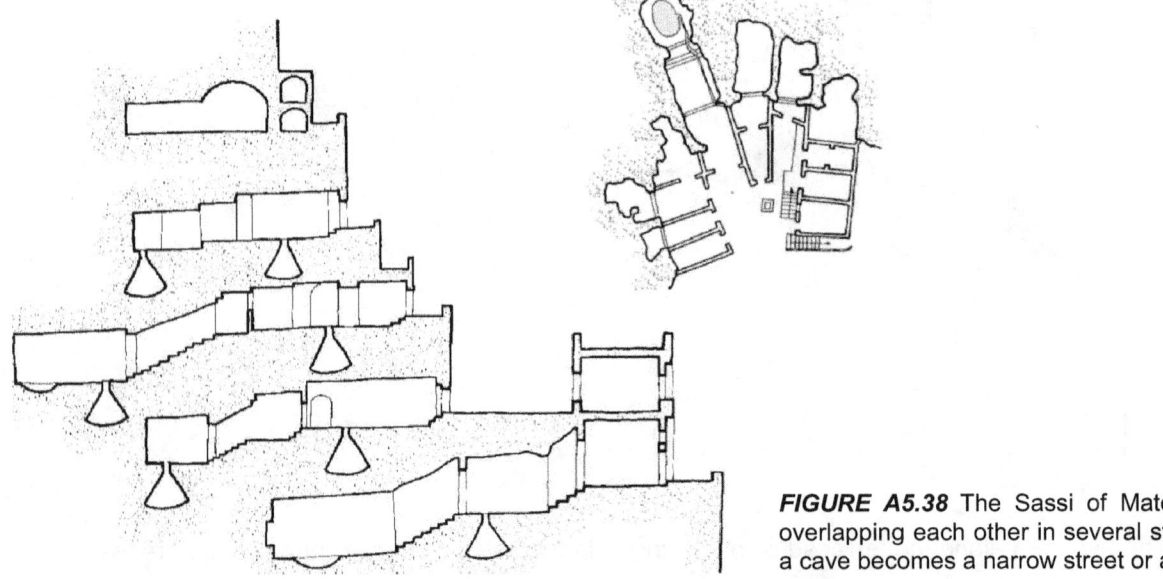

FIGURE A5.38 The Sassi of Matera. The hypogea overlapping each other in several storeys. The roof of a cave becomes a narrow street or a hanging garden.

A5.3 From Water Collection to Urban Ecosystems: Nabatean Farming

In the Negev desert, along the Wadi Araba and in Jordan the prehistoric remains of innumerable hydraulic devices prove the existence of appropriate techniques for making the desert fertile and life-supporting by capturing humidity and protecting the soil. Similar devices are found in the Saharan Neolithic, in the Arabian Desert and in the Yemen; and they subsequently spread all over the Mediterranean. Petra is their most impressive city, and for this reason they have been called Hedomite and Nabatean agriculture from the two ancient peoples who had this city as their centre. Contacts with southern Arabia by means of the Incense Road explain their similarity with the Sabean water techniques, the most important of which is the so-called Marib Dam, which is in fact a system of water dividers or gates. The probable Mesopotamian origin of the technique for diverting floodwater explains why they spread as far as the Indus Valley, and along the Silk Road in China.

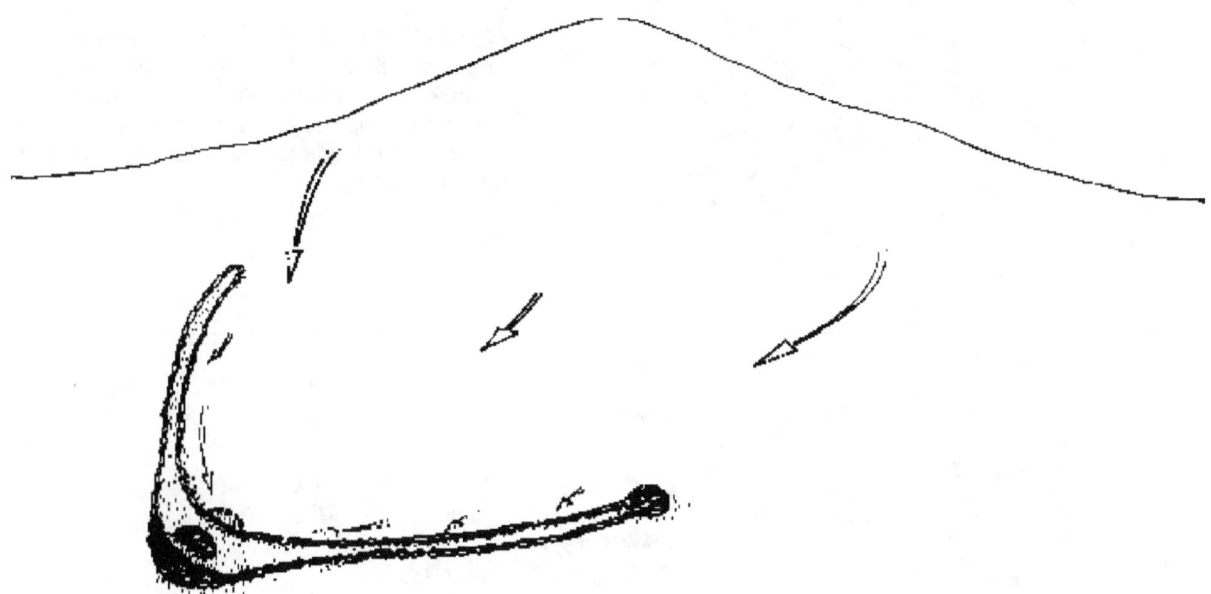

FIGURE A5.39 Saharan mausoleum used as a collector of moisture and water run-off along the slope. The rows of stone convey the flows towards the area protected by the barrow.

FIGURE A5.40 Mounds of stones in the shape of a crescent, circles and rows of stones, found during archaeological excavations in the Hedomite and Nabatean hydroagriculture, common in all arid and Mediterranean areas for plant preservation.

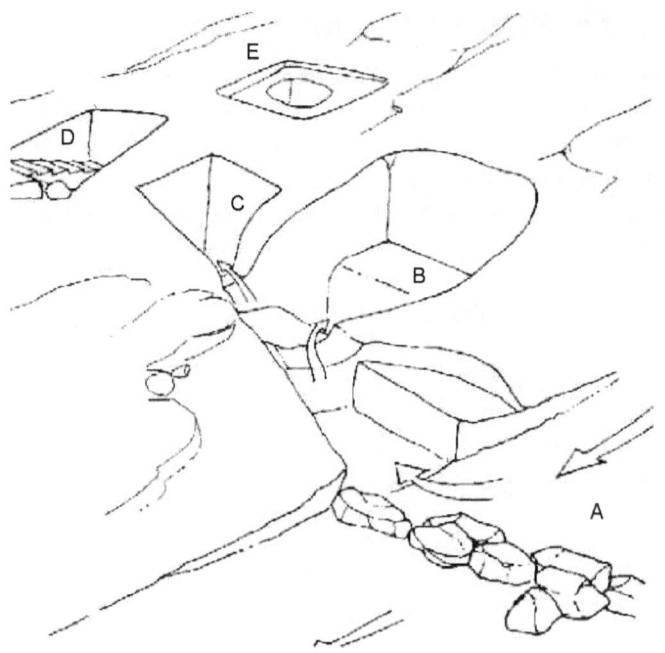

FIGURE A5.41 Flood trap at Bir Huweimel (Petra). The water flow deviated by a wall of pebbles (A) is cleaned by means of spillways in consecutive basins (B) and fills up the large underground cistern (C). A staircase (D) leads to the cistern and water is drawn up from a well (E).

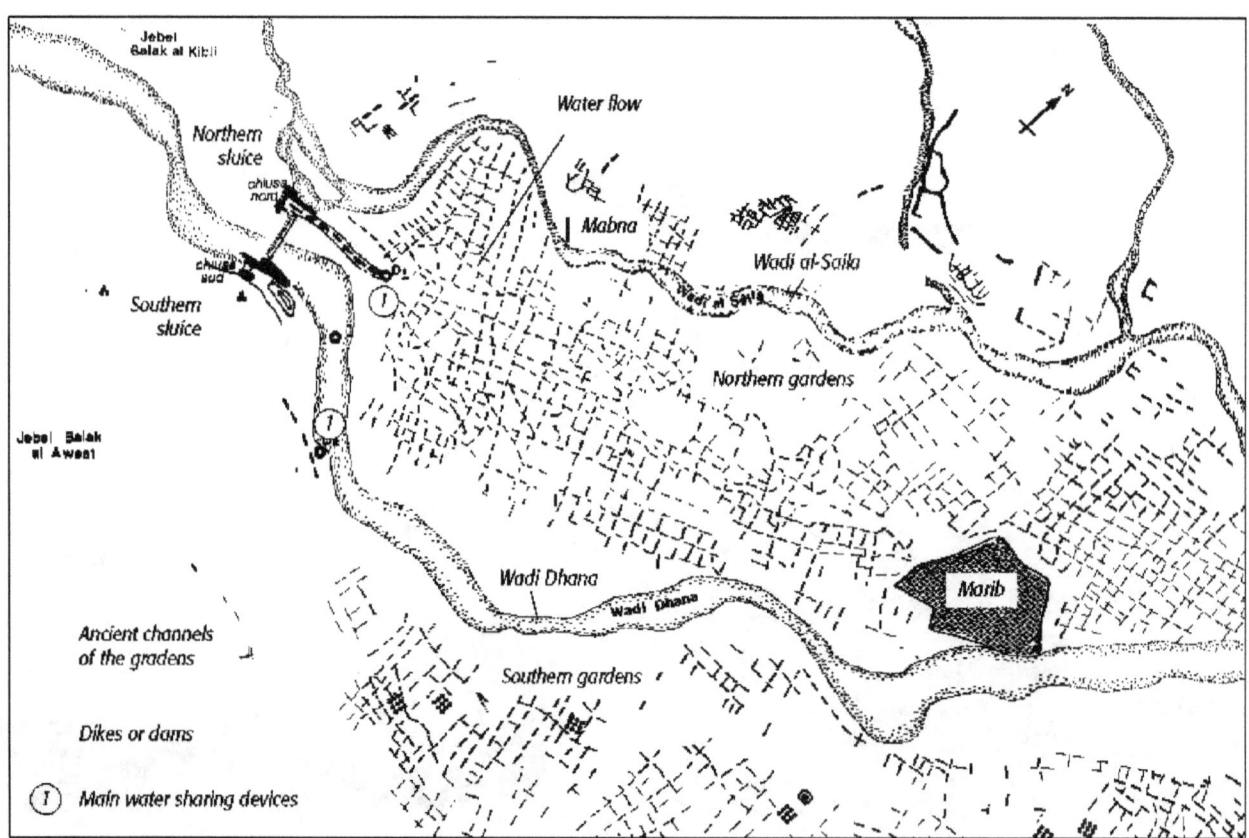

FIGURE A5.42 The irrigation system of Marib (Yemen) consisting of a large dam and a series of sluices and water-flow sharing systems allowed the northern and southern well-known gardens to be created on both sides of the bed of wadi Dhana.

A5.4 Water Systems of Petra, Shibam, and Thula

The urban ecosystems are the synthesis of traditional knowledge that has developed in the different environments, starting with the first caves, lines of stones and artificial streams, and increasingly complex water systems. Petra, the stone city oasis, is the highest point in the evolution of systems built on the arid and rocky upland plains, where methods of excavation and water catchment predominated. Thula in the Yemen is an example of a fortified acropolis where atmospheric water is collected, conveying it downhill by means of an imposing system of channels on terraced slopes. Shibam, a city oasis built of raw bricks in the loess of the Hadramaut Valley, is the sum of the experience accumulated in building banks and channels in the big flood plains of the Indus, the Nile, Mesopotamia, the Yellow River. All of these are places where the first civilisations grew up thanks to skill in controlling flood waters and managing hydromorphic soils.

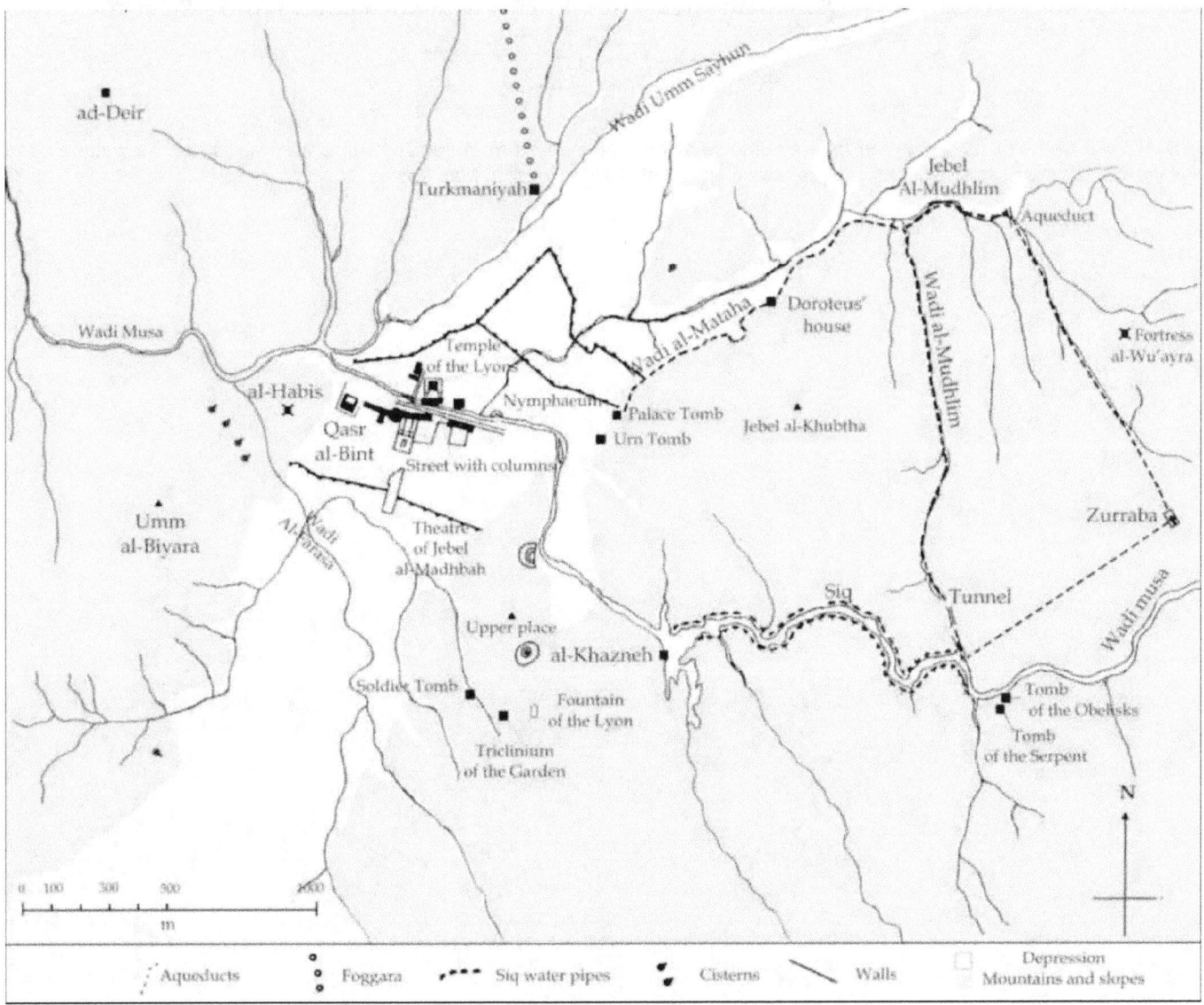

FIGURE A5.43 Petra (Jordan). The monumental organisation of the town depends on its natural morphology and on the use of the latter for harvesting and distributing water. An intricate network of hydraulic devices supplies the most important hypogeal structures.

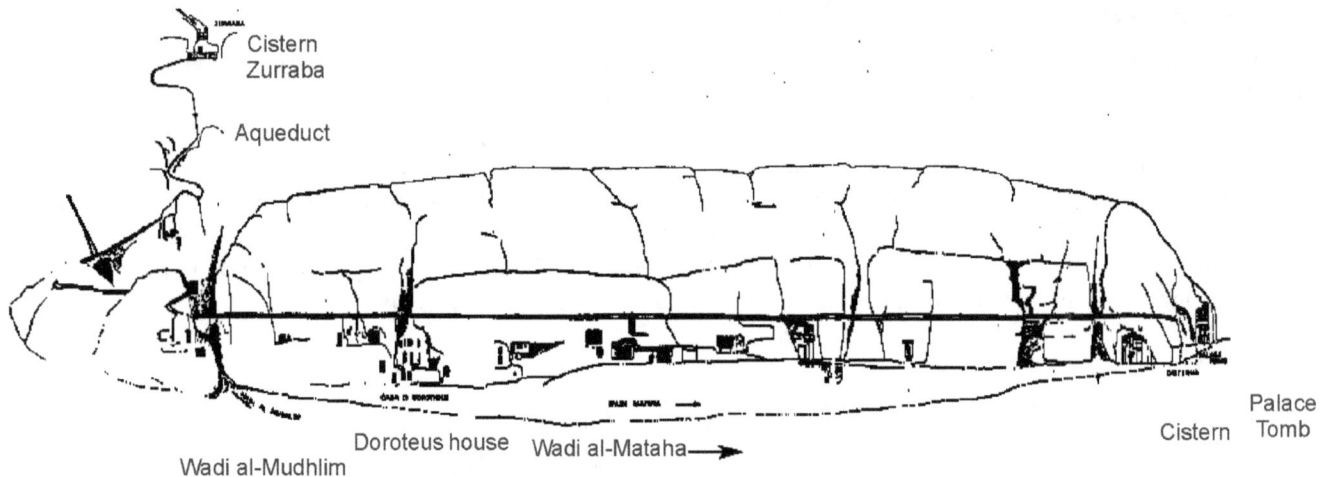

FIGURE A5.44 Petra (Jordan). The long aqueduct, which branched off from the Zurraba cistern as far as the waterfall and Palace Tomb cistern, supplied the hypogeal dwellings situated along wadi al-Mataha.

FIGURE A5.45 A proposal for rebuilding the water system and the tilled terraces of wadi al-Mataha (Petra). The restoration of the ecosystem and the revival of the vegetation are not only a new archaeological attraction managed by the bedu groups, but also the defence of the environment against the erosion and demolition of the sandstone walls.

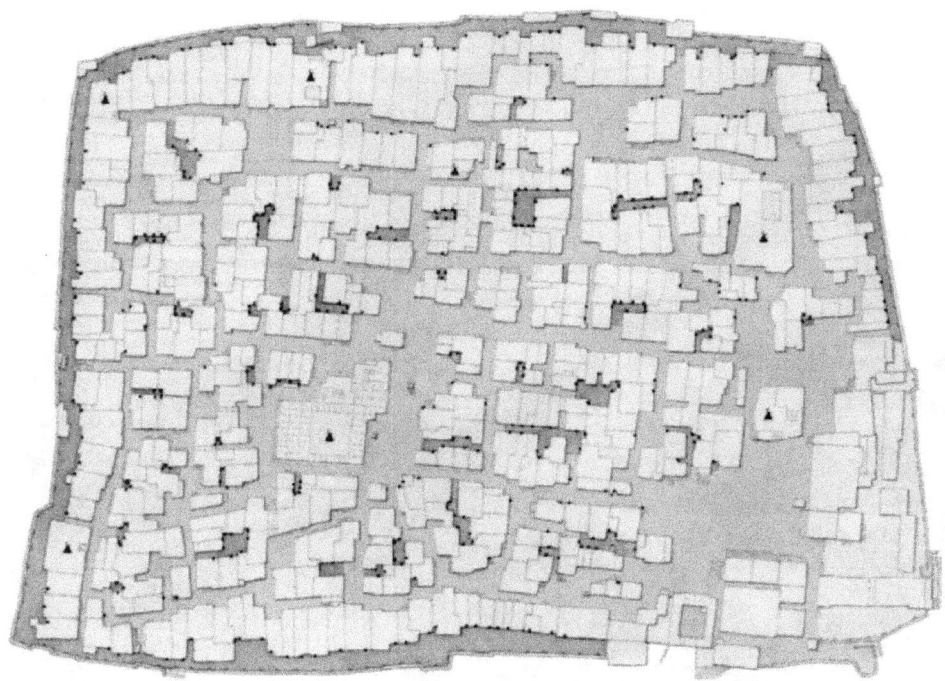

FIGURE A5.46 Urban plan of Shibam (Yemen). The harmonious distribution of squares, streets, and blind alleys is the result of the sewage collection used as fertilizer. Each house has a waste disposal system provided with external outlets (marked in black). The latter overlook narrow back streets, blind alleys, or perimeter paths (grey shaded).

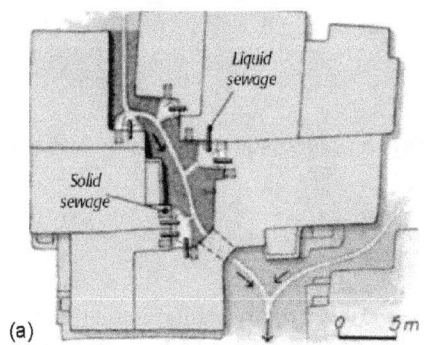

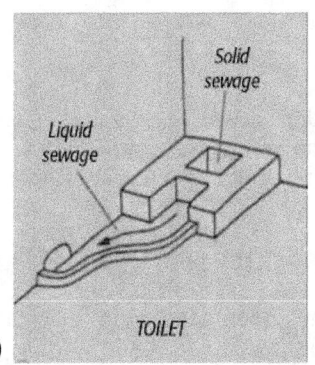

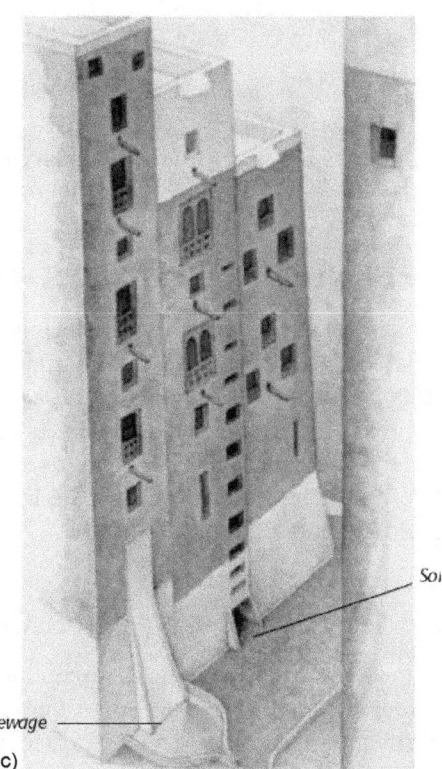

FIGURE A5.47 Shibam (Yemen). The sewage disposal system: (a) organisation of a blind alley (shaded on the urban plan, Fig. A5.46) to discharge the solid and liquid waste dropping from the houses; (b) the two-outlet toilet which allows the separation of liquid and solid excrement; (c) the façade of a building equipped with sewage shafts and excrement collection baskets.

FIGURE A5.48 Thula (Yemen), reconstruction of water-harvesting systems, open-air cisterns, underground cavities and tunnels which from the citadel provide the terraced gardens and the ablution rooms of the mosque with water. The hydraulic installation still in use is very similar to that of the ancient Sabean towns.

APPENDIX 6: LOCAL KNOWLEDGE IN HYDRAULIC SOCIETIES

Large-scale water management techniques have been developed by great civilisations known as hydraulic societies for this reason. They are the ancient empires that grew up on the alluvial sediments of silt, loess and sand along the Afro-Asian river basins and also in the karst regions of the meso-American rainforests. The geographic extension and the impressiveness of the hydraulic works led to political despotism, bureaucratic hypertrophy and militarisation of the state. Nonetheless the techniques used by these societies evolved from a traditional knowledge system, the fruit of local knowledge tested on a small scale by those communities based on models of self-sustainability that we have defined hydroagricultural and autopoietic.

A6.1 Structures for Water Collection, Purification, and Management in India

In the tradition of the Indian sub-continent, knowledge of water is abundant and often linked to strong spiritual sentiments. The holiness of water is part of the religious value attributed to the great rivers and to the practices of ablution and purification. Complex devices are set up for this purpose, in which the functional and the religious motivation coincide. Since the 3rd millennium urban water systems were used in the civilisations of the Indus Valley, equipped with hygiene and water systems and wells reinforced by walling introduced here for the first time. On a territorial scale, in Beluchistan with the devices called gabar-band, there are even older experiences of flood water management and distribution.

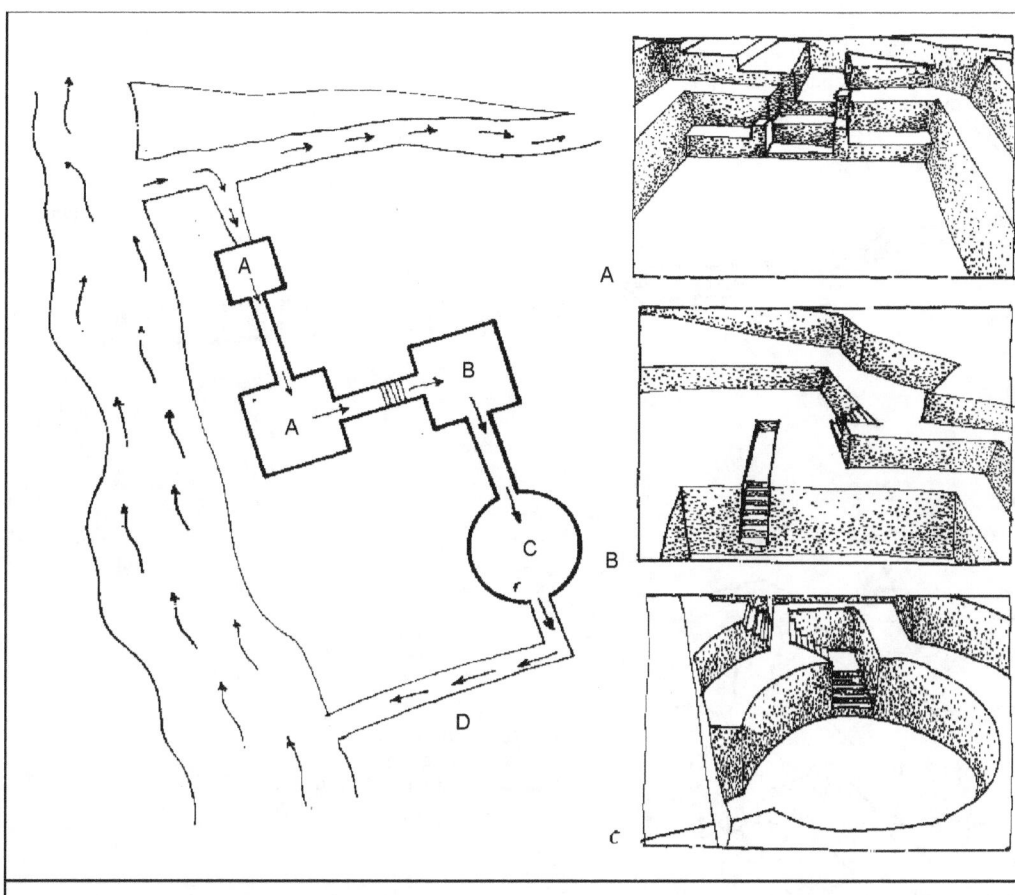

A. Sedimentation and flood water cleaning tanks
B. Water storage tank
C. Ceremonial basin for ablutions
D. System of chambers for filtering water by means of spillways to enable purified water to be put back into the river

FIGURE A6.1 Water purification system which was brought to light at Sringaverapura, near the holy city of Allahabad, at the confluence of the sacred rivers Ganges and Jumna, 1st century BC.

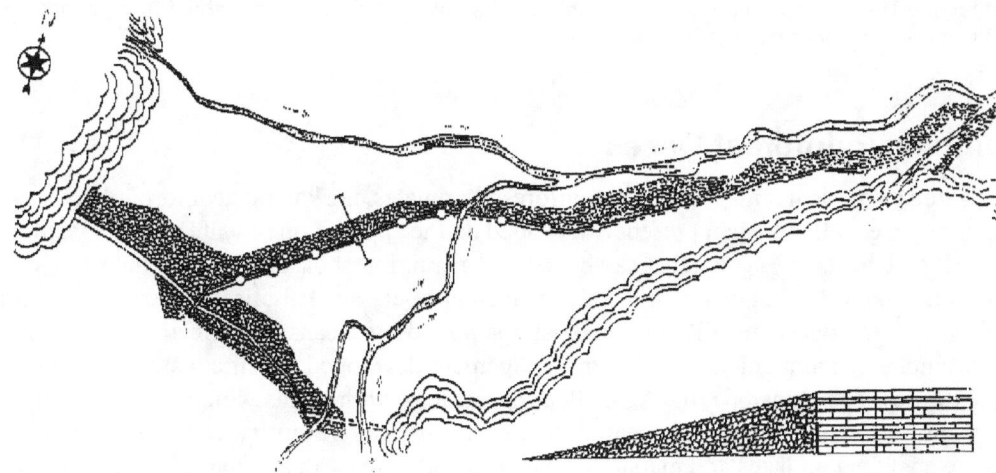

FIGURE A6.2 Gabarband of Pir Munaghara (Belucistan). Dating back to before the Harappa civilization, the device consisted of a series of 60–120 cm high terraced platforms made out of pebbles which decreased in height as they went upwards. This device was used to keep the floods under control and stop the alluvial sediments coming down the hill.

Appendices **275**

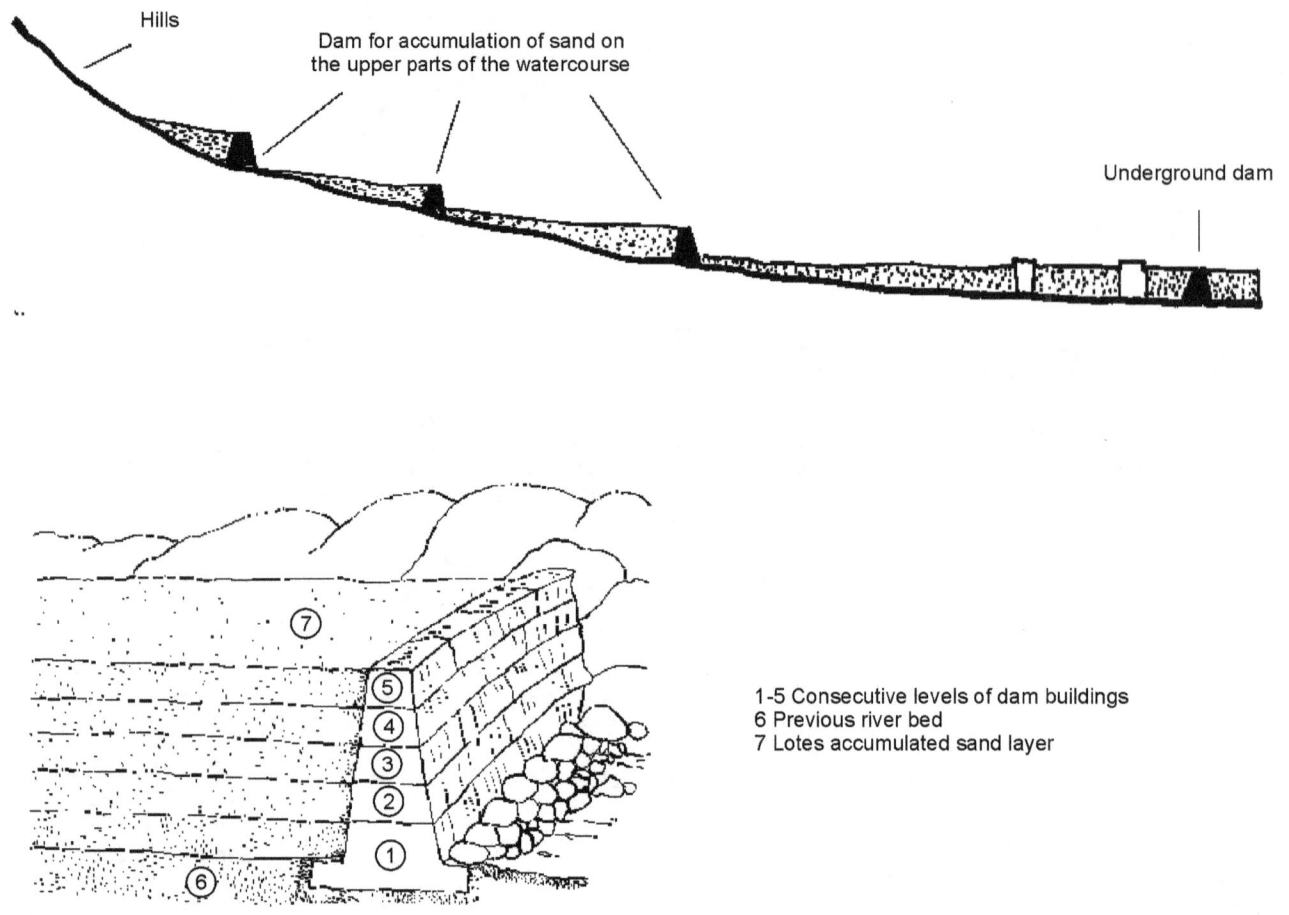

FIGURE A6.3 Combined system of sand accumulation dams and underground dams. The first (b) are generally built by overlapping different levels. The underlying principle is to limit the height of each level so that lighter material is transported by water out of the basin whereas heavier material accumulates.

A6.2 Pre-Columbian Rainforest Oases

In areas naturally irrigated by tropical rains, where the rainforest dominates, the karstic geomorphology lacking in streams and surface water courses, meant that human presence depended on the application of water control techniques. This was the case with the Maya settlements in Yucatan that can be defined as rainforest oases. The original water control practices date back to the 2nd millennium BC, but it is with the classical and pre-classical civilisations that the natural depressions and cavities full of water were systematically organised and supplied by means of collection areas, that were no less than the pyramids and monumental architecture. Water management developed specific water control practices, for the purpose of limiting excesses. The chinampa, the Aztec floating gardens, with plants which directly absorb the necessary water through their roots, are an example of the creation of a space that can be cultivated when there is water in excess. Large wooden rafts are anchored on lakes and marshes. A layer of soil with earth and manure is spread on top. Humidity passes directly from the wood to the roots of the plants, which thus obtain the water they need without irrigation.

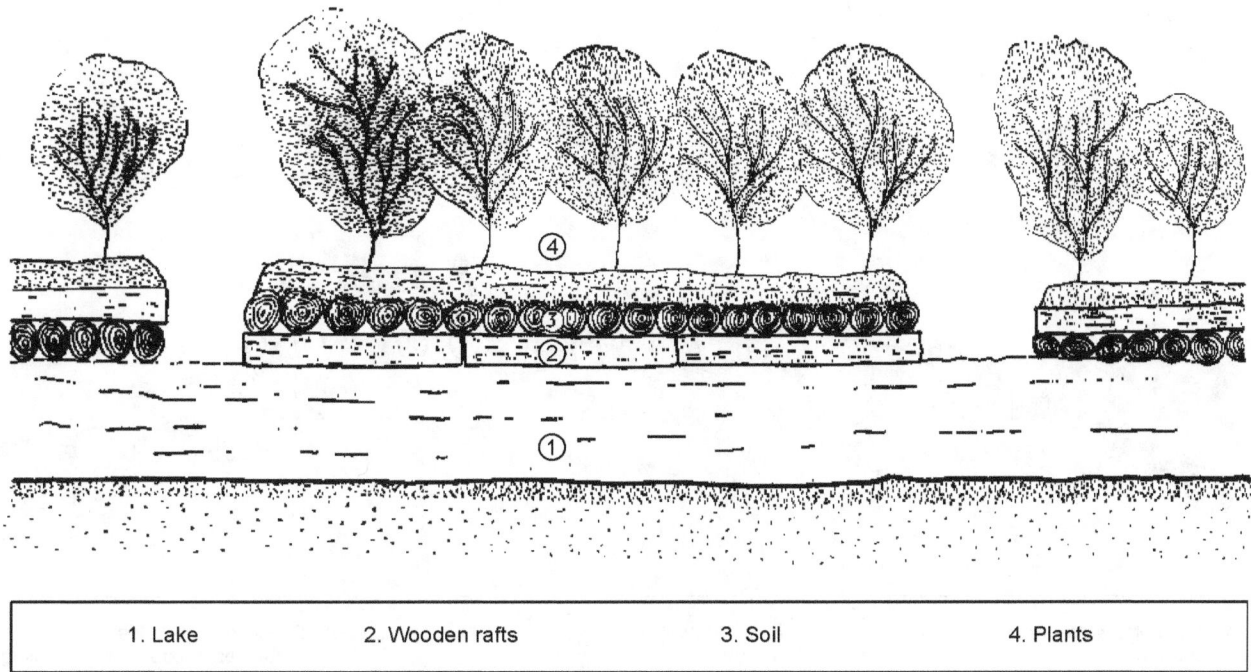

| 1. Lake | 2. Wooden rafts | 3. Soil | 4. Plants |

FIGURE A6.4 Chinampa, Aztec irrigation technique carried out directly from the subsoil by means of floating gardens arranged on rafts in fresh water lakes.

FIGURE A6.5 The aguada of Rancho Jabal (Northern Yucatán) with the shafts (A) and the chultun (B) which retain water when the aguada (C) dries up.

Appendices 277

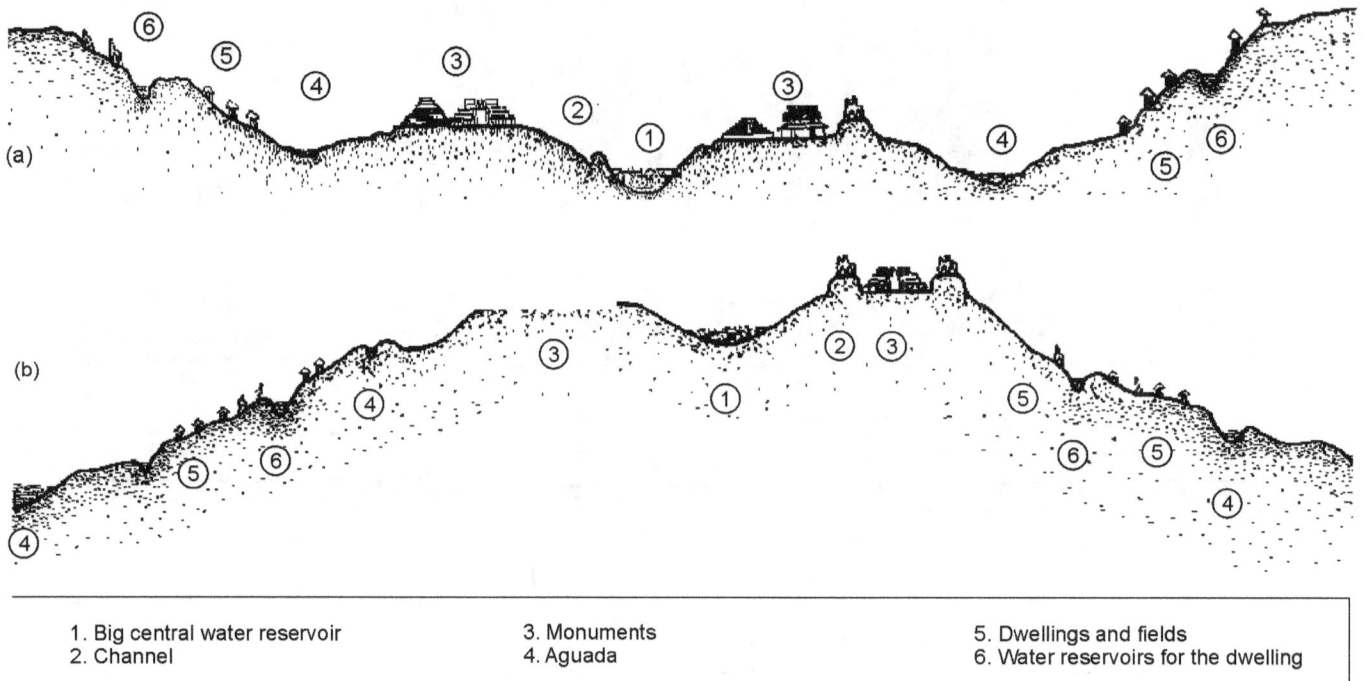

1. Big central water reservoir
2. Channel
3. Monuments
4. Aguada
5. Dwellings and fields
6. Water reservoirs for the dwelling

FIGURE A6.6 Maya hydraulic technology. (a) Before the classic age the settlements were carried out at the bottom in natural depression used as water reservoirs. (b) In the late classic age hydraulic technology made it possible to build in high places, using the roofs and the monuments of the town as water catchment devices which filled a big central reservoir with water.

A6.3 The Evolution of Hypogeal Constructions in China

The arid zones in China, the Taklamakan and Gobi deserts, the Loess high plateau and the course of the Huang Ho and the Yellow River are a reservoir of traditional knowledge. Carried along the ramifications of the Silk Road, almost all the water catchment and soil-protection techniques are present, from the villages with Neolithic ditches to the creation of oases and underground drainage tunnels. In particular, concerning the hypogeal practices, it is possible to follow all the forms of passive architecture from the first ditch hypogea to semi-hypogeal dwellings, and the imposing courtyard hypogeum systems that are still inhabited, here acquiring rigorous geometric shapes. A particularly interesting circular shape is still present: the adobe village-house called hwai yuen lo, the continuation and maximum evolution of the archaic rounded forms with a central impluvium.

FIGURES A6.7–6.9 Evolution of the prehistoric dwelling structures in China (fig. 3.58) compared with a pit-house of the peblo (New Mexico, fig. 359) and a hypogeal dwelling in Tunisia (fig. 360). Adapted from a drawing by loubes, 1993. (p. 231)

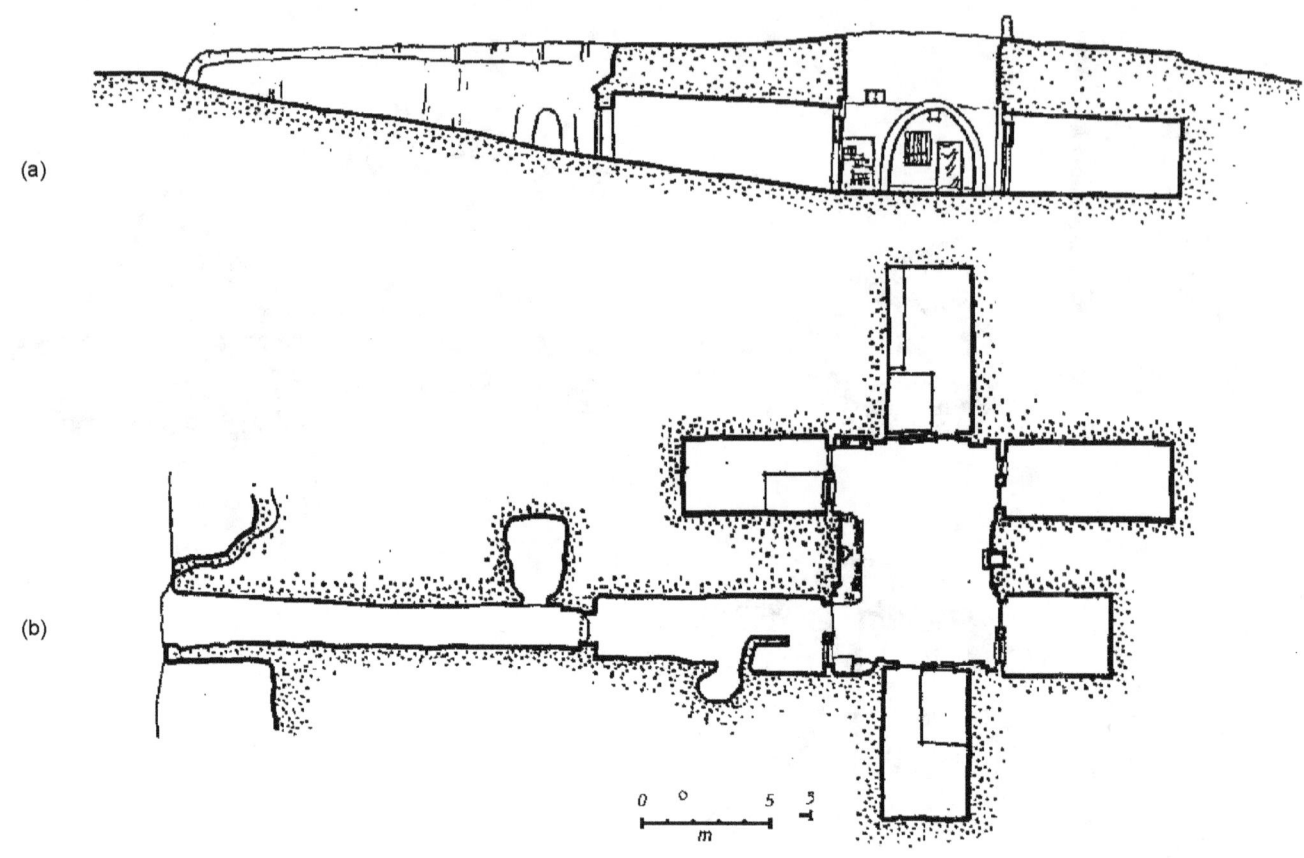

FIGURE A6.10 Troglodyte pit-dwelling in Shaanxi; (a) cross, section, (b) plan. [pp. 68, 231]

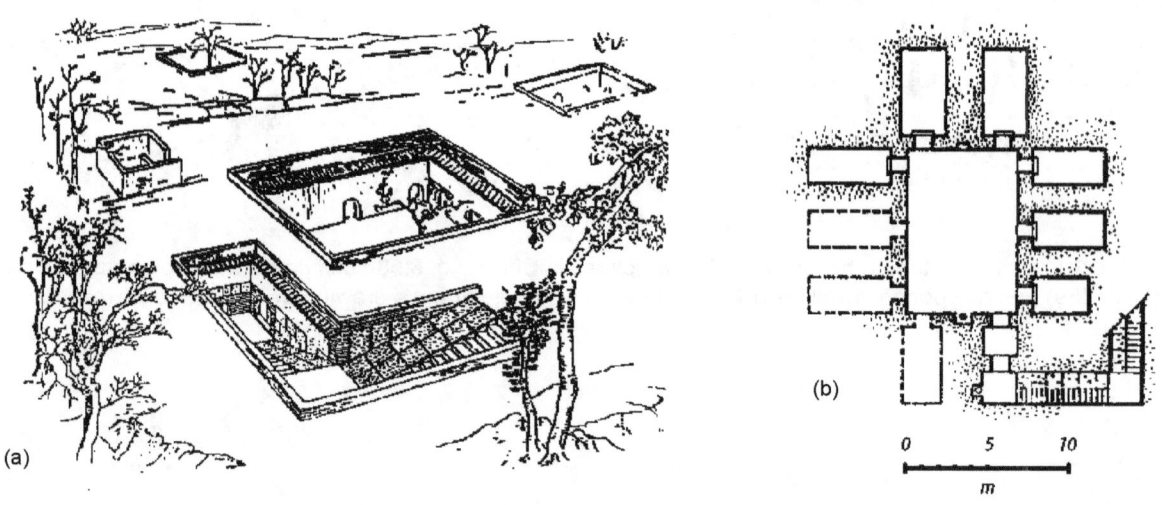

FIGURE A6.11 Troglodyte pit-dwelling on the Loess highland along the Yellow River: (a) cross section, (b) plan.

FIGURE A6.12 Planimetry of the Chinese village on the Loess highland that shows the large population density thanks to the pit-courtyard habitat [pp. 68, 231]

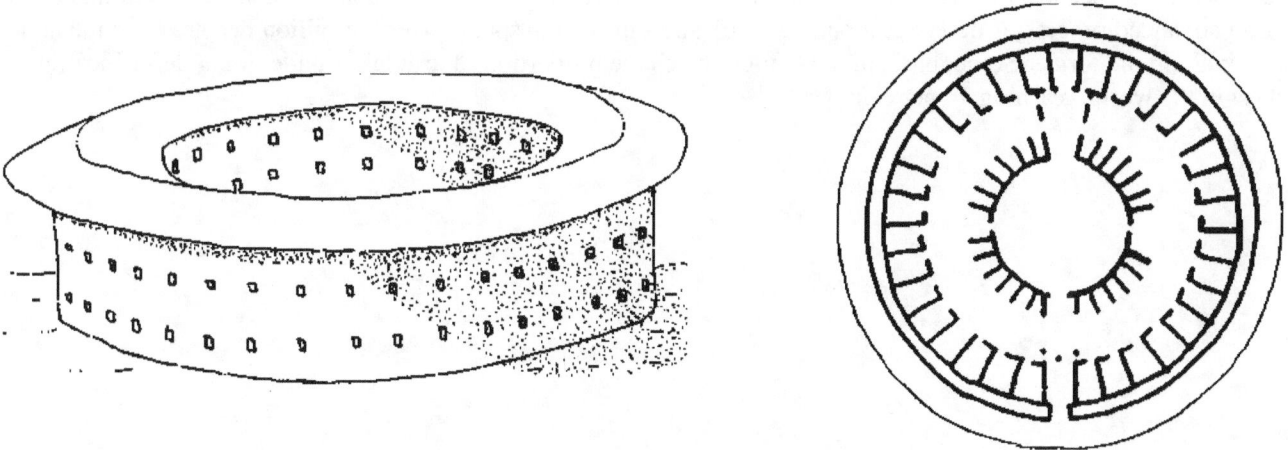

FIGURE A6.13 Circular dwelling called hwai yuen lo, a typical example of the ring buildings made of concrete and built by the hakka inhabitants of Nanjing (Fujian): (a) elevation, (b) plan.

Appendices **281**

APPENDIX 7: THE NEW PARADIGM

Global warming, the loss of biodiversity and desertification are processes that can be ascribed to human action, beginning with the industrial revolution and accelerating enormously in the last 50 years. Three different United Nations conventions have the aim of counteracting these phenomena. But if the greenhouse effect, determined by industrial emissions, has to be tackled with global agreements, the problem of desertification requires local actions that provide an example of a different way of existing. Rains are beneficial or destructive according to the management of the soil, that is the degree of organisation of the slopes, the plant cover, and urban aggression on the territory. Traditional knowledge that for centuries had guaranteed the environmental and landscape order, balancing the alternating climatic conditions and natural, seasonal or catastrophic adversities, and ensuring the renewability of resources, has now been lost because of development based on the destruction of nature, migrations of peoples, and unlimited production growth. The prevailing technology used is that of industrialisation pushed by modernism and consumerism, though it is now clear that the same choice on the part of all countries would be incompatible with life on a planetary scale.

A different model based on appropriate innovative technologies can be derived from traditional knowledge. These technologies are already available, but to develop and spread they require a cultural and social change. It has always been so in human history. The Neolithic transformation was not brought about by the technology used in agriculture and animal husbandry, which was already familiar and was applied only in the face of environmental pressures. The present emergency is caused by the water crisis in the form of an excess or scarcity of water, soil erosion and environmental and urban collapse. It will change the living conditions of millions of individuals in the near future, imposing an alternative vision of the economy, a human development founded on cultural diversities, a new technological paradigm guided by the multifunctional and holistic wisdom of tradition.

A7.1 Desertification and Soil Degradation in the World

Desertification concerns every area of the planet, rapidly increasing the threat to 30 per cent of the available land. The United Nations Convention to combat desertification (Unccd) defines it thus: degradation of the land in arid, semiarid and sub-humid zones due to various causes, including variations in climate and to human activity. The coloured areas on the maps are those subject to degradation and the different shading shows how humid or dry each area is.

The most intense forms of desertification can be found in over 100 countries, threatening the survival of more than a billion people. Every year 24 billion tons of topsoil is lost. In the course of the last two decades the worldwide loss was the equivalent of all the arable land in the United States. The situation is particularly dramatic in the arid zones, where about 70 per cent of the areas, corresponding to a quarter of the entire earth's surface, are threatened. In Italy 27 per cent of the territory is exposed to a high risk of erosion. The regions of Apulia, Basilicata, Calabria, Sicily, and Sardinia show signs of an advanced process of desertification. Desertification in Asia is spread over 1.4 billion hectares and the areas most at risk are in the former Soviet bloc. In the United States the proportion of arid lands undergoing desertification is the highest in the world, reaching 74 per cent.

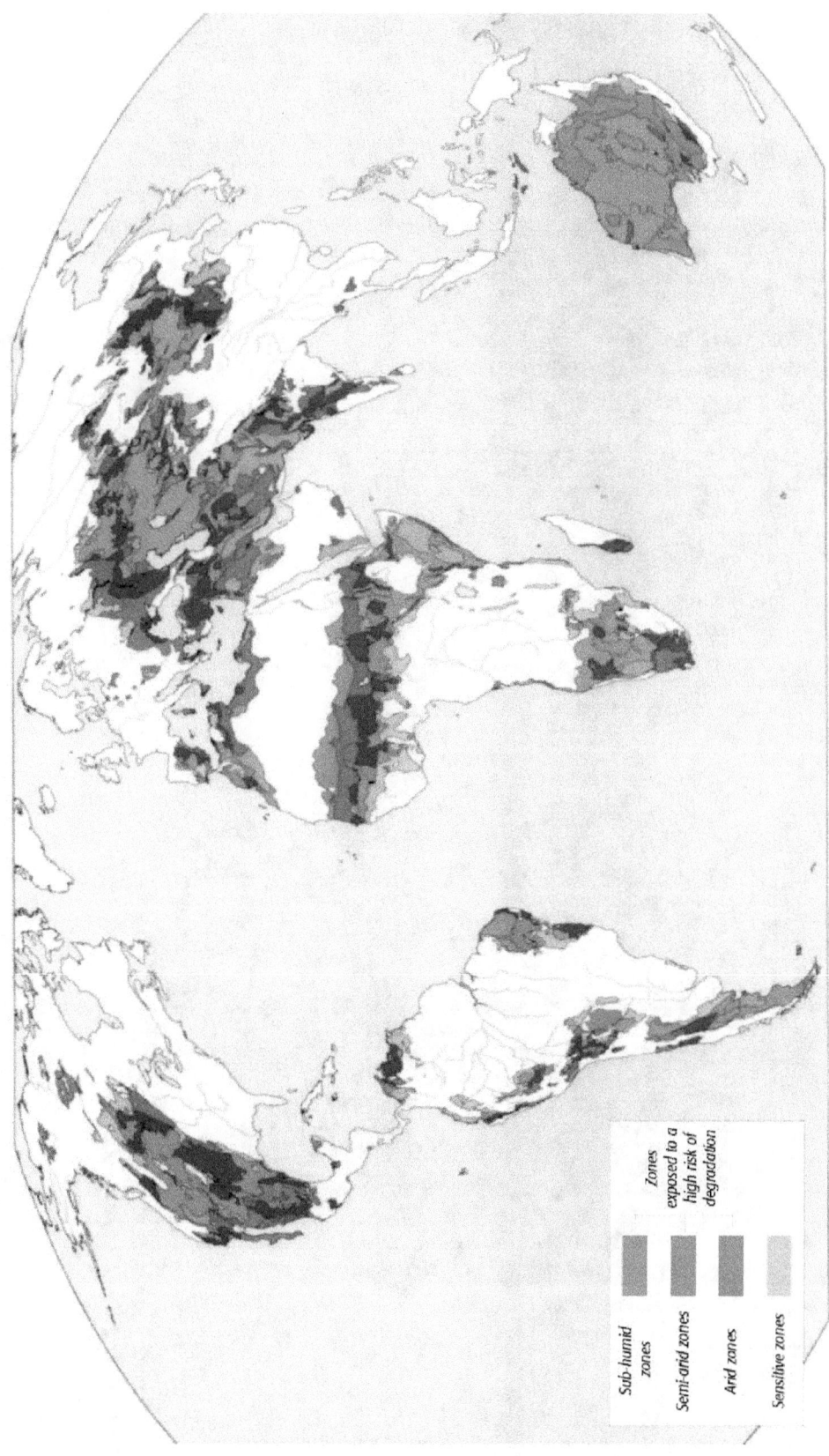

FIGURE A7.1 Zones exposed to a risk of high degradation.

Appendices

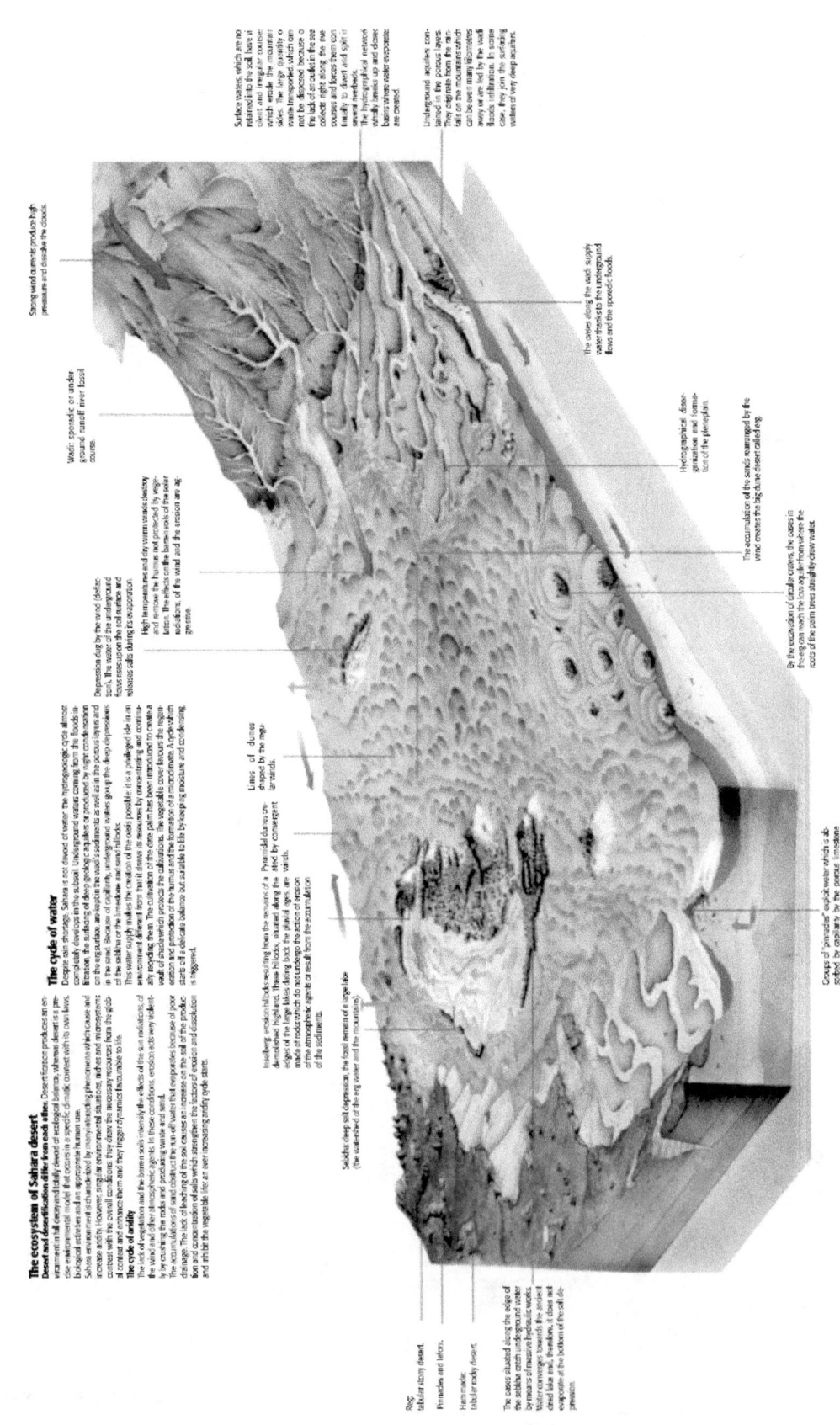

FIGURE A7.2 The ecosystem of Sahara desert.

A7.2 The Cycle of Water

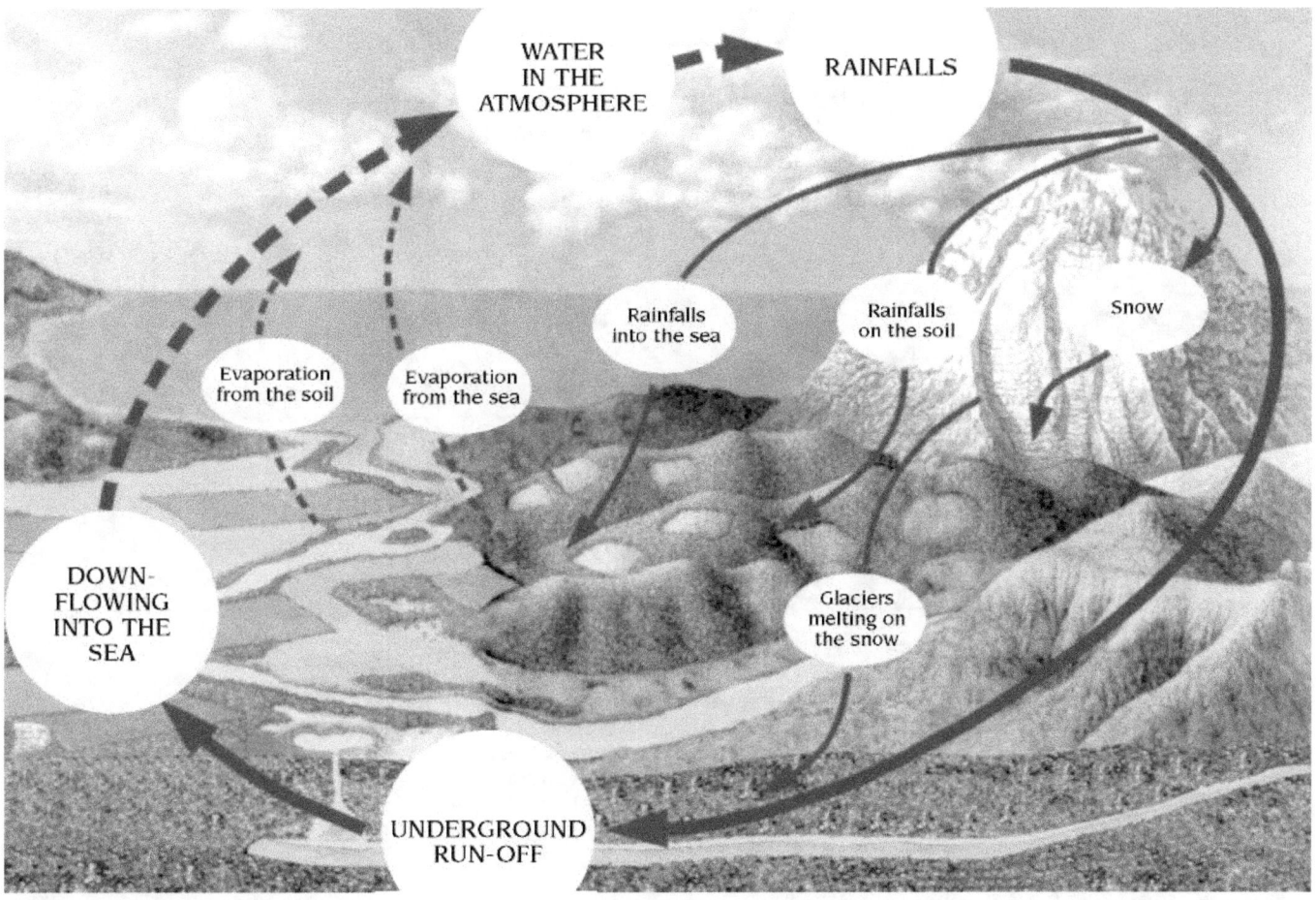

FIGURE A7.3 Our planet is a closed ecosystem which receives from the outside the sun's energy that feeds all the processes. The latter works within cycles involving stable quantities of resources that are not consumed and exhausted but rather are constantly used. The residues of a process or organism are the main resource to start up a new activity as well as a different form of life. Self-regulation and an active balance, without a hypertrophic and expensive growth, are the main characteristics of the cycles which can be both organic and inorganic and both forms can coexist. In particular, the water cycle is based on an inorganic element, i.e. water that thanks to solar energy evaporates from the oceans, loses salt and is purified; water determines weather and soil conditions; it moulds, carves, hollows out, or erodes landscape. In its constant presence in the air, on the soil, in the subsoil, and in the sea water, it interacts with all forms of life to which it is absolutely necessary.

A7.3 Complex Traditional System: The Oasis Model

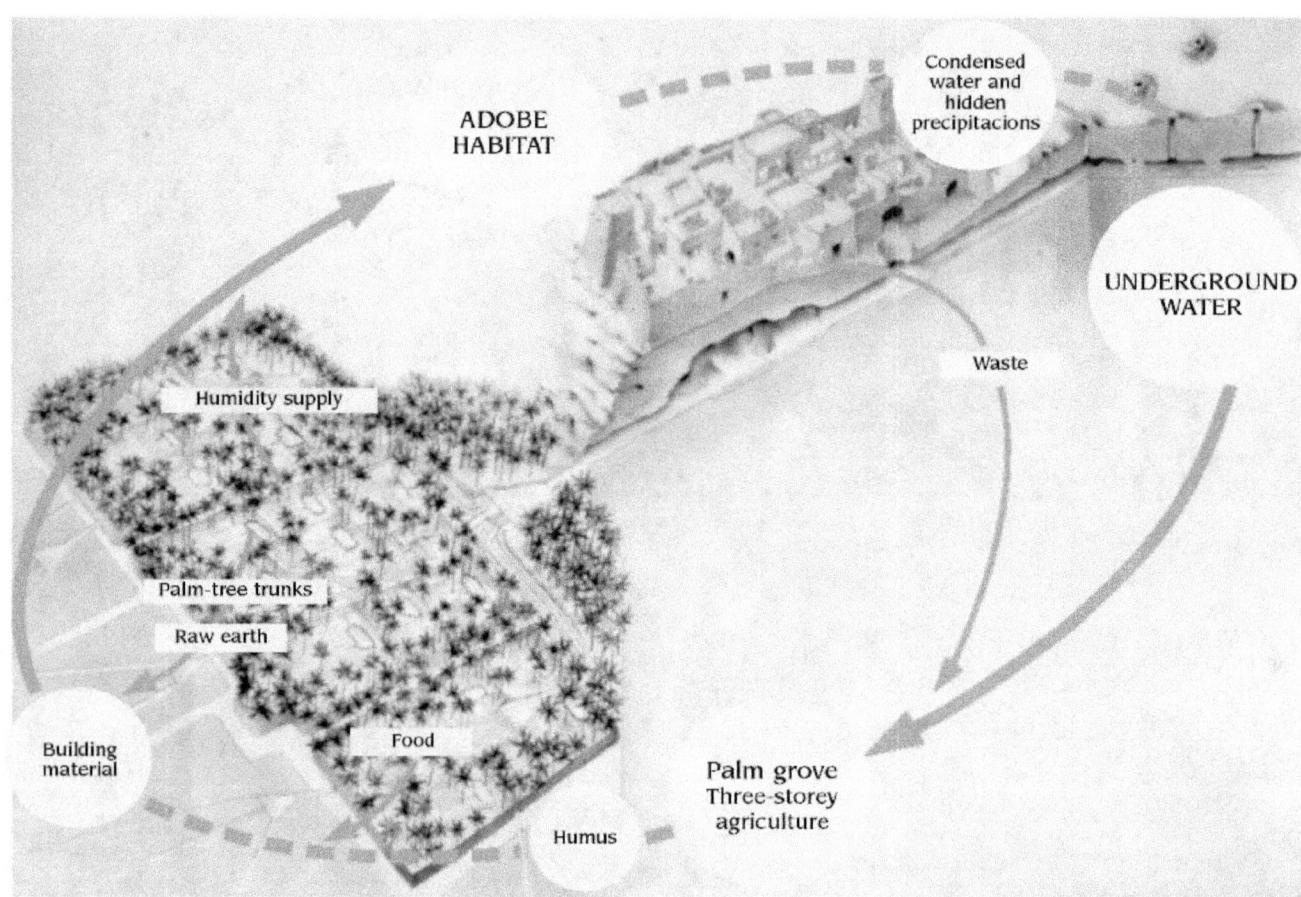

FIGURE A7.4 The oasis is a self-catalytic system in which the first supply of water condensation and moisture is increased by the installation of palm trees which produce shade, attract organisms, and form humus. The palm-grove determines a humid microclimate fed by hidden precipitations, water condensation, and underground drainage through the underground passageways of the foggaras. The adobe habitat does not waste wood for firing bricks, it is kept cool by the underground water passageway and provides waste to fertilise the fields. The system runs the water resource in a cycle of use which is not only compatible with the renewable quantities available but also increases them.

A7.4 Complex Traditional System: the Ecosystem of Shibam

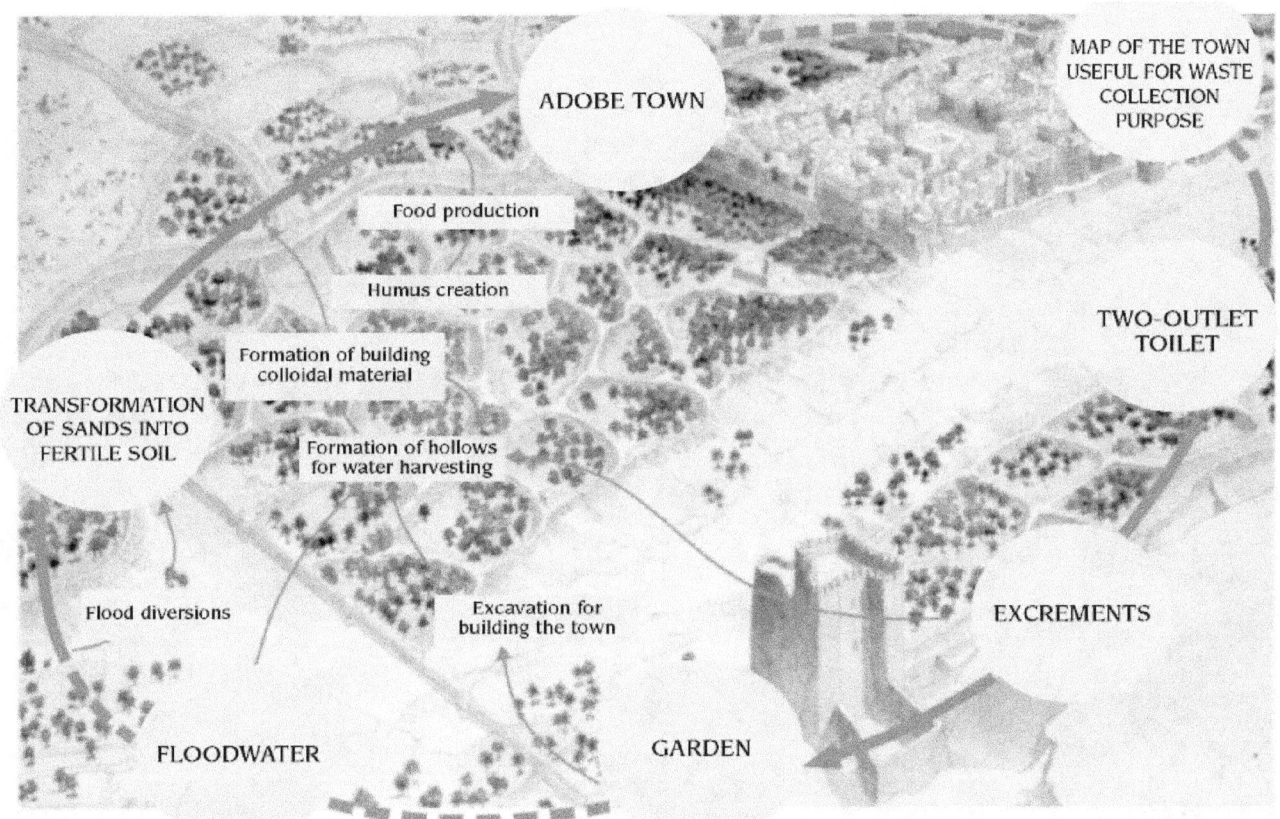

FIGURE A7.5 In Shibam the habitat is important for the fertilisation of the fields with which it interacts in an indissoluble cycle of careful use of the resources. The town is able to meet the need of collecting human excrements, thanks to the kind of closet, the fabric of the houses, and the whole planimetry. Excrement, essential in order to cultivate the desert, is dried in the sun. Thanks to the supply of flood waters impounded by deviation dams, the excrement turns into humus and colloidal material, which is dug out and used for building and periodically renovating the tall adobe houses of the town. Depressions are made, surrounded by embankments and channels, and shaded by the palm-grove. Their function is that of providing agricultural foodstuffs and protecting the habitat from the floods by absorbing and storing quantities of water.

A7.5 Complex Traditional System: the Ecosystem of Matera

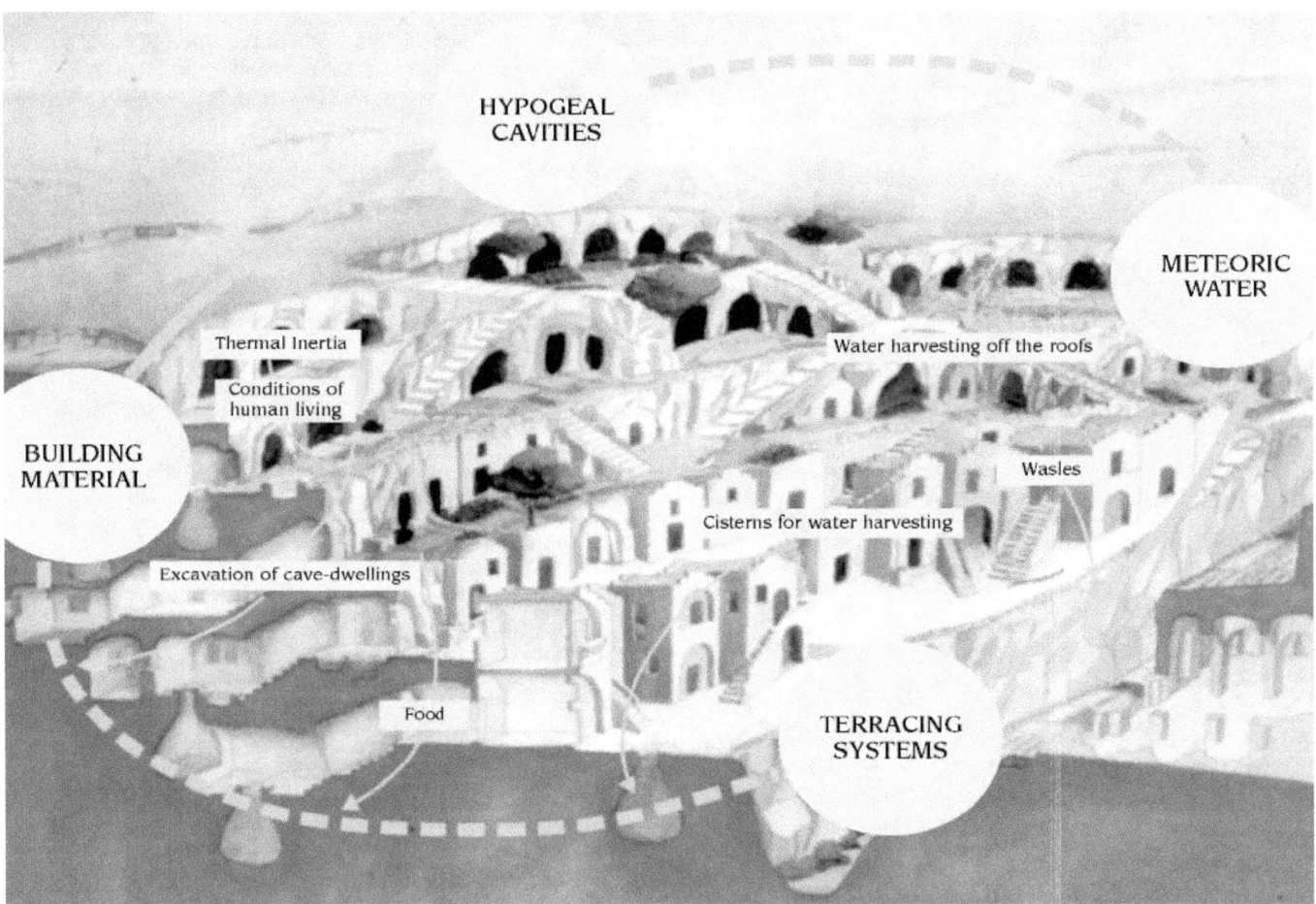

FIGURE A7.6 In the Sassi of Matera the digging of caves drains the slope and the inside of the rock thus making the cavities useful and providing water storage for the inhabitants and the terrace crops. The digging material is used for building the cave-dwellings by extending forward the lateral caves of each terrace and for building the protected courtyards. The rainwater off the roofs is harvested in the well inside the courtyard. In order to accomplish this task the pitches of the roofs do not protrude from the houses but they are rather built within the walls, where the community life of the neighbourhood takes place. The hypogeums, whose temperature is constantly 15°C, provide heat in winter time and cool in summer time. The layout of small streets and stairs is useful to channel rainwater for farming the terraces, which because of the urban development become saturated with houses or turn into hanging gardens.

A7.6 The Traditional Model for A New Technological Paradigm

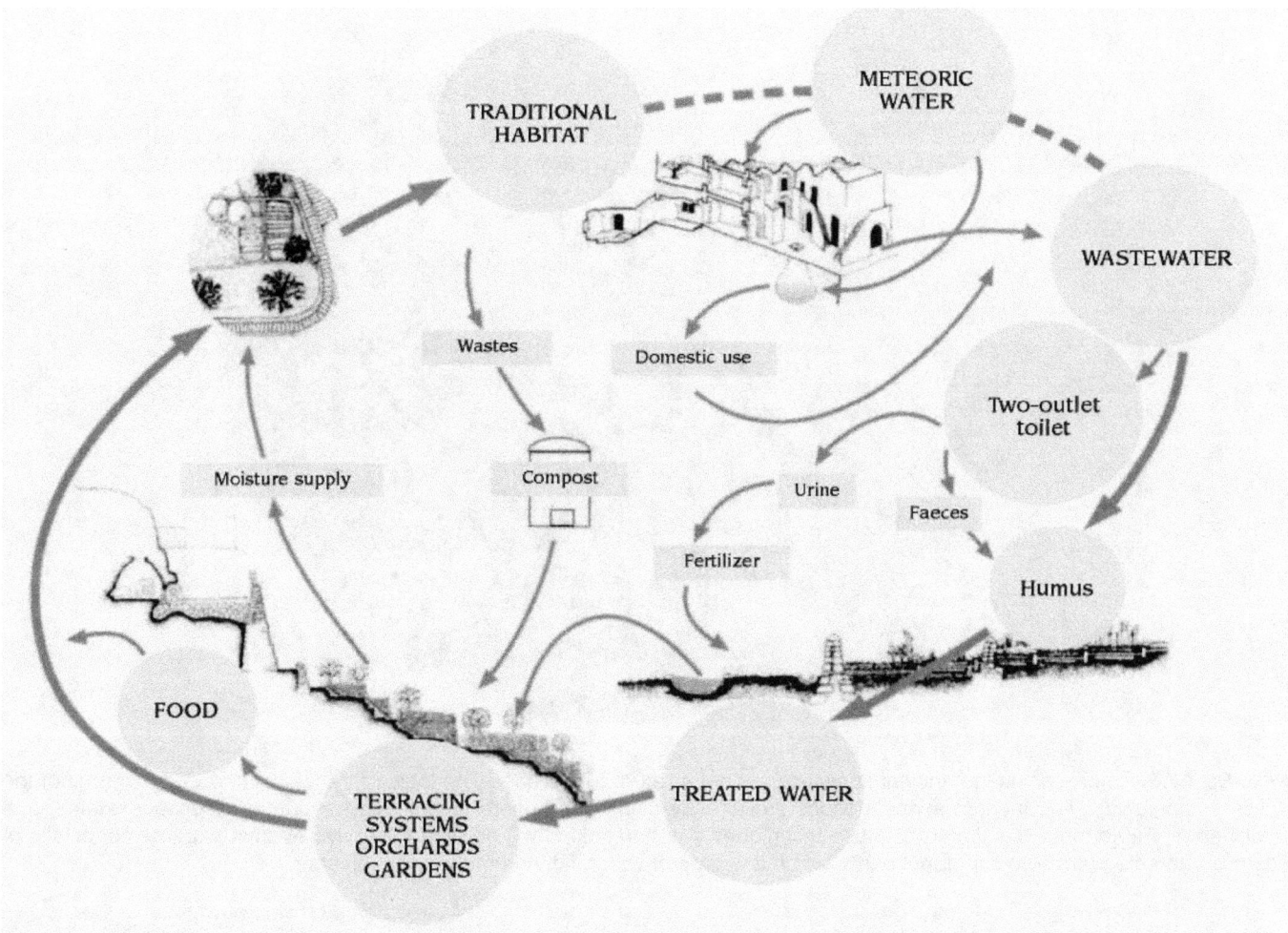

FIGURE A7.7 Each traditional technique, classified and safeguarded, is an exceptional heritage of experience and knowledge which is in danger today but which may be spread and reused. However, it is not a question of reproducing exactly the solutions in each context but rather of adopting the logic within which they operate also by using advanced technologies. Natural cycles and traditional urban ecosystems show processes based on a harmonious use of resources wherein each manufacturing process produces wastes which are not a problem but are a source of materials for the other components of the overall activity. Sustainable management of the territory and of the towns derives from the application of these principles learnt from tradition. The latter has always been a dynamic system able to incorporate innovation put to the test of long-term use and of local and environmental sustainability. Traditional knowledge is, therefore, re-proposed as innovative, appropriate, and advanced knowledge for the elaboration of a new technological paradigm.

FIGURE A7.8 Re-proposing the ancient knowledge is not a return to the past. The logic of traditional knowledge is that of the future technologies. The modern space stations are already using appropriate techniques, resources disposal systems, and a fully energy autonomy. It is thanks to these techniques that humankind will be able to survive even in extreme conditions of cosmos and safeguard also our planet earth, which is a drop of water in the immensity of universe.

APPENDIX 8: TECHNOLOGIES AND PROJECTS FOR THEIR APPLICATION
A8.1 Reuse of Traditional Techniques

In the cycle of nature the elements water, air, earth, and fire are linked. This principle is part of traditional knowledge and should be maintained when restoring the landscape and planning the territory and the self-sustainable city. The lack of resources is the result of destruction and waste. Enormous quantities of rainwater are not collected, and valuable drinking water is used for personal hygiene. The sun's energy has always been present in tradition and today, with modern photovoltaic techniques, it could solve the energy problems of a whole nation. The mountains of refuse and the quantities of water used, which are a problem today, could become a resource. With innovative techniques, suited to the environment and to local society, it is possible to implement programmes for obtaining water from the atmosphere, energy from the sun, soil and fertilisers from recycling: a harmonious human development that is compatible with culture and nature.

A8.1.1 Water from the Atmosphere

Starting from the experience of the traditional converters made of stone various innovative forms of water production have been tried.

Atmospheric condenser – The device consists of a dome 12 m high and 12 m in diameter, built on a hilltop. The stone walls are 2.5 m thick and contain seven rows of apertures, two of which near the base and five near the top. Inside there is an impermeable hollow cylindrical column, through which porous pipes pass. The central column is equipped with sharp edges made of pieces of slate pointing down towards the ground to increase the contact surface with the air and help drops to form. In the centre there is a cylindrical cavity 1 m in diameter and 9 m high, with a metal pipe inserted into its axis, acting as a chimney with an outlet to the air at a height of 50 cm above the dome. Below ground there is a cistern, equipped with a water pump, which can be inspected from the bottom of a flight of steps. During the day the inner chamber, insulated by the thickness of the walls, stays low. The hot air outside enters upper the air pipes, runs along the inside walls, is cooled and, helped by the humidity absorbed by the porous pipes that maintain a more saturated layer on the surface, reaches condensation point. Drops form on the sharp edges and fall into the collecting cistern. The cooled air comes out through the lower pipes. The central metal pipe has the task of intercepting air during the night to keep the condensing mass cool. The condensation capacity depends on keeping the inside temperature low. In order for the condenser to function properly, there must be a difference of at least 15 degrees centigrade between the outside and inside temperatures. In traditional condensers this situation, with the condenser producing as much as 16 cubic metres of water, was guaranteed by the huge mass of stones.

The Knapen air well – This system works in the same way as the previous device. Unlike the traditional water-capturing devices (Appendix 3, Fig. 20) that work both day and night, these systems condense only the water vapour contained in the air during the day. They are impermeable to the outside, and they can only capture daytime atmospheric water. Thus the quantity of water produced is not affected by night frost.

Humidity collector – The system consists of irregular lumps of limestone, piled up to a height of 2.5 m on a 3 m square platform. The construction has the appearance of a truncated pyramid covered with an impermeable cement layer, in which there are air holes from top to bottom. The platform leans slightly towards the centre, where a conduit leads to the underground collection chamber that can be reached from an external staircase. The system works in the daytime when the air is warmer and the limestone is colder than the outside temperature. However, the temperature difference alone would not be enough to reach condensation point: the action of the stones is also necessary. The limestone, by absorption, fixes the humidity on the porous surface, creating a more saturated layer in which the water vapour present in the air condenses at an even higher temperature than that of the dew formation gradient. Therefore through heat inertia the limestone mass has the role of a condenser, and thanks to its porosity it acts as a humidity absorber and catalyst. A structure of this kind, Chaptal's collector, has produced 87,833 litres of water during the hot season.

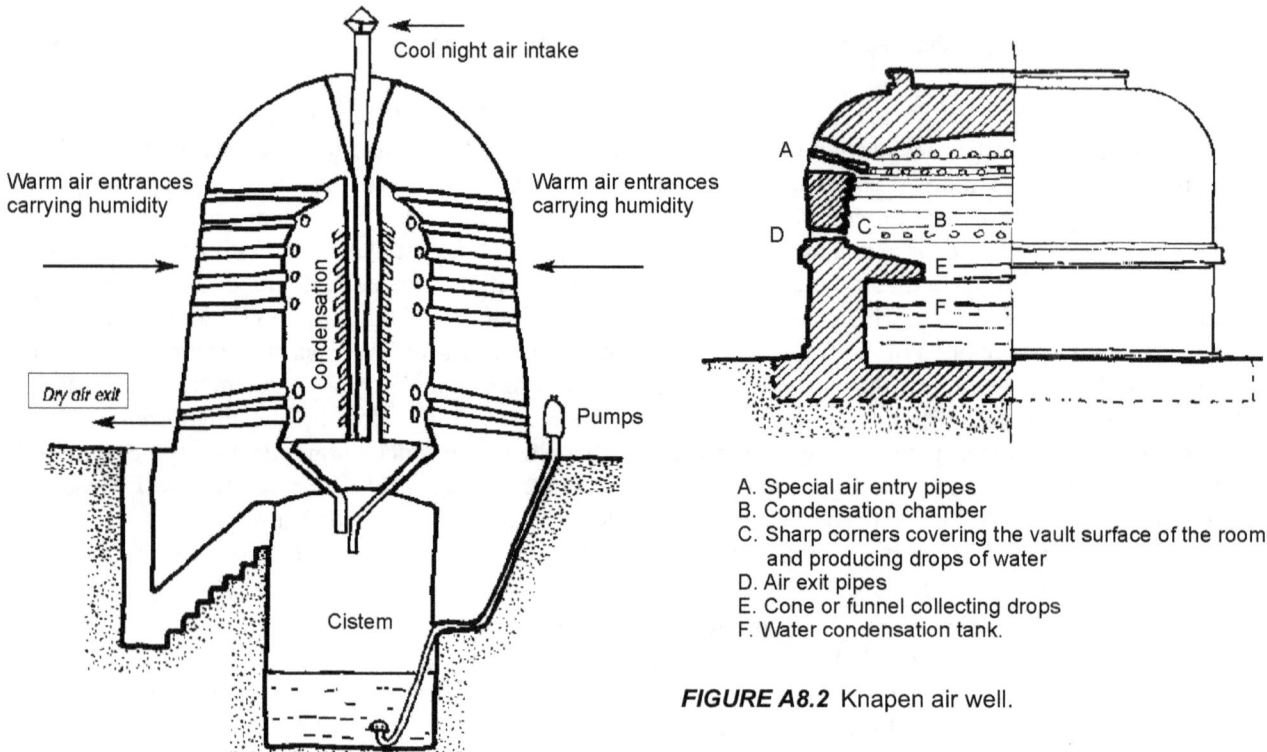

FIGURE A8.1 Atmospheric condenser.

A. Special air entry pipes
B. Condensation chamber
C. Sharp corners covering the vault surface of the room and producing drops of water
D. Air exit pipes
E. Cone or funnel collecting drops
F. Water condensation tank.

FIGURE A8.2 Knapen air well.

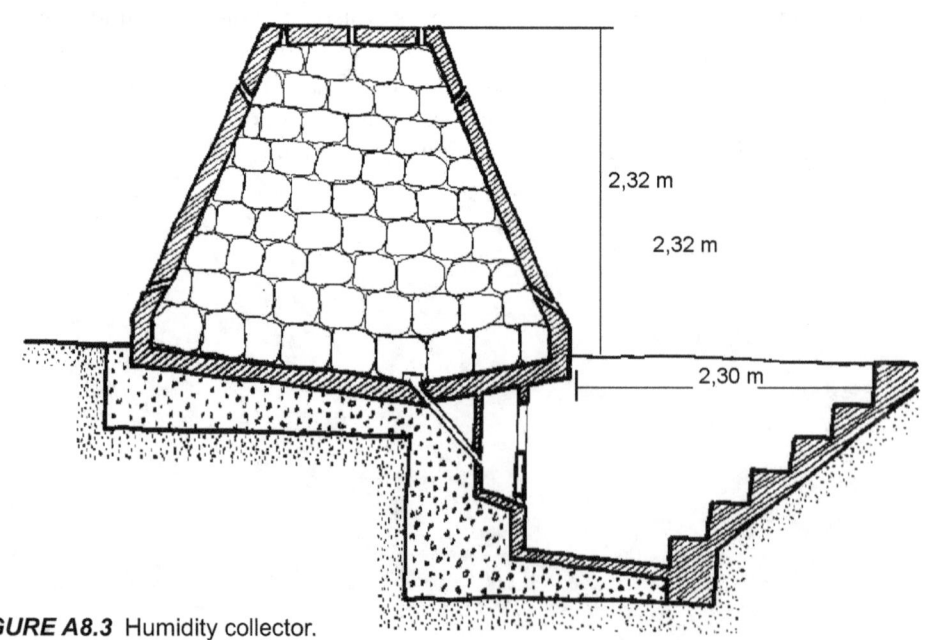

FIGURE A8.3 Humidity collector.

292   Water conservation techniques in traditional human settlements

A8.1.2 Energy from the Sun

By analysing the bio-climate of a place it is possible to draw the maximum benefit from its natural conditions. Passive architecture techniques are preferred, including natural ventilation, cooling by evaporation or drying or shielding, chimneys and underground piping. Moreover, passive solar heating is achieved, thanks to masses that accumulate an enormous amount of heat or that produce a greenhouse effect with photovoltaic cells. The bio-climatic diagram indicates the most appropriate actions according to the humidity and temperature. Following these principles it is possible to build an ecological house suited to the local conditions. Photovoltaic cells can be inserted in the roof as tiles or cover a porch or be inserted into the windowpanes. They are able to produce the necessary energy for a house and surplus energy that is returned to the network. The house can be equipped with water collectors on the roof for washing purposes and for watering the hanging gardens. A living area is created below the roof garden, naturally cooled by the vegetation above. Refuse collection with a biological waste bin and the resulting compost provide the soil for the hanging gardens. Shields and windows facing the same direction as the walls provide heating during the cold season and cooling in the summer.

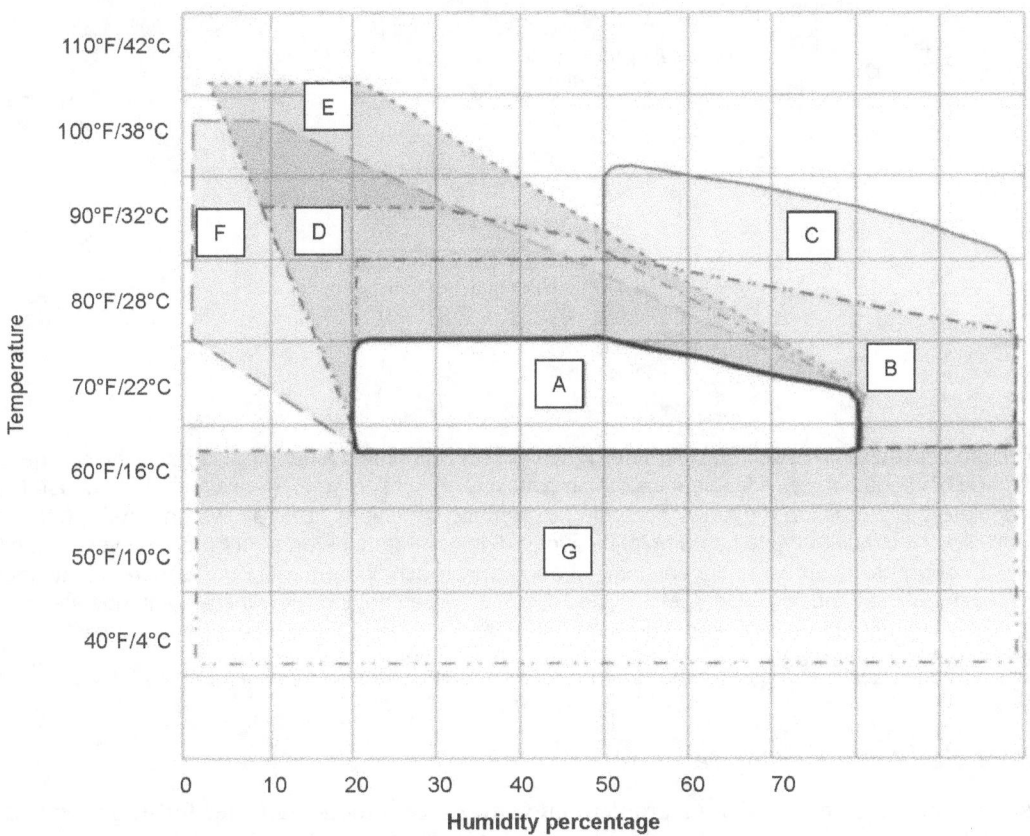

The necessary works according to the gradient temperature/humidity

A. Comfort zone
B. Natural ventilation
C. Cooling by drying and underground piping
D. Mass with a huge thermal accumulation
E. Mass with a huge thermal accumulation with night ventilation
F. Cooling by evaporation
G. Passive solar heating

Passive heating and cooling
– Solar check
– Natural ventilation (chimneys effect)
– Cooling by evaporation (by means of underground pipes)
– Mass with a huge thermal accumulation (pool roof)
– Systems of passive solar heating

FIGURE A8.4 Bio-climatic abacus indicating the devices to be adopted according to the environmental conditions.

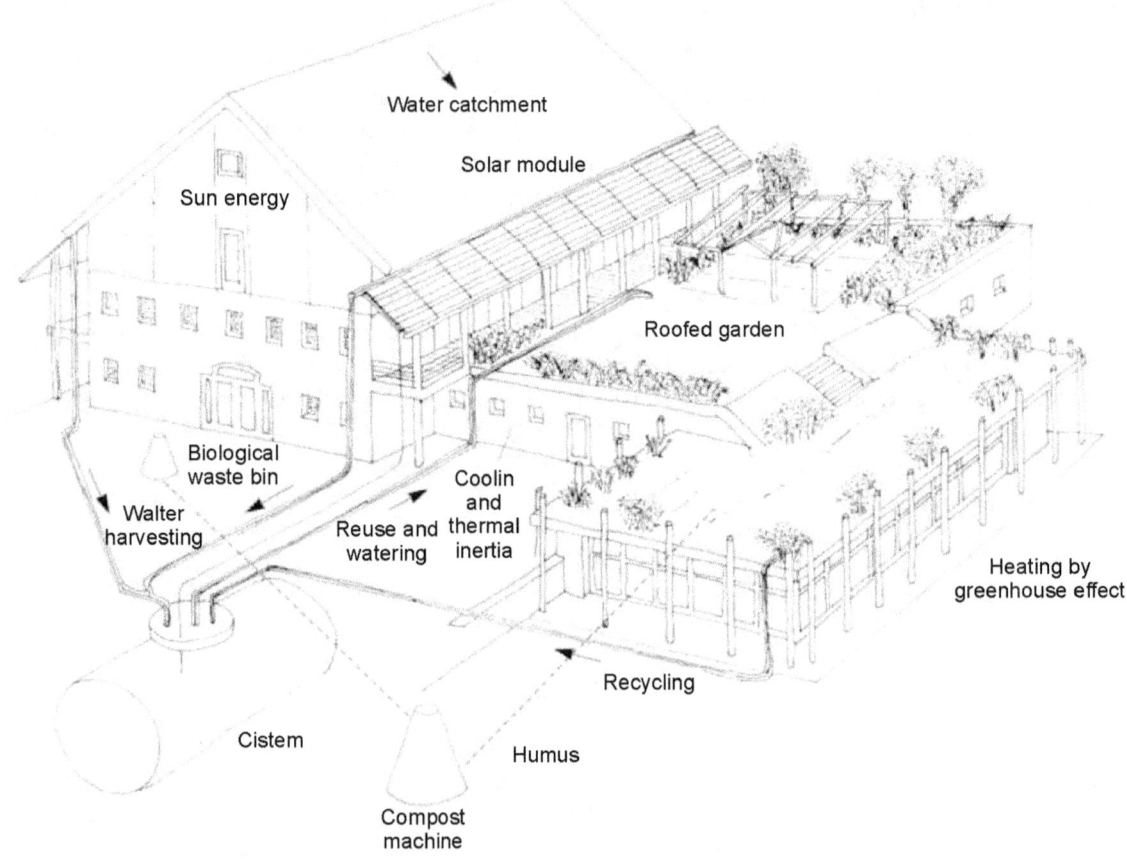

FIGURE A8.5 Ecological dwelling based on solar energy, water harvesting, and a hanging garden. The roof garden consisting of a hanging roof made of vegetation provides heat insulation both in winter in summer. Thanks to their homeostatic qualities, plants automatically regulate the protection they give according to climatic conditions. This allows energy for heating to be reduced by up to 50% and electric conditioning to be completely avoided. In summer time on a roof made of vegetation the temperature does not exceed 25 degrees, whereas a conventional covering may reach 80 degrees. Furthermore, plants improve the quality of the air by producing oxygen and retaining dust particles. From an urban point of view the advantages are so significant that in Tokyo, where the mean temperature increased 3 degrees in the last few years, the city council has forced people to replace roof tiles and cement with the roof gardens.

A8.1.3 Fertile Soil from Recycling

Disposal of excrement can be turned from a problem into a resource, producing water for irrigation and fertile land. In urban areas nowadays there are many systems that can directly process excrement, without having to build big sewage systems. These toilets that produce compost are based on the "aerobic digestion" of waste. Aerobic systems are odourless, and the air emitted is composed of carbon dioxide and water vapour, unlike the anaerobic process that, taking place without oxygen, has a bad smell and releases methane gas. Compost production takes place in a decomposition chamber where organic soil is created, and must be placed under the bathroom and kitchen outlets; it must be possible to inspect the chamber in order to be able to remove the humus produced. The compost obtained has a bacterial content, consistency, and colour similar to the surface layer of the soil. Similar systems have been devised to transform organic kitchen waste into compost. Larger scale systems include phytodepuration, directing the water along cultivated terraces that purify the liquid using the physiological processes of the plants that it irrigates. Phytodepuration systems on terraces are the most suitable and often the only possible solution in arid and semiarid or karst regions such as in southern Italy, and in general regions lacking in rivers for water disposal and where purification in lagoons is a strain on the environment.

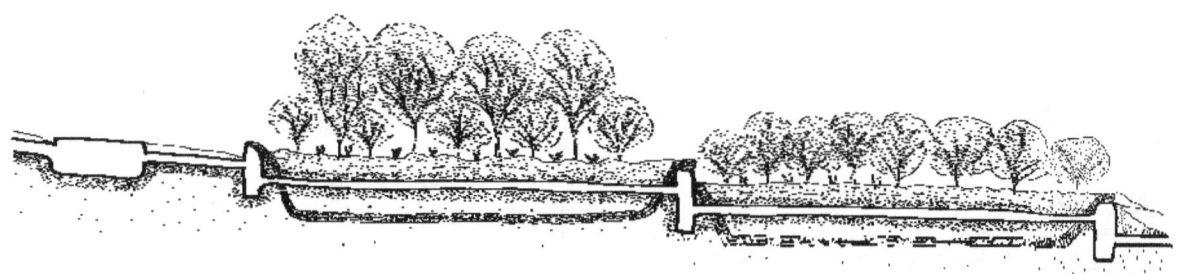

FIGURE A8.6 Water disposal system on terraces and phytodepuration.

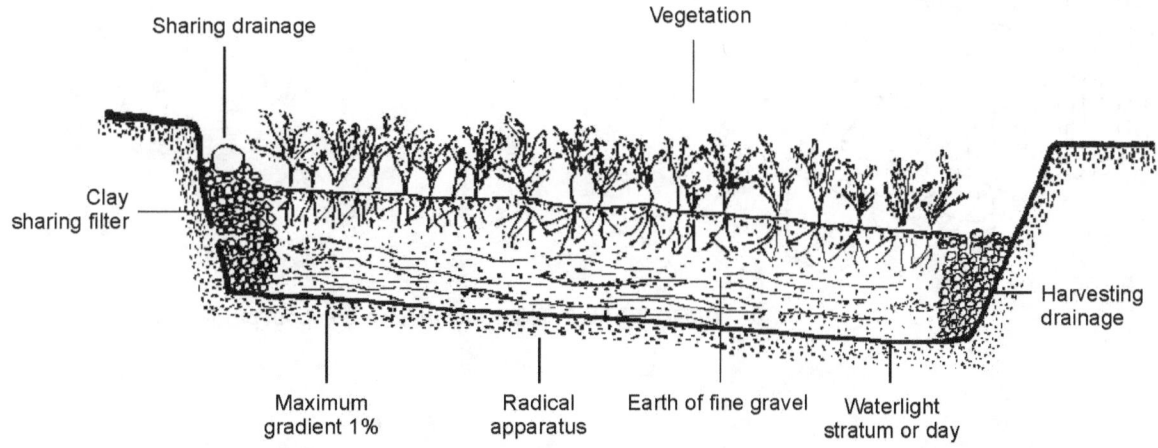

FIGURE A8.7 A detail of the disposal system of wastewater: percolation bed used to create subsurface flow systems.

FIGURE A8.8 A detail of the wastewater disposal system: hollow pipes disperse water into the soil.

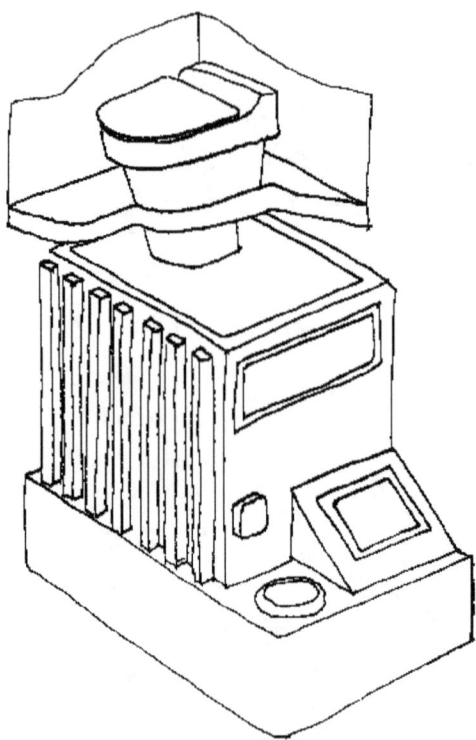

FIGURE A8.9 Toilet with its own compost production system.

FIGURE A8.10 Restoration of the hanging gardens and the terraced steps of the gravina of Laterza (Laureano, 1999). The traditional practice of hanging cultivations is confirmed by the restoration and amplified by the organisation of terraced slopes used in the phytodepuration system.

FIGURE A8.11 Application of the phytodepuration system by means of terraces in wadi Hadramaut (Yemen). Below the town a system of consecutive terraces (A) in harmony with the traditional landscape drains wastewater that would otherwise stagnate in the environment that lacks rivers able to collect them (Laureano, 1993).

A8.2 Projects for A Sustainable World

After the Rio Conference on the environment and development (Unced, 1992), in the light of the new economic, technological, and environmental changes, it is necessary to assess the application of the resolutions passed in Rio, known as Agenda 21. This resolution had the merit of asserting the transnational nature of problems such as the water crisis and pollution, which affect countries and regions beyond their place of origin. Climate change, the thinning of the ozone layers, the management of water in the oceans and drinking water, deforestation, desertification and soil degradation, the spreading of waste, the loss of biodiversity and cultural diversity, massive urbanisation, and agricultural industrialisation: these are all problems that must be tackled with the concerted action of the whole world. Both general agreements such as those on greenhouse gas emissions to combat global warming and local actions are needed.

In particular, unanimous agreement has been reached about the impossibility of separating environmental protection from the fight against poverty and the lack of human and social progress. For this reason the concept of sustainable development has been adopted. The World Commission on environment and development has defined it: "development that fulfils present needs without compromising the possibility for future generations to fulfil their needs". This concept has been recognised as a primary objective at both local and international level, an imperative for the perpetuation of human life on Earth. To achieve this there must be integration between the economic, social, and environmental dimensions and new ways of conceiving productive and consumer activities. The next task is on the one hand to assess the extent to which this process called "visions for sustainable development" (Johannesburg Summit, 2002) has been implemented, and on the other hand to carry out concrete actions towards the project's completion. These projects are promoted everywhere in the world, based on a commitment to protect the environment, and the will to return to the traditional techniques, processes, and landscape, or imposed by compelling needs for water. The aim of these experiments is to create a new, ethical economy and a technology that is able to incorporate the revolutionary values of tradition.

A8.2.1 Project for an Ecological Residential Complex in Vasteras (Sweden)

The project was completed in the 1990s, 150 km from Stockholm and involves a residential complex of six buildings with four to six storeys for a total of seventy apartments, built by the Hsb (Institute for funding public housing). The project introduces an ecological way of living in an urban environment, and is an experiment that can be generalised with the principal aim of enabling individuals to be part of the natural cycle and actively protect the environment. The project is based on building a courtyard and creating spaces that allow ecological waste management: from the toilet based on the separation of solids and liquids according to the ancient tradition of the Yemen, and separate kitchen waste collection, to the use of compost in the condominium's vegetable garden.

Part of the water, collected from the roofs by means of gutters goes directly to the apartments for domestic uses; the remainder, coming from domestic drains and from the paved areas in the garden, is used for irrigation, after being stored in a cistern and filtered.

For solid waste there is a compost production system, located beneath the buildings.

The project is a return to nature on an urban scale. It does not require particular effort or costs, and it contributes to the creation of self-supporting living areas within urban settlements.

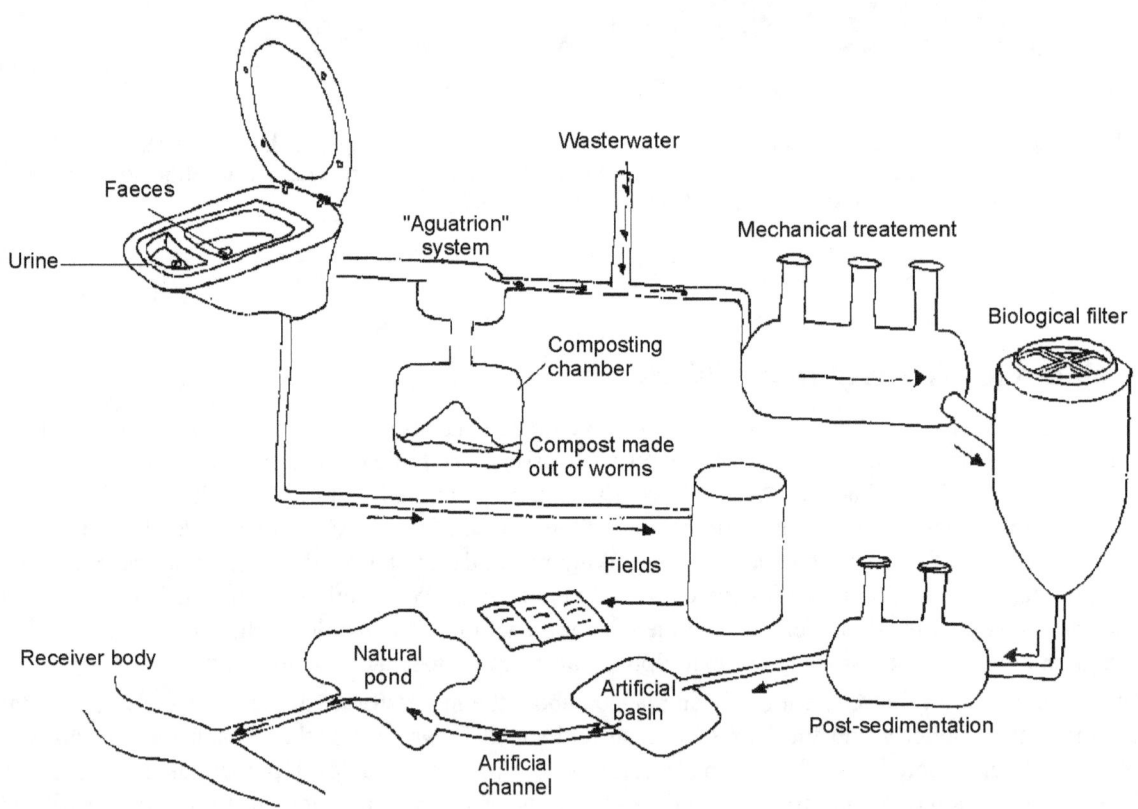

FIGURE A8.12 Diagram of the waste treatment system. Modern use of a traditional Yemenite two-outlet toilet.

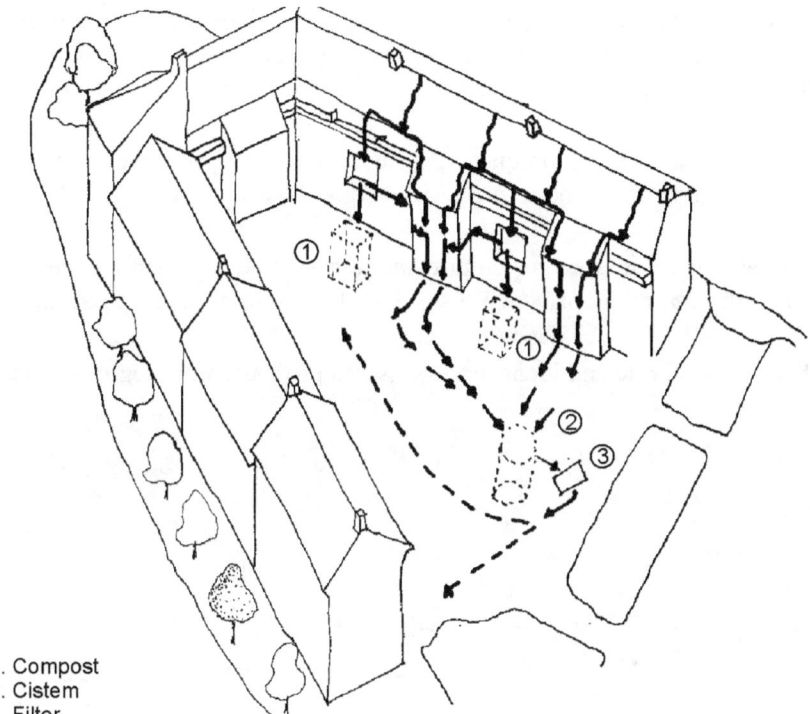

1. Compost
2. Cistern
3. Filter

FIGURE A8.13 The residential complex of Hsb in Vasteras, the ecological courtyard and the waste- and wastewater-management systems.

A8.2.2 Restoration of the Ecosystem of the Gravina di Palagianello (Italy)

Gravine are deep, eroded valleys cut into the edges of upland plains in the Murge in Basilicata and Apulia. Today they appear as natural systems, places with spontaneous vegetation, and a wild environment. On the contrary they are the result of continuous action by man, who uses and models the natural geomorphological context to build systems of habitats and cultural landscapes. The constant work of terracing slopes, controlling water flows, creating fertile land, cultivation, digging out caves, carving out stairways, and maintaining pathways creates the landscape of the gravine and contributes to the conservation of biodiversity. Without this work, which continued from the remote prehistoric past until the recent 1950s, the gravine evolved in a situation of degradation and desertification. The slope was exposed to sudden rains alternating with completely dry seasons, and where it was not protected by water collection and control systems, showed signs of erosion when wet and was arid in the dry months. The soil completely disappeared and the vegetation was reduced to residual scrub in the deepest part of the riverbed, where the original wealth of biodiversity made way for single crops of the most resilient species in situations of deterioration.

In the Palagianello gravina this process has caused a series of collapses and landslides. The landscape with cultivated terraces and a karstic environment, with limestone outcrops amid the Mediterranean scrub vegetation has given way to a deteriorated situation with alluvial cones, on which an alien and ephemeral flora grows. The project produced by the author with IPOGEA (Research Center on Local and Traditional Knowledge) consolidates and protects the side of the gravina by restoring the ecosystem. The solutions and means of intervention have been drawn from the past and present of the Palagianello environment, applying traditional knowledge and techniques and re-introducing the original landscape. The latter, with its water control systems, terraced fields and agricultural maintenance, used to protect the slope, safeguarding it from degradation and from disastrous collapse.

The project fulfils the following aims:
1. Environmental rehabilitation in the area of the Palagianello gravina by means of systems of consolidation using traditional technology and adapted new techniques, acting as a pilot project for actions of environmental sustainability in the ecological and cultural context of the gravina systems and of the slopes undergoing desertification.
2. Consolidation and protection of the chosen area, using techniques of great cultural value and interest, that at the same time require methods of execution that have high labour intensity and quality, with positive effects for local employment.
3. Thanks to the consolidation it provides an area of interest for culture and tourism and a garden for the city and for visitors, creating new employment both in bringing private plots of land back into productive use and in the overall management of the area.
4. Revival of local know-how, giving back a social role and identity to skills and professional categories discarded by modern construction systems.

FIGURE A8.14 Environmental restoration project on the prospect of the front of the gravina of Palagianello (Laureano, 2000).

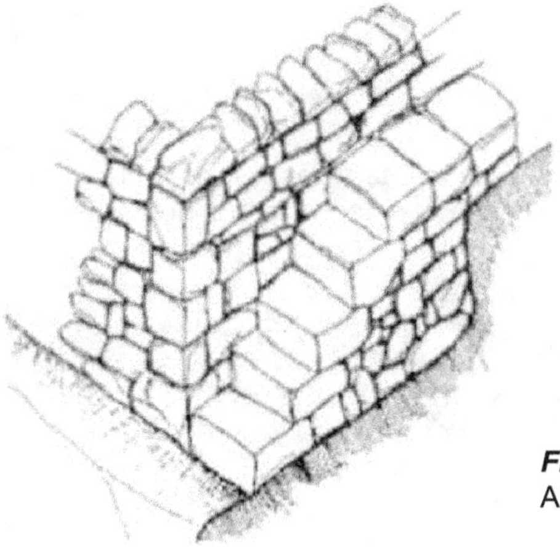

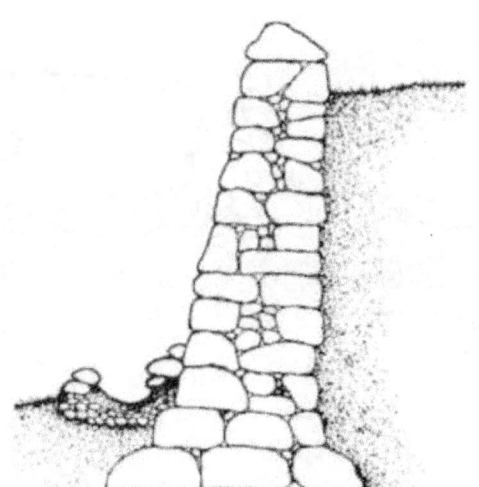

FIGURE A8.15–16. Details of the soil protection systems used in the project. Figures A8.18–19 represent the terraced slope and the addition of steps, respectively.

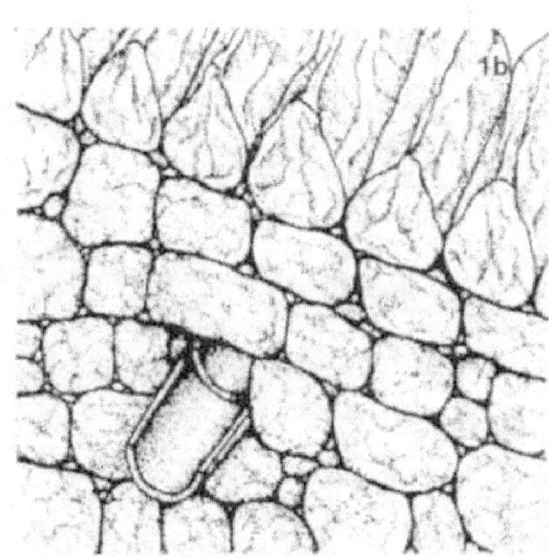

FIGURE A8.17 Supporting wall and channel.

FIGURE A8.18 Gutter.

Appendices **301**

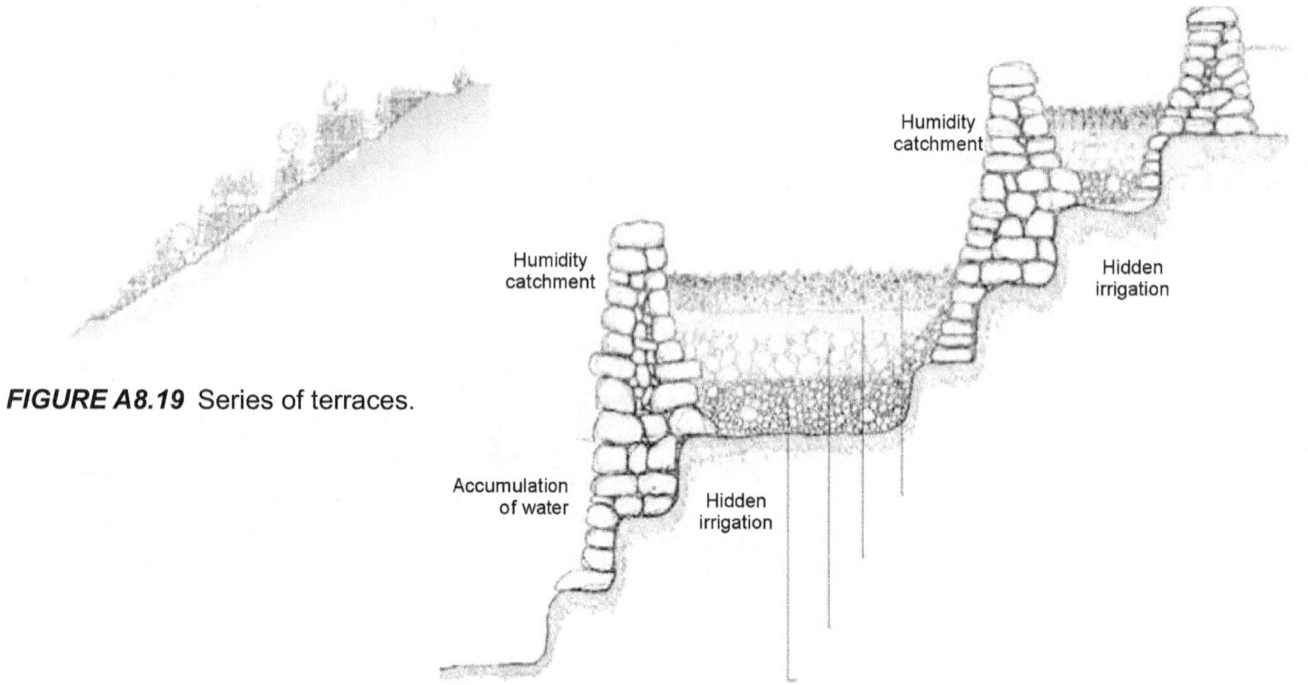

FIGURE A8.19 Series of terraces.

FIGURE A8.20 Functioning of the terraces as humidity-collection devices, irrigation systems from below and formation of humus.

FIGURE A8.21 Water system crossing the terraced slope.

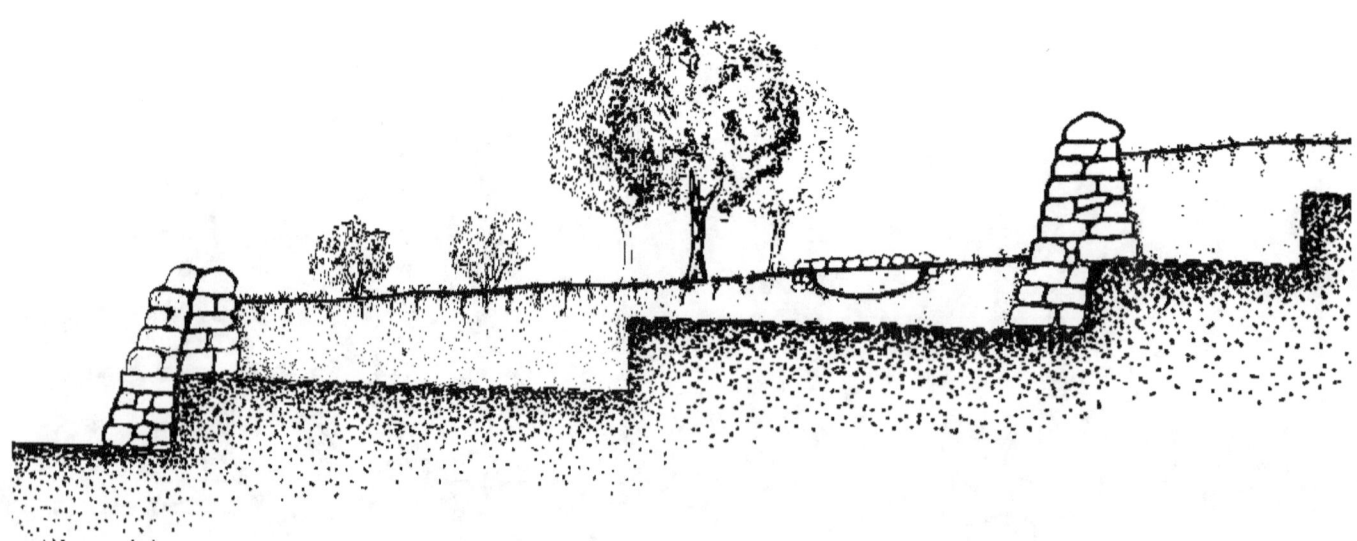

FIGURE A8.22 Creation of a microclimate reducing evaporation from the soil and starting up of a virtuous cycle of self-propulsion and self-regeneration.

A8.2.3 Restoration of the Environmental and Urban Ecosystem of the Walled City of Harar (Ethiopia)

Harar is situated 500 km from the Ethiopian capital, and for a long time was the most important and indeed the only urban settlement in the horn of Africa. Girded with imposing walls in the 16th century, the city became the commercial and spiritual centre for Muslims in Africa, a synthesis of the autochthonous hydroagricultural tradition and the southern Arabian hydraulic experience. The historical existence of the city of Harar is due to its special quality as an urban ecosystem able to fully exploit the available natural resources. Today the situation with regard to water supplies in Harar is dramatic. The water for the modern city comes from Lake Alemaya, 14 km away. It is brought by a 30-year-old pipeline that loses about 35 per cent of the water through leakage. Due to desertification the lake is also becoming shallower, and risks disappearing completely.

The ancient system for the disposal of human excrement, which was collected by donkeys and used to manure the fields, is no longer functioning and the lack of water means that western style toilets with water closets cannot be installed. On the contrary the ancient town had its own techniques for obtaining water and had impressive water systems that stretched out into the surrounding countryside and to the terraced gardens. In the rainy season the torrents swell and the water was directed by deviators and ditches towards the town to supply the water table. Interpreting Harar's hydrographic network, one can see that certain streets follow the course of the torrents that supplied the aquifers close to the houses and allowed the excess water to flow away through the doorways.

The project, produced by the author for UNESCO, presents innovative methods for applying the logic for the harmonious management of resources that belongs to Harar's historical tradition, applying the following procedures:

- Return to the floodwater control system in order to replenish the aquifers and reorganise the water reserves
- Restoration of the houses with terrace roofs as surfaces for collecting rainwater, to be stored in family cisterns
- Creation of a system for the toilet and for disposing of wastewater with dry toilets that produce manure and by phtyodepuration
- Creation of a green belt around the wall perimeter as a protection area, park, plant nursery for reforestation and as an area for the disposal of used water using phytodepuration terraces
- Involvement of the traditional corporate associations in process organisation and management.

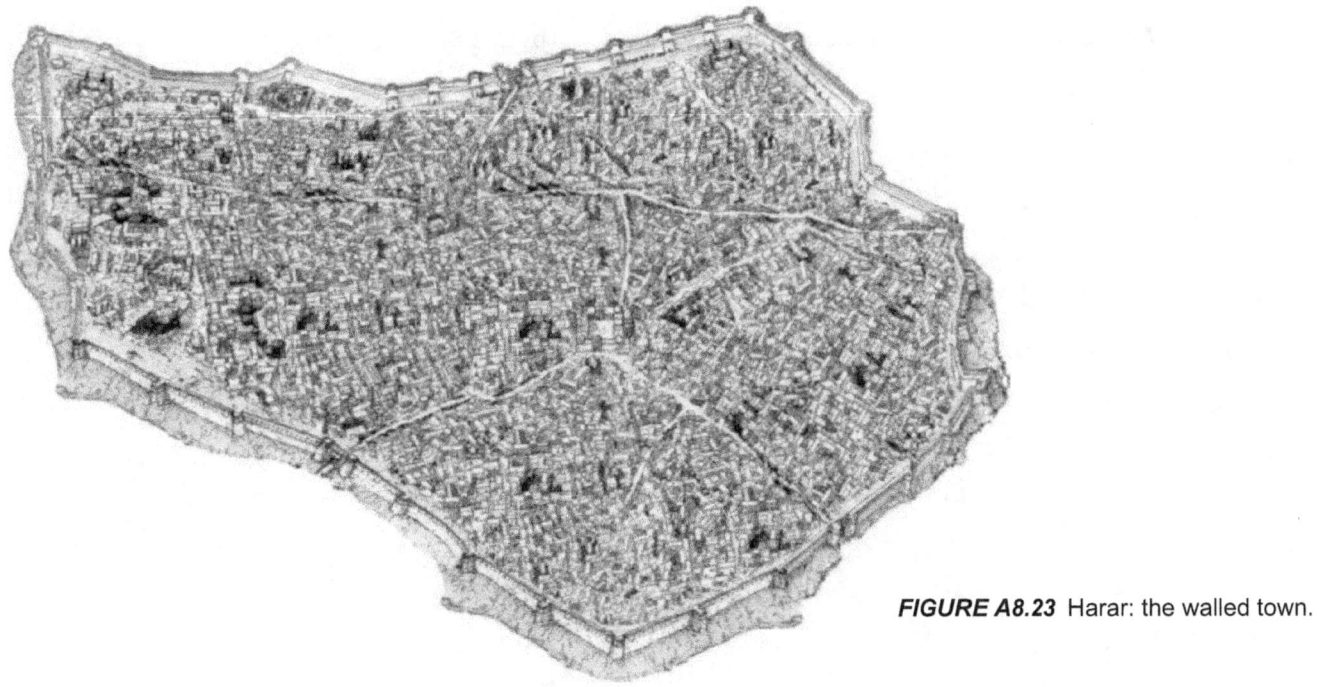

FIGURE A8.23 Harar: the walled town.

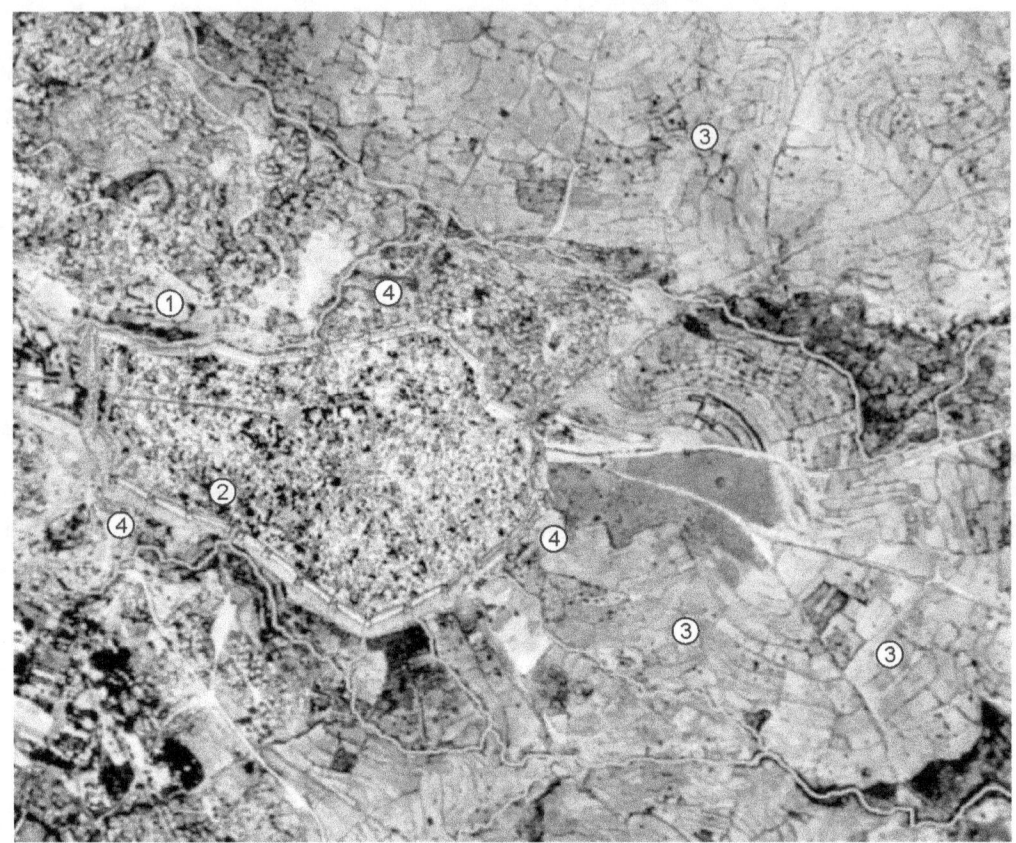

1. Water intake to replenish the aquifers in the town
2. Rearrangement of the torrent-streets and the run-off
3. Terraces
4. Green bel equipped with plant nursery for reforestation and crops
5. Regeneration of the urban area with the introduction of composting toilets

FIGURE A8.24 Environmental rehabilitation project carried out by UNESCO (Laureano, 2001).

BIBLIOGRAPHY

AA.VV.

1992 *Appropriate Technology in Post-Modern Times,* German Appropriate Technology Exchange (Gate).

1993 *Biotecnologia, recursos fitogenéticos y agricultura en los Andes,* Ccta, Peru.

1995 *Actes du colloque international sur les bisses* (Sion, 15-18 settembre 1994), in «Annales valaisannes. Bulletin annuel de la Société du Valais romand», ser. 2, LXX, Schmidt, Sion.

1996 *Elles et l'eau*, Unesco, Programme hydrologique international, Paris

1997 *Dare to Share!*, Dare-to-Share Fair at the 9th Conference of the International Soil Conservation Organisation (Isco) (Bonn, 26-30 agosto 1996), Margraf, Weikersheim

1997 *L'enjeu de l'eau,* Marinor, Paris

1997 *El curs de les aigües. Treballs sobre els pagesos de Ibiza*, in «Quaderns d'arqueologia Pitiùsa», n. 3, Consell insular d'Eivissa i Formentera February 1980, *Water Management*, in «World Archeology», II, 3

2000 *Forest, Chiefs and Peasants in Africa. Local Management of Natural Resources in Tanzania, Zimbawe and Monzambique*, in «Silva Carelica», n. 34 (numero monografico), University of Joensuu (Finland)

2000 *Il Parco della pietra e dell'acqua. Risultati della campagna internazionale di ricerca, studio e valorizzazione dell'area Sidin e recupero e restauro del Parco Bruno (1996-1998)*, sotto la direzione di P. Laureano, Gravina in Puglia

2000 *Women and Water Management*, Oxford University Press, New Delhi.

Agarwal A. e Narain S.

1997 *Dying Wisdom. Rise, Fall and Potential of India's Taditional Water Harvesting Systems*, State of India's Environment, Centre for Science and Environment, New Dehli.

Allen E

1969 *Stone Shelters*, Mit, Cambridge (Mass.) [trad. it. *Pietre di Puglia. Dolmen, trulli e insediamenti rupestri*, Adda, Bari 1979].

el-Amami S

1983 *Les aménagements hydrauliques traditionnels en Tunisie,* Centre de recherche du génie rural, Tunis.

Ambrosi A., Degano E. e Zaccaria C. A.

1990 *Architettura in pietra a secco*, Schena, Fasano.

Amiran R

1970 *The Beginnings of Urbanization in Canaan,* in J.A. Sanders, *Near Eastern Archaeology in Twentieh Century*, Doubleday, Garden City (ny).

Anati E.

1994   *Il linguaggio delle pietre. Valcamonica: una storia per l'Europa*, Centro camuno di studi preistorici, Capo di Ponte (Brescia).

Anfray F

1980   *La civilisation d'Axoum du ier au viie siècle,* in G. Mokhtar, *Histoire générale de l'Afrique*, vol. 2, *Afrique ancienne*, Unesco, Paris [trad. it. *La civiltà di Axum dal i au VII secolo*, in G. Mokhtar, *Storia generale dell'Africa*, vol. 2, L'Africa antica, Jaca Book, Milano 1988].

Aurenche O

1982   *Préhistoire des sociétés hydrauliques du Proche-Orient ancien*, in aa.vv., *L'homme et l'eau en Méditerranée et au Proche-Orient*, vol. 2, Maison de l'Orient, Presses Universitaires de Lyon, Lyon.

Barich B

1992   *L'uomo e la ricerca dell'acqua presso le società sahariane dell'Olocene,* in aa.vv., *La religione della sete. L'uomo e l'acqua nel Sahara*, Centro di studi di archeologia africana, Milano.

Barker G

1981   *Landscape and Society. Prehistoric Central Italy*, Academic Press, London [trad. it. *Ambiente e società nella preistoria dell'Italia centrale*, Carocci, Roma 1984]

1988-9 *Forme e sistemi dell'insediamento nella valle del Biferno nel ii millennio a.C.*, estratto da «Origini: preistoria e protostoria delle civiltà antiche», XIV, Multigrafica, Roma

1996   *Farming the Desert. The Unesco Libyan Valleys Archeological Survey*, Unesco, Department of Antiquities, Tripoli, e Society for Libyan Studies, London.

Barrois A. G

1937   *Les installations hydrauliques de Megiddo*, estratto da «Syria», n. 3, Librairie orientaliste Geuthner, Paris.

Beaumont P., Bonine M. e McLachlan K

1989   *Qanat, Kariz and Khattara. Traditional Water Systems in the Middle East and North Africa*, Menas, London.

Benveniste E

1969   *Le vocabulaire des institutions indo-européennes*, Editions de Minuit, 2 voll., Paris [trad. it. *Il vocabolario delle istituzioni indoeuropee*, 2 voll., Einaudi, Torino 1976].

Bernal M.

1987-91 *Black Athena. The Afroasiatic Roots of Classical Civilization*, 2 voll., Free Association Book, London [trad. it. *Atena nera. Le radici afroasiatiche della civiltà classica*, 2 voll., Pratiche, Parma 1992-94].

Bethemont J

1982   *Sur les origines de l'agriculture hydraulique*, in aa.vv., *L'homme et l'eau en Méditerranée et au Proche-Orient*, vol. 2, Maison de l'Orient, Presses Universitaires de Lyon, Lyon.

Bhalla, A. S

1977   *Towards Global Action for Appropriate Technology*, Pergamon, Oxford.

Bietti Sestieri A., Lentini M.C. e Voza G.

1995   *Guide archeologiche. Preistoria e protostoria in Italia: Sicilia orientale e Isole Eolie*, Abaco, Forlì.

Bonnin J

1984 *L'eau dans l'antiquité. L'hydraulique avant notre ère*, Eyrolles, Paris.

Bouayard-Agha, Malia

1996 *Dimension socio-culturelle et projets de développement*, in aa.vv., *Elles et l'eau*, Unesco, Programme hydrologique international, Paris.

Bousquet B., Laureano P. e altri

1993 *Petra Archaeological & Natural Park-Management Plan*, Unesco, Paris.

Brancati A

1969 *Il regime delle acque nell'Antichità*, La Nuova Italia, Firenze.

Brandt C.J. e Thornes J.

1996 *Mediterranean Desertification and Land Use*, Wiley, New York.

Bratt G

1995 *The Bisses of Valais*, Amadeus Press, Huddersfield (UK).

Brokensha D., Warren D. M. e Werner O.

1980 *Indigenous Knowledge Systems and Development*, University Press of America, Washington (DC).

Brown L.R

1991 *Saving the Planet. How to Shape an Environmentally Sustainable Global Economy*, Norton, New York.

Camps G

1974 *Les civilisations préhistoriques de l'Afrique du Nord et du Sahara*, Doin, Paris

1982 *La préhistoire. A la recherche du paradis perdu*, Perrin, Paris.

Cantelli C

1994 *Misconosciute funzioni dei muretti a secco, in Umanesimo della pietra*, n. 9, Martina Franca.

Cassano F

2001 *Modernizzare stanca*, il Mulino, Bologna.

Castellani V. e Dragoni W

1989 *Opere idrauliche ipogee nel mondo romano. Origine sviluppo e impatto sul territorio*, in «L'Universo», LXIX, 2

1992 *Opere arcaiche per il controllo del territorio. Gli emissari artificiali dei laghi Albani*, in *Gli etruschi maestri di idraulica*, Electa, Milano.

Cauvin J

1994 *Naissance des divinités, naissance de l'agricolture*, Cnrs, Paris.

Cavalli Sforza L. L., Menozzi P. e Piazza A

1994 *The History and Geography of Human Genes*, Princeton University Press, Princeton (nj) [trad. it. *Storia e geografia dei geni umani*, Adelphi, Milano 1997].

Chaptal L

1932 *La lutte contre la sécheresse. La capatation de la vapeur d'eau atmosphérique*, in «La Nature», LX, 2.

Chelhod J

1984 *L'Arabie du Sud. Histoire et civilisation*, 3 voll., Maisonneuve/Larose, Paris.

Childe V. Gordon

1954 *Early Forms of Society*, in C. Singer e altri, *A History of Technology*, vol. 1, Clarendon, Oxford [trad. it. *Prime forme di società*, in C. Singer e altri, *Storia della tecnologia*, vol. 1, *La preistoria e gli antichi imperi*, Bollati Boringhieri, Torino 1961, 19923].

China National Committee for the Implementation of United Nations Convention to Combat Desertification (Cciccd) Secretariat

1999 *Desertification, Rehabilitation and Ecology Restoration in China Highlight*, Beijing.

Cipolloni Sampò M

1987 *Tomba 3 dell'acropoli di Toppo Daguzzo (Potenza). Elementi per uno studio preliminare*, in «Aion», VIII.

1999 *L'Eneolitico e l'Età del Bronzo, in Storia della Basilicata*, vol. 1, *L'Antichità*, D. Adamesteau, Laterza, Roma-Bari.

Cleuziou S

1988 *Dilmoun-Arabie*, in J. F. Salles, *L'Arabie et ses mers bordières*, Maison de l'Orient, Presses universitaires de Lyon, Lyon.

Cleuziou S. e Laureano P.

1999 *Oases and Other Forms of Agricultural Intensification, in Papers from the European Association of Archeologists. Third Annual Meeting at Ravenna 1997*, Archeopress, Oxford.

Cosgrove W. J. e Rijsberman F. R

2000 *World Water Vision, for the World Water Council*, Earthscan Publications, London.

Crumley C.L.

1994 *Historical Ecology. Cultural Knowledge and Changing Landscapes*, School of American Research Press, Santa Fe.

Dainelli G. e Marinelli O

1912 *Risultati scientifici di un viaggio nella colonia eritrea*, Regio Istituto di studi superiori, Firenze.

Davis S

1995 *Traditional Knowledge and Sustainable Development*, in «Environmentally Sustainable Development Proceedings», n. 4, The World Bank, Washington (dc).

Dayton E

1979 *A Discussion on the Hydrology of Marib*, in «Proceedings of the Seminar for Arabian Studies», IX.

Dentzer M. e altri

1989 *Contribution française à l'archéologie jordanienne*, Ifapo, Amman.

Diamond J

1997 *Guns, Germs, and Steel. The Fates of Human Societies*, Norton, New York - London [trad. it. *Armi, acciaio e malattie*, Einaudi, Torino 2001].

Di Lernia S. e altri

1990 *Gargano Prehistoric Mines Project.The State of Research in the Neolithic Mine of Defensola-Vieste (Italy)*, in «Origini», XV.

Di Salvo M

1999 *Chiese di Etiopia*, Skira, Milano.

Dowdeswell E

1993 *Walking in Two Worlds,* intervento alla «InterAmerican Indigenous Peoples Conference» (Vancouver, 18 settembre).

Drower M. S

1954 *Water-Supply, Irrigation, and Agriculture*, in C. Singer e altri, *A History of Technology*, vol. 1, Clarendon, Oxford [trad. it. *Fornitura di acqua, irrigazione e agricoltura*, in C. Singer e altri (a cura di), *Storia della tecnologia*, vol. 1, *La preistoria e gli antichi imperi,* Bollati Boringhieri, Torino 1961, 19923].

Dupont G

1938 *L'eau dans l'Antiquité*, Paris.

Dupre G

1991 *Savoirs paysans et développement*, Paris, Karthala/Orstom.

Dutton R.W.

1988 *The Scientific Results of the Royal Geographical Society's Oman Wahiba Sands Project, 1985-1987*, in «The Journal of Oman Studies», n. 3 (numero monografico), Muscat (Oman).

Eea (European Environment Agency)

1999a *Environmental Indicators. Typology and Overview*, Technical Report, n. 25, Copenhagen.

Enne G., D'Angelo M. e Zanolla C.

1998 *Indicators for Assessing Desertification in the Mediterranean,* «Proceedings of the International Seminar Held in Porto Torres, Italy, 18-20 September 1998», Ministero dell'Ambiente, Osservatorio nazionale sulla desertificazione, Roma.

Enne G., Pulina G. e Aru A

1994 *Land Use and Soil Degradation: medalus in Sardinia*, in «Proceedings of the Conference Held in Sassari, 25 May 1994».

European Commission

2000a *Desertification in Europe. Mitigation Strategies, Land-Use Planning*, Advanced Study Course, Brussels.

2000b *Mediterranean Desertification. Research Results and Policy Implications*, «Proceedings of the International Conference, 29 October to 1 November 1996, Crete, Greece», voll. 1-2, Brussels.

Evenari M., Shanan L. e Tadmor N

1971 *The Negev. The Challenge of a Desert*, Harvard University Press, Cambridge (Mass.) - London.

Fagan B

1999 *Floods, Famines and Emperors. El Niño and the Fate of Civilization*, Basic Books, New York

2000 *The Little Ice Age. The Prelude to Global Warming 1300-1850*, Basic Books, New York.

Fao (Food and Agriculture Organization of the United Nations)

1997   *Irrigation in the Near East Region in Figures*, Water Report, n. 9, Fao, Rome.

Garnier M. e Renault P

1993   *Souterrains et captages traditionnnels dans le Mont d'Or Lyonnais*, Association Connaissance du Mont d'Or, St Didier au Mont d'Or, Lyon.

Gauthier E. F

1928   *Le Sahara,* Payot, Paris.

Gérard R. D. e Worzel J. L

1967   *Condensation of Atmospheric Moisture from Tropical Maritime Air Masses as a Freshwater Resources,* in «Science», CLVII.

Geyer B.

1990   *Techniques et pratiques hydro-agricoles traditionnelles en domaine irrigué. Actes du colloque de Damas 1987,* voll. 1-2, Librairie orientaliste Geuthner, Paris.

Gill R.B

2000   *The Great Maya Droughts. Water, Life and Death*, University of New Mexico Press, Albuquerque.

Ginestous G

1932   *Hydogenèse aérienne au Sahara*, in «Revue agricole de l'Afrique du Nord», n. 670.

Goblot H

1979   *Les qanats. Une technique d'acquisition de l'eau*, Mouton, Paris.

Grandguillaume G

1975   *Le droit de l'eau dans les foggara du Touat au xviiie siècle*, estratto dalla «Revue des études islamiques», XLIII, Librairie orientaliste Geuthner, Paris.

Grassi D. e altri

1991   I*ndagine sull'acquedotto del Triglio*, in «Itinerari speleologici», n. 5, Nuova editrice Apulia, Castellana.

Gruet M.

1955   *Amoncellement pyramidal de spheres calcaires dans une source fossile moustérienne à El Guettar (Sud tunisien)*, in *Actes du II Congrès panafricain de préhistoire et de protohistoire*, Arts et Métiers Graphiques, Paris.

Guilaine J. e Cremonesi G

1985   *L'habitat néolithique de Trasano (Matera, Basilicate). Premiers resultats*, in *Atti delle Riunioni scientifiche dell'Istituto italiano di preistoria e protostoria*, XXVI, Firenze.

Hartmann F

1923   *L'agriculture dans l'ancien Égypte*, Geuthner, Paris.

Hassan A. Y. e Hill D. R

1986   *Islamic Technology,* Cambridge University Press, London.

Hillel D

1997   *Small-Scale Irrigation for Arid Zones. Principles and Options,* Fao Development Series 2, Rome.

Hitier H

1935 *Condensateurs des vapeurs atmosphériques dans l'Antiquité*, in «Compte rendu des séances de l'Académie d'agriculture de France», XI.

Hobsbawm E. e Ranger T.

1999 *The Invention of Tradition*, Cambridge University Press, Cambridge (UK).

Huot J., Thalmann J. e Valbelle D.

1990 *Naissance des cités*, Nathan, Paris.

Ibn al-Awwam

Kitab al-filaha (sec. XII) [trad. fr. *Livre de l'agricolture,* 3 voll., Mullet, Paris 1864; rist. Bouslama, Tunis 1977].

Ibn Wahsiya

Al-filaha en Nabatiya, manoscritto del ix secolo della Biblioteca nazionale di Algeri, traduzione in arabo dell'opera del iv-v secolo *L'agricoltura nabatea*, compilata in siriaco antico.

Ilo (International Labour Organization)

1985 *Technologies Which Are Appropriate for Meeting Social Objectives of Developing Countries*, Ilo, Geneva, e Institute of Ethnology, Zurich.

Jequier N. e Blanc G

1983 *The World of Appropriate Technology. A Quantitative Analysis*, Oecd, Paris.

al-Karagi

Kitab inbat al-miyah al-hafiyya [L'arte di fare sgorgare le acque nascoste, sec. XI], Haiderabad 1940 [trad. fr. in P. Landry, *Eaux souterraines et qanats d'après un livre arabe du xi siècle*, in B. Geyer, *Techniques et pratiques hydro-agricoles traditionnelles en domaine irrigué*, Librairie orientaliste Geuthner, Paris 1990, vol. 2].

Keys D

2000 *Catastrophe. An Investigation into the Origins of Modern World*, Ballantine, New York.

Keller W

1955 *Und die Bibel hat doch Recht,* Econ, Wien [trad. it. *La Bibbia aveva ragione*, Garzanti, Milano 1980].

Khouri J., Amer A. e Sali A.

1995 *Rainfall Water Management in the Arab Region*, Unesco/Rostas Working Group, Rostas, Cairo.

Kobori I

1976 *Notes on Foggara in the Algerian Sahara*, in «Bulletin of Department of Geography University of Tokio», n. 8.

Latin American and Caribbean Commission on Development and Environment

1997 *Amanecer en los Andes*.

Latouche S

1989 *L'occidentalisation du monde. Essai sur la signification, la portée et les limites de l'uniformation planénatire*, La Découvert, Paris [trad. it. *L'occidentalizzazione del mondo*, Bollati Boringhieri, Torino 1992].

Laureano P

1985 *Wadi Villages and Sebkha Villages in the Saharan Ecosystem*, in «Environmental Design», n. 2, Carucci, Rome
1986 *The Oasis. The Origin of the Garden*, in «Environmental Design», n. 1, Carucci, Rome

1987 *Les ksour du Sahara algerien. Un exemple d'architecture globale*, in «Icomos Information», n. 3
1988 *Sahara, giardino sconosciuto*, Giunti, Firenze
1993 *Giardini di pietra. I Sassi di Matera e la civiltà mediterranea*, Bollati Boringhieri, Torino
1995 *La piramide rovesciata. Il modello dell'oasi per il pianeta Terra*, Bollati Boringhieri, Torino
1998 *Proper Uses of Natural Resources, Environmental Architecture and Hydraulic Technologies for Self-Sustainable and Resources-Sparing Projects*, in «Human Evolution», XIII, 1
1999 *The System of Traditional Knowledge in the Mediterranean Area and Its Classification with Reference to Different Social Groupings,* relazione (iccd/cop(3)/cst/Misc. 1) presentata alla «Conference of the Parties» organizzata dal Committee on Science and Technology della Unccd, Recife (Brasile), 16-18 novembre 1999 (sul sito web: www.unccd.int)
1999 *Water: The cycle of life*. Laia Libros and Agbar. Barcelona.
2000 *Inventario delle conoscenze tradizionali e locali*, in *Azioni italiane a sostegno della Convenzione delle Nazioni Unite per combattere la desertificazione*, atti del 2° Forum internazionale, Matera 1998, a cura del Ministero italiano dell'Ambiente e della Unccd, vol. 2.

Lazarev G.

1993 *Vers un eco-développement participatif. Leçons et synthèse d'une étude thématique*, L'Harmattan, Paris.

Lee R. B

1969 *Kung Bushman Subsistence. An Input-Output Analysis*, in A. P. Vayda, *Environment and Cultural Behaviour*, Natural History Press, New York.

Lee R. B. e De Vore I.

1968 *Man the Hunter*, Aldine, Chicago.

Leuci G

1991 *Ancora sulle opere neolitiche a Passo di Corvo (Foggia)*, in *L'Appennino meridionale, Annuario del Club alpino italiano, sezione di Napoli*, Napoli.

Lhote H

1976 *Les gravures rupestres de l'oued Djerat, Tassili-n-Ajjer,* Centre de Recherches anthropologiques, préhistoriques et ethnographiques, Alger.

Liere W.J. van

1980 *Traditional Water Management in the Lower Mekong Basin*, in «World Archeology», n. 3.

Lilliu G

1984 *La civiltà nuragica*, Delfino, Sassari.

Loguercio C.

1999 *Il ruolo dell'Italia nella lotta alla desertificazione. Iniziative del nostro paese per attuare la Convenzione delle Nazioni Unite*, Cuen, Napoli.

Loubes J.-P

1993 *La formation d'un type architectural: l'habitation creusée en puit*, in *Actes du Symposium international «Patrimoine souterrain creusé»*, Saumur.

Louis P. e Métral J. e F.

1987 *L'homme et l'eau en Méditerranée et au Proche Orient*, vol. 4, *L'eau dans l'agricolture*, Maison de l'Orient, Presses universitaries de Lyon, Lyon.

Lourandos H

1980 *Change or Stability? Hydraulics, Hunter-Gatherers and Population in Temperate Australia*, in «World Archeology», II, 3.

Mairota P., Thornes J. e Geeson N.

1998 *Atlas of Mediterranean Environments in Europe. The Desertification Context*, Wiley, New York.

Marino De Botero M

1990 *Des déchets et des hommes. Expériences urbaines de recyclage dans le Tiers Monde, Enda Tiers Monde*, Dakar.

Marouf N

1980 *Lecture de l'espace oasien*, Sindbad, Paris.

Masson H

1954 *La rosée et la possibilités de son utilisation*, in «Annales de l'École supérieure de sciences», Unesco, Institut des hautes études de Dakar, I.

Mayerson Ph

1959 *Ancient Agricultural Remains in the Central Negeb*, in «Basor», n. 153.

Mazaheri A

1973 *La civilisation des eaux cachées*, Université de Nice (Ideric), Nice.

Mellaart J

1967 *Çatal Hüyük. A Neolithic Town in Anatolia*, Mortimer Wheeler, London.

Métral J. e Sanlaville P

1981 *L'homme et l'eau en Méditerranée et au Proche Orient*, Maison de l'Orient, Presses universitaries de Lyon, Lyon.

Miller R

1980 *Water Use in Syria and Palestine from Neolithic to the Bronze Age*, in «World Archeology», n. II.

Mit Club di Roma

1972 *I limiti dello sviluppo*, Est Mondatori, Milano.

Moravetti A. e Tozzi C.

1995 *Guide archeologiche. Preistoria e protostoria in Italia: Sardegna*, Abaco, Forlì.

Mori F

2000 *Le grandi civiltà del Sahara antico*, Bollati Boringhieri, Torino.

Nebbia G

1961 *Il problema dell'acqua nelle zone aride. L'estrazione dell'acqua dall'atmosfera*, in «Annali della Facoltà di Economia e Commercio», Bari, n.s., XVII.

Neveux V

1928 *Pour puiser l'eau de l'atmosphère dans les pays chauds. Le puits aérien, systeme knapen*, in «La Nature», n. 2.

Ngaba-Waye A.

1996 *The Sahara Is Coming! Die Sahara kommt! Le Sahara arrive!*, Proceedings of the International Seminar on Environmental Education (Amburgo, 13-14 ottobre 1995), Unesco Institute for Education, Hamburg.

Nicod J

1992 *Muretti e terrazze di coltura nelle regioni carsiche mediterranee*, in «Itinerari speleologici», n. 6, Nuova editrice Apulia, Castellana.

Orme B

1981 *Anthropology for Archaeologists*, Duckworth, London.

Ortloff C. R. e Kolata A. L

1989 *Hydraulic Analysis of Tiwanaku Aqueduct Structures at Lukurmata and Pajchiri, Bolivia,* in «Journal of Archaeological Science».

Palmisano P. e Fanizzi A

1992 *I laghi di Conversano. Il fenomeno degli stagni stagionali dei territori carsici pugliesi,* in «Itinerari speleologici», n. 6, Nuova editrice Apulia, Castellana.

Parancola S. e Trevisiol E.

1996 *L'acqua salvata. Utilizzo integrato in una prospettiva di biofitodepurazione*, Daest - Dipartimento di Analisi economica e sociale del territorio, Convegni, n. 2, Venezia.

Pasteur E

1933 *Hydrogenèse aérienne et terrestre*, in «La Nature», n. 2902.

Pauli G

1999 *Il progetto Zeri,* Il Sole 24 Ore, Milano.

Peretto C.

1991 *Isernia La Pineta. Nuovi contributi scientifici,* Istituto regionale per gli studi storici del Molise, Isernia.

Petrassi L

2001 *Un passato senza traccia,* in AA.VV.., *Luoghi e paesaggi archeologici del suburbio orientale di Roma*, Bibliotheca Land, Roma.

Petrassi L. e Pracchia S

2000 *Le isole votive di strada Santo Stefano,* in AA.VV., *Il Parco della pietra e dell'acqua. Risultati della campagna internazionale di ricerca, studio e valorizzazione dell'area Sidin e recupero e restauro del Parco Bruno (1996-1998)*, sotto la direzione di P. Laureano, Gravina in Puglia.

Pignauvin G

1932 *L'hydraulique en Tunisie d'après les Romains*, Tunis.

Piña Chan R.

1992 *Chichen Itza. The City of the Wise Men of Water*, Dante, Mérida (México).

Pirenne J

1977 *La maitrise de l'eau en Arabie du sud antique*, Geuthner, Paris
1990 *Fouilles de Shabwa*, Geuthner, Paris.

Planhol X. de

1977 *Qanats et structure urbaine*, in «Annales de géographie».

Pracchia S

2001 *Note per un'archeologia dei paesaggi agrari*, in AA.VV., *Luoghi e paesaggi archeologici del suburbio orientale di Roma*, Biblioteca Land, Roma.

Prinz D

1996 *Water Harvesting. History, Techniques and Trends*, in «Zeitschrift für Bewüsserungswirtschaft»

1999 *Water Harvesting in the Mediterranean*, relazione presentata al forum dell'Unesco International School of Science for Peace su «Water Security in the Third Millenium. Mediterranean Countries towards a Regional Vision» (Italia, 12-15 aprile).

Prinz D. e altri

Water Harvesting for Crop Production, Fao Training Course.

Rewerski J

1999 *Lart des troglodytes,* Arthaud, Paris.

Richter J., Wolff P., Franzen H. e Heim F

1997 *Strategies for Intersectorial Water Management in Developing Countries. Challenges and Consequences for Agriculture,* Proceedings of the International Workshop (Berlino, maggio 1996), Berlin.

Ridola D

1926 *Le grandi trincee preistoriche di Matera*, estratto dal «Bullettino di paleoetnologia italiana», Roma.

Roberts N

1977 *Water Conservations in Ancient Arabia*, in «Seminar of Arabian Studies», III.

Robins F. W

1946 *The Story of Water Supply*, Oxford University Press, London.

Rossi E

1940 *Vocaboli sud-arabici nelle odierne parlate arabe del Yemen*, in «Rivista di studi orientali», XX, 18

1953 *Note sull'irrigazione, l'agricoltura e le stagioni nel Yemen*, in «Oriente moderno», n. 33.

Roux H

1953 *Notes sur l'hydrogénie*, in «Bulletin de Mayenne - Sciences» (1952).

Roys R.L.

1933 *The Book of Chilam Balam of Chumayel*, University of Oklahoma Press, Norman.

Ryckmans J

1979 *Le barrage de Marib et les jardins du royaume de Saba*, in «Dossier de l'archéologie», XXXIII.

Sachs W.

1992 *The Development Dictionary. A Guide to Knowledge as Power*, Zed Books, London [trad. it. *Dizionario dello sviluppo*, Gruppo Abele, Torino 1998].

Sahlins M

1968   *Notes on the Original Affluent Society*, in R. B. Lee e I. De Vore, *Man the Hunter*, Aldine, Chicago

1972   *Stone Age Economics*, Tavistock, London [trad. it. *Economia dell'età della pietra*, Bompiani, Milano 1980].

Saint-Non J. C. R. de

1781-86 *Voyage pittoresque ou description du royaume de Naples et de Sicile*, Lafosse, Paris; rist. Dufour, Paris 1829.

Sajjadi S. M

1982   *Qanat/kariz. Storia, tecnica costruttiva ed evoluzione*, Istituto italiano di cultura, Sezione archeologica, Teheran.

Sakaguchi A

2000   Contributo presentato alla «Unep's Ietc e-mail Conference», inedito.

Saouma E

1993   *Indigenous Knowledge and Biodiversity*, in *Harvesting Nature's Diversity*, Fao, Rome.

Scarborough V.L. e Isaac B.L.

1993   *Economic Aspects of Water Management in the Prehispanic New World*, Jai Press, Greenwich (Conn.).

Schmitt K. e altri

1994   *Appropriate Technology in Post Modern Times*, Gtz-Gate, Frankfurt.

Schoeller H. J

1962   *Les eaux souterraines*, Masson, Paris.

Semeraro G

1984-94 *Le origini della cultura europea*, 4 voll., Olschki, Firenze

2001   *L'infinito. Un equivoco millenario*, Bruno Mondadori, Milano.

Sen A.

1999   *Development as Freedom*, Oxford University Press, Oxford [trad. it. *Lo sviluppo è libertà,* Mondadori, Milano 2000].

Sherrat A.

1980   *Water, Soil and Seasonality in the Early Cereal Cultivation*, in «World Archeology», n. 3.

Shiva V

1993   *Monocultures of the Mind. Perspectives on Biodiversity and Biotechnology*, Zed Books, London [trad.it. *Monoculture della mente. Biodiversità, biotecnologia e agricoltura scientifica*, Bollati Boringhieri, Torino 1995].

Soldi A. M

1982   *La agricultura tradicional en hoyas*, Pontificia universidad católica del Perú, Lima.

Spyropoulos T

1972   *Aigiptiakos epoikismos en Boiotiai*, in «Archaiologika analekta ex Athenon», V. Tinè S

1967   *Alcuni dati circa il sistema di raccolta idrica nei villaggi neolitici del Foggiano*, in *Atti della XI e XII Riunione scientifica dell'Istituto italiano di preistoria e di protostoria*, Firenze

1983   *Passo di Corvo e la civiltà neolitica del Tavoliere*, Sagep, Genova.

Tinè S. e Isetti E

1980   *Culto neolitico delle acque e recenti scavi nella grotta Scaloria*, in «Bollettino di paletnologia italiana», n. 82.

Tirfe Mammo

1999   *The Paradox of Africa's Poverty. The Role of Indigenous Knowledge, Traditional Practices and Local Institutions: The case of Ethiopia*, Red Sea Press, Asmara.

Tobin B., Torres Guevara J. e Tapia M. E

1998   *Ecosistemas de montaña. Un nuovo banco de oro?*, Friedrich-Ebert-Stiftung, Lima.

Todaro P

1988   *Il sottosuolo di Palermo*, Flaccovio, Palermo.

Tölle Kastenbein R

1990   *Antike Wasserkultur*, Beck, München [trad. it. *Archeologia dell'acqua*, Longanesi, Milano 1993].

Tortajada C

2000   *Women and Water Management. The Latin American Experience*, Oxford University Press, New Delhi.

Tresse R

1929   *L'irrigation dans la Ghouta de Damas*, estrato dalla «Revue des études islamiques», Librairie orientaliste Geuthner, Paris.

Trevisiol E.R. e Parancola S.

1996   *L'acqua salvata. Utilizzo integrato in una prospettiva di biofitodepurazione*, Daest - Dipartimento di Analisi economica e sociale del territorio, Convegni, n. 2, Venezia.

Unccd (United Nations Convention to Combat Desertification)

1998a   *Synthèse des rapports sur les connaissances traditionnelles*, ICCD/COP(2)/cst/5 (sul sito web: www.unccd.int)

1998b   *Traditional Knowledge and Practical Techniques for Combating Desertification in China*, Beijing (sul sito web: www.unccd.int)

1999a   *Building Linkage between Environmental Conventions and Initiatives*, ICCD/COP(3)/ cst/3/add.1 (sul sito web: www.unccd.int)

1999b   *Synthesis on Important and Widely Applied Traditional Knowledge on a Sub-Regional and Regional Basis and on Traditional Scale*, ICCD/COP(3)/cst/3 (sul sito web: www.unccd.int)

1999c   *The System of Traditional Knowledge in the Mediterranean*, ICCD/COP(3)/cst/Misc.1), (sul sito web: www.unccd.int)

1999d   *Traditional Knowledge. Report of the ad Hoc Panel*, ICCD/COP(3)/cst/3 (sul sito web: www.unccd. int).

Unesco (United Nations Educational, Scientific and Cultural Organization)

1994a   *Traditional Knowledge in Tropical Environments*, in «Nature and Resources», XXX, 1

1994b   *Traditional Knowledge into the Twenty-First Century*, in «Nature and Resources», XXX, 2.

Unesco Nuffic

1999   *Best Practices on Indigenous Knowledge*, Unesco, Paris.

Vaufrey R

1939   *L'art rupestre nord-africain*, Masson, Paris.

Vautier A

1997 *Au pays des bisses et inventaire des bisses valaisans*, Ketty & Alexandre, Suisse.

Vernon P

1989 *Technological Development. The Historical Experience,* Washington (DC).

Vincent L

1995 *Hill Irrigation, Water and Development in Mountain Agriculture*, Overseas Development Institute, London.

Wacker C

1997a *Traditional Water Management System in Ladakh, India*, contributo al «Working Group on Community Management and Partnership with Civil Society» del Water Supply and Sanitation Collaborative Council (Wsscc), presentato al Fourth Global Forum del Wsscc (Manila, novembre)

1997b *Traditional Water Management System in Ladakh, India*, University of Zurich.

Webb P. e Iskandarani M

1998 *Water Insecurity and the Poor. Issues and Research Needs* (n. 2), ZEF Bonn.

Weber M.

1905 *Die protestantische Ethik und der Geist des Kapitalismus,* in *Gesammelte Aufsätze zur Religionssoziologie*, Mohr, Tübingen 1922 [trad. it. *L'etica protestante e lo spirito del capitalismo*, Rizzoli, Milano 1991].

Willcocks W. e Craig J. J

1913 *Egyptian Irrigation*, Spon, London

1917 *The Irrigation of Mesopotamia*, Spon, London.

Wilson E. O

1998 *Consilience. The Unity of Knowledge*, Knof, New York [trad. it. *L'armonia meravigliosa*, Mondadori, Milano 1999].

Winser N.

1989 *The Sea of Sands and Mists*, Century, London.

Wittfogel K. A.

1957 *Oriental Despotism,* Yale University Press, New Haven [trad. it. *Il dispotismo orientale*, Vallecchi, Firenze 1968].

Yassoglou N.J

2000 *History and Development of Desertification in the Mediterranean and Its Contemporary Reality,* in AA.VV., *Desertification in Europe. Mitigation Strategies, Land-Use Planning*, Advanced Study Course, Brussels.

Yoffee N. e Cowgill G.L.

1988 *The Collapse of Ancient States and Civilizations*, University of Arizona Press, Tucson.

Zapata Peraza R. L

1989 *Los chultunes sistemas de captación y almacenamiento de agua pluvial*, Instituto nacional de antropologîa e historia (Inah), México.

Zarattini A. e Petrassi L

1997 *Casale del Dolce. Ambiente, economia e cultura di una comunità preistorica della Valle del Sacco*, Baioni, Roma.

INDEX

A

Abraham, 64
Adobe bricks, 35, 37
Adrar, the Algerian oasis of, 113
Aeneolithic Age, the, 42
Afar (Eritrea), 43
Agau, 45
Agnuak, 235
Andalusian, 35, 129, 169, 174, 191, 207
Hedomite, 33, 60, 121, 143, 269
Nabatean and Sabean, 171
Alberobello (Apulia), 84, 180, 226, 242, 243
Alemaya, lake (Ethiopia), 303
Aleppo (Syria), 84
Alexander the Great, 2, 152
Alghero (Sardinia), 260, 261
Allahabad (India), 174, 275
Alquerie, 126
Altamura (Apulia), 43
Alto Adige, 214
Amalfi (Campania), 174
Amazon, 19, 196
Amphion and Zetes, the tomb of, 84
Anasazi, 44, 259
Anaximander, 222
Andalusia, 102, 126, 129
Angkor (Cambodia), 11
Aqaba, the Gulf of, 18, 60, 166
Arabah Valley, 60

Arcadia, 84
Aristotle, 2, 222
Artificial basins, 13
Artificial craters, 81, 100, 140
Artificial lake, 152
Aryan, 178
Aswan, dam (Egypt), 191
Atlantic Mata (Brazil), the, 200
Atmospheric condenser, 291–92
Attica, 168
Australian aborigines, 20
Autopoiesis (self-reproduction), 11, 14, 94, 121, 220
Autopoietic communities, 187
Axum (Ethiopia), 131
Aztecs, 169

B

Babylon, 58
Bahrein (the Persian Gulf), 94
Baibars, the sultan, 202
Balearic Islands (Spain), 84
Banpo (China), 187
Barcane, 98
Basilicata, 40, 42, 196, 201, 282
Bedu, 272
Beida (Jordan), 37, 39, 40, 41, 121, 127, 229
Belucistan (Pakistan), 275
Bengal, western (India), 181
Beni Isguen (Algeria), 124–25
Bersabea (Israel), 260
Beyt Bows (Yemen), 63

Bhopal, lake of (India), 181
Bible, 60, 144, 152, 222
Bisse, 169, 174–76, 210–11, 214, 254
Botromagno (Apulia), 158, 161, 170
Botswana, 134
Bronze Age, the, 41–42, 60–61, 64, 81–82, 84, 157, 178, 187, 219, 243, 247, 257–58, 260–61
Bulla Regia (Tunisia), 43
Burkina Faso, 56, 194
Burren (Ireland), 174, 179

C

Cadmus, the founder of Thebes, 84
Calabria, 196, 282
Calcutta (India), 212
Calcutta's wetlands, 212
Cambise, Emperor, 76
Canary Islands (Spain), 94
Chandragupta, the Indian emperor, 180
Cappadocia, 44–45, 47, 257
Capsians, the, 34
Casaldolce (Lazio), 52
Çatal Hüyük (Turkey), 35–37, 230
Catchment, 9, 24, 32, 63, 66, 94, 110, 121, 152, 157, 174, 177, 189, 202, 206, 210, 216, 219, 232, 234, 266, 271, 278; *see also* kundis
Cenote, 181–85
Chac Mool, 186
Chaco Canyon (North America), 44
Chichén Itzá (Yucatan), 181–82, 184, 186, 200, 202
Chilam Balam, 181
Chinampa, 169, 183–84, 276–77
Chultun, 184–85, 277
Cinque Terre (Liguria), 174, 188, 213–15
Cisternali, 157, 184; *see also* cutini, laghi
Cisterns, 32, 43, 49, 64–67, 69, 74–75, 78, 81, 92, 126, 140, 142, 144, 150, 153, 156–57, 161, 164–65, 174, 178, 181, 189, 202, 219, 226–27, 232, 47–49, 257, 264, 303
 bell-like or bell-shaped, 81, 145, 158, 184, 225, 263, 265; *see also* chultun
 open-air, 64, 75, 76, 274; *see also* artificial basins; tanks

 pit, 43, 266
 linear, 49
 rectangular, 144
 tholos, 265
Concentric circles or double ring, 23, 25, 40, 49, 90, 121, 160
Confucius, 187
Conversano (Apulia), 43, 156–57, 226
Coren of the Valento (Valcamonica), 243
Cromleck, 174, 179
Cueva Pintada, (Baja California, Mexico), 17, 19

D

Dahlac, isles, (Eritrea), 80
Damascus (Syria), 64, 74 Dammusi, 44
Danaus, the Egyptian King, 84
Daunia, 40, 41, 84
Dead Sea, 18, 33, 60, 76, 166
Deforestation, 167, 193, 196, 216, 297
Delos (Greece), 76
Dhahr, wadi (Yemen), 124, 128
Dhana, wadi (Yemen), 67–68, 270
Diodorus, the Sicilian, 84, 142
Ditches, 11, 26, 32, 40–42, 45, 49, 50, 52, 56, 58, 81, 84, 121, 133, 154, 158, 165, 168, 187, 219, 223, 227, 228, 278, 303
Dolinas, 43, 156, 157; *see also* laghi; puli
Dongollo (Ethiopia), 45
Dorze, 236
Dravidian, 178
Dromos, 81
Dunes, 4, 8, 14, 98–99, 101–02, 194, 216, 250
 artificial, 189, 249; *see also* afreg

E

Ellora (India), 262
Eritrea, 3, 43, 52, 117, 126, 132
Etruria, 84
Euphrates, 60
European Union, 196
Ezekiel, 63

F

Falaj, 32, 102
Family clans, 60, 81, 129, 157
Fantiano in Grottaglie (Apulia), 89
Farmer-breeders, 14, 31, 224
Feixe, 169, 172, 184, 254, 256
Foggara, 32, 98, 103–107, 110, 112–13, 158, 207, 209–10, 249, 252–53, 286
Fogge, 202
Food and Agriculture Organization (FAO), 205
Fumaroles, 43; *see also* boina

G

Gabarband, 180, 275
Gafsa, the oasis of (Tunisia), 21
Ganges, river (India), 174, 275
Gargano (Apulia), 41–43, 157
Gegard (Armenia), 261
Ghardaia, oasis of (Algeria), 108, 120–24, 126–27, 219
Ghuta (Syria), 64, 76
Gindah, the valley of (Eritrea), 132
Gobi desert, the, 187, 278
Gobrikarez, 180
Gourara (Algeria), 103, 107
Grabiglioni, 165, 202
Gravina in Puglia, 85, 158, 170
Great Eastern Erg, the, 98
Great Mother Goddess, the, 36, 61
Great Western Erg, the, 8, 99
Greece, 84, 158, 174
Greek civilisation, the, 158
Grottaglie (Apulia), 89, 156
Guelta, 12, 13
El-Guettar (Tunisia), 21
Guinea, 19
Gujarat (India), 181

H

Habba, 112
Habitat for Humanity, 216
Hadramaut (Yemen), 57–58, 67, 133–34, 136, 141, 180, 216–218, 271, 297
Al-Hajarain (Yemen), wadi of, 141
Hakka, 281
Hallafa, 112–13
al-Hamdani, 67
Harappa (India), 178, 180, 275
Harar (Ethiopia), 131, 133, 303
Harrah, 69, 72, 232
Harran (Mesopotamia), 84
Hedomites, the, 33, 60, 121
Hegra (Medain Saleh, Arabia), 76
Helladic period, 84
Heracles, 84
Hermaion, 21
Hermes Trismegistus, 2
Herodotus, 76
Hidden precipitations, 103, 286; *see also* condensation, precipitations
Historical centres, 16, 158, 174, 214
Holes or hollows, 32, 259, 285
Holland, 216
Homeostasis, 121, 220
Homer, 247
Hoyas, 102
Huang Ho, 187, 191, 278; *see* Yellow River
Hunter-fishers, 20
Hwai yuen lo (the Chinese adobe village-house), 187, 278, 281
Hydraulic civilisations, 7
Hydraulic law, 124
Hydraulic societies, 184, 187, 189, 274; *see also* hydraulic civilisations
Hydraulic systems, 76, 129, 144, 161
Hydrogenesis, 203, 219
Pit-courtyards, 44, 45; *see also* dammusi; damùs;
Hypogeums in the wadi, 251; see also underground chambers in the wadi

I

Ibadite, the community, 121
al-Idrisi, 102

IETC, *see* International Environmental Technology Centre, 205
Ighzer, oasis of (Algeria), 102
Iglamah, 69, 71
Incas, the, 187
Incense route, 64, 76, 219
India, 174, 178, 180, 181, 184, 206, 212, 249, 262, 274
Indonesia, 206, 216
Integrated traditional cycle, 216; *see also* organic wastes, collection and recycle of; zai
International Council for Science (ICSU), 205
International Labour Organisation (ILO), 205
Isernia (Molise), 20
Israel, 76, 216, 260
Ituri (Congo), 38

J

Janet, the oasis of (Algeria), 18, 107
Japan, 205, 212
Jarmo (Iraq), 35, 37
Jawa (Jordan), 64, 247–48
Jazzo, 89, 268
Jenna, 116
Jerat, wadi (Algeria), 28, 224
Jericho (Palestine), 33, 35, 40, 41, 102
Jerud, 76
Jerusalem (Israel), 102
Jheel, 181
Johannesburg, world conference, 221, 297
Jordan valley, the, 64
Jumna, river (India), 174, 275

K

al-Karagi, 103
Kautilya, Indian minister, 180
Kebran Gabriel (Ethiopia), 238
Kenadsa dam (Algeria), 207
Kenya, 22
Kerak, 202
Kesria, 112, 114, 253
Khaur, 76, 79
Khottara, 96–97, 102, 144, 147

Kiva, 44
Konya, 35
Koran, the, 64
Kos (Greece), 76
Kuis, 181
Kundis, 181
Kurgan, 61
Kurii, 133

L

La Venta (Yucatan), 184
Labyrinth, 22, 25, 26, 28, 84, 223, 224, 244
Ladakh (India), 181, 206
Laghi, 43, 157, 226
Lamione, 162, 264, 265
Laterza (Apulia), 135, 213, 384
Lebanon, 166, 219
Loess highland (China), 187, 280
Loess, 32, 44, 134, 140, 187, 224, 271
Loire valley, the (France), 210, 224
Loltun (Yucatan), 23, 28, 181

M

Madagascar, 194, 216
Madjirat, 102, 249
Madrid (Spain), 102
Maghreb, 214
Ma'had, 69, 234
Mahfid, 69–70, 233
Maihabar, 126, 129
Majen, 111–113
Malaak, 133
Malabar, the coast of (India), 181
Maldharis, the, 223
Mali, 194, 199
Malta, 36, 158, 168, 257, 264
Manduria (Apulia), 42
Manhal, 232
Mao Zedong, 187
Marbid, 69, 72, 232
Marco Polo, 187
al-Masudi, 64

al-Mataha (Jordan), the wadi, 144, 154, 272
Mauritania, 194, 216
Itzá, 181, 182, 184, 186, 200, 202
Medracen, 84, 88
Megiddo, the oasis of, 102
Menes or Mendes, 84
Menhir, 84
Mesolithic Age, the, 33
Mesopotamia, 35, 84, 94, 117, 189, 219, 222, 247, 269, 271
Messapians, the, 84
Metal Age, the, or Age of Metals, the, 59, 60, 62, 63, 92, 117, 157
Mexico City, 183–85
Neolithic flint, 43
Minoans, the, 84
Minos, 84
Modica (Sicily), 158, 160
Mohenjodaro (India), 178
Mongolia, 187
Monoculture, 14, 194
Monolith, 45, 48, 61
Mont d'Or (France), 169
Montezuma Castle (Mesa Verde, United States), 259
Morocco, 102, 207, 209
Moses, 76, 144
Motswelo, 134
al-Mudhlim (Jordan), the wadi, 144
Murge, highlands of the, 43, 89, 91, 155, 157, 299
Murgia Timone (Basilicata), 41, 42, 54, 81, 82, 239
Musa (Jordan), the wadi, 142, 144
Mycenae (Greece), 81, 84, 86, 158, 241
Mycenaean civilizations, 84

N

Nabateans, the, 33, 43, 60, 64, 76, 121, 140, 142, 149, 166
Nakuto Laab (Ethiopia), 24
Namibia, 35, 216
Nanjing (China), 281
Natufians, the, 33, 34
Natural cavities, 12, 224
Natural drips, 144

Neqaba, 69
New Guinea, 24
New Mexico, 279
Nicobar Islands (India), the, 181
Niger, the river, 49, 199
Nineveh, 102
Nomadism, 18, 35, 60, 76, 115
Nouakchott (Mauritania), 194
Nuraghi, 69, 70, 84, 90, 235, 239, 242, 244
an-Nuwairi, 202

O

Oasis effect, 14, 112, 210, 249
Olive tree, 76, 89, 90, 167
Olmec, the, 184
Orcomeno (Greece), 84
Organisation for Economic Co-operation and Development (OECD), 205
Orkney Islands (Scotland), the, 174

P

Paestum (Campania), 92
Pairidaeza, 152; *see also* garden, paradise
Pakistan, 35, 178
Palaeolithic, 16, 17, 19–22, 24, 26, 29, 32, 34, 35, 84, 121, 222–24
Palagianello (Apulia), 299–300
Palermo (Sicily), 69, 102
Palestine, 33, 63, 84, 219, 257
Palmavera (Sardinia), 70, 244
Parieti, 90
Peloponnese, the, 84
Percolation in the caves, 110, 219
Pertosa (Campania), 22
Perù, 102, 216, 222
Petra (Jordan), 37, 44–46, 52, 60, 76, 79, 121, 140–54, 158, 167, 169, 200, 202, 219, 257, 258, 269, 70–72
Peucetians, the, 84
Philippines, the, 206
Philistines, the, 84
Phoenicians, the, 84, 129
Phytodepuration, 294–297, 303

Piancada di Palazzolo dello Stella (Friuli), 52
Piedmont, 214, 254
Pisé, 35
Pisticci (Basilicata), 201
Plato, 222
Pliny the Elder, 76
Plutarch, 7
Pollution, 41, 297
Polybius, 102
Pozzuoli (Campania), 76
Pre-Neolithic age, 33
Ptolemy II Philadelphus, Egyptian King, 150
Pueblo, 44, 259

Q

Qana (Yemen), 64, 65, 75, 76, 102, 247, 248
Qanat or kariz, 32, 102, 103, 144, 180, 207, 249
Qasr el-Abd (Jordan), 150
Quetzalcoatl or Kukulkan, 181, 184, 186
Qumran (Palestine), 76

R

Ragusa Ibla (Sicily), 158, 159
Rajasthan (India), 181
Ramlat as Sabatayn desert, 76
Ras Djebel (Tunisia), 206
Red Sea, 3, 12, 18, 76, 80, 131, 132, 173, 181, 257
Resaf (risefa), 69, 74, 75
Rift Valley, 18, 35, 43, 49, 60, 131
Rig Veda, 178
Rio de Janeiro, the World Conference in, 7
Roufi (Algeria), 128

S

Sabean, 64, 67, 69, 75, 137, 171, 269, 274
Sadd al-Ma'jan, wadi (Jordan), 186
Sahel, 6, 194–197, 216, 249
Saint Lorenz (Yucatan), 184
Salillas de Jalon (Spain), 262, 263
salinity, increase of, 129, 184, 197, 207
San'a (Yemen), 124

Santa Cristina (Sardinia), 239
Saoura, wadi (Algeria), 97, 250
Sardinia, 36, 69, 84, 117, 174, 196, 242, 282
Sargon II, the Assyrian King, 102
Sas Concas (Sardinia), 257
Scicli (Sicily), 158, 160
Scotland, 174
Seasonal mobility, 24; *see also* nomadism sebkha
Sedrata (Algeria), 121
Self-catalytic, system, 286
Senegal, 34, 194, 195
Sennacherib, Sargon's son, 102
Shaanxi (China), 187, 280
Shabwa (Yemen), 67, 76, 140, 200, 202
Shaduf, 96, 97, 204
Shakaret Museied (Jordan), 204
Shaubak (Jordan), 166
Sheba, 64, 66, 69
Sidama, 236
Sigilmasa (Morocco), 121
Silk Road, 121, 166, 189, 257, 269, 278
Silviculture, 7, 10
Sinai, 60, 76
Sion (Switzerland), 215, 217, 330, 332
Siwah (Lybia), 76
Sleisel, 76
Sluice gates or sluices, 52, 68, 124
Social cohesion, 17, 174, 187, 203, 206, 214, 221, 226
Socio-cultural formations, 11, 16
Solomon, 87, 94, 96
Souf (Algeria), 132, 134, 327 Sowing, 60, 64, 69
Specchie, 84, 88, 90, 174, 179
Srefe, 117; "*see also* agriculture; cultivation"
Sringaverapura (India), 174, 275
Stalactites and stalagmites, 4
Steppes, 10, 223
Stockholm (Sweden), 298
Stonehenge (England), 1, 90, 240
Sumerians, the, 45, 60, 94, 247
Surangam, 181
Sustainability, 7, 205, 206, 217, 219–21, 274, 289, 300
Sweden, 217, 289
Symbiosis, 11, 14, 94, 121, 134, 174

T

Taghit, oasis of (Algeria), 34, 38, 99
Tahert (Algeria), 121
Taklimakan, the desert of (China), 187
Talayotes, 84, 90
Tamil Nadu, 181
Tana, Lake (Ethiopia), 117, 237–38
Tanka, 174, 178
Tanks, 144, 174, 202, 253
Tanzania, 35
Taranto, 102, 154, 156, 158
Tassili of Ajjer (Algeria), 94
Teleylat al-anab, 76, 90
Tenochtitlán (Yucatan), 183
Terracing (systems), 9, 74, 79, 121, 129, 134, 138, 144, 159, 166, 177, 187, 188, 213, 215, 216, 218, 220, 232
Thapsos (Sicily), 260
Thar, the desert of (India), 181
Thebes (Egypt), 62, 84, 96, 152, 251
Tholos, 61, 81, 84, 86, 87, 158, 174, 235, 241, 242, 265
Thutmosis I, Pharaoh, 62, 251
Tiberias, Lake, 18
Tiddis, (North Africa), 43
Tigris, 60
Timimoun, oases of the Sebkha of (Algeria), 9, 10, 11, 102, 104, 105, 114, 252
Tin Tazarift (Algeria), 26
Tin Tegherghent (Algeria), 25
Tobias, the governor of the valley of the Jordan, 150, 152
Toilet, *compost production system*, 296, 298
    two-outlet, 217, 273, 298
Toltec, the, 184
Toppo Daguzzo (Basilicata), 42, 258
Torrent-streets, 128, 285
Touat (Algeria), 103
Toya, 133
Tozeur, oasis of (Tunisia), 15
Traditional knowledge 2, 6, 8–11, 15, 20, 58, 121, 124, 158, 161, 169, 195, 204–210, 282, 299
Traps, 20
Troy, 60
Trulli, 84, 86, 90, 92, 174, 235, 242
Tuareg, 13, 18, 19, 115–119
Tula (Mexico), 184
Tunisia, 15, 21, 43, 44, 45, 76, 168, 169, 206, 208, 24, 262, 279
Turpan, the depression of (China), 187, 189
Tuscany, 210, 214
Tyrsenois, 84

U

Ucrò (Ethiopia), 45
Udine, 52
Umm al-Jamal (Jordan), 64
United Nations Convention to combat desertification (Unccd), 2, 7, 282
United Nations Educational, Scientific and Cultural Organization (UNESCO), 205
United Nations Programme for the Environment (UNEP), 196
United States, 196, 216, 282
Ura Kidana Merhat (Ethiopia), 237
Urartu (Armenia), 102
Urban ecosystems, 11, 14, 216, 120–165, 174, 220, 257, 269, 271, 289
Urban settlements, 64, 178, 229, 247, 298
Uxmal (Yucatan), 158, 185

V

Valais (Switzerland), 169, 175, 176, 210, 211, 214, 254
Valcamonica (Lombardia), 92, 243
Valle d'Aosta, 254
Valley of Kings (Egypt), the, 249
Vegetable barriers to fix the soils, 216
Vicinato a pozzo, 44; *see also* hypogeal pit-courtyards
Victoria (Australia), 24
Vineyards, 76, 84, 116, 224
Vitruvius, 7, 43, 103

W

Water extraction, 81
Waqara (to dig), 45
Water masters (kiel el-ma), 112

Water vapour, 14, 103, 193, 291, 294
Wei, river (China), 187
Woodhenge (Great Britain), 228
World Bank, 205
World Commission on environment and development, 297

X

Xochimilco (Mexico), 184

Y

Yangtze, the (China), 187, 191
Yellow River, the, (the Huang Ho), 44, 187, 191, 271, 278, 280
Yemen, 58, 63, 64–81, 124, 128, 136–140, 180, 216, 233, 234, 248, 249, 257, 269–274, 297, 298
Yü, founder of the Chinese dynasty Xia, 187
Yucatan, 15, 23, 28, 158, 181–186, 276, 277

Z

Zabur, 69
Zafar (Yemen), 69
Zai, 56
Ziggurat, 60, 84
Ziz, wadi (Morocco), 207
Zoroaster, 180
Zosimus, 5